8-5

AMERICAN
ISSUES FORUM:
A COURSES BY
NEWSPAPER READER

VOLUME ONE

ISSUES FORUM:
A COURSES BY NEWSPAPER READER

VOLUME ONE
Edited by
**Daniel Aaron, Michael Parrish
Jane L. Scheiber, Allen Weinstein**

COURSES BY NEWSPAPER
is a project of
UNIVERSITY EXTENSION
UNIVERSITY OF CALIFORNIA, SAN DIEGO
Funded by
THE NATIONAL ENDOWMENT FOR THE HUMANITIES

PUBLISHER'S INC.

ACADEMIC COORDINATOR
Daniel Aaron, Professor of English and American Literature, Harvard University

ASSISTANT COORDINATORS
Michael Parrish, Associate Professor of History, University of California, San Diego
Allen Weinstein, Associate Professor of History and Director, American Studies Program, Smith College

FACULTY COMMITTEE, UNIVERSITY OF CALIFORNIA, SAN DIEGO
Paul D. Saltman, Chairman; Vice-Chancellor for Academic Affairs and Professor of Biology
Robert C. Elliott, Professor of English Literature
Donald A. Norman, Professor of Psychology
Jacqueline P. Wiseman, Professor of Sociology
Herbert F. York, Professor of Physics

PROJECT DIRECTOR
Caleb A. Lewis, Director of Media Programs, University Extension, UCSD

ASSOCIATE PROJECT DIRECTOR
George A. Colburn, UCSD

EDITORIAL DIRECTOR
Jane L. Scheiber, UCSD

AMERICAN ISSUES FORUM I:
AMERICAN SOCIETY IN THE MAKING

★

Unit One:
"A Nation of Nations"

Unit Two:
The Land of Plenty

Unit Three:
"Certain Unalienable Rights"

Unit Four:
"A More Perfect Union":
The American Government

CONTENTS

UNIT FOUR
"A MORE PERFECT UNION":
THE AMERICAN GOVERNMENT

ACKNOWLEDGMENTS

Courses by Newspaper would not have been possible without the efforts of many people and organizations. We should like to acknowledge them here. Hundreds of newspaper editors and publishers across the country have contributed precious newspaper space to bring the specially prepared articles to their readers. The faculties and administrations of the many colleges and universities participating in the program have cooperated to make credit available to students throughout the nation.

Deserving special mention at the University of California, San Diego, are Caleb A. Lewis, Project Director and Director of Media Programs at University Extension, who originated the idea; and C. David Hellyer, University Editor, now retired, who helped develop the program in its earliest phases. George A. Colburn, Associate Project Director, has energetically administered the program this year and has offered valuable suggestions in the preparation of this Reader.

Paul D. Saltman, Vice-Chancellor for Academic Affairs and Professor of Biology at UCSD, has enthusiastically supported Courses by Newspaper from its inception and served as the first Academic Coordinator and as Chairman of the UCSD Faculty Committee. The other members of the Faculty Committee—Professors Robert C. Elliott, who coordinated the second course, Donald Norman, Jacqueline Wiseman, and Herbert York—also deserve special thanks, as do Professors Harry N. Scheiber and Ricardo Romo of the UCSD History Department for their suggestions. Cecilia Solis, Vickie Wilkerson, and Yvonne Hancher of the Courses by Newspaper staff performed many services that were indispensable to the operation of this national educational program.

We also wish to thank Dean Martin Chamberlain, Mary Walshok, and John Brooks of University Extension, UCSD; Oscar Kaplan of the Center for Survey Research at San Diego State University; Barbara Phillips, secretary for the Committee on Higher Degrees in the History of American Civilization at Harvard University; and Nancy Sjoberg and Linda Rill, photo researchers. The authors of the newspaper articles—John Higham of Johns Hopkins University; John B. Jackson of Harvard and the University of California, Berkeley; Alan Barth, retired editorial writer for the Washington *Post*; and Doris Kearns of Harvard University—consulted with us in the preparation of this book.

Finally, we wish to thank the National Endowment for the Humanities for funding Courses by Newspaper. The Endowment, a

x

federal agency created in 1965 to support education, research, and public activity in the humanities, has generously supported this nationwide program from its beginning. We wish particularly to acknowledge the support and advice of Ronald Berman, the NEH Chairman; Robert Kingston, the Deputy Director; Armen Tashdinian, the Director of the Office of Planning and Analysis; and James Kraft, Program Officer in the Office of Planning and Analysis. Mr. Kraft has worked particularly closely with us on this third course and on coordination with the American Issues Forum.

Although Courses by Newspaper was supported by the National Endowment for the Humanities, the views expressed in this course and the accompanying materials are those of the authors only and do not necessarily reflect those of the Endowment or the University of California.

INTRODUCTION

This is the third in a series of books prepared for Courses by Newspaper. Developed and administered by University Extension, University of California, San Diego, with funding from the National Endowment for the Humanities, Courses by Newspaper presents college-level courses to the public through the cooperation of newspapers and local colleges and universities throughout the nation.

The Reader supplements the eighteen articles written for the Bicentennial course, *American Issues Forum I: American Society in the Making,* and published weekly in newspapers across the country in the fall of 1975. It is divided into four units, each of which relates directly to one of the four topics treated by our newspaper "faculty." Many of the selections touch upon topics and issues raised by the authors of the newspaper articles, but others are included to encourage venturesome readers to strike out on their own. Documents of various sorts—letters, memoirs, photographs, cartoons—add an authentic, contemporary flavor to the events discussed. Excerpts from books and journals provide a useful historical background and scholarly commentary.

Both this book of readings and the Course by Newspaper for which it was prepared are essential components of the American Issues Forum, the national program for the Bicentennial Year. The Forum, designed to encourage a national dialogue on issues fundamental to the development and future of American society, features a calendar of monthly topics. These topics will be the focus of discussions from the community level to that of the national media. The Course by Newspaper has been synchronized with the first four months of the Forum calendar. (A sequel course, and a companion volume of this Reader, will treat the remaining issues of the Forum.)

A comparison of the calendar, reprinted in the following pages, with the Table of Contents of this Reader will reveal how the Course by Newspaper complements the American Issues Forum. Each unit of the Course and the Reader comments upon the same questions posed by the designers of the Forum. Each contributes to a national dialogue about our country's past and present condition. Together they reveal the setbacks as well as the successes of American democracy, while at the same time offering clues to its future.

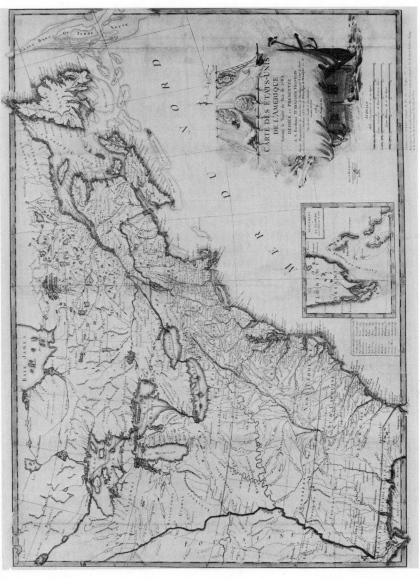

Map of the United States of America following the Peace Treaty of 1783. Dedicated and presented to His Excellency Mr. Benjamin Franklin by his very humble and obedient servant Lattré, 1784.

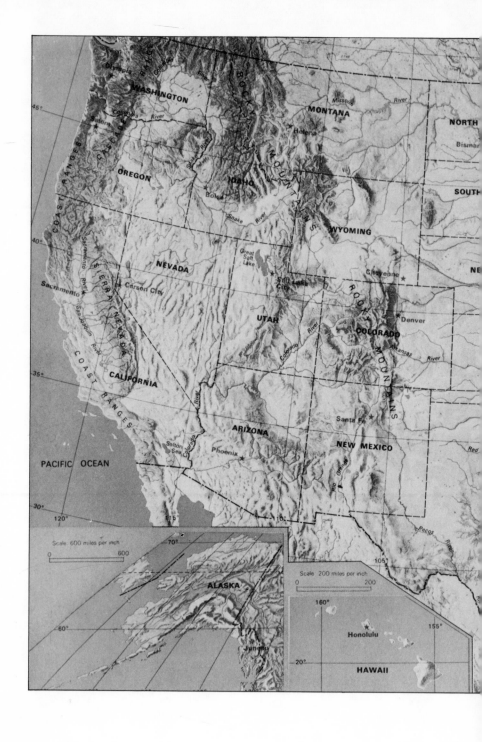

THE UNITED STATES OF AMERICA

Scale 208 miles per inch

0   208

© 1960, JEPPESEN & CO. DENVER, COLO. U.S.A.
ALL RIGHTS RESERVED

★★★
The American Issues Forum: CALENDAR 1975-1976
★★★

INTRODUCTION

This introduces the American Issues Forum, a national program for the Bicentennial year.

The American Issues Forum invites the entire population of the country to engage in a serious exploration of some of the issues that are fundamental to our American society. What it plans for the Bicentennial year is a nationwide dialogue about our country—what it is, how it got that way, where it is headed. And the invitation to participate is extended to every individual American and to every organization and every institution, large or small: groups of every kind—television, radio, and the press; libraries, schools, colleges; churches and synagogues; labor and professional organizations; corporations and foundations; service clubs and discussion groups; communities, neighborhoods, and families—all are invited to join in using the Forum as a framework for their Bicentennial planning. . . .

The mechanics of the project are simple. The calendar for the Forum covers just nine months, from September 1975 through May 1976. On the following pages, one major issue is presented for each of these months—an issue that has affected American life from the beginning, that affects it today, and that will surely affect it for generations to come. With each issue, a few sample questions are proposed, to suggest possible lines of approach; some examples and quotations are presented, too, just to show how often and under what different circumstances the American people have faced these issues in the past. And because some groups, and some of the media, and some of the schools may want to make this exploration of our national life a weekly rather than a monthly event, the following pages also suggest a sequence of four weekly approaches to each of the nine issues.

Beyond that, the design of the Forum is up to the participants. How each of us addresses the issues will depend on how we interpret them: the general topics described in this calendar are meant only to suggest ideas. . . .

The essential thing, however, is to spark a nationwide discussion of fundamentals. To do this, it is useful, as a matter of procedure, that all participants agree to address the same general issues at the same time. The calendar of the American Issues Forum will help us to give each aspect of our national life the serious attention it deserves. An effort at orderly public discourse seems an especially fitting way to commemorate the nation's founding, for the Declaration of Independence was itself the product of well-ordered debate.

There is one final reason for embarking on the American Issues Forum. A free people, to remain free, must continually reexamine itself. Patrick Henry once said: ''I know of no way of judging the future but by the past.'' Through the American Issues Forum we shall be looking at America, asking what *is* America, how did it come to be what it is and what are the problems that disturb each one of us Americans today. We shall be looking, sometimes, at the past—to find out where we came from.

From *The Calendar of the American Issues Forum*, Washington, D.C., 1975.

We shall be looking at the traditions of America—and asking about ways of renewing those traditions—or of changing them. We shall sometimes find diversity and discord, compromises and conflicts. Doubtless we shall also find some disparities between our ideals and our practices, evidence of failure and mere muddling through. But we shall also find ideals that move us and prospects that excite. And we may finally find the continuity of our experience, a sense of our tradition, to affirm and renew.

Our subject, then, will be as broad as America. And as immediate as our own lives.

THE AMERICAN ISSUES FORUM
is a program developed for the nation's Bicentennial under the auspices of
THE NATIONAL ENDOWMENT FOR THE HUMANITIES
and with the co-sponsorship of the
AMERICAN REVOLUTION BICENTENNIAL ADMINISTRATION

Posterity! You will never know how much it cost the present generation, to preserve your Freedom! I hope you make a good use of it. If you do not, I shall repent in Heaven that ever I took half the pains to preserve it.

—John Adams
Second President of the United States
Philadelphia, 1777

Let us all, during the coming months, study carefully the character, study the qualities of the men who founded this Nation. Let us try to grasp the stuff that was inside of each of them and all of them collectively. And then, let us release, if we can, the same spirit within ourselves. We have the same capacity for unity, discipline and sacrifice. Let us show the world that the character and quality of the American people has not changed in 200 years.

—Gerald R. Ford
Thirty-eighth President of the United States
Philadelphia, 1974

THE AMERICAN ISSUES FORUM: OUTLINE OF TOPICS 1975-1976

THE FIRST MONTH:
"A NATION OF NATIONS"
1. The Founding Peoples
2. Two Centuries of Immigrants
3. Out of Many, One
4. We Pledge Allegiance . . .

THE SECOND MONTH:
THE LAND OF PLENTY
1. A Shrinking Frontier?
2. The Sprawling City
3. Use and Abuse in the Land of Plenty
4. Who Owns the Land

THE THIRD MONTH:
"CERTAIN UNALIENABLE RIGHTS"
1. Freedom of Speech, Assembly and Religion
2. Freedom of the Press
3. Freedom from Search and Seizure
4. Equal Protection Under the Law

THE FOURTH MONTH:
"A MORE PERFECT UNION":
THE AMERICAN GOVERNMENT
1. "In Congress Assembled. . .":
A Representative Legislature
2. A President: An Elected Executive
3. "The Government": The Growth of Bureaucracy
4. "By Consent of the States. . ."

THE FIFTH MONTH:
WORKING IN AMERICA
1. The American Work Ethic
2. Organization of the Labor Force
3. The Welfare State: Providing a Livelihood
4. Enjoying the Fruits of Labor

THE SIXTH MONTH:
"THE BUSINESS OF AMERICA. . ."
1. Private Enterprise in the Marketplace
2. Empire Building: Cornering the Market
3. Subsidizing and Regulating: Controlling the Economy
4. Selling the Consumer

THE SEVENTH MONTH:
AMERICA IN THE WORLD
1. The American "Dream" Among Nations
2. The Economic Dimension
3. A Power in the World
4. A Nation Among Nations

THE EIGHTH MONTH:
GROWING UP IN AMERICA
1. The American Family
2. Education for Work and for Life
3. "In God We Trust"
4. A Sense of Belonging

THE NINTH MONTH:
LIFE, LIBERTY AND THE PURSUIT OF HAPPINESS
1. The Rugged Individualist
2. The Dream of Success
3. The Pursuit of Pleasure
4. The Fruits of Wisdom

6

★ ★ ★
THE AMERICAN ISSUES FORUM: ANNOTATED CALENDAR FOR THE FIRST FOUR MONTHS
★ ★ ★

"A Nation of Nations"

"We, the people . . . " These familiar words begin our Constitution. For America is, first of all, a people—a group of peoples, really. "Here is not merely a nation," as Walt Whitman put it, "but a teeming nation of nations." Most nations are organized around a single people, or a particular piece of real estate. Yet America is very much based on an idea, a dream of freedom and well-being that was embraced by men and women of many tongues and traditions. Where did they come from? And what led so many to abandon what was familiar and strike out for what was totally unknown? Was it courage or fear that drove them on? Hope or despair? What sort of people were they to be able to overcome hardship and, in the face of long odds, create a new nation? What kept them together, despite their differences, through revolution and Civil War, Depression and World War? What keeps us together now: what is the basis of the brotherhood we feel?

My neighbors—what makes them different from me and yet similar to me? Are our differences fading as the memory of other lands and other traditions fades? And how are we to answer the questions: "What do I mean when I call myself an American? What do I want out of being an American?"

1. The Founding Peoples

Yankee Doodle, keep it up, / Yankee Doodle, dandy, /
Mind the music and the step / And with the girls
be handy. —(circa 1767)

There were human beings aboard the Mayflower, not
merely ancestors. —Stephen Vincent Benet

I always consider the settlement of America with
reverence and wonder, as the opening of a grand
scene and designe . . . for the illumination of
the ignorant, and the emancipation of the slavish
part of mankind all over the earth. —John Adams

Who were they, these early Americans? Some, of course, had been in the
country for generations: the Indians, who were the native peoples of America.
Some were black slaves who came not of their own will but in chains. Some were
"temporary slaves"—indentured servants and apprentices—who had to put in
years of hard labor before they could earn their freedom. Some were colonizers
who came to find land, to produce and trade, to grow rich. And some came in
search of freedoms that they couldn't enjoy elsewhere. Explorers, colonizers,
adventurers, criminals, rebels, runaways, and religious dissidents—together they
settled a new world and forged a new nation. We still think of them as our
"ancestors," Founding Fathers, even though few of us have any direct relationship to them, and our backgrounds and experiences are much different from
theirs. Why should what they did and what they dreamt still affect us so
deeply? Has the dream dimmed, or changed for the better?

- Before debarking from the *Mayflower* on November 11, 1620,
the men signed an agreement to create a body politic in which
majority rule would prevail. The voyage of the *Arabella*
and John Winthrop's speech *"A Modell of Christian Charity"*
also exemplify the motives and aspirations of early settlers of
New England.

- The rigors of colonization: the Roanoke Island Settlement
of 1585 vanishes entirely, a mystery to this day; nearly
60 percent of the Jamestown colonizers perish in 1607; half of
Plymouth is wiped out in the first winter after its settlement
in 1620.

- King Philip's war of 1675-76 foretells the bloody confrontations
between Europeans and the native population during the next
two centuries. Olaudah Equiano, a seventeenth-century black
slave, provides a rare first-hand account of forced migration and
bondage in *Equiano's Travels.*

2. Two Centuries of Immigrants

Give me your tired, your poor, your huddled masses
yearning to breathe free . . .
—Emma Lazarus, inscription on the Statue of Liberty

No Irish need apply.—nineteenth-century advertisement

Remember, remember always that all of us . . . are
descended from immigrants and revolutionists.
—Franklin D. Roosevelt

Most Americans today are closer to the immigrants who poured through our portals in the last 150 years than to the Founding Fathers. The impact of this human tidal wave was overwhelming. Northern Europeans from Germany and Scandinavia, Catholics from Ireland and Italy, Jews from Central Europe and Russia, Chinese laborers and Japanese farmers—they came, many of them, out of despair and in hope. Most new Americans found a better life, but they did not always realize their hopes. Some found lands to farm and businesses to build, and became rich. But for many there was only the ghetto and sweatshop, the marginal acre—and prejudice. Crowded into the growing cities, these were the ones who created our modern industrial society—the raw, cheap labor that built the railroads, dug the sewers, kept the textile factories of New England humming,and manned the packing-houses of Chicago. Their descendants built our modern cities—and our suburbs—helped revitalize our arts and transform our politics. Our urban industrial society grew to a large extent out of their efforts. How did they affect the values and attitudes of their adopted land? Even today, one-third of our increase in population comes from immigration. How do *we* treat new immigrants, and other newcomers to our communities today?

- The Irish potato famines, the pogroms of Eastern Europe, the poverty of the Italian south and the activities of American labor contractors in Asia and Europe spur the great waves of immigration. Between 1860 and 1900, some 14 million immigrants arrive. Ellis Island, the sweatshops in major cities, the building of the Erie Canal and the Union Pacific, the ghettos and Chinatowns, portray the newcomers' life.

- So do *The Americanization of Edward Bok,* Jacob Riis' *The Making of an American,* and Leo Rosten's *The Education of H*y*m*a*n K*a*p*l*a*n.*

- Immigrant intellectuals infuse American life with new ideas, new energy, new leadership. In 1848 many highly educated Europeans flee from the continent's political upheavals. In another great influx in the 1930's, a reaction to the rise of fascism, a great number of scientists and educators arrive, but also artists, architects, musicians, writers. DeKooning and Stravinsky, Balanchine and Albers, Gropius and Saarinen are all immigrants.

3. Out of Many, One

We must all hang together, or most assuredly we shall all hang separately. —Benjamin Franklin

I could point out to you a man whose grandfather was an Englishman, whose wife was Dutch, whose son married a French woman, and whose present four sons have now four wives of different nations. —Carl Bode

America, my country, is almost a continent and hardly yet a nation. —Ezra Pound

What indeed is an American? Our roots are as tangled as those of an ancient tree, our blood a mix that can be found in no other country. Our national motto is *E Pluribus Unum*—out of many, one. Yet it is not easy to see how the very different groups that settled America were able to establish one nation. Indeed, Mark Twain once wrote that the only feature of "the American character" that he had ever discovered was a fondness for ice water. What is the "American character"? What values and symbols do we share? For all our talk of integration, assimilation, "the melting pot," we often insist, by and large, on going our separate ways. Theodore Roosevelt once said, "There is no room in this country for hyphenated Americanism." But more and more people *want* to be known as Italian-Americans, Mexican-Americans, Afro-Americans—for reasons of pride and identity. Should we emphasize the differences that set us apart or the similarities that bind us together? Is it better to remember—or to forget—that "I am Polish, or Irish, or Italian, or Black, or English, or Jewish . . . "?

- In 1891, eleven Italians are lynched in New Orleans after being acquitted of complicity in the murder of a police Commissioner, yet local authorities praise the lawlessness.

- Ole E. Rolvaag's 1927 novel of Norwegian-American life, *Giants in the Earth,* analyzes the immigrant's transition from the Old World to the New. In her novels—*My Antonia, O Pioneers*— Willa Cather depicts Czechoslovakian and Swedish immigrants plowing the unbroken land of the American frontier, as they progress from peasants to proprietors.

• In his 1908 play about Jewish life in New York City, Israel Zangwill coins the term "melting pot." The phrase catches on as a concise description of a society composed of so many peoples. But those who want America to remain more homogeneous dislike the notion and challenge it, as in Henry Pratt Fairchild's *The Melting Pot Mistake*. Still, our diversity and the complex relationships like religious and racial intermarriage that grow out of it are oft-explored themes in literature: the play *Abie's Irish Rose* and films like *Guess Who's Coming to Dinner*.

4. We Pledge Allegiance . . .

I pledge allegiance to the flag . . . and to the Republic for which it stands . . .—Salute to the flag

I am a 100 percent American. I am a super-patriot.
—William Woolcott

America—Love It or Leave It!—Popular slogan

If we are all conscious of our ethnic, or racial, or philosophical differences, how can we agree on what makes "a good American"? The question has recurrently haunted—and bloodied—America: during the War for Independence, when the population was bitterly divided between Tory loyalists and revolutionaries; during the Civil War, still our most wrenching experience as a nation; during the Cold War and its by-product, the Vietnam War. Trials for treason and criticism of "unAmerican" activities have spotted our history from the first. People have long owed multiple loyalties—to family, community, religion, country. Such allegiances enrich our culture, yet keeping all of them in harmony is sometimes impossible. What happens when loyalties collide? What are the requirements of the loyal citizen? Just how much civil disobedience can a society tolerate? Do we like America because we were born here or because we like what it stands for? Who is the real patriot? Stephen Decatur is credited with the maxim, "Our country, right or wrong!" Carl Schurz changed it to: "Our country, right or wrong! When right, to be kept right, when wrong, to be put right!"

• Nathan Hale and Benedict Arnold. Hale, a young schoolteacher commissioned in the Connecticut militia, is captured in New York City and hanged without trial as a spy. His last words, "I only regret that I have but one life to lose for my country." Arnold, a revolutionary hero, turns traitor after a 1780 court-martial on charges of using military forces for his own purposes. When his plot to surrender West Point is exposed and foiled, he joins the British forces and in 1781 sails for England, where he is scorned.

• With the onset of the Civil War, Robert E. Lee, Jefferson Davis, Moncure Conway suffer the anguish of conflicting loyalties—as many have in many wars since.

• The rise of Senator Joseph McCarthy in the 1950's manifests the anti-Communist hysteria that engulfs the U.S. from 1946 to 1954. It affects the press, schools, courts, churches and Congress—and, of course, thousands of individuals—stimulating the conviction that it is safer to conform than to disagree with the majority.

The Land of Plenty

America is also a place—a land to be settled, owned, rented, mined, seeded, plowed under, asphalted over, built upon, played on, lived in. It began as thin slivers of civilization along the coasts—colonial settlements on the Atlantic, Spanish missions on the Pacific. Now it spans a continent, embraces an archipelago in the mid-Pacific, reaches into the Arctic Circle, thrusts into the Caribbean. The land drew our forefathers here, and our wealth as a nation derives from it: our use of it has given us the world's most productive system of agriculture and industry. How have we shaped this land and how has it shaped us? What explains our different regional cultures, the growth of our cities and suburbs? Have we used the land wastefully? Do we need to put limits on our growth to recapture a reverence for nature? Of course we must use the land for cities and suburbs, to sustain life and make it worth living. To what extent can we have the best both of growth and of harmony with nature by planning, zoning, and land-use management? Who decides? Who really owns the land?

1. A Shrinking Frontier?

Go West, young man, and grow up with the country.
—Horace Greeley

Come all ye yankee farmers who wish to change your lot. /
Who've spunk to travel beyond your native spot . . .
—Folk song circa 1800

Where today are the Pequot? Where are the Narragansett, the
Mohican, the Pokanoket, and many other once powerful tribes
of our people? They have vanished before the avarice and the
oppression of the White Man, as snow before a summer sun.
—Tecumseh of the Shawnees

The broad land beckoned, and the early settlers took up its invitation. Even before the East was conquered and cleared, pioneers were pushing west of the Alleghenies into the Midwest, spanning the Mississippi to cross the Great Plains, then struggling across the Continental Divide and surmounting the high Sierras to reach the Pacific. In Washington's time America was the "new-found land," a virgin continent that offered rich possibilities for settlement. Farms, ranches, plantations, towns and trading posts were carved out from the wilderness. Each kind of settlement supported a quite different way of life: the life of the southern planter, sustained by a slave economy, the New England townsman, The Midwestern wheat farmer, the Western rancher, the Pacific fur trapper. How did each area affect them, and how did they change each place they settled? The frontier molded resilient men and women—or it drained them and destroyed them! Is the whole colonizing, pioneering, prospecting spirit still a significant element in our character? Did a propensity for violence grow out of it . . . a wanderlust . . . a sense of community . . . or of intolerance? Does a frontier spirit still spur us on?

• Accounts from early settlers, like the Reverend Alexander Whittaker's *Good News from Virginia* (1913) and John Hammond's *Leah and Rachel, or The Two Fruitful Sisters, Virginia and Maryland* (1656), portray America as an earthly paradise.

• The Lewis and Clark Expedition is commissioned by Jefferson to explore the resources of the Louisiana Purchase. This and other expeditions initiate an important genre of literature in America— Francis Parkman's famous account of the journey, Frederick Jackson Turner's theory of the frontier as *the* central factor in shaping the American character, Owen Wister's novel, *The Virginian,* as a romanticization of that new American, the Westerner.

• The Donner Party and its trials symbolize the Westward rush, the hunger for land and riches, the hazards of pioneering and the eventual conquest—not without heavy cost—of the continent.

2. The Sprawling City

Hog butcher for the world, / Tool maker, stacker of wheat,
Player with railroads and the nation's freight handler;
stormy, husky, brawling, city of the big shoulders.
—Carl Sandburg, "Chicago"

Little boxes on the hillside / Little boxes made of ticky tacky, /
Little boxes on the hillside, / Little boxes all the same.
—Malvina Reynolds

How you gonna keep 'em down on the farm after they've seen
Paree?—Title and refrain, 1919

In the America of the young immigrants' dreams, the cities were paved with gold. They offered a new kind of frontier, where people built up rather than out. Though the American city could not fulfill the rosiest expectations, its most squalid neighborhoods often seemed to offer more hope than the back-breaking toil and stifling insularity of rural Europe—or, for that matter, of rural America. And once we had tamed the land and made it productive, we began congregating more and more in cities, until prosperity after World War II touched off the spectacular growth of suburbs. The result: 7 out of 10 Americans now live in cities or their suburbs, compared with 5 percent 200 years ago. Are our biggest cities becoming places where only the rich and poor live, while the middle class commutes from suburbia? Will the sophistication and bright lights of the cities continue to lure people from all economic levels? To a great extent, urban man has lost touch with nature, yet he remains nostalgic about rural America.

Does Jefferson's old vision of an agrarian society have any meaning for us today? Or does modern urban living require a new mood, a new communal ethic? Why do we live in cities, anyway—because we want to, or because we have to? Is urban America really all that different from rural America—in this age of high-speed communication, interstate highways, and nation-wide chain stores?

• The city in fiction: Dreiser's Chicago in *Sister Carrie,*
Henry Roth's New York in *Call It Sleep,* Jack Kerouac's San
Francisco, J.P. Marquand's Boston.

• Jane Addams and Ellen Gates Starr establish Hull House, one
of the first settlement houses in America, in 1889, to help
what Addams calls "the city's disinherited." This pioneering
effort in Chicago influences many other cities.

• The skyscraper is born in America in the last quarter of the
nineteenth century. Early examples are the Equitable Life and
Western Union Buildings in New York, which make full use of
the elevator. In this century, large suburban developments like

Levittown grow up, as do new towns such as Columbia, Maryland and Reston, Virginia, Lake Havasu City, Lysander, New York, which attempt to bring the conveniences of urban life to rural settings.

3. Use and Abuse in the Land of Plenty

Give me land, lots of land, under starry skies above . . .
—Cole Porter, "Don't Fence Me In"

And I brought you into a plentiful country, to eat the fruit thereof and the goodness thereof; but when ye entered, ye defiled my land . . .—Jeremiah, Chapter 2, Verse 7

In the United States there is more space where nobody is than where anybody is. This is what makes America what it is.
—Gertrude Stein

Once it was the limitless land, the land of plenty. And so we used it—felling forests, working farmland, drawing minerals from the earth. The land is our most fundamental resource: everything comes, one way or another, from it. We have used the land to make us prosperous: our farms produce more of the world's exportable grain than the Middle East does of the World's oil; and our factories produce an enormous amount of the world's goods. But we use great amounts of natural resources. Have we pushed too far? Must we now be mindful not of exploiting nature but conserving it? Is there enough for all? Conservationists like Teddy Roosevelt sounded early alarms, but they went largely unheeded. Must we now conserve dwindling resources by making do with less? Or can we count on our technology to bail us out as it so often has?

How should we respond to insistent demands from a starving world that we distribute our resources more equitably? Will we have to arrest the spread of the suburbs to put more land back into farming? Hard choices may lie ahead. Will our grandchildren still sing of "America the Beautiful"?

• Tennessee Valley Authority, Hoover Dam, Lake Mead, Lake Powell: public works to achieve flood control provide new sources of energy, conservation, and, not so incidentally, recreation.

• Despite the flight to cities and suburbs, the farm remains one of America's drive-shafts, and agriculture one of its biggest businesses. Even in the two most populous states, California and New York, agriculture is the major "industry."

• In 1962, Rachel Carson's *Silent Spring* launches the environmentalist movement by warning the nation of the damage caused by DDT and other pesticides. by 1973 the U.S. Environment Protection Agency has banned DDT for most uses, citing its potential health hazard to man.

4. Who Owns the Land?

*This land is your land/This land is my land/From
California/To the New York highlands . . ./This land was made
for you and me.*—Woody Guthrie

*Sell a country! Why not sell the air, the clouds and the
great sea, as well as the earth? Did not the Great Spirit
make them all for the use of his children?*—Tecumseh

The instinct of ownership is fundamental in man's nature.
—William James

Whose land is it? The question goes to the heart of debates that are as old as
the Republic: the rights of property, private versus public ownership, government regulation, the need for centralized planning. Virtually every American
has sought to acquire a piece of land. Two of every three Americans do in fact
own their own homes, and some own vacation property as well. A few hold vast
tracts of land. Why is the ownership of land so important to us? What are the
chances of us all owning a piece of land in the future, anyway? A nineteenth-
century versifier named Jesse Hutchinson, Jr., said in one of his popular songs,
"Uncle Sam is rich enough to give us all a farm." There are 3 *billion* acres of
land in America, but could Uncle Sam really afford to be that generous? The
ownership of land has been tied to notions of privacy, self-reliance, and
individualism. But how should we balance our individual rights over our own
plots of land with the rights of those around us?

The worth of one parcel of land depends on the uses to which the surrounding
parcels are put. We often talk of property rights. What responsibilities go along
with these rights? Are these as "real" as civil rights? Should we be entitled to
use land in any way we fancy because we own it? How are the rights of private
ownership balanced against the good of society as a whole?

- The Homestead Act of 1862 offers "quarter-sections"—160 acres—
  to any head of a family who agrees to till the land for five years.
  Free land, a goal sought by Westerners for generations, is attained.
  The measure helps settle the American West but falls short of its
  goals because most good land is already settled.

- In 1872 Congress creates the National Parks System, preserving
  vast wilderness areas. Yellowstone is the first park established "for
  the benefit and enjoyment of the people." Yosemite, only one of
  dozens of national and state parks, is bigger than the state of
  Rhode Island.

- Zoning laws protect the interests of the community at large and
  affect the quality of lives. Some laws bar commercial and industrial

development from residential areas or set minimum acreage requirements to prevent overcrowding, setting limits to what an owner is permitted to do with his property.

"Certain Unalienable Rights"

Now why did these people, in this land, seek independence to begin with? And why is the Fourth of July so important to us? This month we will be concerned with the freedoms that the new Republic guaranteed to its citizens. We'll examine some of the basic freedoms for which the War of Independence was fought—and which affect our everyday lives as Americans. Or are *supposed* to! "We hold these truths to be self-evident, that all men are created equal, that they are endowed by their Creator with certain unalienable rights . . ." So read the familiar words of the Declaration of Independence; and Jefferson wrote, two years before his death: "Nothing, then is unchangeable but the inherent and unalienable rights of man." Yet all through our history, it has proved harder than it might seem to defend these rights—and even to define them. Some of our most fundamental freedoms were not initially written into the Constitution, and even today, the exercise of our freedoms is a matter of debate, regularly contested in our courts. Are our ideals diluted in practice? By what standards do we interpret and extend equality? Are some of us more equal than others? If liberty and duty, rights and responsibilities, go hand in hand, how unfettered can freedom be? To what extent is freedom limited by responsibility?

1. Freedom of Speech, Assembly and Religion

Congress shall make no law respecting an establishment of religion or prohibiting the free exercise thereof, or abridging the freedom of speech or of the press, or the right of the people peaceably to assemble, and to petition the government for a redress of grievances.
—First Amendment to the Constitution

Is life so dear, or peace so sweet, as to be purchased at the price of chains and slavery? Forbid it, Almighty God! I know not what course others may take, but as for me, give me liberty or give me death!—Patrick Henry

Restriction of free thought and free speech is the most dangerous of all subversions. It is the one un-American act that could most easily defeat us.—William O. Douglas

Among the "unalienable rights" that we cherish, perhaps the most basic are the rights to say what we want, when we want, and where we want; to assemble with others to talk freely; and to worship in the way we choose. Our Founding Fathers, who had seen the corrupt side of governmental power, insisted on First Amendment liberties as a bulwark against tyranny. But are these rights absolute? Most of us don't really want others to be able to say or write *anything, anywhere,* at *any time,* so we limit these basic rights. Hanging witches, banning books, jailing dissidents, and requiring or prohibiting prayers—this "free country" has done all of these. And the practices of some religious sects have been prohibited by the nation's laws. Is freedom so fragile that we sometimes must—or think we must—defend it by denying it to others? Or is the surest way to defend it through what Oliver Wendell Holmes called the "free trade in ideas"? On the other hand, are there no limits at all to freedom? What is the dividing line between art and pornography? Between reasonable protest and impermissible violence? Between religious principle and antisocial practice? When does the expression of an opinion become treason, endangering the common good or the rights of others? What makes up an "unlawful assembly"?

- The Sedition Act of 1798 threatens anyone who utters or writes "false, scandalous and malicious" comments against the government of the United States with fine and imprisonment.

- In *U.S.* v. *Cruikshank* (1876) the Supreme Court holds that the right of the people to assemble peacefully for lawful purposes existed long before the Constitution was adopted. The Court traces the right to English law and describes it as a distinct, separate, and independent right.

- The 1963 March on Washington, led by Dr. Martin Luther King, Jr., demonstrates the importance of mass assemblies as a way of shaping public policy in the area of civil rights. Such meetings become an important tactic again during the Vietnam War, sometimes marked by violence.

2. Freedom of the Press

Our liberty depends on the freedom of the press, and that cannot be limited without being lost.—Thomas Jefferson

Freedom of the press is not an end in itself but a means to the end of a free society.—Felix Frankfurter

If all printers were determined not to print anything till they were sure it would offend nobody, there would be very little printed.—Benjamin Franklin

Without a free press, it is doubtful whether there could have been an American Revolution. The Revolution didn't just happen; preachers, pamphleteers and journalists were generating—and publishing—revolutionary ideas for many years. Some of the founding fathers wrote articles and essays that inflamed opinion, and the Constitution itself contributed to great public controversy. But if a free press helped to create America, on many occasions since, it has seemed to divide it. From Tom Paine to the Pentagon Papers, the press and the Establishment have been adversaries, sometimes cordial, more often not. Some of the Founders feared that the spirit of the revolution would vanish without independent voices of conscience; by contrast, other ardent supporters of the Constitution have seen the commercial press as fragmenting and undermining the Republic. Is the press too powerful? Does it jeopardize the rights of others—especially the right to privacy? The media can make, and unmake, public opinion, values, and personalities. Because it wields such power, should the press be licensed, or monitored in some way? If so, by whom? Can a free press monitor society if it is monitored itself?

- John Peter Zenger, a New York publisher, is tried in 1735 for libeling the royal government. His acquittal, on the grounds that he had printed the truth in his newspaper, leaves writers free to criticize the government.

- "Yellow journalism": The Hearst papers so inflame public opinion that the Government is encouraged to go to war with Spain over Cuba in 1898. At one point Publisher William Randolph Hearst cables an artist for his papers in Cuba: "You furnish the pictures and I'll furnish the war."

- The Government in 1971 seeks to halt publication of the Pentagon Papers on national security grounds. The Supreme Court rules against this attempted "prior restraint" by a six-to-three vote.

3. Freedom from Search and Seizure

The rights of the people to be secure in their persons, houses, papers, and effects, against unreasonable searches and seizures, shall not be violated.
—Fourth Amendment to the Constitution

The right to be let alone, the most comprehensive of rights and the right most valued by civilized men.—Louis D. Brandeis

Liberty is the only thing you cannot have unless you are willing to give it to others.—William Allen White

The nation's founding peoples feared a nighttime knock on the door by British soldiers; they appreciated the danger of laws enforced without due process. Freedom from search and seizure particularly mattered to them. Modern technology has added new and disturbing dimensions to the fears that prompted the adoption of the Fourth Amendment. Concealed cameras with telescopic lenses, tapped telephones, listening devices that can hear through walls, computer data banks that recall the most minor details of our lives—all are instruments that could be used by tax auditors, credit investigators, and personnel managers to snoop on us. Small wonder that the courts have been broadening the Fourth Amendment to support a right to privacy against many new forms of search and seizure. Yet there *are* searches and seizures, with and without court orders. In as large and complex a society as ours, the Government obviously needs information, as do industry, banks, and employers. But how much? How is the collection and use of private information to be controlled? When does the right to privacy cease to be a right? When does its exercise interfere with the rights of others?

- Writs of assistance, general search warrants issued to the customs officers of the various colonies, first come into use in Massachusetts in 1751. They are used to ferret out all merchandise that has been slipped into the colonies without being taxed. The writs arouse such passion that their issuance is listed in the Declaration of Independence as a common grievance.

- In the wake of the Russian Revolution, Attorney General A. Mitchell Palmer launches "Red-hunts" for subversive aliens and Communists, using forcible entry and deportation without cause.

- Excessive use of telephone tapping, and abuse of "no-knock" and "stop-and-search" laws cause controversy in the 1970's and prompt Government agencies to reexamine how these practices should be revised.

4. Equal Protection Under the Law

No person shall be . . . deprived of life, liberty, or property, without due process of law, nor shall private property be taken for public use without just compensation.—Fifth Amendment to the Constitution

We hold these truths to be self-evident: that all men and women are created equal . . .—Seneca Falls Declaration of Sentiments, 1848

For de little stealin' dey gits you in jail soon or late. For de big stealin' dey makes you emperor and puts you in the Hall of Fame . . .
—Eugene O'Neill, *Emperor Jones*

Laws, exceptions, compromises! What makes them all work is a basic guarantee that we have as Americans: equal protection under the law for every citizen. Much of our legal and political tradition has been occupied with giving concrete, practical meaning to the ideal of equality. Yet laws are made by fallible legislators and enforced by fallible police, judges, and juries. Women, Blacks, migrants, immigrants, religious dissidents—many groups have sometimes suffered second-class treatment at the hands of the majority. Have they also received second-class treatment from the courts, or equal protection and justice? "We are under a constitution," wrote Charles Evans Hughes, onetime Chief Justice of the United States, "but the Constitution is what the judges say it is." What if the judges don't measure up? If the ideal standard of equality before the law is compromised, isn't everything else in jeopardy? What recourse does the wronged citizen have but the law? Are we in practice equal before the law? Or are some "more equal" than others? Is there one rule for the rich and another for the poor; one for the influential and another for the obscure? How, over 200 years, has America preserved the rights of those who wrong society?

- Progress in the concept of equality: John Winthrop's *A Modell of Christian Charity* (1630) declares all persons unequal; Jefferson's *Declaration of Independence* (1776) declares *men* are equal; *The Seneca Falls Declaration* (1848) proclaims all *men and women* equal. Constitutional amendments extend the vote to Blacks (Fifteenth), women (Nineteenth), and persons aged eighteen to twenty-one (Twenty-sixth).

- The Dred Scott case of 1857 rules that a black slave cannot establish his freedom by residence in a free territory and that slavery cannot be excluded from territories as Congress had legislated. After the Civil War, the Thirteenth and Fourteenth Amendments to the Constitution overturn the Supreme Court's rulings.

- The *Plessy* v. *Ferguson* case in 1896 results in a Supreme Court decision that state laws giving Blacks "separate but equal" facilities on railroads in constitutional. This doctrine is reversed by the historic *Brown* v. *Board* of Education case in 1954.

"A More Perfect Union": the American Government

America, too, is a political life. A very rare, risky, even fragile kind of political life—a democracy, in which (or so the theory goes) every citizen has an equal voice in the affairs of the country through his vote. What is unique about *our* form of democracy? The framers of our Constitution felt the need for "a more perfect Union" among the newly independent states and attempted to institute a political regime that would uniquely combine the advantages of liberty *and* stability. "Power checks power" was a maxim they followed, and they crafted a delicate balance among the institutions of the new Republic so that none would become too strong. How well has the doctrine of separation of powers among executive, legislative and judicial branches worked? Our theory of judicial review of the Constitution? Our political parties? For a long time not everybody had a vote. Now that the franchise is nearly universal, how much does the vote of a single individual matter? The men who wrote the Constitution thought that one key to a good society was to vest power in the people. But under democracy's system of "representative government," the people then delegate that power to elected officials whose performance may—or may not—please them. What can the people do if their displeasure grows too great?

1. "In Congress Assembled . . ." : A Representative Legislature

*Every man [in the Congress] is a great man, an orator, a critic,
a statesman; and therefore every man upon every question must show
his oratory, his criticism, and his political abilities.* —John Adams

Bad officials are elected by good citizens who do not vote.
—George Jean Nathan

Can this National Legislature be competent to make laws for the free
*internal government of one people, living in climates so remote
and whose "Habits and Particular Interests" are and probably always
will be so different?* —Samuel Adams

In a sense, Congress is even older than the Republic. The Constitutional Congress of representatives from the states met in Philadelphia in 1774, and since then we have regularly elected representatives to serve and speak for us. But how far can the 535 legislators who assemble in that magnificently domed building on Capitol Hill really represent us as individuals? "Government of the people, by the people, and for the people" is one of our favorite catchphrases. But with each member of the House representing an average of 500,000 constituents, is it a hollow phrase? When should a Congressman follow his constituents? When should he lead them? The House has been called "the forge of democracy," legislating for the common good. Does it really? Or do its deliberations and legislation reflect narrower concerns, the needs of particular constituencies? Can it be otherwise? Some argue that there is a serious confusion of roles in the three branches. With the Executive Branch steadily growing in power, what chance does Congress have to make its influence felt?

- In the Constitutional debates, the South wants to count slaves as part of the population for purposes of representation in Congress but not for direct taxation. The North wants the opposite. Through compromise, three-fifths of the slaves are counted for both representation and taxation.

- Senators are originally elected by state legislatures. After the Seventeenth Amendment is ratified in 1913, they are elected by popular vote.

- The Kansas-Nebraska Bill of 1854, opening the Western territories to slavery, causes such popular revulsion in the Northeast and the upper Midwest that a new political party springs up. First gathering at Jackson, Michigan, in 1854, it calls itself the Republican Party. The Whig Party, divided since 1850 over slavery, all but vanishes by 1860, leaving in commanding position the two major parties that still control American politics—Democrats and Republicans.

2. A President: An Elected Executive

When a man assumes a public trust, he should consider himself as public property.—Thomas Jefferson

The buck stops here.—Harry S. Truman

My God! What is there in this place that a man should ever want to get into it?—James Garfield

Somebody has to "run" the government, so the founders made provision for a President. But they knew the dangers of kings and dictators, so they saw to it that the President would have no hereditary rights and that his power would be circumscribed by law. For the framers of the Constitution feared above all the concentration of power in one man or one organ of government. How has their design stood up in our century? Our spectacular growth has helped make the presidency increasingly powerful and complex. On the night he was inaugurated in 1801, Thomas Jefferson had to wait like everybody else at his boarding house until there was a table for him in the dining room. Quite a difference from what has lately been called "the imperial presidency"! How can so remote and overworked an executive respond to the people's will? How can he even know what our will may be? Does the President really run the government? In 1789, Washington went on tour to convince Americans that they really had a national government. Nobody needs convincing today, but few Americans now know their President personally. Television gives the illusion of familiarity, but does it also lead to an overemphasis on image? On what basis do we cast our votes for him?

• Andrew Jackson becomes the first "people's President." With several states abolishing property qualifications for voting, he is elected by Western farmers and Eastern workers. Mobs descend on Washington for the inauguration of their hero in 1829, and Jackson throws the White House open to them.

• Presidents clash frequently with the other branches: Wilson with the Senate over ratification of the League of Nations (he calls his chief opponents "a little group of willful men, representing no opinion but their own"); FDR with the Supreme Court, which he tried to pack with his appointees; Truman with what he dubbed the "Do-Nothing" 80th Congress in 1947-48.

• A tradition against a third term grows from Washington onward, but FDR breaks it in 1940 with a third term, and again in 1944. In reaction, Congress in 1947 moves to make a two-term limit constitutional. The Twenty-second Amendment, ratified in 1951, puts a two-term limit on the presidency and sets ten years as the maximum number a person may serve in the office.

3. "The Government": The Growth of Bureaucracy

Government, even in its best state, is but a necessary evil; in its worst state, an intolerable one.—Thomas Paine

I saw the Civil Service debauched and demoralized. I saw offices distributed to incompetent and unworthy men as a reward for the lowest of dirty partisan work. I saw many men employed to do the work of one man. I saw the money of the people shamefully wasted to keep up electioneering funds . . .—George H. Pendleton, 1883

I don't make jokes: I just watch the government and report the facts.—Will Rogers

Little more than a century ago, 51,000 civilians worked for the United States government. Today 3,000,000 do so. This vast bureaucracy administers and enforces laws, collects taxes, pays pensions, insures bank deposits, operates dams, regulates farms and industries, busts trusts, investigates crimes, prosecutes offenders, gathers intelligence. Is this what we mean when we talk about "the Government"? How did this unelected Government grow up? Does it in fact wield excessive powers? Certainly it can irritate us with its red tape and its remoteness. But it also administers programs that reach practically every American—from the widow on Social Security and the indigent on Medicaid to the college student in need of a loan and the airline in need of a subsidy. In effect, it implements the laws and policies of the nation. Can we do with less of it? Or should we accord a higher standing to the "bureaucrat"? Should we be paying more attention to recruiting good people into the government—and to rewarding those who are there? Can government take care of the common good without people, offices, agencies with which to do it?

- Loyalty and party service are at first the chief qualifications for government positions—the "spoils system." Under the Pendleton Act in 1883 competitive examinations are required for branches of the public service that are "unclassified" by the President or the Congress. The Act establishes a Civil Service Commission and a merit system.

- The life and death of a government agency: Lyndon Johnson creates the Office of Economic Opportunity in 1964 to wage his "war on poverty." Richard Nixon virtually dismantles it in 1973, scattering its surviving functions among other agencies.

- Early in this decade, the Department of Agriculture learns that it has more employees than there are American farmers. At almost the same time, however, the official Government bureaucracy is shrunk by a postal reform measure creating an independent U.S. Postal Service, ending direct Government control of the mails in 1971.

4. "By Consent of the States"

The powers not delegated to the United States by the Constitution nor prohibited by it to the States, are reserved to the States respectively, or to the people.—Tenth Amendment to the Constitution

I needed the good will of the legislature of four states. I "formed" the legislative bodies with my own money. I found that it was cheaper that way.—Jay Gould

I am not a Virginian, but an American.—Patrick Henry

Having fought a war against a remote central authority, the framers of the Constitution were sensitive to criticisms of the new Federal government as not sufficiently close to the people. They might, then, be pleased to know that there are now more than 90,000 other governmental units in the United States. Besides the fifty states, there are countless elected representatives in cities, towns, counties, villages, school boards, port and tunnel authorities, highway commissions, sewage districts, power boards, and water regions. There are also metropolitan and regional authorities that enable us to deal with interstate problems without going to Washington. Plainly, a great deal of America's government is not at the Federal level. We are all citizens of our towns and states, as well as of the nation, even if we don't hold "town meetings" any more. Would we have a better society if more power and responsibility were retained locally? What would we sacrifice thereby? In what areas should each state have the right to decide what's best for its inhabitants? Should we be limited by inherited local and state boundaries, given present conditions? Do we need more or less uniform national standards?

- At the Hartford convention of 1814, Federalists who disapprove of the War of 1812 advocate states' rights and nullification—the doctrine that any state has the right to oppose a Congressional action that it believes is a violation of the Constitution. They are accused of verging on secession.

- William M. Tweed symbolizes the growing power and corruption of big-city political machines in the nineteenth century. "Boss" Tweed's Tammany Hall steals millions, is in absolute control of New York Politics; Tweed himself says, "As long as I count the votes, what are you going to do about it?" From 1900 to 1917, municipal reformers work for more modern, honest city governments.

- In the early 1960's the Supreme Court moves to end the disproportion among districts in state legislatures which permitted rural legislators to control state assemblies and senates long after a majority of the population had become urban. *Reynolds* v. *Sims* establishes the "one-man, one-vote" rule, requiring seats in both houses of a state legislature to be apportioned on the basis of population.

★ ★ ★

UNIT ONE
"A NATION OF NATIONS"

★ ★ ★

DeBry Engraving of an Indian Town, 1590, showing (A) the house serving as a tomb for chieftains, (B) place of prayer, (C) ceremonial dance, (D) feast, (E) tobacco field, (F) watchman, (G) corn, (H) squash, (I) pumpkins, (K) ceremonial fire, (L) water.

"Throughout the Southeast . . . a highly successful agriculture permitted the growth of large population centers . . . [with] an elaborate art and ceremonial life."—McNickle

Scene in the Hold of the "Blood-Stained Gloria." (Middle Passage.)

"Aboard ship . . . the men were all put in irons, two and two shackled together, to prevent their mutiny."—Phillips

Welcome to All By J. Keppler, 1880

". . . Give me your tired, your poor, Your huddled masses yearning to breathe free, The wretched refuse of your teeming shore. . . ."—Lazarus, quoted in Higham

Immigrants on the Steerage Deck of the S.S. Pennland, 1893.

"And so suffering, fearing, brooding, rejoicing, we crept nearer and nearer to the coveted shore."—Antin

Immigrants at Ellis Island Awaiting Processing

"Ellis Island was little more than a prison in those days."—Mangione

Immigrants in New York City's Lower East Side, about 1900.

"The one thing you shall vainly ask for in the chief city of America is a distinctively American community. There is none; certainly not among the tenements. . . . In their place has come this queer conglomerate mass of heterogeneous elements."—Riis

Cartoonist Thomas Nast comments on the anti-Chinese sentiment of the 1870s.

February 8, 1879

"Every Dog" (No Distinction of Color) "Has His Day."

RED GENTLEMAN TO YELLOW GENTLEMAN: "Pale face 'fraid you crowd him out, as he did me."

Cheyenne Indian Village, 1895.

"The reservations did not disappear, and the Indians—demonstrating that no people can be stripped involuntarily of their culture—continued to be Indians."—Josephy

Albert Einstein and his daughter, Margot, right, take oath of citizenship in New Jersey Court, October, 1940.

"The concept of America as a refuge from European oppression supplied one of the original, fertilizing elements of our national consciousness. . . . The efforts [of Jewish refugees] to escape Nazi barbarism coincided with a growing revulsion of American opinion against racism."—Higham

Americans Called Indians

D'Arcy McNickle

The first of the many migrations that contributed to the American nation took place some 30,000 years ago. Moving eastward from Asia, primitive peoples spread throughout the Americas over a period of thousands of years, adapting to the changing climate and environments. By the time Columbus landed in the New World and bestowed the word "Indians" on its inhabitants, there were, in what is now the United States, hundreds of tribes, differing in physical appearance, language, and civilization. Some were primarily hunters and gatherers; others depended more heavily on agriculture and had established permanent villages.

The complete story of the development of the Indian cultures will probably never be known, but in the following article D'Arcy McNickle, a member of the Confederated Salish and Kootenai Tribes of Montana, introduces us to "Americans Called Indians."

The Americans called Indians wrote no histories, and their past was only dimly told in oral tradition and legend. When strangers came to write about the land that had been theirs, the Indians somehow turned into flora and fauna and were hardly visible as men. Their global experience had been reduced to scattered footnotes in world history. Yet the crossing into a new world and the long trek spanning two continents and 9,000 miles of mountain and prairie, desert and jungle, were in their magnitude the equivalent of anything man had experienced elsewhere.

The Americans called Indians shared what is probably man's oldest characteristic—his inclination to wander. . . . As a hunter and gatherer of foodstuffs, man explored the fearful unknown of all climates and regions, including the troublesome world within himself. He became adventurer and poet.

These qualities the Indian people shared. It is not necessary to speculate on how early man, the predecessor of the American Indian, stumbled into the Western Hemisphere northeastward out of Asia in pursuit of game animals. He simply radiated into all beckoning biospheres of the Old World and continued into the New, without any awareness that he had bridged two worlds. Wherever he paused along the way, he named the land and learned to live within it. . . .

D'Arcy McNickle, "Americans Called Indians," from *North American Indians in Historical Perspective*, edited by Eleanor Burke Leacock and Nancy Oestreich Lurie, Copyright © 1971 by Random House, Inc. Reprinted by permission of the publisher. The preparation of this paper was made possible by a faculty grant from the University of Saskatchewan, Regina Campus.

The Search for Beginnings

The question of when the first migrations occurred may ultimately be determined by comparative studies of technological development. A scattering of evidence throughout the two continents suggests occupation as early as 30,000 years ago or even earlier. . . .

When New World settlement is viewed from the point in time for which firm dates have been established, two features are apparent: The technology was capable of producing a variety of finely wrought tools, and man had spread all over North America south of lingering ice masses and perhaps over much of South America as well.

The time range involved here, supported by numerous radiocarbon dates, is between 15,000 B.C. and 5000 B.C. The culture stage is variously referred to as Paleo-Indian, Upper Lithic, and Big Game Hunting, among others. . . .

While the economy was presumably based on big game hunting and the remains of mammoth and other extinct mammals are invariably associated with the human artifacts of the period, the ecological adaption was not limited to a single-minded pursuit of big game. . . . Certainly small game was taken, and quite possibly other natural food substances were used, although no milling stones for grinding wild seeds are associated with the period. . . .

A major readaptation was forced upon these early hunters by the disappearance of certain of the game animals upon which they had subsisted. The mammoth, for example, whose dismembered skeletons are found so frequently in association with the fluted spear points of this period, had disappeared by about 8000 B.C. . . . Hunting continued as a way of life into historic times, at least in the Great Plains, but the animals pursued were the modern bison and various deer and antelope species. Hunting persisted also in the nonagricultural North, of course, again with the substitution of modern animal species for those that became extinct.

There is as yet no satisfactory explanation for this relatively sudden disappearance of animal species, which had the effect of profoundly re-shaping human life in the postglacial age.

The Archaic Mode

The succeeding period or cultural stage, designated the Archaic, is characterized by fuller exploitation of resources, with regional variations, and by an expanding population. The period began about 6000 B.C., earlier in some areas, and for some historic tribes it remained the basic scheme of life into modern times, with refinements in technology and social practice.

. . . It was a gathering or foraging economy, in which game animals might still have provided a major food supply, but all manner of wild seeds, fruits, berries, nuts, roots, and fleshy plants were utilized. Along fresh-water streams and lakes and salt-water shores, fish and shellfish were taken in abundance with traps and weirs and specialized gear. Substances other than stone and bone were fabricated into utility objects. Especially common . . . are devices for grinding wild seeds or other vegetable matter. . . .

In the Far West, where large game animals of the Ice Age were first to

39

disappear or never flourished, the Desert Culture, which is equated with the Archaic, had its beginnings as early as 8000 B.C. Because of the extreme aridity of much of the area, as in the Great Basin, southeastern California, southern Arizona, and northern Mexico, agriculture never became established (except in some local situations), and the historic tribes occupying these desert environments have retained much of the basic cultural adaptations of their ancient forebears. . . .

The Archaic period saw the beginnings of more settled communities. Even where people of necessity followed seasonal cycles of food gathering, supplemented by small game hunting, their movements were scheduled and purposeful. The rootless nomadic tribesman of later literature was already a fiction. . . . Every ecological niche, to use the biologist's term, appears to have been occupied during the course of the Archaic stage, that is, by 2000 B.C. . . .

There is good evidence that trade routes were established during this period, which would mean that individuals or small groups traveled to other regions and learned about other people—a familiar pattern in later Indian society. . . . Another characteristic that would seem to have significance for the future was a factor of technology itself. In their foraging activities the people learned to identify varieties of plants and their economic uses. . . . These cultural acquisitions, taken together, contributed to the transition that would lead to the practice of agriculture and to larger, stable communities of people—to the Indian world as it came to be.

The First Farmers

Beginning at about 1000 B.C., the cultural stream that had carried man and material artifacts southward out of northern North America reversed itself, like channeled tidewater at the end of its run. Thereafter, the flow was northward. . . .

Desert culture subsistence, with characteristic milling stones, storage baskets, digging sticks, and related food-gathering equipment, appeared in the Mexican highlands before 7000 B.C.; between that date and 2000 B.C. the economy had shifted from hunting-gathering to an agricultural base in which domesticated plants provided an ever-expanding proportion of food production. . . . After about 2500 B.C. plant cultivation throughout Mesoamerica* expanded rapidly. . . . By 1000 B.C. squash and the red kidney bean had followed corn into the Southwest, and agriculture had made its beginnings along with settled villages and pottery. . . .

Except in the East, where rich soils and abudant rainfall favored plant growth, agriculture never entirely displaced the Archaic foraging adaptation in other areas of North Amercia. A major exception was in the desert valleys of southern Arizona, where the Hohokam people practiced and intensive irrigation agriculture. . . .

Elsewhere in the West and Southwest, farming was marginal and , after an initial spread over the region, tended to withdraw to watered valleys. . . . In the Great Basin and the Plateau country, where the Desert Culture was the initial adaptation, as well as in the High Plains, river and creek bottom farming was simply an addition to the old foraging-hunting style of life.

---

*Ed. note: Central America.

It was a life-style that fitted perfectly the kind of social organization that must have been developing throughout the West and northward to the Arctic. This was an unstratified, egalitarian, kinsmen-oriented group, cooperating in small units, and maintaining an intimate association with the natural environment. The people of these regions remained apart from the agriculturally induced urbanization that, in the Southeast and in Meso-america, divided populations into ruling hegemonies and voiceless masses.

The People
The Americans called Indians had physical form; they were not abstract phantoms. They had words for themselves and for other people they knew or encountered. They moved within, and were adapted to, a physical environment. . . .

In even the earliest descriptions by incoming Europeans it was recognized that the Indians were physically a distinct people with "copper-colored skins" and coarse black hair—"almost like the hairs of a horse's tail," Columbus remarked. Only much later, when more Indians had been observed, was it recognized that the Indian population was not, in fact, all of a single type. Skin color varied from ivory to the darkest brown. Hair form ranged from the coarse black of Columbus' observation to shades of brown and degrees of waviness. Stature and body build showed great variability. With respect to the Mongoloid features that are generally considered to be typically Indian—the slanting eye fold, the low-bridged nose, the smooth, straight brow, prominent cheek bones, scantiness of beard and body hair—these are not all equally manifested by all Indian population groups. . . .

Language
The variability expressed in physical form has it counterpart in groupings of some half-dozen basic language stocks, each containing a broad band of cognate tongues ranging from locally differing dialects, with some interchange of communication possible, to mutually unintelligible languages. . . . The gross number of more than 2,000 separate, identifiable languages spread throughout the two continents gives an idea of the possibilities for interpreting movement in time and space. . . .

From Prehistory to History
The native world that existed before permanent settlers moved in from Europe is less remote and inscrutable than it seemed last century when the great mounds of the Ohio and Mississippi Valleys and the monumental works of Middle America were first contemplated. . . . The better understanding we now have of aboriginal America can be traced to a lessened parochialism growing out of wider knowledge of man's evolutionary development, but it also traces to the extensive ethnographic studies and historical reconstructions published within the century. . . .

Throughout the Southeast, for example, a highly successful agriculture permitted the growth of large population centers, which in some instances approached the true urban developments. The cultural florescence that accompanied this population growth resulted in an elaborate art and ceremonial life and marked social stratification that endured from about A.D. 500 until as late as A.D. 1650. . . .

. . . [Among] the Iroguoian people of the lower Great Lakes and central New York . . . from about A.D. 1000 the Owasco culture flourished, a regional adaptation of the Woodland tradition. . . . Some domesticated food plants were grown, at least corn and beans, supplementing the basic hunting and gathering way of life. By A.D. 1200 the longhouse was in use, and palisaded village clusters began to appear, indicating an expanding semi-sedentary population. Squash was added to the garden crops, forming the Indian trinity of plants, and a localized pottery style had emerged. All of these were were distinguishing features of the Iroquois people when they were first encountered by Europeans, as by Cartier in the St. Lawrence Valley in 1534. . . .

The earliest recorded encounter between Europeans and Indians living between the Rocky Mountains and the Mississippi was chronicled by the Coronado Expedition of 1541, in what is now western Kansas. . . .

Occupation of the Plains can be traced back at least 12,000, possibly 15,000 years, and through a series of developmental stages. . . . In the latest of these, the Plains Village stage, beginning before A.D. 1000,. . . corn-growing Indians occupied the fertile valleys of all the major streams flowing eastward out of the Rockies, in permanent villages of earth-covered houses. They made a sturdy, durable pottery and utilized a variety of materials in fashioning household tools and utensils. After the horse reached the Plains from Spanish settlements in the Southwest at the beginning of the eighteenth century, some tribal groups abandoned farming (which provided a precarious economic base in some areas) and became highly mobile hunters; but others among the Plains Village tribes maintained their fixed settlements and used the horse only on semiannual hunts into the neighboring countryside. . . .

. . . The record of cultural development in the Southwest is . . . better know than in any other region of native America, and in at least one instance the record of continuous occupation to historic times is only exceeded perhaps by recent discoveries in the Tehuacan Valley of southern Mexico. . . .

A similarly continuous chronology, though of shorter time span, can be demonstrated for the modern Pueblo peoples of the Rio Grande Valley, western New Mexico, and the Hopi villages of Arizona. These and their predecessors, the Basket Maker people, together referred to as the Anasazi (a Navaho word meaning "ancient ones"), have occupied approximately the same territory since the early years of the Christian era. Through all this time, they have been village-dwelling farmers, gradually elaborating their technologies and style of life until the coming of European settlement at the end of the sixteenth century. At a slightly earlier time, beginning about 300 B.C., the Mogollon culture of southwestern New Mexico and southeastern Arizona had acquired agriculture and pottery, presumably from Mexico, and these and other traits were carried north to the Anasazi country. . . .

The Arctic

Sequences of settlement and adaptation in the Arctic and the Subarctic interior have not been clearly defined as yet. . . . It would seem that once

42

man had developed the essential tools and technologies for life along the Arctic sea, in tundra country, and in the boreal forest, he had little reason and scant inducement to experiment with new devices. Gaining a livelihood became highly specialized, and maintaining an ecological balance was the essential concern. . . .

Retrospect

What has been reviewed here, all too briefly is a long history of ecological adaptation, of people learning the infinite variety of the land and accommodating| themselves to it. Though details have been generalized or omitted (sometimes for the simple reason that they are not known), certain characteristics or themes are strikingly apparent.

Foremost, perhaps, is an underlying homogeneity that persists as a kind of nucleating core with great diversity—of physical type, language, subsistence base, social form, ceremonial style, and technological level. . . .

It would almost seem that something in the land itself and in its challenges compelled a certain kind of human adaptation. Perhaps it is not fortuitous that the Indians in their creation stories conceive of a man as emerging from the underworld, the earth. First Man and First Woman do not spring fully formed from the sea or from the head of a God, and not from any Word. They are weak and imperfect beings faced with imminent doom, which they escape by calling upon their brothers of the earth, sky and water—badger, beaver, turtle, ant, raven, chipmunk, blue jay, dragonfly—the cast of characters varies from region to region, but the theme is well-nigh universal. Man and the animals are equally involved in making the world. . . .

The land in its infinite variety, its immensity of space, stretching to empty horizons, and its first loneliness, compelled respect, and moving through it man saw himself in perspective against thundering waterways and crashing mountains. Not only was his stature held to lifesize, but he recognized himself as but one of the features of that infinite landscape, and he made no prior claim because he was alive and sentient. What he was, he owed to that which was around him, and he gave back what he could of himself. The idea of reciprocity became the core of his social existence.

That was the nature of the adaptation that the Americans called Indians achieved in the New World. . . .

"A Hideous and Desolate Wilderness"

William Bradford

The Europeans who braved the Atlantic crossing in the seventeenth century, like later immigrants, came to America for a variety of reasons—economic, religious, political, and personal. The combination of factors that drove them from the Old World and drew them to the New varied with individuals, with time, and with place. Nevertheless, almost all immigrants shared certain common experiences: the uprooting from what was familiar, a long and hazardous ocean voyage, and the adaptation to a foreign land.

Hope for the future was frequently mingled with fear of the unknown, and a profound sense of isolation often marked the immigrants' experience. For the first colonists, struggling for physical survival in a hostile environment, this isolation was a harsh reality. In the following selection, William Bradford, governor of the Plymouth Colony for thirty years, describes the voyage of the Pilgrims aboard the Mayflower *in 1620 and their reactions upon first landing in the New World.*

. . . So being ready to depart, they had a day of solemn humiliation, their pastor taking his text from Ezra viii. 21: "And there at the river, by Ahava, I proclaimed a fast, that we might humble ourselves before our God, and seek of him a right way for us, and for our children, and for all our substance." . . . They were accompanied with most of their brethren out of the city, unto a town sundry miles off called Delftshaven, where the ship lay ready to receive them. So they left that goodly and pleasant city which had been their resting place near twelve years; but they knew they were pilgrims, and looked not much on those things, but lift up their eyes to the heavens, their dearest country, and quieted their spirits. . . .

After they had enjoyed fair winds and weather for a season, they were encountered many times with cross winds and met with many fierce storms with which the ship was shroudly* shaken, and her upper works made very leaky; and one of the main beams in the midships was bowed and cracked, which put them in some fear that the ship could not be able to perform the

---

*Ed. note: "Shrewdly." This word originally meant "wickedly."

From William Bradford, *Of Plymouth Plantation, 1620–1647*, ed., Samuel Eliot Morison. (New York: Alfred A. Knopf, Inc., 1966); pp. 47, 58–63. © 1952 by Samuel Eliot Morison. Reprinted by permission.

voyage. So some of the chief of the company, perceiving the mariners to fear the sufficiency of the ship as appeared by their mutterings, they entered into serious consultation with the master and other officers of the ship, to consider in time of the danger, and rather to return than to cast themselves into a desperate and inevitable peril. . . . But in examining of all opinions, the master and others affirmed they knew the ship to be strong and firm under water; and for the buckling of the main beam, there was a great iron screw the passengers brought out of Holland, which would raise the beam into his place; the which being done, the carpenter and master affirmed that with a post put under it, set firm in the lower deck and otherways bound, he would make it sufficient. And as for the decks and upper works, they would caulk them as well as they could, and though with the working of the ship they would not long keep staunch, yet there would otherwise be no great danger, if they did not overpress her with sails. So they committed themselves to the will of God and resolved to proceed. . . .

But to omit other things (that I may be brief) after long beating at sea they fell with that land which is called Cape Cod; the which being made and certainly known to be it, they were not a little joyful. After some deliberation had amongst themselves and with the master of the ship, they tacked about and resolved to stand for the southward (the wind and weather being fair) to find some place about Hudson's River for their habitation. But after they had sailed that course about half the day, they fell amongst dangerous shoals and roaring breakers, and they were so far entangled therewith as they conceived themselves in great danger; and the wind shrinking upon them withal, they resolved to bear up again for the Cape and thought themselves happy to get out of those dangers before night overtook them, as by God's good providence they did. And the next day they got into the Cape Harbor where they rid in safety. . . .

Being thus arrived in a good harbor, and brought safe to land, they fell upon their knees and blessed the God of Heaven who had brought them over the vast and furious ocean, and delivered them from all the perils and miseries thereof, again to set their feet on the firm and stable earth, their proper element. . . .

But here I cannot but stay and make a pause, and stand half amazed at this poor people's present condition; and so I think will the reader, too, when he well considers the same. Being thus passed the vast ocean, and a sea of troubles before in their preparation (as may be remembered by that which went before), they had now no friends to welcome them nor inns to entertain or refresh their weatherbeaten bodies; no houses or much less towns to repair to, to seek for succour. It is recorded in Scripture as a mercy to the Apostle and his shipwrecked company, that the barbarians showed them no small kindness in refreshing them, but these savage barbarians, when they met with them (as after will appear) were readier to fill their sides full of arrows than otherwise. And for the season it was winter, and they that know the winters of that country know them to be sharp and violent, and subject to cruel and fierce storms, dangerous to travel to known places, much more to search an unknown coast. Besides, what could they see but a hideous and desolate wilderness, full of wild beasts and wild men—and what multitudes there might be of them they knew not. Neither could they, as it were, go up to the top of Pisgah* to view from this wilderness a more goodly country to feed their hopes; for which way soever they turned their eyes (save upward to the heavens) they could have little solace or content in respect of any outward objects. For summer being done, all things stand upon them with a weatherbeaten face, and the whole country, full of woods and thickets, represented a wild and savage hue. If they looked behind them, there was the mighty ocean which they had passed and was now as a main bar and gulf to separate them from all the civil parts of the world. If it be said they had a ship to succour them, it is true; but what heard they daily from the master and company? But that with speed they should look out a place (with their shallop) where they would be, at some near distance; for the season was such as he would not stir from thence till a safe harbor was discovered by them, where they would be, and he might go without danger; and that victuals consumed apace but he must and would keep sufficient for themselves and their return. Yea, it was muttered by some that if they got not a place in time, they would turn them and their goods ashore and leave them. Let it also be considered what weak hopes of supply and succour they left behind them, that might bear up their minds in this sad condition and trials they were under; and they could not but be very small. It is true, indeed, the affections and love of their brethren at Leyden was cordial and entire towards them, but they had little power to help them or themselves. . . .

What could now sustain them but the Spirit of God and His grace? May not and ought not the children of these fathers rightly say: "Our fathers were Englishmen which came over this great ocean, and were ready to perish in this wilderness; but they cried unto the Lord, and He heard their voice and looked on their adversity," etc. "Let them therefore praise the Lord, because He is good: and His mercies endure forever." . . .

*Ed. note: Mountain range from which, according to the Bible, Moses saw the Promised Land.

They Came in Chains

Thomas Phillips,
Commander of the *Hannibal*

Although some colonists—notably prisoners and debtors— were sent to the New World by the civil authorities in the mother country, for most European immigrants the decision to come to America was a voluntary one. But for some nine million blacks, from the fifteenth to the nineteenth centuries, the trip from Africa to the Americas was part of the largest forced migration in history. Of this number, approximately 345,000 were imported into what is now the United States before the slave trade was prohibited in 1808.

For the black immigrants who came to America in chains, horror followed upon horror: capture by other Africans, in war or perhaps by kidnapping; the march to the coast in "coffles" or caravans; the sale to European slave traders; the voyage to the New World in overcrowded, disease-ridden ships; and the auction to new owners. It was a deliberately dehumanizing process in which people became merely "black cargo." Some of these hardships are illustrated in the following account by the commander of a ship engaged in the slave trade in the late seventeenth century. It should be noted that many captains were less humane than the author of this narrative.

The cappasheirs* each brought out his slaves according to his degree and quality, the greatest first, etc. and our surgeon examin'd them well in all kinds, to see that they were sound wind and limb, making them jump, stretch out their arms swiftly, looking in their mouths to judge of their age; for the cappasheirs are so cunning, that they shave them all close before we see them, so that let them be never so old we can see no grey hairs in their heads or beards; and then having liquor'd them well and sleek with palm oil, 'tis no easy matter to know an old one from a middle-age one, but by the teeths decay; but our greatest care of all is to buy none that are pox'd, lest they should infect the rest aboard. . . .

Ed. note: Caboceers, or lesser chiefs.

From "A Journal of a Voyage Made in the *Hannibal* of London, 1693-1694," by Thomas Phillips, Commander of Said Ship, in Elizabeth Donnan, ed., *Documents Illustrative of the Slave Trade.* Publication No. 409, Carnegie Institution of Washington, 1930. Vol. I, pp. 399-410.

When we had selected from the rest such as we liked, we agreed in what goods to pay for them, the prices being already stated before the king, how much of each sort of merchandize we were to give for a man, woman, and child, which gave us much ease, and saved abundance of disputes and wranglings, and gave the owner a note, signifying our agreement of the sorts of goods; upon delivery of which the next day he receiv'd them; then we mark'd the slaves we had bought in the breast, or shoulder, with a hot iron, having the letter of the ship's name on it, the place being before anointed with a little palm oil, which caus'd but little pain, the mark being usually well in four or five days, appearing very plain and white after. . . .

When our slaves were come to the seaside, our canoes were ready to carry them off to the longboat, if the sea permitted, and she convey'd them aboard ship, where the men were all put in irons, two and two shackled together, to prevent their mutiny, or swimming ashore.

The negroes are so wilful and loth to leave their own country, that they have often leap'd out of the canoes, boat and ship, into the sea, and kept under water till they were drowned, to avoid being taken up and saved by our boats, which pursued them; they having a more dreadful apprehension of Barbadoes than we can have of hell, tho' in reality they live much better there than in their own country; but home is home, etc: we have likewise seen divers of them eaten by the sharks. . . .

We had about 12 negroes did wilfully drown themselves, and others starv'd themselves to death; for 'tis their belief that when they die they return home to their own country and friends again.

I have been inform'd that some commanders have cut off the legs and arms of the most wilful, to terrify the rest, for they believe if they lose a member, they cannot return home again: I was advis'd by some of my officers to do the same, but I could not be perswaded to entertain the least thought of it, much less put in practice such barbarity and cruelty to poor creatures, who, excepting their want of christianity and true religion (their misfortune more than fault) are as much the works of God's hands, and no doubt as dear to him as ourselves; nor can I imagine why they should be despis'd for their colour, being what they cannot help, and the effect of the climate it has pleas'd God to appoint them. I can't think there is any intrinsick value in one colour more than another, nor that white is better than black, only we think so because we are so, and are prone to judge favourably in our own case, as well as the blacks, who in odium of the colour, say, the devil is white, and so paint him. . . .

When we come to sea we let them all out of irons, they never attempting then to rebel, considering that should they kill or master us, they could not tell how to manage the ship, or must trust us, who would carry them where we pleas'd; therefore the only danger is while we are in sight of their own country, which they are loth to part with; but once out of sight out of mind: I never heard that they mutiny'd in any ships of consequence, that had a good number of men, and the least care; but in small tools where they had but few men, and those negligent or drunk, then they surpriz'd and butcher'd them, cut the cables, and let the vessel drive ashore, and every one shift for himself. However, we have some 30 or 40 gold coast negroes, which we buy, and are procur'd us there by our factors, to make guardians and overseers of the Whidaw negroes, and sleep among them to keep them from quarrelling; and in order, as well as to give us notice, if they can discover any caballing or plotting among them, which trust they will discharge with great diligence: they also take care to make the negroes scrape the decks where they lodge every morning very clean, to eschew any distempers that may engender from filth and nastiness; when we constitute a guardian, we give him a cat of nine tails as a badge of his office, which he is not a little proud of, and will exercise with great authority. We often at sea in the evenings would let the slaves come up into the sun to air themselves, and make them jump and dance for an hour or two to our bag-pipes, harp, and fiddle, by which exercise to preserve them in health; but notwithstanding all our endeavour, 'twas my hard fortune to have great sickness and mortality among them. . . .

We spent in our passage from St. Thomas to Barbadoes two months eleven days, from the 25th of August to the 4th of November following: in which time there happen'd much sickness and mortality among my poor men and negroes, that of the first we buried 14, and of the last 320, which was a great detriment to our voyage, the royal African company losing ten pounds by every slave that died, and the owners of the ship ten pounds ten shillings, being the freight agreed on to be paid them by the charter-party for every negroe deliver'd alive ashore to the African company's agents at Barbadoes; whereby the loss in all amounted to near 6560 pounds sterling. The distemper which my men as well as the blacks mostly die of, was the white flux, which was so violent and inveterate, that no medicine would in the least check it; so that when any of our men were seiz'd with it, we esteem'd him a dead man, as he generally proved. . . .

The negroes are so incident to the small-pox, that few ships that carry them escape without it, and sometimes it makes vast havock and destruction among them: but tho' we had 100 at a time sick of it, and that it went thro' the ship, yet we lost not above a dozen by it. All the assistance we gave the diseased was only as much water as they desir'd to drink, and some palm-oil to anoint their sores, and they would generally recover without any other helps but what kind nature gave them.

. . . But what the small-pox spar'd, the flux swept off, to our great regret, after all our pains and care to give them their messes in due order and season, keeping their lodgings as clean and sweet as possible, and enduring so much misery and stench so long among a parcel of creatures nastier than swine; and after all our expectations to be defeated by their mortality. No gold-finders can endure so much noisome slavery as they do who carry negroes; for those have some respite and satisfaction, but we endure twice the misery; and yet by their mortality our voyages are ruin'd, and we pine and fret our selves to death, to think that we should undergo so much misery, and take so much pains to so little purpose. . . .

Paying Off
the Passage

Gottlieb Mittelberger

The trade in human cargo was by no means limited to Africans. During the seventeenth and eighteenth centuries between one-half and two-thirds of all European immigrants came to America as servants. Unable to pay for their passage, indentured servants bound themselves by "indentures" or contracts to a ship's captain for a specified term, usually four to seven years. The captain would, in turn, sell the indentures to planters or merchants in the colonies. When the period of service was over, the servant was usually given a small sum of money and perhaps title to some land.

A second class of servants, redemptioners, also bound themselves to work off the cost of their passage; but their terms of servitude were not specified in advance. They were transported to the colonial seaports where their services were sold to the highest bidder. The system of servitude was often harsh, but it helped to meet both the needs of Europeans too poor to pay their way to America and the needs of the New World, chronically short of labor.

Among those who availed themselves of the redemption system in the mid-eighteenth century were thousands of Germans, fleeing the political and religious intolerance and poverty that had followed in the wake of the Thirty Years' War. They were attracted in particular to Pennsylvania, where they numbered between 110,000 and 150,000 on the eve of the Revolution. They became successful farmers and were in the forefront of the westward movement.

The following account by Gottlieb Mittelberger, a teacher and organist who sailed to Philadelphia with a boatload of German servants in 1750, describes the experiences faced by those selling themselves into servitude to pay off their passage.

When the ships have weighed anchor for the last time, usually off Cowes in Old England, then both the long sea voyage and misery begin in earnest.

Reprinted by permission of the publisher from *Journey to Pennsylvania* by Gottlieb Mittelberger, edited and translated by Oscar Handlin and John Clive, Cambridge, Mass.: The Belknap Press of Harvard University Press, © 1960 by the President and Fellows of Harvard College.

For from there the ships often take eight, nine, ten, or twelve weeks sailing to Philadelphia, if the wind is unfavorable. But even given the most favorable winds, the voyage takes seven weeks.

During the journey the ship is full of pitiful signs of distress—smells, fumes, horrors, vomiting, various kinds of sea sickness, fever, dysentery, headaches, heat, constipation, boils, scurvy, cancer, mouth-rot, and similar afflictions, all of them caused by the age and the highly-salted state of the food, especially of the meat, as well as by the very bad and filthy water, which brings about the miserable destruction and death of many. Add to all that shortage of food, hunger, thirst, frost, heat, dampness, fear, misery, vexation, and lamentation as well as other troubles. Thus, for example, there are so many lice, especially on the sick people, that they have to be scraped off the bodies. All this misery reaches its climax when in addition to everything else one must also suffer through two to three days and nights of storm, with everyone convinced that the ship with all aboard is bound to sink. In such misery all the people on board pray and cry pitifully together. . . .

I myself was afflicted by severe illness at sea, and know very well how I felt. These people in their misery are many times very much in want of solace, and I often entertained and comforted them with singing, praying, and encouragement. Also, when possible, and when wind and waves permitted it, I held daily prayer meetings with them on deck, and, since we had no ordained clergyman on board, was forced to administer baptism to five children. I also held services, including a sermon, every Sunday, and when the dead were buried at sea, commended them and our souls to the mercy of God.

Among those who are in good health impatience sometimes grows so great and bitter that one person begins to curse the other, or himself and the day of his birth, and people sometimes come close to murdering one another. Misery and malice are readily associated, so that people begin to cheat and steal from one another. And then one always blames the other for having undertaken the voyage. Often the children cry out against their parents, husbands against wives and wives against husbands, brothers against their sisters, friends and acquaintances against one another.

But most of all they cry out against the thieves of human beings! Many groan and exclaim: "Oh! If only I were back at home, even lying in my pig-sty!" Or they call out: "Ah, dear God, if I only once again had a piece of good bread or a good fresh drop of water." Many people whimper, sigh, and cry out pitifully for home. Most of them become homesick at the thought that many hundreds of people must necessarily perish, die, and be thrown into the ocean in such misery. And this in turn makes their families, or those who were responsible for their undertaking the journey, oftentimes fall almost into despair. . . .

One can scarcely conceive what happens at sea to women in childbirth and to their innocent offspring. Very few escape with their lives; and mother and child, as soon as they have died, are thrown into the water. . . .

Children between the ages of one and seven seldom survive the sea voyage; and parents must often watch their offspring suffer miserably, die, and be thrown into the ocean, from want, hunger, thirst, and the like. I myself, alas, saw such a pitiful fate overtake thirty-two children on board our vessel, all of whom were finally thrown into the sea. . . .

On one of these voyages a father often becomes infected by his wife and children, or a mother by her small children, or even both parents by their children, or sometimes whole families one by the other, so that many times numerous corpses lie on the cots next to those who are still alive, especially when contagious diseases rage on board.

Many other accidents also occur on these ships, especially falls in which people become totally crippled and can never be completely made whole again. Many also tumble into the sea.

It is not surprising that many passengers fall ill, because in addition to all the other troubles and miseries, warm food is served only three times a week, and at that is very bad, very small in quantity, and so dirty as to be hardly palatable at all. And the water distributed in these ships is often very black, thick with dirt, and full of worms. . . . True, great hunger and thirst teach one to eat and drink everything—but many must forfeit their lives in the process. It is impossible to drink sea water, since it is salty and bitter as gall. If this were not the case, one could undertake such an ocean voyage with far less expense and without so many hardships.

When at last after the long and difficult voyage the ships finally approach land, when one gets to see the headlands for the sight of which the people on board had longed so passionately, then everyone crawls from below to the deck, in order to look at the land from afar. And people cry for joy, pray, and sing praises and thanks to God. The glimpse of land revives the passengers, especially those who are half-dead of illness. Their spirits, however weak they had become, leap up, triumph, and rejoice within them. Such people are now willing to bear all ills patiently, if only they can disembark soon and step on land. But, alas, alas!

When the ships finally arrive in Philadelphia after the long voyage only those are let off who can pay their sea freight or can give good security. The others, who lack the money to pay, have to remain on board until they are purchased and until their purchasers can thus pry them loose from the ship. In this whole process the sick are the worst off, for the healthy are preferred and are more readily paid for. The miserable people who are ill must often still remain at sea and in sight of the city for another two or three weeks—which in many cases means death. Yet many of them, were they able to pay their debts and to leave the ships at once, might escape with their lives. . . .

This is how the commerce in human beings on board ship takes place. Every day Englishmen, Dutchmen, and High Germans come from Philadelphia and other places, some of them very far away, sometime twenty or thirty or forty hours' journey, and go on board the newly arrived vessel that has brought people from Europe and offers them for sale. From among the healthy they pick out those suitable for the purposes for which they require them. Then they negotiate with them as to the length of the period for which they will go into service in order to pay off their passage, the whole amount of which they generally still owe. When an agreement has been reached, adult persons by written contract bind themselves to serve for three, four, five, or six years, according to their health and age. The very young, between the ages of ten and fifteen, have to serve until they are twenty-one, however.

Many parents in order to pay their fares in this way and get off the ship must barter and sell their children as if they were cattle. Since the fathers and mothers often do not know where or to what masters their children are to be sent, it frequently happens that after leaving the vessel, parents and children do not see each other for years on end, or even for the rest of their lives.

People who arrive without the funds to pay their way and who have children under the age of five, cannot settle their debts by selling them. They must give away these children for nothing to be brought up by strangers; and in return these children must stay in service until they are twenty-one years old. Children between five and ten who owe half-fare, that is, thirty florins, must also go into service in return until they are twenty-one years old, and can neither set free their parents nor take their debts upon themselves. On the other hand, the sale of children older than ten can help to settle a part of their parents' passage charges. . . .

No one in this country can run away from a master who has treated him harshly and get far. For there are regulations and laws that ensure that runaways are certainly and quickly recaptured. Those who arrest or return a fugitive get a good reward. For every day that someone who runs away is absent from his master he must as a punishment do service an extra week, for every week an extra month, and for every month a half year. But if the master does not want to take back the recaptured runaway, he is entitled to sell him to someone else for the period of as many years as he would still have had to serve. . . .

Red, White, and Black

Gary B. Nash

By the eve of the Revolution, three large and distinct cultural groups, each with many subgroups, peopled the Atlantic seaboard of North America. Of the 2.3 million persons living east of the Alleghenies in 1770, some 1.7 million were Europeans, half a million were Africans, and probably less than 100,000 were Indians. There was, to be sure, both cultural borrowing and some interracial mixing of blood lines. But the dominant European group exhibited little real desire to assimilate the other cultures.

The Europeans had made an initial attempt to "civilize" the Indians, but the native peoples had clung tenaciously to their own cultures, even in the face of military defeat. As early as 1646, the beginning of a system of "reserving" certain territories for Indians emerged as the white man's "solution" to the "Indian problem."

The Africans, brought to this country as slaves, were treated from the first as unfit for assimilation. As their numbers increased, so did the restrictions against their full participation in society.

The attitudes developed toward Indians and blacks in the colonial period were to shape the nation's policy toward these minorities throughout much of its history; clearly, the democratic ideals expressed in the Declaration of Independence were to apply to white men only.

Gary Nash, who explores the relationships between red, white and black in the following selection, is professor of history at UCLA.

The colonial period of our history is the story of a minority of Englishmen interacting with a majority of Iroquois, Delawares, Narragansetts, Pequots, Mahicans, Catawbas, Tuscaroras, Creeks, Cherokees, Choctaws, Ibos, Mandingos, Fulas, Yorubas, Ashantis, Germans, French, Spaniards, Swedes, and Scotch-Irish, to mention only some of the cultural strains present on the continent. . . .

English-Indian Relations

. . . From the time that the first Jamestown expedition touched land,

From Gary B. Nash, *Red, White, and Black: The Peoples of Early America,* © 1974. Reprinted by permission of Prentice-Hall, Inc., Englewood Cliffs, New Jersey.

Indians and Englishmen were in continuous contact in North America. Moreover, permanent settlement required acquisition of land by white settlers—land which was in the possession of the Indian. That single fact was the beginning of a chain of events which governed the entire sociology of red-white relations. . . .

. . .

Notwithstanding misconceptions, suspicion, and violence on both sides, the English and the Powhatans lived in close contact during the first decade of English settlement and cultural interchange occurred on a broad scale. Although it has been a commonplace in the popular mind since the moment when Europeans and native Americans first met that the Europeans were "advanced" and the Indians were "primitive," the technological differences between the two cultures, as anthropologist Nancy Lurie has recently reminded us, were equaled or outweighed by the similarities between these two agricultural societies. The main technological advantages of the English were their ability to traverse large bodies of water in wooden ships and their superiority in the use of iron to fashion implements and weapons. But the Indians quickly incorporated such iron-age items as kettles, fishhooks, traps, needles, knives, and guns into their material culture. In return they provided Englishmen with an understanding of how to use nets and weirs to catch the abundant fish and shellfish of the Chesapeake waters and introduced the Europeans to a wide range of agricultural products that were unknown in Europe before the New World was reached. . . .

. . .

After the increase of population that accompanied the rapid growth of tobacco production, relations between the two peoples underwent a fundamental alteration. While giving Virginia a money crop of great potential, the cultivation of tobacco created an enormous new demand for land. As more and more men pushed up the rivers that flowed into the Chesapeake Bay to carve out tobacco plantations, the Indians of the region perceived that what had previously been an abrasive and sometimes violent relationship might now become a disastrous one. Powhatan had died in 1618, just as the tobacco culture was beginning to expand rapidly. His cousin Opechancanough watched the English expansion uneasily for four years. Then in 1622 he set about to coordinate a unified attack on all the English settlements. It was the murder of a greatly respected Indian of the Powhatan Confederacy that ignited the assault on the Virginia settlements in 1622, but the highly combustible atmosphere generated by a half-dozen years of white expansion and pressure on Indian hunting lands was the more fundamental cause.

Although it did not achieve its goal of ending English presence in the Chesapeake area, the Indian attack of 1622 wiped out almost one-third of the white population. . . . Those who survived the attack were left free to pursue a ruthless new Indian policy. Even though several leaders in the colony confided to men in England that the real cause of the Indian attack was "our own perfidious dealing with them," it was generally agreed that henceforward the colonists would be free to hunt down the Indian wherever he could be found. No longer would it be necessary to acknowledge an obligation to "civilize" and Christianize the native. . . .

It was . . . tough, self-made, ambitious men, unhindered by religious or humanitarian concern for the Indians and unrestrained by government, that the Chesapeake tribes had to confront after 1630. They also had to face the rapidly shifting demographic balance—the drastic decline of their population by disease and war during the first quarter-century of English presence and the rapid increase of English after 1624. These were factors beyond the control of the Chesapeake tribes. But even though they did not auger well for the future the natives continued to follow their traditional way of life. The years of contact with European culture did little to convince them that they should remodel their religion, social and political organization, or values and beliefs on English patterns. Only the technological innovations and material objects of the newcomers were incorporated into Indian culture; the other aspects of European culture were resisted or rejected.

The Indian uprising of 1644 is additional proof, as Lurie has recently written, "that the Indians' method of adjusting to changes wrought by the Europeans continued to be an attempt to prevail over or remove the source of anxiety—the settlers—rather than to adapt themselves to the foreign culture. . . . Their determination apparently convinced the Virginians that Indians could rarely be cowed into submissiveness. Rather than risk future wars, the colonists reversed the policy of the 1620s and in 1646 signed a formal treaty with the survivors of the Powhatan Confederacy which drew a line between red and white territory and promised the Indians safety in their areas. It was the beginning of the modern reservation system, for it recognized that assimilation of the two peoples was unlikely and guaranteed to the indigenous people a sanctuary from white land hunger and aggression. . . .

Decay of Indian Strength

When a census was taken in Virginia in 1669, only 11 of the 28 tribes described by John Smith in 1608 and only about 2,000 of the 30,000 Indians present when the English arrived were still left in the colony. That the English prevailed in the clash of cultures was partly due to the continued immigration of new settlers to the colony at a time when the Indians were suffering population decline. The waning strength of the Indians may also have been related to the technological inferiority of their weapons although this is uncertain since the bow and arrow could be at least as effective as the musket in forest fighting. More important in the Indians' decline was their inability to unify against the incoming European peoples. . . .

Another factor played an equal if not more important role in the slow decay of Indian strength: the functionlessness of the Chesapeake tribes within the English economic and social system. This can be best understood by looking comparatively at the English and Spanish systems of colonization. In the Spanish colonies, the densely settled Indians had been utilized effectively as a subjugated labor force, both in the silver mines and in agriculture. The Spanish had unerringly located the native population centers in Mexico and Peru and made them the focal point of their colonizing efforts. Because the Indians supplied the bulk of the labor for colonial extractive and productive enterprises in the early decades, it was not only desirable but necessary to assimilate them into the European culture. Moreover, the Spanish church had a vested interest in the Indians. They sent hundreds of missionaries to the colonies with the express purpose of obtaining as many conversions as possible for the greater glory of the church. Thirdly, because the Spanish emigrants were overwhelmingly male, Indian women came to serve the indispensable function of mistress, concubine, and wife. . . . Of course none of these services could be obtained until the native societies had been subordinated to Spanish authority. And the most merciless forms of mass killing and terrorization were employed by the Spanish to insure their ascendancy in the first period of contact. Thereafter, however, the Indians were seen not primarily as a threat to Spanish colonization, though the possibility of native uprisings was always present, but as a population that could answer the economic, religious, and biological needs of the European newcomers. Important incentives existed for drawing the natives into Spanish culture, for mixing with them, and protecting them. In spite of catastrophic spread of European diseases, which may have reduced the Indian population by as much as 75 percent in the first century of contact, an impressive degree of acculturation and assimilation took place in the colonial period.

In Virginia none of these factors pertained except in the most limited way. The English brought no military force comparable to the conquistadors to subjugate the sparsely settled Chesapeake tribes and drive them into agricultural labor. The Anglican church sent only a handful of clergymen to the colony and they made only token efforts to mount a missionary campaign. Their power over local settlers so far as relations with the Indians was concerned was minimal. Nor was there a prolonged need for Indian women that might have brought about greater assimilation. The imbalance of males and females, though it existed in the early decades of settlement, was redressed by about mid-seventeenth century because English women were imported and emigration after mid-century tended to be by family far more often than in the Spanish case. Inter-racial marriages were almost unknown in Virginia and the few contacts between white men and Indian women that did take place were limited to the frontier areas where trappers and traders occasionally consorted with native women.

The only way in which the Indian served the needs of the white colonist was in the fur trade where the Indian served as trapper and hunter. But the fur trade was always of negligible importance in the early Virginia settlements, and by the 1620s tobacco dominated the Virginia economy. What the colonist primarily wanted from the Indian was his cleared land, as was made manifest in the aftermath of the 1622 attack. Within the first generation of European settlement, it was demonstrated that neither side possessed the military capacity to subjugate the other. But for the English subjugation was unnecessary. The Indian, it was understood, had little to contribute to the goals of English colonization and was therefore regarded merely as an obstacle. Once defined in these terms, the Chesapeake tribes became the subject not of assimilative policies but apartheid plans which called for separation or removal. In almost a perfect reversal of Spanish Indian policy the English in Virginia after 1622 worked to keep the two cultures apart, to minimize assimilation and acculturation. Like the Spanish policy it was a plan based on the calculation of self-interest. Differences in the exploitable resources of the Spanish and English colonies, in the density of Indian population, in the demographic composition of the colonizing and colonized societies, and in the social backgrounds of the colonists, rather than differences in national character, attitudes toward the indigenous people, or in national policy, were chiefly responsible for the pursuit of assimilation in Spanish America and the pursuit of racial separation in Virginia.

The African Response to Slavery

It is easy to assume that Africans, once sold into slavery and brought to the New World, were simply fitted into a closed system of forced labor where they lived out their lives, abject and de-Africanized, as best they could. So much attention is lavished on the kind of slave system fashioned by slave owners—the black codes they legislated, their treatment of slaves, the economic development they engineered—that the slaves themselves are often forgotten as active participants in a cultural process. How did they live their daily lives in a vastly different culture? To what degree were they acculturated into white European society? How did they experience and respond to the loss of their freedom and the separation from all that was familiar in their native culture? To what degree did they mold a new Afro-American culture, distinct from the European culture surrounding them? . . .

The first instinct of the slave who found himself on a Virginia tobacco plantation or a Jamaican sugar plantation was simply to survive. To do this he was obliged, like all of the oppressed, to study carefully the ways of his oppressor. In many cases other slaves were already on the plantation where the slave was taken and it was from them that the techniques of survival were learned. If other slaves were numerous, as on many Southern plantations by the mid-eighteenth century, and if new slaves were frequently arriving from Africa, then it was easier and more relevant to keep elements of the African culture alive and vibrant. But in no case could the African culture simply be erased, for new cultures always effloresce from previous cultures in a gradual process of syncretic change. . . . Music, dance, games, and folktales were among the most persistent cultural survivals, but religion, speech patterns, taboos, and superstitions were also retained in some measure. White slave owners were not unaware of the attempts of their slaves to maintain their cultural heritage and they undoubtedly allowed this insofar as it did not interfere with the "seasoning" of the new immigrants. When it impeded adaptation to the new system of life and work, attempts were made to obliterate such Africanisms. But never in the long history of slavery could memory, habit, and belief be entirely wiped away. The old was altered to suit the demands of a new situation and a new environment. What emerged was a blend of African and European cultural elements. . . .

Cultural Interaction of Red, White and Black

At the end of the colonial period, American society, some 2.5 million strong, was far from a homogeneous culture. Almost two hundred years of European colonization and the continuous interaction of three large and internally diverse cultural groups had left a conglomeration of cultural entities. Each had its own goals and to a large extent its own values. Two of the groups, European and Indian, retained a considerable degree of autonomy, although both were somewhat limited in what they could do by the presence of the other and by the political and economic relationships that they had contracted during the colonial epoch. The third group, the Afro-Americans, was necessarily limited by the fact that most of its members were enslaved. But Afro-Americans also retained a measure of autonomy, though it appeared in more subtle forms.

The complex interaction of the three cultural groups was filled with paradoxes. Europeans in America claimed that they wished to assimilate Indians and Africans but they found that the most effective way to exploit the land of one and the labor of the other was to follow a nonassimilationist policy. Bringing Christianity to non-Christians was an expensive and time-consuming enterprise, useful only to the extent that it better enabled Europeans to make use of the resources of those they sought to dominate. Since it often gave little promise of accomplishing that—and in fact frequently threatened to make the utilization of Indian land and African labor more difficult—it was given a low priority. . . . Southern slaves were widely exposed to Christian doctrine in the upper South where the threat of slave revolt was not so keenly felt, but were carefully shielded from the potentially radical message of Christianity in South Carolina and Georgia. That slaves in the North were broadly inculcated with Protestantism only reflected the belief that where slaves were vastly outnumbered by whites instruction in the precepts of Protestantism, with emphasis on dutiful work in one's present station, would act as a damper on rebelliousness. In education it was the same: slaves were educated in those things that enabled them to function in their work more effectively; but education as a concept, as a process of inquiry, was shunned for it promised only to cultivate aspirations that were inappropriate to those whose servitude was lifelong.

A handful of reformers and churchmen kept alive the humanitarian impulse, based on the theory that Africans and Indians should be assimilated into Anglo-American society. But though hardly admissible in public discussion, most colonists regarded the two cultural minorities in their midst as most useful when unassimilated or semiassimilated. Indeed, a large majority of the colonists came to regard slaves as unassimilable, as was to be clearly revealed when the emancipation of slaves in the Revolutionary era brought cries for their repatriation to Africa. So far as the assimilation of Indians was concerned, nothing could have been less desirable to European settlers, who coveted Indian land but not land with Indians on it. Nor did Indians seek entry into white society, for there was little they wanted from Europeans that they could not obtain through bartering skins and furs. Thus the problem for European colonists was how to obtain Indian land and exploit the presence of these ''obstacles'' to colonial expansion. Because they were almost as internally divided as the Indian nations and rarely in the colonial period had enough power to force the interior tribes to give up their land or political autonomy, the colonists based their Indian policy on the principle of keeping tribes divided against each other. . . .

Also working against assimilation was the inner need of white colonists to justify their exploitation of Africans and Indians by an insistence on the wide gap that separated "barbarian savages" from "civilized" Europeans. By definition, assimilation would narrow this gap, making Africans and Europeans or Indians and Europeans more alike. . . .

A second paradox was that white American culture developed the most pervasively negative attitudes toward the cultural minority in its midst that was indispensably valuable to it—the Afro-Americans—and held the more positive attitudes toward the cultural minority which stood only as an obstacle to white society once their military assistance was no longer needed —the Indians. Colonial society grew in size and strength in direct relationship to an increase in slaves and a decrease in "land-cluttering" Indians. Yet it was the black man upon whom the colonists fastened the most indelibly negative images. The key to this irony was that the colonist almost always encountered the black man as a slave and thus came to think of him as an abject and less than human creature; but the English settler met the Indian as an adversary or a half-trusted ally. The Indian maintained the freedom and power to come and go, to attack and kill, to give and withhold support, and to retain his political sovereignty. Though he was hated for many of these things, they earned him a grudging respect. . . .

A third paradox in the convergence of cultures was that the cultural group that was enslaved, degraded, and despised survived and flourished demographically in America, while the group that maintained its freedom, much of its power, and a considerable amount of European respect suffered depopulation and gradual decline. It is in no way to minimize the pain, humiliation, and brutality of slavery to point out that Africans in America were remarkably successful in a demographic sense, particularly in contrast to most other areas of the New World. Probably not more than 250,000 slaves were imported into the mainland colonies in the colonial period and yet on the eve of the Revolution the black population stood at close to .5 million. Although careful studies of slave fertility and mortality have not yet been made, the limited data we have suggest that while black mortality was far higher than white mortality, black fertility may have been rather close to the white norm. . . .

By contrast, the Indian tribes east of the Appalachian Mountains suffered major population declines in the first two centuries of contact with Europeans. Although they were not struck down in the same catastrophic proportions as the indigenous people of Mexico and most parts of Latin America, their mortality rates and natural decline stood in stark contrast to the natural increase of the enslaved Africans. Particularly in areas of white settlement, along the coastal plain from Maine to Georgia, only remnants of the Indian population remained on the eve of the Revolution. Connecticut, for example, counted 930 Indians in a census in 1762; Massachusetts found 1,681 in 1761; Virginia listed only 130 in 1774; and Rhode Island tabulated 1,482 in the same year. At the same time the black population, even setting aside increases through importation, was growing rapidly. This was due to a number of factors. First, Africans were far more resistant to European epidemic diseases and by the mid-eighteenth century were being immunized, like whites, against the biggest killer of all—smallpox. Hardly an Indian tribe or nation in the eastern part of the continent escaped the dread killer. . . . Far less important as a killer were the wars which tribes fought with European settlers and with each other at the instigation of their trading partners. But these too took a toll on life that was not duplicated in the slave experience. Still another cause of depopulation was alcohol, which though it killed slowly in contrast to smallpox and other epidemic diseases, also took its toll.

All the lethal factors that decimated Indian villages throughout eastern North America, while touching slaves only incidentally, were linked to white calculations of the usefulness of blacks as opposed to Indians. White colonists did not, of course, possess direct control over bacteriological and demographic factors. But they eagerly sought to increase the black slave population while reducing the Indian population. To this end they instituted policies which influenced, if they did not control, population curves. Blacks, for example, were inoculated against smallpox and given medical treatment in case of sickness. . . . If Indians, however, contracted an epidemic disease, the colonist could only give thanks that God had seen fit to diminish their numbers in order to make more room for "civilized" men. . . . With alcohol it was the same. . . . Rum was a liquid form of control for white colonists in their dealings with both Africans and Indians. But it was intended to sustain life among blacks while destroying life among Indians.

The third killer, war, was also controlled to some extent by whites. Black rebellion was, of course, quelled as quickly as possible, for it was a direct threat to the labor system and to social dominance by whites. But war with Indians and war among Indians was often a carefully calculated objective in white minds. . . .

Thus, while escaping slavery in most cases, native Americans found themselves confronting a mushrooming European population that sought the land they occupied and could conceive of no way that Indians could be useful to white society except to aid in the process of their own collective decimation and dispossession of land. This had not been true for most of the colonial period, for when the European population was small, while it had been divided among Spanish, French, and English contenders for continental supremacy, and while the fur and skin trade had been a major factor in the colonial economy, the Indian had been a functional part of the process of building a new society in the New World. By the mid-eighteenth century, however, the Indian trade had become a minor part of the colonial economy. Fishing and ship building in New England, grain and livestock production in the Middle Colonies, and tobacco, rice, and indigo production on Southern plantations had become the principal forms of economic activity. By 1763 the elimination of France as an imperial rival eliminated the need for Indian military support. Finally, the tremendous growth of population in the two generations before the Revolution made acquisition of the interior river valleys of the continent the preoccupation of both eastern entrepreneurs, for whom population growth had created a new source of wealth far greater than the fur trade, and the swarming settlers who poured through the mountain gaps into the Trans-Appalachian region.

A final paradox was that many Indian societies embodied what Englishmen and other Europeans had come to find in the New World but were destroyed or driven westward while daring to be what Europeans could not. It is true that many colonists came venturing across the Atlantic for nothing more than material gain; but many others saw the "wilderness" of North America as a place where tired, corrupt, materialistic, self-seeking Europeans might begin a new life centered around the long-lost but ever-valuable concepts of reciprocity, spirituality, and community. From John Winthrop to William Penn to John Adams the notion of transplanted Europeans building a virtuous society in cities on the hill coursed through the dreamlife of the newcomers. Yet as time passed and Europeans became more numerous, it became more and more evident that the people in North America who were best upholding these values and organizing their society around them were the people who were being driven from the land.

It was not simply the romantic side of eighteenth-century Enlightenment thinking that caricatured the Indians as the possessors of a better formula for living. As early as the 1660s Thomas Traherne, an English poet, was writing that

> Earth was better than Gold, and. . . Water was, every Drop of it, a Precious Jewel. And that these were Great and Living Treasures: and that all Riches whatsoever els was Dross in Comparison. . . The Sun is Glorious. A Man is a Beautifull Creature. . . The Stars Minister unto us, the World was Made for you. . . But to say This Hous is yours, and these Lands are another Mans and this Bauble is a Jewel and this Gugaw a fine Thing. . . is deadly Barbarous and uncouth. . . becaus the Nature of the Thing contradicts your Words. . . . By this you may see who are the Rude and Barbarous Indians. For verily there is no Salvage Nation under the Cope of Heaven that is more absurdly Barbarous than the Christian World.

These thoughts would echo down the corridors of seventeenth- and eighteenth-century history. Even hard-bitten, unsentimental colonists often recognized that Indian society, though by no means without its problems and its own disreputable characters, put white society to shame. . . .

This was a kind of innocence that beckoned destruction. By embodying some of the virtues around which Europeans had hoped to reorganize their cultural system, but could not, the Indian was a disturbing reminder of the retrogression rather than the progress of European man in his New World setting. Englishmen, Germans, Scotch-Irish, Swedes, Finns, Dutch, French Huguenots, and others might congratulate themselves on the eve of the American Revolution for "taming the wilderness"; for building thriving seaports where none had previously existed; for raising towns, churches, schools, and governments along a thousand miles of coastal plain from Maine to Georgia. They had chosen productivity and acquisitiveness, both of which proceeded far. But it was obvious from looking in any direction that this had been accomplished at a terrible price in exploitation and human suffering, enslavement and alienation.

Letters to Sweden

Mary Helena Stephenson

Beginning with colonial times, "America letters"—letters written to the homeland by those who had ventured to the New World—were influential in stimulating emigration from Europe. Some letters made extravagant claims about the riches to be found in America, where the ditches flowed with wine; others contained more sober appraisals but stressed the opportunities available to settlers who were willing to work hard. In the nineteenth century such letters were circulated among the relatives and friends of those to whom they were addressed, and they were sometimes printed in local newspapers, infecting entire parishes with "America fever."

Typical of such America letters is the one reprinted below, written by a Swedish woman in Iowa. A small number of Swedes had been among the early colonists, settling New Sweden—now Delaware—in 1638. But it was not until the 1840s that Swedes, encouraged by steamship and railway companies, arrived in America in appreciable numbers. They usually headed west immediately where, along with other Scandinavians, they were among the pioneers who conquered the high prairies.

Mount Pleasant, Iowa, June or July, 1868.

To Jonas P. Zackrison.
Dear parents, brothers, and sisters:—

The peace of God be with you! . . .
Dear brother-in-law Carl and sister Johanna, you ask how you can put your money to the best advantage. You cannot buy a farm, because land is too high-priced, but you can get a start by renting a farm. Renters get ahead much faster here than in Sweden. Those who want to own land go farther west, where the land is free. If you settle in this community, however, you can soon get started by buying colts and calves and harvesting fodder. Livestock develops rapidly, and it will not be long before you can realize on them. Oliver says he will help you all he can. You will not regret coming here if you do not encounter misfortunes—and misfortunes are met with in every country. Day laborers are able to save money here—an impossibility in

From "Typical 'America Letters,'" ed., George M. Stephenson, Swedish Historical Society of America, *Year Book*, 1921–1922, pp. 91–93.

Sweden. I know of many who own farms who didn't even have gruel in Sweden. I am reminded of Jonas Peter whose possessions on his arrival consisted only of his clothing. Now if his property were converted into money he could buy a good estate in Sweden, and this in spite of the fact that he married a poor girl, suffered misfortunes, and had no one to help him. But he is industrious and has a good wife. There are many similar cases. A house-keeper has few worries, because food is so plentiful. There is no necessity for begging.

A few weeks ago seventeen emigrants from Nydala parish arrived and made their headquarters with us. We housed and fed them, as they had no relatives or acquaintances. One family is still with us. The husband has been engaged to work two months for an American for $20 per month, his wife and two children staying with us. She assists me in various ways. People are arriving from Sweden and from other countries and sections in large numbers; but do not worry over the danger of overpopulation, as Iowa is as large as Sweden and only half settled. Then think of the other states! People come and go constantly.

I want to warn you that the voyage is trying, and some become seasick. I escaped that. Now, however, the voyage is so brief that it is a pleasure trip compared to what it was in former days. The sooner you go the better.

Addressing Sven and Christine, let me say that, accustomed as you are to the ways of Sweden, I doubt that you would be satisfied here, unable to understand the language of the country. But you would do well by your children, and Christine would no doubt have things better.

Now a few words with my parents. We are glad to know America is in your thoughts, but I am sorry that mother is so reluctant. One of you will have to yield, and that of course will be difficult. But whatever you do, don't separate: if father came without mother, he would be so lonesome that he would see the dark side of everything and finally return. An old man who left his wife in Sweden came with Peter Gustaf. In this community there is a lonesome and dissatisfied man making his home with his son who left his wife, who in spite of the most urgent letters refuses to join him. He cannot return to her because they lived unhappily and had little in common. I advise you to come together, and I believe you will spend a happy old age here.

It may be that you are afraid we will expect some recompense from you, but that has never entered our minds. Don't let that worry you. If in the providence of God sickness should come upon you, we will perform our duty as your children and care for you. It is doubtful if Sven and Christine will stay at Bredagard until your days are ended. If you think it desirable, you might rent your farm and order the money sent to America in case you need it. But you know what is best, and it is hardly necessary to lay plans a hundred years ahead. I am sure that you will get along better here; you will not have to grind and cook and bake. Weigh the matter carefully. I am sorry for mother if she is persuaded to go against her will. If Johanna is in the party, she can be of assistance in case of need. I hope what I have written will be taken in the right spirit. I do not want to take the responsibility of causing you to undertake something for which you will be sorry.

Our son thanks his grandfather for the present . . . and I thank you for the yarn. Our little daughter is the best baby I have ever seen. She is growing fast, and, although only five months old, sits alone. I have a great deal of work, but my health remains good. We get ten gallons of milk from four cows. We sold a cow two weeks ago. I got over thirty pounds of wool this year.

I close with greetings to all. Write soon, and we will reply immediately.

Mary Helena Stephenson.

Good-bye to Ireland

Padraic Colum

No matter how eager the European peasant or laborer might be to pursue the opportunities described in "America letters," the actual leavetaking of family and friends was a painful experience—one shared by all immigrants.

In the following account, writer/author/poet Padraic Colum, himself an Irish immigrant, paints a poignant picture of a farewell in his homeland. It was a scene frequently repeated in Ireland, which lost more than 4,250,000 immigrants to the United States between 1820 and 1920. The Irish immigrants in the early part of this period were mainly poor but independent farmers, seeking better economic opportunity and freedom from the political and religious domination of England. They were eagerly recruited by American contractors working on canals, roads—and later, railroads.

Starting in 1847, however, the number of Irish immigrants mounted sharply, reaching almost 200,000 in that year, and by 1860 there were more than 1,610,000 Irish in the United States. These were the years of the potato blight in Ireland, and for most of these immigrants there had been little choice between starvation at home and flight. Arriving penniless, with no marketable skills and no means to proceed westward to take up farming, most of them became marginal workers in the seaboard cities where they docked. Crowded into tenements, exploited by politicians, construction bosses and mill-owners, they became the object of anti-Catholic, anti-immigrant sentiment. Gradually, however, the Irish were able to work their way into more secure positions, and America continued to lure the poor of Ireland.

A girl whom I knew came into the shop I frequented. Her greeting was constrained and she stood silent and apart, with a shawl across her head. She had taken me to many festivities during the months I was in that place. I came over and spoke to her in Irish: "When will there be a dance in your village?" I asked. "There's a dance to-night," she said, "if you would care to come." "Is it at the Stones?" "No, it's at our house. It's the night of my own wake."

Reprinted with permission of Macmillan Publishing Co., Inc., from *The Road Round Ireland* by Padraic Colum. Copyright 1926 by Macmillan Publishing Co., Inc., renewed 1954 by Padraic Colum.

She did not use the word in its generally accepted sense. In some of the Irish-speaking districts the word "wake" has come to signify the last gathering around the boy or girl who is leaving the village for Boston or New York. Grania was in the shop, to buy provisions for her American wake. I had seen another part of peasant Ireland denuded of its vitality by emigration and I thought of Grania as typical of the robust and high-spirited youth who go away and are lost to the country, or return to Ireland for a while, changed and dissatisfied. She bade good-bye to those in the shop and gave me the word to come with her. Our path was between walls of loose stones that went across a country strewn with boulders. On account of these bare surfaces of rock the landscape was toned with greyness. There was no luminary in the early night; the full moon was gone and the new moon had not made its appearance. It is customary in this part of the country to use the English word "village" as the equivalent of their area of community. But the picture brought up by the word has no relation to their scattered hamlet. The houses were scattered through miles of uneven territory, and no roof was visible from the door of another house.

We met Grania's mother before we came to the house. She was one of those women who smile as though they did not understand what was happening or what was being said. She was silent and smiled as though speech had been frightened from her. The father greeted me at the door and brought me to the circle that was round the fire. He was a stolid and silent man. Another old man at the fire spoke eloquently and passionately in Irish. "Every man has his rearing, except the poor Irishman. This is the way with him. When his children grow up, they scatter from him like the little birds." Grania had taken off her shawl and was busy in the household duties. There was some intensity in her manner, but she made herself pleasant and capable. . . .

Visitors had been coming, singly and in couples, and on going back to the kitchen I encountered something like a mob. People were standing three-deep from the walls. I heard a discord of music and song, the clash of grave speaking with loud-tongued humour, of gossip and boisterous flirtation, of American nasals and full-sounding Gaelic vowels. The children crowded together in the recess of the wide chimney, and the old people kept going into and coming out of the inner room. People were speaking of a dance, but a stranger would wonder whether there was room for a dance between the dresser and the fire on the hearth, between the table and the meal bins. Grania drew out the partners for the girls, arranged the dance, and induced a quiet man to play on the flute. The figures in the dance were complicated, but even the swinging of the partners was accomplished with safety.

After some rounds of dancing, songs were given. English words were most in the fashion. Some of the songs were in the Irish tradition, some had been brought home by the workers in Scotland or England, and some had come from America. . . .

The night wore on with dance and song, with challenge and repartee. Grania left us and stayed in the upper room for a while. When she returned she was in wild spirits and set about forming another dance. The orchestra was changed for this. She brought down a fiddle and a young man undertook to play. Only the wildest spirits were in this last dance that was on the skirts of the creeping day. Before the dance ended Grania's brother went from us, and we saw him take the harness down from the wall. It was an action as significant as anything in drama. The dance went on, but we heard the stamp of the awakened horse and the rattle of the harness as the conveyance was made ready for the journey. The dance fluttered out. Through the little window the trees became visible, then we saw colour, the green of the grass and the green of the leaves. Grania left the revellers and went into the room where her mother was busy. All of us who were in the kitchen went outside, so that those who were parting would have the place to themselves. In the morning world the corncrakes were crying through the meadows. They were quiet in the house now, and the chill of dawn made me wish for the overcoat I had left within. I went inside. After the vivid life I felt the emptiness of the kitchen; the fire had burnt to ashes and the broad light through the window was on the flame of the lamp. As I was going out Grania came down, dressed for the journey. The poor girl was changed. She was dazed with grief.

She sat on the cart that went down the stony road, and the remnant of the company followed. Farther·on they would meet more carts with other emigrants, boys and girls. The cart jogged itself on to the main road; as yet there was only a single figure on the way, a man driving a cow to some far-off fair. We bade good-bye to Grania and separated. On my way back I passed her house; it was soundless and closed in as if the house had not yet wakened into life.

Life in the Back Alleys

Jacob Riis

Most of the immigrants who had come to America prior to 1880 were from northern and western Europe—England, the Scandinavian countries, Germany, and Ireland. With the exception of the Irish, this "old immigration," as it came to be called, had been lured by the opportunities for farming on the westward-moving frontier. But toward the end of the nineteenth century the era of free lands came to an end; the census of 1890 officially noted the closing of the frontier. At the same time industrial growth in northern Europe opened new opportunities. The tide of old immigration began to ebb, and a new tide of immigrants from southern and eastern Europe flowed to American shores.

The new immigrants differed markedly from the old in language, culture, and customs. Peasants and laborers, they were fleeing poverty at home, and their standards of living were of necessity low. Most of the new immigrants were Catholics, Greek Orthodox, or Jews, in contrast to the predominantly Protestant old immigration. Arriving in an increasingly industrial and urbanized America, they congregated in the cities of the East and Midwest. The tenement districts that had been the province of the Irish in the mid-nineteenth century became crowded with Italians, Greeks, Poles, Hungarians, and Russians. By 1890, one-fourth of Philadelphians and one-third of Chicagoans and Bostonians were foreign-born; in Greater New York, four-fifths of the population had foreign-born parents or were foreign-born themselves.

As successive waves of immigrants landed in the cities, they filled the lowest positions in society, allowing those who had preceded them to move into semi-skilled and skilled trades and businesses. The immigrants provided an ever-ready reservoir of cheap labor for the mines and factories of the new industrial society; but all too many immigrants found that they had merely exchanged the poverty of their old-world villages for that of the American tenement.

Jacob Riis, a Danish-born immigrant who had first-hand knowledge of the slums of New York City in the 1870s, did much to expose the conditions of tenement life in How the Other Half Lives, *published in 1890.*

Excerpted from Jacob Riis, *How the Other Half Lives* (New York: Charles Scribner's Sons, 1906).

. . . One may find for the asking an Italian, a German, a French, African, Spanish, Bohemian, Russian, Scandinavian, Jewish, and Chinese colony. Even the Arab, who peddles "holy earth" from the Battery as a direct importation from Jerusalem, has his exclusive preserves at the lower end of Washington Street. The one thing you shall vainly ask for in the chief city of America is a distinctively American community. There is none; certainly not among the tenements. Where have they gone to, the old inhabitants? . . .

. . . They are not here. In their place has come this queer conglomerate mass of heterogeneous elements, ever striving and working like whisky and water in one glass, and with the like result: final union and a prevailing taint of whisky. . . .

It is not to be assumed, of course, that the whole body of the population living in the tenements, of which New Yorkers are in the habit of speaking vaguely as "the poor," or even the larger part of it, is to be classed as vicious or as poor in the sense of verging on beggary.

New York's wage earners have no other place to live, more is the pity. They are truly poor for having no better homes; waxing poorer in purse as the exorbitant rents to which they are tied, as ever was serf to soil, keep rising. The wonder is that they are not all corrupted, and speedily, by their surroundings. If, on the contrary, there be a steady working up, if not out of the slough, the fact is a powerful argument for the optimist's belief that the world is, after all, growing better, not worse, and would go far toward disarming apprehension, were it not for the steadier growth of the sediment of the slums and its constant menace. Such an impulse toward better things there certainly is. The German ragpicker of thirty years ago, quite as low in the scale as his Italian successor, is the thrifty tradesman or prosperous farmer of today.

The Italian scavenger of our time is fast graduating into exclusive control of the corner fruit stands, while his black-eyed boy monopolizes the bootblacking industry in which a few years ago he was an intruder. The Irish hod carrier in the second generation has become a bricklayer, if not the Alderman of his ward, while the Chinese coolie is in almost exclusive possession of the laundry business. The reason is obvious. The poorest immigrant comes here with the purpose and ambition to better himself and, given half a chance, might be reasonably expected to make the most of it. To the false plea that he prefers the squalid homes in which his kind are housed there could be no better answer. The truth is, his half chance has too long been wanting, and for the bad result he has been unjustly blamed.

As emigration from east to west follows the latitude, so does the foreign influx in New York distribute itself along certain well-defined lines that waver and break only under the stronger pressure of a more gregarious race or the encroachments of inexorable business. A feeling of dependence upon mutual effort, natural to strangers in a strange land, unacquainted with its language and customs, sufficiently accounts for this.

. . . A map of the city, colored to designate nationalities, would show more stripes than on the skin of a zebra, and more colors than any rainbow. The city on such a map would fall into two great halves, green for the Irish prevailing in the West Side tenement districts, and blue for the Germans on the East Side. But intermingled with these ground colors would be an odd variety of tints that would give the whole the appearance of an extraordinary crazy quilt. From down in the Sixth Ward, upon the site of the old Collect Pond that in the days of the fathers drained the hills which are no more, the red of the Italian would be seen forcing its way northward along the line of Mulberry Street to the quarter of the French purple on Bleecker Street and South Fifth Avenue, to lose itself and reappear, after a lapse of miles, in the "Little Italy" of Harlem, east of Second Avenue. Dashes of red, sharply defined, would be seen strung through the Annexed District, northward to the city line. On the West Side the red would be seen overrunning the old Africa of Thompson Street, pushing the black of the negro rapidly uptown, against querulous but unavailing protests, occupying his home, his church, his trade and all, with merciless impartiality. . . . The negroes have made a stand at several points along Seventh and Eighth Avenues; but their main body, still pursued by the Italian foe, is on the march yet, and the black mark will be found overshadowing today many blocks on the East Side, with One Hundredth Street as the center, where colonies of them have settled recently.

Hardly less aggressive than the Italian, the Russian and Polish Jew, having overrun the district between Rivington and Division Streets, east of the Bowery, to the point of suffocation, is filling the tenements of the old Seventh Ward to the river front, and disputing with the Italian every foot of available space in the back alleys of Mulberry Street. . . . Other nationalities that begin at the bottom make a fresh start when crowded up the ladder. Happily both are manageable, the one by rabbinical, the other by the civil law. Between the dull gray of the Jew, his favorite color, and the Italian red, would be seen squeezed in on the map a sharp streak of yellow, marking the narrow boundaries of Chinatown. Dovetailed in with the German population, the poor but thrifty Bohemian might be picked out by the somber hue of his life as of his philosophy, struggling against heavy odds in the big human beehives of the East Side. Colonies of his people extend northward, with long lapses of space, from below the Cooper Institute more than three miles. The Bohemian is the only foreigner with any considerable representation in the city who counts no wealthy man of his race, none who has not to work hard for a living, or has got beyond the reach of the tenement.

Down near the Battery the West Side emerald would be soiled by a dirty stain, spreading rapidly like a splash of ink on a sheet of blotting paper, headquarters of the Arab tribe, that in a single year has swelled from the original dozen to twelve hundred, intent, every mother's son, on trade and barter. Dots and dashes of color here and there would show where the Finnish sailors worship their djumala (God), the Greek peddlers the ancient name of their race, and the Swiss the goddess of thrift. And so on to the end of the long register, all toiling together in the galling fetters of the tenement. . . .

* * *

Down below Chatham Square, in the old Fourth Ward, where the cradle of the tenement stood, we shall find New York's Other Half at home, receiving such as care to call and are not afraid. Not all of it, to be sure, there is not room for that; but a fairly representative gathering, representative of its earliest and worst traditions. There is nothing to be afraid of. In this metropolis, let it be understood, there is no public street where the stranger may not go safely by day and by night, provided he knows how to mind his own business and is sober. His coming and going will excite little interest, unless he is suspected of being a truant officer, in which case he will be impressed with the truth of the observation that the American stock is dying out for want of children. . . .

Leaving the Elevated Railroad where it dives under the Brooklyn Bridge at Franklin Square, scarce a dozen steps will take us where we wish to go. With its rush and roar echoing yet in our ears, we have turned the corner from prosperity to poverty. We stand upon the domain of the tenement. . . .

Enough of them everywhere. Suppose we look into one? No—Cherry Street. Be a little careful, please! The hall is dark and you might stumble over the children pitching pennies back there. Not that it would hurt them; kicks and cuffs are their daily diet. They have little else. Here where the hall turns and dives into utter darkness is a step, and another, another. A flight of stairs. You can feel your way, if you cannot see it. Close? Yes! What would you have? All the fresh air that ever enters these stairs comes from the hall door that is forever slamming, and from the windows of dark bedrooms that in turn receive from the stairs their sole supply of the elements God meant to be free, but man deals out with such niggardly hand. That was a woman filling her pail by the hydrant you just bumped against. The sinks are in the hallway, that all the tenants may have access—and all be poisoned alike by their summer stenches. Hear the pump squeak! It is the lullaby of tenement-house babes. In summer, when a thousand thirsty throats pant for a cooling drink in this block, it is worked in vain. But the saloon, whose open door you passed in the hall, is always there. The smell of it has followed you up. Here is a door. Listen! That short hacking cough, that tiny, helpless wail—what do they mean? They mean that the soiled bow of white you saw on the door downstairs will have another story to tell—Oh! a sadly familiar story—before the day is at an end. The child is dying with measles. With half a chance it might have lived; but it had none. That dark bedroom killed it.

"It was took all of a suddint," says the mother, smoothing the throbbing little body with trembling hands. There is no unkindness in the rough voice of the man in the jumper, who sits by the window grimly smoking a clay pipe, with the little life ebbing out in his sight, bitter as his words sound: "Hush, Mary! If we cannot keep the baby, need we complain—such as we?"

Such as we! What if the words ring in your ears as we grope our way up the stairs and down from floor to floor, listening to the sounds behind the closed doors—some of quarreling, some of coarse songs, more of profanity. They are true. When the summer heats come with their suffering, they have meaning more terrible than words can tell. Come over here. Step carefully over this baby—it is a baby, in spite of its rags and dirt—under these iron bridges called fire escapes, but loaded down, despite the incessant watchfulness of the firemen, with broken household goods, with wash tubs and barrels, over which no man could climb from a fire. This gap between dingy brick walls is the yard. That strip of smoke-colored sky up there is the heaven of these people. Do you wonder the name does not attract them to the churches? That baby's parents live in the rear tenement here. She is at least as clean as the steps we are now climbing. There are plenty of houses with half a hundred such in. The tenement is much like the one in front we just left, only fouler, closer, darker—we will not say more cheerless. The word is a mockery. A hundred thousand people lived in rear tenements in New York last year. Here is a room neater than the rest. The woman, a stout matron with hard lines of care in her face, is at the wash tub. "I try to keep the children clean," she says, apologetically, but with a hopeless glance around. The spice of hot soapsuds is added to the air already tainted with the smell of boiling cabbage, of rags and uncleanliness all about. It makes an over-powering compound. It is Thursday, but patched linen is hung upon the pulley line from the window. There is no Monday cleaning in the tenements. It is wash day all the week round, for a change of clothing is scarce among the poor. They are poverty's honest badge, these perennial lines of rags hung out to dry, those that are not the washerwoman's professional shingle. The true line to be drawn between pauperism and honest poverty is the clothesline. With it begins the effort to be clean that is the first and the best evidence of a desire to be honest.

What sort of an answer, think you, would come from these tenements to the question "Is life worth living?" were they heard at all in the discussion? It may be that this, cut from the last report but one of the Association for the Improvement of the Condition of the Poor, a long name for a weary task, has a suggestion of it: "In the depth of winter the attention of the Association was called to a Protestant family living in a garret in a miserable tenement in Cherry Street. The family's condition was most deplorable. The man, his wife, and three small children shivering in one room through the roof of which the pitiless winds of winter whistled. The room was almost barren of furniture; the parents slept on the floor, the elder children in boxes, and the baby was swung in an old shawl attached to the rafters by cords by way of a hammock. The father, a seaman, had been obliged to give up that calling because he was in consumption, and was unable to provide either bread or fire for his little ones."

Perhaps this may be put down as an exceptional case, but one that came to my notice some months ago in a Seventh Ward tenement was typical enough to escape that reproach. There were nine in the family: husband, wife, an aged grandmother, and six children; honest, hard-working Germans, scrupulously neat, but poor. All nine lived in two rooms, one about ten feet square that served as parlor, bedroom, and eating room, the other a small hall room made into a kitchen. The rent was seven dollars and a half a month, more than a week's wages for the husband and father, who was the only breadwinner in the family. That day the mother had thrown herself out of the window, and was carried up from the street dead. She was "discouraged," said some of the other women from the tenement, who had come in to look after the children while a messenger carried the news to the father at the shop. They went stolidly about their task, although they were evidently not without feeling for the dead woman. No doubt she was wrong in not taking life philosophically, as did the four families a city missionary found housekeeping in the four corners of one room. They got along well enough together until one of the families took a boarder and made trouble. Philosophy, according to my optimistic friend, naturally inhabits the tenements. The people who live there come to look upon death in a different way from the rest of us—do not take it as hard. He has never found time to explain how the fact fits into his general theory that life is not unbearable in the tenements. Unhappily for the philosophy of the slums, it is too apt to be of the kind that readily recognizes the saloon, always handy, as the refuge from every trouble, and shapes its practice according to the discovery.

The Promised Land

Mary Antin

As appalling as slum conditions might be, America was still viewed by many as the Promised Land. This was particularly true for the Jews.

An early group of German Jews had been among the large German immigration to America in the mid-nineteenth century. But a much larger influx of Jews came from eastern Europe, particularly Russia, in the later nineteenth and early twentieth centuries. In the fifty years from 1877 to 1927, the Jewish population in the United States increased from under one quarter of a million to more than four million.

The Jews had been peddlers and small-scale traders, tailors and shoemakers in Russia; in America they became pushcart peddlers and small shopkeepers, garment workers and cigar-makers. Many of them had fled from pogroms and other forms of religious and economic persecution, and for them America was a haven of freedom if not immediately a land of milk and honey. Having never felt patriotism toward their homeland, they were eager to embrace their new country. In the process of Americanization, for the Jews as for other immigrant groups, the public school played a central role.

Mary Antin, who was a child when she left Russian Poland for Boston in 1894, eloquently describes her experiences—and those of millions of her generation—upon arriving in the Promised Land.

Memory may take a rest while I copy from a contemporaneous document the story of the great voyage. In accordance with my promise to my uncle, I wrote, during my first months in America, a detailed account of our adventures between Polotzk and Boston. . . .

The Journey

Our route lay over the German border, with Hamburg for our port. . . .

On the German side our course joined that of many other emigrant groups, on their way to Hamburg and other ports. We were a clumsy enough crowd, with wide, unsophisticated eyes, with awkward bundles hugged in our arms, and our hearts set on America. . . .

The phrases "we were told to do this" and "told to do that" occur again

From Mary Antin, *The Promised Land* (Boston: Houghton-Mifflin, 1911), pp. 169, 174-75, 177-84, 202-207, and 222-28. Copyright © 1912 by Houghton-Mifflin, 1940 by Mary Antin. Reprinted by permission of the publisher.

and again in my narrative, and the most effective handling of the facts could give no more vivid picture of the proceedings. We emigrants were herded at the stations, packed in the cars, and driven from place to place like cattle. . . .

The plight of the bewildered emigrant on the way to foreign parts is always pitiful enough, but for us who came from plague-ridden Russia the terrors of the way were doubled.

In a great lonely field, opposite a solitary house within a large yard, our train pulled up at last, and a conductor commanded the passengers to make haste and get out. . . . He hurried us into the one large room which made up the house, and then into the yard. Here a great many men and women, dressed in white, received us, the women attending to the women and girls of the passengers, and the men to the others.

This was another scene of bewildering confusion, parents losing their children, and little ones crying; baggage being thrown together in one corner of the yard, heedless of contents, which suffered in consequence. . . .

. . . Here we had been taken to a lonely place where only that house was to be seen; our things were taken away, our friends separated from us; a man came to inspect us, as if to ascertain our full value; strange-looking people driving us about like dumb animals, helpless and unresisting; children we could not see crying in a way that suggested terrible things; ourselves driven into a little room where a great kettle was boiling on a little stove; our clothes taken off, our bodies rubbed with a slippery substance that might be any bad thing; a shower of warm water let down on us without warning; again driven to another little room where we sit, wrapped in woollen blankets till large, coarse bags are brought in, their contents turned out, and we see only a cloud of steam, and hear the women's orders to dress ourselves,—"Quick! Quick!—or you'll miss the train!"—Oh, so we really won't be murdered! They are only making us ready for the continuing of our journey, cleaning us of all suspicions of dangerous sickness. Thank God! . . .

We arrived in Hamburg early one morning, after a long night in the crowded cars. . . .

. . . On the outskirts of the city, . . . we were once more lined up, cross-questioned, disinfected, labelled, and pigeonholed. . . .

This last place of detention turned out to be a prison. "Quarantine" they called it, and there was a great deal of it—two weeks of it. Two weeks within high brick walls, several hundred of us herded in half a dozen compartments,—numbered compartments,—sleeping in rows, like sick people in a hospital; with roll-call morning and night, and short rations three times a day; with never a sign of the free world beyond our barred windows; with anxiety and longing and homesickness in our hearts, and in our ears the unfamiliar voice of the invisible ocean, which drew and repelled us at the same time. The fortnight in quarantine was not an episode; it was an epoch, divisible into eras, periods, events. . . .

Our turn came at last. We were conducted through the gate of departure, and after some hours of bewildering manoeuvres, described in great detail in the report to my uncle, we found ourselves—we five frightened pilgrims from Polotzk—on the deck of a great big steamship afloat on the strange big waters of the ocean.

For sixteen days the ship was our world. My letter dwells solemnly on the details of the life at sea, as if afraid to cheat my uncle of the smallest circumstance. It does not shrink from describing the torments of seasickness. . . . Then came happy hours on deck, with fugitive sunshine, birds atop the crested waves, band music and dancing and fun. I explored the ship, made friends with officers and crew, or pursued my thoughts in quiet nooks. It was my first experience of the ocean, and I was profoundly moved. . . .

And so suffering, fearing, brooding, rejoicing, we crept nearer and nearer to the coveted shore, until, on a glorious May morning, six weeks after our departure from Polotzk, our eyes beheld the Promised Land, and my father received us in his arms.

Arrival

Having made such good time across the ocean, I ought to be able to proceed no less rapidly on *terra firma*, where, after all, I am more at home. And yet here is where I falter. Not that I hesitated, even for the space of a breath, in my first steps in America. There was no time to hesitate. The most ignorant immigrant, on landing, proceeds to give and receive greetings, to eat, sleep, and rise, after the manner of his own country; wherein he is corrected, admonished, and laughed at, whether by interested friends or the most indifferent strangers; and his American experience is thus begun. The process is spontaneous on all sides, like the education of the child by the family circle. . . .

During his three years of probation, my father had made a number of false starts in business. His history for that period is the history of thousands who come to America, like him, with pockets empty, hands untrained to the use of tools, minds cramped by centuries of repression in their native land. Dozens of these men pass under your eyes every day, my American friend, too absorbed in their honest affairs to notice the looks of suspicion which you cast at them, the repugnance with which you shrink from their touch. You see them shuffle from door to door with a basket of spools and buttons, or bending over the sizzling irons in a basement tailor shop, or rummaging in your ash can, or moving a pushcart from curb to curb, at the command of the burly policeman. "The Jew peddler!" you say, and dismiss him from your premises and from your thoughts, never dreaming that the sordid drama of his days may have a moral that concerns you. What if the creature with the untidy beard carries in his bosom his citizenship papers? What if the cross-legged tailor is supporting a boy in college who is one day going to mend your state constitution for you? What if the ragpicker's daughters are hastening over the ocean to teach your children in the public schools? Think, every time you pass the greasy alien on the street, that he was born thousands of years before the oldest native American; and he may have something to communicate to you, when you two shall have learned a common language. . . .

Anybody who knows Boston knows that the West and North Ends are the wrong ends of that city. They form the tenement district, or, in the newer phrase, the slums of Boston. Anybody who is acquainted with the slums of any American metropolis knows that that is the quarter where poor immigrants foregather, to live, for the most part, as unkempt, half-washed, toiling, unaspiring foreigners; pitiful in the eyes of social missionaries, the despair of boards of health, the hope of ward politicians, the touchstone of American democracy. The well-versed metropolitan knows the slums as a sort of house of detention for poor aliens, where they live on probation till they can show a certificate of good citizenship.

He may know all this and yet not guess how Wall Street, in the West End, appears in the eyes of a little immigrant from Polotzk. . . . I saw two imposing rows of brick buildings, loftier than any dwelling I had ever lived in. Brick was even on the ground for me to tread on, instead of common earth or boards. Many friendly windows stood open, filled with uncovered heads of women and children. I looked up to the topmost row of windows, and my eyes were filled with the May blue of an American sky! . . .

Going to School

Education was free. That subject my father had written about repeatedly, as comprising his chief hope for us children, the essence of American opportunity, the treasure that no thief could touch, not even misfortune or poverty. It was the one thing that he was able to promise us when he sent for us; surer, safer than bread or shelter. On our second day I was thrilled with the realization of what this freedom of education meant. A little girl from across the alley came and offered to conduct us to school. My father was out, but we five between us had a few words of English by this time. We knew the word school. We understood. This child, who had never seen us till yesterday, who could not pronounce our names, who was not much better dressed than we, was able to offer us the freedom of the schools of Boston! No application made, no questions asked, no examinations, rulings, exclusions; no machinations, no fees. The doors stood open for every one of us. The smallest child could show us the way.

This incident impressed me more than anything I had heard in advance of the freedom of education in America. It was a concrete proof—almost the thing itself. One had to experience it to understand it. . . .

Father himself conducted us to school. He would not have delegated that mission to the President of the United States. He had awaited the day with impatience equal to mine, and the visions he saw as he hurried us over the sun-flecked pavements transcended all my dreams. Almost his first act on landing on American soil, three years before, had been his application for naturalization. He had taken the remaining steps in the process with eager promptness, and at the earliest moment allowed by the law, he became a citizen of the United States. It is true that he had left home in search of bread for his hungry family, but he went blessing the necessity that drove him to America. The boasted freedom of the New World meant to him far more than the right to reside, travel, and work wherever he pleased; it meant the freedom to speak his thoughts, to throw off the shackles of superstition, to test his own fate, unhindered by political or religious tyranny. . . .

. . . He had very little opportunity to prosecute his education, which, in truth, had never been begun. His struggle for a bare living left him no time to take advantage of the public evening school; but he lost nothing of what was to be learned through reading, through attendance at public meetings, through exercising the rights of citizenship. Even here he was hindered by a natural inability to acquire the English language. In time, indeed, he learned to read, to follow a conversation or lecture; but he never learned to write correctly, and his pronunciation remains extremely foreign to this day.

If education, culture, the higher life were shining things to be worshipped from afar, he had still a means left whereby he could draw one step nearer to them. He could send his children to school, to learn all those things that he knew by fame to be desirable. The common school, at least, perhaps high school; for one or two, perhaps even college! His children should be students, should fill his house with books and intellectual company; and thus he would walk by proxy in the Elysian Fields of liberal learning. As for the children themselves, he knew no surer way to their advancement and happiness.

So it was with a heart full of longing and hope that my father led us to school on that first day. . . .

At last the four of us stood around the teacher's desk; and my father, in his impossible English, gave us over in her charge, with some broken word of his hopes for us that his swelling heart could no longer contain. . . . I think Miss Nixon guessed what my father's best English could not convey. I think she divined that by the simple act of delivering our school certificates to her he took possession of America.

It is not worth while to refer to voluminous school statistics to see just how many "green" pupils entered school last September, not knowing the days of the week in English, who next February will be declaiming patriotic verses in honor of George Washington and Abraham Lincoln, with a foreign accent, indeed, but with plenty of enthusiasm. It is enough to know that this hundred-fold miracle is common to the schools in every part of the United States where immigrants are received. . . .

There were about half a dozen of us beginners in English, in age from six to fifteen. Miss Nixon made a special class of us, and aided us so skilfully and earnestly in our endeavors to "see-a-cat," and "hear-a-dog-bark," and "look-at-the-hen," that we turned over page after page of the ravishing history, eager to find out how the common world looked, smelled, and tasted in the strange speech. The teacher knew just when to let us help each other out with a word in our own tongue,—it happened that we were all Jews,—and so, working all together, we actually covered more ground in a lesson than the native classes, composed entirely of the little tots. . . .

Becoming an American

The public school has done its best for us foreigners, and for the country, when it has made us into good Americans. I am glad it is mine to tell how the miracle was wrought in one case. You should be glad to hear of it, you born Americans; for it is the story of the growth of your country; of the flocking of your brothers and sisters from the far ends of the earth to the flag you love; of the recruiting of your armies of workers, thinkers, and leaders. And you will be glad to hear of it, my comrades in adoption; for it is a rehearsal of your own experience, the thrill and wonder of which your own hearts have felt.

How long would you say, wise reader, it takes to make an American? By the middle of my second year in school I had reached the sixth grade. When, after the Christmas holidays, we began to study the life of Washington, running through a summary of the Revolution, and the early days of the Republic, it seemed to me that all my reading and study had been idle until then. The reader, the arithmetic, the song book, that had so fascinated me until now, became suddenly sober exercise books, tools wherewith to hew a way to the source of inspiration. When the teacher read to us out of a big book with many bookmarks in it, I sat rigid with attention in my little chair, my hands tightly clasped on the edge of my desk; and I painfully held my breath, to prevent sighs of disappointment escaping, as I saw the teacher skip the parts between bookmarks. When the class read, and it came my turn, my voice shook and the book trembled in my hands. I could not pronounce the name of George Washington without a pause. Never had I prayed, never had I chanted the songs of David, never had I called upon the Most Holy, in such utter reverence and worship as I repeated the simple sentences of my child's story of the patriot. I gazed with adoration at the portraits of George and Martha Washington, till I could see them with my eyes shut. And whereas formerly my self-consciousness had bordered on conceit, and I thought myself an uncommon person, parading my schoolbooks through the streets, and swelling with pride when a teacher detained me in conversation, now I grew humble all at once, seeing how insignificant I was beside the Great . . . .

So I was forced to revise my own estimate of myself. But the twin of my new-born humility, paradoxical as it may seem, was a sense of dignity I had never known before. For if I found that I was a person of small consequence, I discovered at the same time that I was more nobly related than I had ever supposed. I had relatives and friends who were notable people by the old standards,—I had never been ashamed of my family,—but this George Washington, who died long before I was born, was like a king in greatness, and he and I were Fellow Citizens. There was a great deal about Fellow Citizens in the patriotic literature we read at this time; and I knew from my father how he was a Citizen, through the process of naturalization, and how I also was a citizen, by virtue of my relation to him. Undoubtedly I was a Fellow Citizen, and George Washington was another. It thrilled me to realize what sudden greatness had fallen on me; and at the same time it sobered me, as with a sense of responsibility. I strove to conduct myself as befitted a Fellow Citizen . . . .

What more could America give a child? Ah, much more! As I read how the patriots planned the Revolution, and the women gave their sons to die in battle, and the heroes led to victory, and the rejoicing people set up the Republic, it dawned on me gradually what was meant by *my country*. The people all desiring noble things, and striving for them together, defying their oppressors, giving their lives for each other—all this it was that made *my country*. It was not a thing that I *understood*; I could not go home and tell Frieda about it, as I told her other things I learned at school. But I knew one could say "my country" and *feel* it, as one felt "God" or "myself." My

81

teacher, my schoolmates, Miss Dillingham, George Washington himself could not mean more than I when they said "my country," after I had once felt it. For the Country was for all the Citizens, and *I was a Citizen*. And when we stood up to sing "America," I shouted the words with all my might. I was in very earnest proclaiming to the world my love for my new-found country.

> " *I love thy rocks and rills,*
> *Thy woods and templed hills.* "

Boston Harbor, Crescent Beach, Chelsea Square—all was hallowed ground to me. As the day approached when the school was to hold exercises in honor of Washington's Birthday, the halls resounded at all hours with the strains of patriotic songs; and I, who was a model of the attentive pupil, more than once lost my place in the lesson as I strained to hear, through closed doors, some neighboring class rehearsing "The Star-Spangled Banner."...

Where had been my country until now? What flag had I loved? What heroes had I worshipped? The very names of these things had been unknown to me. Well I knew that Polotzk was not my country. It was *goluth*—exile. On many occasions in the year we prayed to God to lead us out of exile. ... In very truth we were a people without a country. Surrounded by mocking foes and detractors, it was difficult for me to realize the persons of my people's heroes or the events in which they moved. ... For the conditions of our civil life did not permit us to cultivate a spirit of nationalism. ...

So it came to pass that we did not know what *my country* could mean to a man. And as we had no country, so we had no flag to love. It was by no far-fetched symbolism that the banner of the House of Romanoff became the emblem of our latter-day bondage in our eyes. Even a child would know how to hate the flag that we were forced, on pain of severe penalties, to hoist above our housetops, in celebration of the advent of one of our oppressors. And as it was with country and flag, so it was with heroes of war. We hated the uniform of the soldier, to the last brass button. On the person of a Gentile, it was the symbol of tyranny; on the person of a Jew, it was the emblem of shame.

So a little Jewish girl in Polotzk was apt to grow up hungry-minded and empty-hearted; and if, still in her outreaching youth, she was set down in a land of outspoken patriotism, she was likely to love her new country with a great love, and to embrace its heroes in a great worship. Naturalization, with us Russian Jews, may mean more than the adoption of the immigrant by America. It may mean the adoption of America by the immigrant. ...

Talking
American—Italian Style

Jerre Mangione

The process of "Americanization"—of adaptation to a new land—was fraught with pain and difficulties. Although they might become American citizens, most immigrants continued to speak their native languages, attend their own churches, and maintain their ethnic ties. The children of these immigrants often felt themselves torn between two cultures; ashamed of the way their parents lived, most of them opted for the "American" way. The parents felt rejected by the children for whom they had sacrificed so much. And the second generation, in denying their origins, often felt a lack of identity and were burdened by a sense of guilt.

The outward sign of adaptation to the new land was, of course, learning and speaking English. In the following vignette, Jerre Mangione, the son of Italian immigrants, gives us a glimpse of both the lighter and the more serious sides of the language problem in immigrant families. A notable feature of his recollection is the family talk of returning to Italy. Although such plans never progressed beyond the talking stage for some, the "bird of passage"—the immigrant seeking to make his fortune and return home—was prominent among the Italian immigrants. Of the more than 2,760,000 Italians who came to America between 1890 and 1910, almost two-thirds were men, and 800,000 Italians had returned home by 1910.

The Italian immigration—which came mostly from rural, Southern Italy—reached its peak in 1907. Few of the immigrants were skilled, and many were illiterate. In America they worked on construction gangs, in mining camps, in steel and textile mills, and in the garment industry, often replacing Irish and Jewish labor in the lowliest tasks. Later, as Mangione indicates, the Italians were to repeat the experience of other immigrant groups in their rise in the business and professional worlds.

Excerpts from a chapter entitled "Talking American" in *Mount Allegro* by Jerre Mangione (Boston, Hill & Wang, 1943; reissued by Crown Publishers, 1972); pp. 49–66 in Crown edition. Reprinted with permission of Jerre Mangione and Crown Publishers.

My father could be more severe than my mother, but usually he was gentle with us and even conspired with us occasionally when we tried to avoid some of the household rules my mother laid down. Probably the most repugnant rule of all was that we eat everything she cooked for us, regardless of whether or not we liked the food or were hungry. . . .

Another unpopular rule she vigorously enforced was that we speak no other language at home but that of our parents. Outside the house she expected us to speak English, and often took pride in the fact that we spoke English so well that almost none of our relatives could understand it. Any English we spoke at home, however, was either by accident or on the sly. My sister Maria, who often talked in her sleep, conducted her monologues in English, but my mother forgave her on the ground that she could not be responsible for her subconscious thoughts.

My mother's insistence that we speak only Italian at home drew a sharp line between our existence there and our life in the world outside. We gradually acquired the notion that we were Italian at home and American (whatever that was) elsewhere. Instinctively, we all sensed the necessity of adapting ourselves to two different worlds. We began to notice that there were several marked differences between those worlds, differences that made Americans and my relatives each think of the other as foreigners.

The difference that pained me most was that of language, probably because I was aware of it most often. Child that I was, I would feel terribly embarrassed whenever my mother called to me in Italian while I was playing on the street, with all my playmates there to listen; or when she was buying clothes for me and would wrangle in broken English with the salesmen about the price.

My mother took no notice of such childish snobbery. As long as I remained under her jurisdiction, she continued to cling to her policy of restricting the family language to Italian. "I might as well not have my children if I can't talk with them," she argued. She considered it sinful for relatives to permit their children to speak a language which the entire family could not speak fluently, and claimed that if she were to cast aside Italian, the language of her forefathers, it would be like renouncing her own flesh and blood.

There was only one possible retort to these arguments but no one dared use it: the language we called Italian and spoke at home was not Italian. It was a Sicilian dialect which only Sicilians could understand . . . .

But if my relatives were under the impression that they were speaking the same dialect they brought with them from Sicily, they were mistaken. After a few years of hearing American, Yiddish, Polish, and Italian dialects other than their own, their language gathered words which no one in Sicily could possibly understand. The most amazing of these were garbled American words dressed up with Sicilian suffixes—strange concoctions which, in later years, that non-Sicilian pundit, H. L. Mencken, was to include in his book, *The American Language*.

Mr. Mencken's collection of Italian-American words is a good indication of what happened to the vocabulary of my relatives. Such words as *minuto* for minute, *ponte* for pound, *storo* for store, *barra* for bar, *giobba* for job were constantly used as Sicilian words.

One word that Mr. Mencken should include in the next edition of his book is *baccauso*, which has been in my relatives' vocabulary as far back as I can remember. My parents probably picked it up from other American Sicilians when they first arrived in Rochester. Certainly, the word had no relation to their current mode of city life. It was used when referring to "toilet" and was obviously derived from the American "backhouse" that flourished in earlier and more rural America. Not until a few years ago when I first visited Italy, a nation without backhouses, and mystified Sicilians there by using the word, did I become aware of its Chic Sale derivation. Yet I had been using *baccauso* for a lifetime, always under the impression it was an authentic Sicilian word. . . .

Even my father felt inhibited by my mother's determination to keep English out of the house, and would only speak the language when it was absolutely necessary or when my mother was not present. My father's English was like no one else's in the world. Yet it could be understood more easily than the English spoken by most of my Sicilian relatives. All that he knew of the language he managed to pick up during his first six months in America. His first factory *bosso*, a noisy Irishman, provided the incentive. My father wanted to learn enough English so that he could talk back to him. He was most successful; the boss fired him the first time he understood what he was saying.

So elated was my father with the amount of English he absorbed in a half-year that he stopped learning the language then and there and never made any further conscious effort to add to his vocabulary or improve his grammar. But he made the most of what he knew, and in a few years had developed a system of speaking English which defied all philological laws but could be understood by most Americans after about five minutes of orientation. Probably the most astonishing aspect of his system was that he used only one pronoun—"she"—and only one tense—the present.

The little English my mother knew she acquired from my father. But she spoke the language without any system, groping for nearly all the words she used, without any of my father's wonderful sureness. Although she had been in America as long as he, she had never had daily contact with persons who spoke only English. The tailor factories, where she worked when she arrived, were nearly all filled with men and women who had recently come from Italy and spoke only their native tongue.

The stores where she did her shopping every day were operated by Italians whose customers were all Italians. The Poles and the Jews who made up a large part of Mount Allegro stuck to their native languages most of the time. My mother had little to do with them. She exchanged greetings with all of them, but you did not need to know much English to keep on friendly terms with a neighbor. A smile or an occasional gift of cooked spaghetti served the purpose just as effectively. . . .

In spite of his superior intellect, Uncle Nino never learned much English— chiefly because of an old grudge he bore against his wife. Whenever he quarreled with her he would shout that he had never intended to come to America in the first place and only did so because she so 'blinded' him that he could not distinguish between love and common sense. Even when he was not quarreling with her, you would have surmised from hearing him talk that he was through with America and was returning to Sicily the very next day.

Since he had ranted in much the same way for nearly twenty years, none of his relatives, least of all his wife, took him seriously. Yet the fact remained that during all that time Uncle Nino considered himself little more than a transient who would some day persuade his wife that it would be far more comfortable to return to Sicily and live on the fat of the land he owned there than to exist in a callow city like Rochester and slave all week for a few strands of spaghetti.

His arguments did not impress his wife, possibly because it was she and not he who slaved all week. My Aunt Giovanna sewed buttonholes in a tailor factory, while he ran a small jewelry trade from his living-room, an occupation that left him with considerable time and energy to play briscola and threaten to leave America.

It was quite true that if he had not met my Aunt Giovanna, he probably would never have set foot outside of Sicily. . . . My Aunt Giovanna . . . was in the throes of conspiring to secure admission into the United States after having failed twice before. Both times her application had been rejected in the belief that she had trachoma, the eye disease that was often contracted by Sicilians living in towns where the water was bad.

On her first attempt to get to America she actually got as far as Ellis Island. But American officials seemed less susceptible to her beauty than the Italian officials who had gallantly helped to smuggle her through the red tape in Palermo. Ellis Island was little more than a prison in those days. For eight days she spent her time looking through iron bars at the Statue of Liberty and the New York skyline, and weeping.

Every morning an Irish policewoman who spoke Italian tried to make her tell how she had got on the boat without a passport. But my aunt never told. Finally the immigration officials realized they were wasting their time and shipped Aunt Giovanna back to Palermo.

When my Uncle Nino proposed three days after he met her, she consented, but only on condition that he take her to America. He give up his thriving business, married her, and took her on a honeymoon to France, where they thought she would stand a better chance of getting a passport. At Havre she was again turned down. Uncle Nino got his passport without any trouble, but he saw little point in leaving his bride behind to go to a country that did not particularly attract him.

My Aunt Giovanna was never lacking in stubbornness. Against his better judgment, she persuaded him to sail alone, arguing that once he was in the United States it would be a simple matter for him to make arrangements to send for her. Was she not his wife? . . . He spent a miserable year in New York filling out endless forms, pining for his bride, and cursing the moment he had given in to her arguments. He was about to return to Europe and take her back to Sicily, when word came that Aunt Giovanna had been able to persuade the French immigration officials that there was nothing wrong with her eyes that a less tearful existence could not remedy.

He had never forgiven her for those lonely months he spent in New York waiting for her. And after twenty years of America he was still angry with her for having wrenched him away from a successful career to a makeshift existence in a strange land where he had to depend largely on his wife's earnings.

86

If it had not been for this old grudge, Uncle Nino might have mastered English.

"He who knows the English language will go forward," he was fond of saying. But he himself made not the slightest effort to learn it. "Why should I try to master a language as difficult as English? By the time I learned to speak it properly, it would be time for me to die. If your demands are as simple as mine, it is not hard to get whatever you want without knowing the language."

He liked to illustrate this point with a story he heard about the first Italians who came to Rochester.

"In the early days Italians were disliked far more than they are now," he said. "They could not speak a word of English; at least I can fool an American into believing that I know what he is talking about, but they didn't even know enough English to do that. Nor did they get much chance to associate with Americans.

"The men were good strong workers but the Americans regarded them as bandits and intruders, and their employers treated them as though they were nothing but workhorses. They all forgot that they had been foreigners once too, and they made life as miserable as possible for them.

"Although the Italians had money, the storekeepers would not sell them food and the landlords would not rent them homes. For many weeks they were forced to live in boxes and tents and depend on *cicoria* for their main food. Now, *cicoria* is one of the most nutritious foods God planted in this earth, but even *cicoria* can become boring as a steady diet.

". . . One afternoon they armed themselves with pickaxes and marched into one of the largest grocery stores in town. While they stood by with their pickaxes poised over their heads, their leader addressed himself to the chief clerk.

"The leader did not know a word of English. He made motions with his hands and his mouth to show that they were all very hungry. He also made it clear that unless the men were allowed to purchase food, they would tear up the store with their pickaxes. The clerk was a very understanding fellow and sold them all the food they wanted.

"Their success went to their heads. Now that they could buy food, they began to wish for real houses to eat it in. Even then Rochester was a miserably damp and rainy town, and a tent or a box was no way to keep snug. Once more the men got out their pickaxes and called on the grocery clerk. Again the clerk had no difficulty making out what they wanted. . . . In a few days the men were moved from their tents and shanties into real homes. These same Italians now have children who are some of the leading doctors, lawyers, and druggists in town. There's no doubt about it: you have to ask for whatever you want in this world, and prayer isn't always the way to ask."

Locking the Door: The Exclusion of Chinese

Immigrants, particularly those with different religions, customs, or standards of living, were not always welcomed by a predominantly Anglo-Saxon, Protestant America. Anti-foreign sentiment was, of course, nothing new. Cotton Mather and John Winthrop of colonial Massachusetts disliked the Scots-Irish, for example; similarly, Benjamin Franklin expressed alarm at the size of the German immigration.

Nativist (anti-foreign) sentiment became a significant political factor in the 1850s with the formation of the American, or Know-Nothing, Party, whose policies were directed primarily against Catholic immigrants then arriving in large numbers from Ireland and Germany. But in most parts of the country, nativism soon gave way, at least for the moment, to traditional American attitudes of religious toleration and democracy, and anti-foreign sentiment was all but forgotten as the nation became absorbed in the conflict over slavery.

On the West Coast, however, a particularly virulent and racist form of anti-foreign sentiment was aimed against the Chinese, who were to become the first ethnic group officially excluded from the United States. Chinese immigration to America began during the gold rush, and it is estimated that by early 1852 some 25,000 Chinese had entered California, forming close to ten percent of the population. Most of the Chinese were men who came as transient workers; they found employment in the mines and domestic trades and on the railroads. But their very industriousness, as well as their willingness to work for low wages, soon aroused the hostility of white laborers and miners. Set apart not only by their race, but by language, dress, and customs, the Chinese were denounced as heathen barbarians. As early as 1852 the Committee on Mines of the California Assembly called upon Congress to exclude the Chinese. But Congress took no action, and in 1868 the Burlingame Treaty guaranteed Chinese free immigration. The result was a sudden growth in Chinese immigration—and in anti-Chinese sentiment. As the Chinese were employed as strike breakers and cheap factory and farm labor in many parts of the country, the hostility toward them became nationwide. In 1880 a new treaty with China permitted mutual exclusion of immigrants, and in 1882 Congress passed a law to exclude Chinese laborers for ten years and deny citizenship to Chinese

*already in the country. The restrictions were periodically ex-
tended, and finally, in 1904, Congress extended indefinitely
the laws excluding Chinese.*

*The anti-Chinese sentiment was reflected in the literature of
the period, including songs and poems. "John Chinaman," a
song that became popular in 1855, expressed the miners' early
fears of Chinese competition. Bret Harte, the well-known
story-writer and poet, wrote the poem reprinted below as a
humorous space-filler; though not intended as an anti-Chinese
poem, "The Heathen Chinee" became an immediate favorite
with those favoring exclusion.*

JOHN CHINAMAN
—Anonymous Song

John Chinaman, John Chinaman,
   But five short years ago,
I welcomed you from Canton, John—
   But wish I hadn't though;

For then I thought you honest, John,
   Not dreaming but you'd make
A citizen as useful, John
   As any in the State

I thought you'd open wide your ports
   And let our merchants in
To barter for their crapes and teas
   Their wares of wood and tin.

I thought you'd cut your queue off, John,
   And don a Yankee coat,
And a collar high you'd raise, John,
   Around your dusky throat.

I imagined that the truth, John
   You'd speak when under oath,
But I find you'll lie and steal too—
   Yes, John, you're up to both.

I thought of rats and puppies, John
   You'd eaten your last fill;
But on such slimy pot-pies, John,
   I'm told you dinner still.

"John Chinaman," *The California Songster* (San Francisco: David E. Appleton & Co., 1855),
p. 44.

Oh, John, I've been deceived in you,
And in all your thieving clan,
For our gold is all you're after, John,
To get it as you can.

THE HEATHEN CHINEE   (1870)
—Bret Harte

Which I wish to remark—
And my language is plain—
That for ways that are dark
And for tricks that are vain,
The heathen Chinee is peculiar
Which the same I would rise to explain.

Ah Sin was his name;
And I shall not deny
In regard to the same
What that name might imply
But his smile it was pensive and childlike,
As I frequent remarked to Bill Nye.

It was August the third;
And quite soft was the skies;
Which it might be inferred
That Ah Sin was likewise;
Yet he played it that day upon William
And me in a way I despise.

Which we had a small game,
And Ah Sin took a hand:
It was Euchre, the game
He did not understand;
But he smiled as he sat by the table,
With the smile that was childlike and bland.

Yet the cards they were stacked
In a way that I grieve,
And my feelings were shocked
At the state of Nye's sleeve:
Which was stuffed full of aces and bowers,
And the same with intent to deceive.

But the hands that were played
By that heathen Chinee,
And the points that he made,

Bret Harte, "The Heathen Chinee," from *Plain Language from Truthful James* (Chicago: Western News Co., 1870).

Were quite frightful to see—
Till at last he put down a right bower,
Which the same Nye had dealt unto me.

Then I looked up at Nye,
And he gazed upon me;
And he rose with a sigh,
And said, "Can this be?
We are ruined by Chinese cheap labor"—
And he went to that heathen Chinee

In the scene that ensued
I did not take a hand
But the floor it was strewed
Like the leaves on the strand
With the cards that Ah Sin had been hiding,
In the game "he did not understand."

In his sleeves, which were long,
He had twenty-four packs—
Which was coming it strong,
Yet I state but the facts;
And we found on his nails, which were toper,
What is frequent in tapers—that's wax.

Which is why I remark,
And my language is plain,
That for ways that are dark,
And for tricks that are vain,
The heathen Chinee is peculiar—
Which the same I am free to maintain.

The New Colossus

John Higham

At the very time that Congress was passing the Chinese Exclusion Act, in 1882, plans were underway in New York to erect the statue that was to become a symbol of refuge for millions of European immigrants. Ironically, the Statue of Liberty was unveiled at a time when many Americans were becoming alarmed at the size and composition of the new immigration. Officially entitled "Liberty Enlightening the World," the statue, a gift from the French, was intended not as a symbol of welcome but as a symbol of republican stability. The transformation in the symbolism of the Statue of Liberty over a period of half a century is traced by John Higham, professor of history at Johns Hopkins University, in the article reprinted below.

For nine frustrating years, from 1877 to 1886, a committee of New York business and society leaders collected funds to pay for a pedestal on which a gigantic Statue of Liberty might stand in New York Harbor. The statue itself, the inspiration and creation of a French sculptor, Frédéric Auguste Bartholdi, was under construction in Paris. It was to be a gift to America from the French people, a symbol and pledge of friendship between the two republics. Americans needed only to erect it properly; yet the task almost exceeded the limits of the sluggish public spirit of the day.

At one point, in 1883, when the statue was almost ready to ship and the pedestal only half-finished, the Pedestal Fund Committee organized a temporary art exhibition as a fund-raising device. Prominent New Yorkers lent some of their treasures, and a number of artists and writers contributed original drawings and letters to a portfolio which was put up for auction. After some urging, Emma Lazarus produced a sonnet for the occasion. The entire portfolio, including the sonnet, sold for $1,500, a disappointing sum.

A finely bred, bookish young lady, Miss Lazarus rarely wrote in a patriotic vein. But this occasion touched obliquely a new and vital concern of hers. Until 1881 she had produced derivative, self-consciously literary verse, the tinkling melodies then fashionable in the world of genteel culture. Belonging to one of the oldest and most secure of New York Jewish families, she had abandoned the synagogue in her youth and had

Reprinted by permission of the University of Chicago Press from John Higham, "Emma Lazarus, 'The New Colossus,'" in Daniel Boorstin (ed.), *An American Primer*. © 1966 by the University of Chicago.

largely lost a sense of Jewish identity. Then the horrifying outbreak of anti-Jewish pogroms in Russia, and the sight of the first bedraggled refugees arriving in New York, gave her a theme and a mission. With a new passion, she wrote henceforth mainly as a champion of the Jews. She became the first modern American laureate of their history and culture. To her the Statue of Liberty, facing seaward, would hold out to uprooted folk the same message of succor that she, Emma Lazarus, was expressing to and for her fellow Jews.

> Not like the brazen giant of Greek fame,[1]
> With conquering limbs astride from land to land;
> Here at our sea-washed, sunset gates shall stand
> A mighty woman with a torch, whose flame
> Is the imprisoned lightning, and her name
> Mother of Exiles. From her beacon-hand
> Glows world-wide welcome; her mild eyes command
> The air-bridged harbor that twin cities frame.

> "Keep, ancient lands, your storied pomp!" cries she
> With silent lips. "Give me your tired, your poor,
> Your huddled masses yearning to breathe free,
> The wretched refuse of your teeming shore.
> Send these, the homeless, tempest-tost to me,
> I lift my lamp beside the golden door!"

Absorbed in the cause of the Jews, Miss Lazarus seems to have taken no further interest in the Statue of Liberty once her poem was written. Nor did her contemporaries pay much heed to "The New Colossus." When she died in 1887, four years after its composition, the obituaries failed to mention it. The reviewers of her collected works, which appeared in 1889, concentrated on her specifically Jewish poems. One critic conceded that "her noble sonnet" on the Bartholdi statue had given many their "first apprehension of the glory in even the more sordid elements in our American life." Others ignored the poem completely. After the turn of the century Miss Lazarus herself was largely forgotten outside a small Anglo-Jewish literary circle.

In 1903, on the twentieth anniversary of the writing of "The New Colossus," another shy, poetry-loving spinster who belonged to the old New York aristocracy, Georgina Schuyler, secured permission to put a bronze tablet containing the entire poem on an interior wall of the statue's pedestal. This she did primarily as a memorial to Miss Lazarus, whom she evidently had known and admired. The event passed without ceremony or public notice. In fact, the poem rested there for another thirty years without attracting any publicity at all.

This long neglect is remarkable; for the ideas that the poem expressed were deeply ingrained in American tradition. The concept of America as a

---

[1]The original manuscript of the poem, which is followed here, is in the possession of the American Jewish Historical Society in New York City. (The "brazen giant" referred to in the first line is the Colossus of Rhodes, a statue of the sun god Helius, which once stood at the harbor of Rhodes; it was known in ancient and medieval times as one of the Seven Wonders of the World.)

refuge from European oppression supplied one of the original, fertilizing elements of our national consciousness. Jefferson, Emerson, Lowell, and many a lesser patriot had voiced its continuing appeal. In the late nineteenth century, however, pride in America's receptive mission dimmed. A gradual liberalization of political institutions throughout most of Europe blurred the once-sharp image of the immigrant as one who had been unfree in his native country. Meanwhile, the new problems of an urban, industrial age inspired a strong movement in America to restrict immigration. By 1886, when the New Colossus was finally unveiled upon her completed pedestal, there was already considerable alarm about the huddled masses streaming through the golden door. The lavish dedication ceremonies took place without a single reference to Miss Lazarus' sonnet and without serious attention to its theme.

Not only the uneasy mood of the time but also the statue itself resisted the generous construction Miss Lazarus placed upon it. The creators of the monument did not intend a symbol of welcome. Bartholdi and the French liberals who supported his work prized America not as an asylum but as an example of republican stability. They constructed a passive figure, austere and unresponsive, a model of frozen perfection, holding a torch high to illuminate the darker world beyond the sea. Its official name was "Liberty Enlightening the World." The meaning of the physical object would have to change before the sonnet could become a living document.

The immigrants themselves wrought that transformation, as they arrived in this country in the years after the statue was erected. The vast majority debarked at New York, and to every exultant heart and straining eye this first American presence was a profoundly moving sight. The immigrants perceived the statue as waiting for them, big with promise. They saw it not as a beacon to other lands but as a redemptive salutation to themselves. The memory of that awesome moment and the unspoken greeting it contained was a thing to cherish, a thing to tell one's children about. In 1906 Edward A. Steiner, an immigrant intellectual who was unaware of Emma Lazarus' poem, predicted that a great poet would someday put into words the inspiring emotions that millions of immigrants felt on encountering "this new divinity into whose keeping they now entrust themselves."

Miss Lazarus' words were rediscovered only after the immigrants' response to the statue penetrated our fund of national myths, revitalizing the old eighteenth-century idea of America as an asylum. While a bitter controversy over immigration pitted older against newer American groups, the Statue of Liberty remained—in the dominant native culture—an aloof, impersonal symbol, conveying a warning rather than a welcome to the outside world. After the restrictive Immigration Act of 1924 was passed, however, fear and rancor subsided; the great influx from overseas was ended. Immigration as a mass movement receded into history. Meanwhile, the children of immigrants from southern and eastern Europe grew up into full participation in American life. To ease their Americanization, public school curricula devoted increasing attention to the immigrants' love for and contributions to America. By 1926 fourth-grade children in St. Louis, Missouri, were studying the Statue of Liberty with the object of understanding what it meant to immigrants. By then some of the school textbooks on American history included pictures of immigrant families gazing joyfully at Bartholdi's Colossus. That immobile figure gradually joined the covered wagon as a symbol of the migrations that had made America.

In the late 1930's, more than fifty years after its composition, Emma Lazarus' poem finally attracted public interest. The event that called it forth from obscurity was a recurrence of the very problem that had moved Miss Lazarus in the first place: the plight of Jewish refugees. Their efforts to escape Nazi barbarism coincided with a growing revulsion of American opinion against racism and with a steady movement of the United States toward war with Germany. In contrast to the situation in the 1880's, when Americans were turning away from a cosmopolitan, humane outlook, the circumstances of the late 1930's united a particular concern for the Jews with a broader movement to strengthen ethnic democracy. Immigration policy did not change significantly. But a nation striving to overcome its own ethnic hatreds, to dignify influential minority groups, and to gird for war against Hitler needed to define itself anew as a bastion against persecution.

Louis Adamic, a Yugoslav-American journalist, did more than anyone else to popularize "The New Colossus." About 1934 he launched a one-man crusade to elevate the status of immigrant groups and to propagate an eclectic sense of American nationality. After 1938 he adopted the Lazarus sonnet as the keynote of practically everything he wrote or said. He quoted it endlessly in books, pamphlets, and public lectures. During the 1940's the words of the poem became a familiar litany in mass-circulation magazines, children's stories, and high-school history texts. In 1945 Georgina Schuyler's commemorative tablet was moved from the second-story landing to the main entrance of the statue. Beginning in 1947, the World Almanac included the poem as a regular feature. Curiosity about its forgotten author awakened. Now she seemed less a Jewish than an American poet, a human statue of liberty. According to the title of one rapturious biography, she was *Emma Lazarus, Woman with a Torch*.

Although the Statue of Liberty was not intended to beckon the tired and the poor, they had come to it. Because it received them no longer in significant numbers, it could enshrine their experience as a transcendental national memory. Because few Americans now were immigrants, all Americans could think of themselves as having been immigrants. Like the myth of the frontier, the myth of the asylum acquired a remembered glory in an age that wished to preserve the spirit of a reality that was largely gone.

Yet the reality of refuge in America has never wholly disappeared, and the myth has not been merely compensatory. Its revival encouraged efforts to live up to the dictates of "The New Colossus." In 1965 Congress repealed the discriminatory features of the Immigration Law of 1924. President Lyndon B. Johnson, signing the new law at the base of the Statue of Liberty, alluded to the Lazarus poem and declared that the nation was returning "to the finest of its traditions." In the same spirit the President used the occasion to announce a large-scale program for reception of refugees from Cuba.

The Melting Pot

As the number of immigrants rose sharply—from an average of 2.6 million per decade between 1850 and 1880 to a high of 8.8 million in the first decade of the twentieth century—many Americans began to question traditional assumptions about their nation's ability to absorb the new immigrant groups.

As early as 1782 the French observer Crèvecoeur had remarked, "He is an American, who, leaving behind him all his ancient prejudices and manners, receives new ones from the new mode of life he has embraced, the new government he obeys, and the new rank he holds. . . . Here individuals of all races are melted into a new breed of men." The Founding Fathers also believed that European immigrants must abandon their ways and adopt those of America. "If they cannot accommodate themselves to the character, moral, political, and physical, of this country," wrote John Adams, ". . . the Atlantic is always open to them to return to the land of their nativity. . . . They must cast off the European skin, never to resume it." Throughout the eighteenth century and much of the nineteenth, Americans believed that European immigrants would be easily absorbed—assimilated to the dominant Anglo-American culture or amalgamated into the new American nationality.

At the height of the period of new immigration, in 1909, the British playwright Israel Zangwill gave new expression to the idea of America as a melting pot, expanding the concept to include all races and nationalities.

But by then large numbers of Americans no longer shared his assumptions. Some, observing the distinct ethnic colonies throughout America, questioned whether it was possible to meld so many disparate ethnic, religious, and racial groups; others, particularly those opposed to unrestricted immigration, questioned whether it was desirable. In 1915, Horace Kallen, then a young philosopher, also took issue with the idea of the melting pot; America was, he argued, a federation of cultures, in which all groups could realize their potentialities and thus enrich the whole. Only gradually has this concept of "cultural pluralism" won acceptance.

Selection 1   Israel Zangwill

It is the fires of God round His Crucible.

There she lies, the great Melting-Pot—listen! Can't you hear the roaring and the bubbling? There gapes her mouth—the harbour where a thousand mammoth feeders come from the ends of the world to pour in their human freight. Ah, what a stirring and a seething! Celt and Latin, Slav and Teuton, Greek and Syrian,—black and yellow—

Jew and Gentile—

Yes, East and West, and North and South, the palm and the pine, the pole and the equator, the crescent and the cross—how the great Alchemist melts and fuses them with his purging flame! Here shall they all unite to build the Republic of Man and the Kingdom of God. Ah, Vera, what is the glory of Rome and Jerusalem where all nations and races come to worship and look back, compared with the glory of America, where all races and nations come to labour and look forward!

Peace, peace, to all ye unborn millions, fated to fill this giant continent—the God of our children give you Peace.

Selection 2   Horace M. Kallen

Immigrants appear to pass through four phases in the course of being automatically Americanized. In the first phase they exhibit economic eagerness, the greedy hunger of the unfed. Since external differences are a handicap in the economic struggle, they "assimilate," seeking thus to facilitate the attainment of economic independence. Once the proletarian level of such independence is reached, the process of assimilation slows down and tends to come to a stop. The immigrant group is still a national group, modified, sometimes improved, by environmental influences, but otherwise a solidary spiritual unit, which is seeking to find its way out on its own social level. This search brings to light permanent group distinctions and the immigrant, like the Anglo-Saxon American, is thrown back upon himself and his ancestry. Then a process of dissimilation begins. The arts, life and ideals of the nationality become central and paramount; ethnic and national differences change in status from disadvantages to distinctions. All the while the immigrant has been uttering his life in the English language and behaving like an American in matters economic and political, and continues to do so. The institutions of the Republic have become the liberating cause and the background for the rise of the cultural consciousness and social autonomy of the immigrant Irishman, German, Scandinavian, Jew, Pole or Bohemian. On the whole, the automatic processes of Americanization have not repressed nationality. These processes have liberated nationality, and more or less gratified it. . . .

From Israel Zangwill, *The Melting Pot* (New York: Jewish Publication Society of America, 1909), pp. 198-199.

From Horace M. Kallen, "Democracy Versus the Melting Pot," *The Nation,*© 1915. Reprinted by permission of *The Nation*.

Democratism and the federal principle have worked together with economic greed and ethnic snobbishness to people the land with all the nationalities of Europe, and to convert the early American nationality into the present American *nation*. For in effect the United States are in the process of becoming a federal state not merely as a union of geographical and administrative unities, but also as a cooperation of cultural diversities, as a federation or commonwealth of national cultures. . . .

. . . America is, in fact, at the parting of the ways. Two genuine social alternatives are before Americans, either of which they may realize if they will. . . . What do Americans *will* to make of the United States—a unison, singing the old British theme "America," the America of the New England School? or a harmony, in which that theme shall be dominant, perhaps, among others, but one among many, not the only one? . . .

In the United States. . . the whole social situation is favorable [for unison] as it has never been at any time elsewhere—everything is favorable but the basic law of America itself, and the spirit of the American institutions. To achieve unison—it can be achieved—would be to violate these. . . .

The attainment of the other alternative, a harmony, also requires concerted public action. But the action would do no violence to the ideals of American fundamental law and the spirit of American institutions nor to the qualities of men. It would seek simply to eliminate the waste and the stupidity of the social organization, by way of freeing and strengthening the strong forces actually in operation. Taking for its point of departure the existing ethnic and cultural groups it would seek to provide conditions under which each might attain the cultural perfection that is *proper to its kind*. The provision of such conditions has been said to be the primary intent of American fundamental law and the function of American institutions. And all of the various nationalities which compose the American nation must be taught first of all this fact, which used perhaps to be, to patriotic minds, the outstanding ideal content of "Americanism"—that democracy means self-realization through self-control, self-discipline, and that one is impossible without the other. . . .

. . . What is inalienable in the life of mankind is its intrinsic positive quality—its psycho-physical inheritance. Men may change their clothes, their politics, their wives, their religions, their philosophies, to a greater or lesser extent: they cannot change their grandfathers. Jews or Poles or Anglo-Saxons, in order to cease being Jews or Poles or Anglo-Saxons, would have to cease to be, while they could cease to be citizens or church members or carpenters or lawyers without ceasing to be. The selfhood which is inalienable in them, and for the realization of which they require "inalienable" liberty is ancestrally determined, and the happiness which they pursue has its form implied in ancestral endowment. This is what, actually, democracy in operation assumes. . . . And as intelligence and wisdom prevail over "politics" and special interests, as the steady and continuous pressure of the "inalienable" qualities and purposes of human groups more and more dominate the confusion of their common life, the outlines of a possible great and truly democratic commonwealth become discernible. Its form would be that of the federal republic; its substance a democracy of nationalities, cooperating voluntarily and autonomously through common institutions in the enterprise of self-realization through the perfection of men according to their kind. The common language of the commonwealth, the language of its great tradition, would be English, but each nationality would have for its emotional and involuntary life its own peculiar dialect or speech, its own individual and inevitable esthetic and intellectual forms. The political and economic life of the commonwealth is a single unit and serves as the foundation and background for the realization of the distinctive individuality of each *natio* that composes it and of the pooling of these in a harmony above them all. Thus "American civilization" may come to mean the perfection of the cooperative harmonies of "European civilization"—the waste, the squalor and the distress of Europe being eliminated—a multiplicity in a unity, an orchestration of mankind. As in an orchestra every type of instrument has its specific *timbre* and *tonality*, founded in its substance and form; as every type has its appropriate theme and melody in the whole symphony, so in society, each ethnic group may be the natural instrument, its temper and culture may be its theme and melody and the harmony and dissonances and discords of them all may make the symphony of civilization . . . .

But the question is, do the dominant classes in America want such a society? The alternative is actually before them. Can they choose wisely? Or will vanity blind them and fear constrain, turning the promise of freedom into the fact of tyranny, and once more vindicating the ancient habit of men and aborting the hope of the world?

Speaking for
Ethnic America

Barbara Mikulski

*In the long run, the concept of cultural pluralism seemed
more appropriate to American society than that of the melting
pot. The various ethnic groups that made America a "nation
of nations" have not lost their separate identities. But while
remaining loyal to their own cultural traditions, most "ethnic
Americans"—the children and grandchildren of southern and
eastern Europeans—readily embraced traditional American
values: patriotism, hard work, obedience to law and order,
and respect for authority. In the mid-sixties, however, many
white ethnics felt that the rules of the game by which they
would enter American society had changed. The Liberal
Establishment and the media often ridiculed their values, while
blacks and Spanish-speaking Americans displaced them from
their jobs and absorbed the major share of the nation's concern
with minority problems. The frustrations of being the "forgotten people" of the sixties are well expressed by Barbara
Mikulski, who represents her ethnic neighborhood on the
Baltimore City Council.*

The Ethnic American is forgotten and forlorn. He is infuriated at being
used and abused by the media, government and business. Pejorative
epithets such as "pigs" and "racists" or slick, patronizing labels like the
"silent majority" or "hard hats" are graphic examples of the lack of respect,
understanding and appreciation of him and his way of life.

The Ethnic Americans are 40 million working class Americans who live
primarily in 58 major industrial cities like Baltimore and Chicago. Our roots
are in Central and Southern Europe. We have been in this country for one,
two or three generations. We have made a maximum contribution to the
U.S.A., yet received minimal recognition.

The ethnics came to America from the turn of the century through the
twenties, until we were restricted by prejudicial immigration quotas—
65,000 Anglo-Saxons to 300 Greeks. We came looking for political freedom
and economic opportunity. Many fled from countries where there had been
political, religious and cultural oppression for 1,000 years.

It was this working class which built the Great Cities—constructed the skyscrapers, operated the railroads, worked on the docks, factories, steel mills and in the mines. Though our labor was in demand, we were not accepted. Our names, language, food and cultural customs were the subject of ridicule. We were discriminated against by banks, institutions of higher learning and other organizations controlled by the Yankee Patricians. There were no protective mechanisms for safety, wages and tenure. We called ourselves Americans. We were called "wop," "polack" and "hunky."

For our own protection, we formed our own institutions and organizations and clung together in our new neighborhoods. We created communities like "Little Italy" and "Polish Hill." The ethnic parish church and the fraternal organizations like the Polish Women's Alliance and the Sons of Italy became the focal points of our culture.

These neighborhoods were genuine "urban villages." Warmth, charm and zesty communal spirit were their characteristics. People knew each other. This was true not only of relatives and friends but of the grocer, politician and priest. The people were proud, industrious and ambitious. All they wanted was a chance to "make it" in America.

Here we are in the 1970's, earning from $5,000 to $10,000 per year. We are "near poor" economically. No one listens to our problems. The President's staff responds to our problems by patronizingly patting us on the head and putting pictures of construction workers on postage stamps. The media stereotype us as gangsters or dumb clods in dirty sweat-shirts. The status of manual labor has been denigrated to the point where men are often embarrassed to say they are plumbers or tugboat operators. This robs men of their pride in their work and themselves.

The Ethnic American is losing ground economically. He is the victim of both inflation and anti-inflation measures. Though wages have increased by 20 per cent since the mid sixties, true purchasing power has remained the same. He is hurt by layoffs due to cutbacks in production and construction. Tight money policies strangle him with high interest rates for installment buying and mortgages. He is the man who at 40 is told by the factory bosses that he is too old to be promoted. The old job is often threatened by automation. At the same time, his expenses are at their peak. He is paying on his home and car, probably trying to put at least one child through college.

In pursuing his dream of home ownership, he finds that it becomes a millstone rather than a milestone in his life. Since FHA loans are primarily restricted to "new" housing, he cannot buy a house in the old neighborhood. He has no silk-stocking lawyers or fancy lobbyists getting him tax breaks.

He believes in the espoused norms of American manhood like "a son should take care of his mother" and "a father should give his children every opportunity." Yet he is torn between putting out $60 a month for his mother's arthritis medication or paying for his daughter's college tuition.

When the ethnic worker looks for some modest help, he is told that his income is too high. He's "too rich" to get help when his dad goes into a nursing home. Colleges make practically no effort to provide scholarships to kids named Colstiani, Slukowski or Klima.

The one place where he felt the master of his fate and had status was in his own neighborhood. Now even that security is being threatened. He wants new schools for his children and recreation facilities for the entire family— not just the token wading pool for pre-schoolers or the occasional dance for teen-agers. He wants his street fixed and his garbage collected. He finds that the only things being planned for his area are housing projects, expressways and fertilizer factories. When he goes to City Hall to make his problems known, he is either put off, put down or put out.

Liberals scapegoat us as racists. Yet there was no racial prejudice in our hearts when we came. There were very few black people in Poland or Lithuania. The elitists who now smugly call us racists are the ones who taught us the meaning of the word: their bigotry extended to those of a different class or national origin.

Government is further polarizing people by the creation of myths that black needs are being met. Thus the ethnic worker is fooled into thinking that the blacks are getting everything.

Old prejudices and new fears are ignited. The two groups end up fighting each other for the same jobs and competing so that the new schools and recreation centers will be built in their respective communities. What results is angry confrontation for tokens, when there should be an alliance for a whole new Agenda for America. This Agenda would be created if black and white organized separately in their own communities for their own needs and came together to form an alliance based on mutual issues, interdependence and respect. This alliance would develop new strategies for community organization and political restructuring. From this, the new Agenda for America would be generated. It could include such items as "new towns in town," innovative concepts of work and creative structures for community control.

What is necessary is to get rid of the guilt of phony liberals, control by economic elitists and manipulation by selfish politicians. Then, let us get on with creating the democratic and pluralistic society that we say we are.

Red Power

Alvin M. Josephy, Jr.

*At the beginning of the twentieth century the Indian popu-
lation of the United States had reached a low point of 237,000,
and much of white America believed that the Indian was
becoming a "vanishing American."*

*But neither the Indians nor their distinctive cultures disap-
peared. Improved health care and a rising birth rate helped
bring Indian population to more than 775,000 by 1960; and
Congressional policies, which since the 1880s had been designed
to hasten assimilation, had proven a dismal failure. As the
following article indicates, an increasing number of Indians
have entered the white man's world and sought employment in
urban America; but at the same time, a new sense of pride in
their heritage and their demands for Red Power have assured
that they will remain a distinct culture in the pluralistic society.*

*Alvin Josephy, Jr., is book editor of the American Heritage
Publishing Company and an authority on Indian history.*

Since the time of Jamestown and Plymouth two principal strains have
characterized the relations between white men and the native inhabitants
of the present-day United States. On the one hand, the white man has
told the Indians that he must become a white—in dress, beliefs, and ways
of life—or perish. On the other hand, he has taken the lands and resources
that the Indians possessed. . . .

Both strains, of course, were aggressive, and both kept the Indian continually on the defensive. If he was not fighting for his lands and life,
he was fighting for the very things that gave meaning to his life, that made
him want to live—his beliefs, his ways of life, his standards, his traditions,
his societies—his right to be what he was, what his ancestors had given him
and made him—a member of his group, an Indian. Shorn of that, he
would be nothing. The continuous pressure of the whites dispossessed
many Indians not only of their lands, but also of their Indianness, and
native Americans were steadily being acculturated and assimilated. But it
was generally a painful process, and many Indians were killed and whole
bands—and even tribes—exterminated because they refused to listen to

Excerpted from Alvin M. Josephy, Jr., "Toward Freedom: the American Indian in the
Twentieth Century." From *Indiana Historical Society Lectures,* 1970–1971, which also includes
"The Image of the Indian in Pre-Civil War America," by Francis Paul Procha and "Indian
Policy after the Civil War," by William T. Hagan.

those among them who counseled that it would be wise to try to live like the white man.

With the final pacification of the tribes, the two strains drew together and became intertwined in a single national policy. Assimilation was the principal goal, and dispossession became the deliberate, unabashed instrument by which to accomplish it. With only minor variations, that development—which became prominently identifiable in 1887—marked the course of Indian affairs in the United States during much of the twentieth century.

. . . The Eleventh Census of the United States in the year 1890 . . . reported that the civilization of the white man at last stretched securely from coast to coast and that there was no longer a frontier in the United States—meaning that there would no longer be serious opposition from Indians to the spread of white men anywhere they chose to expand. . . .

The census found that as of 1890 there were 248,253 Indians in the United States—that is, people who by quantity of "Indian blood," indentification with tribal groups, or descent from native peoples could be considered Indians. Of those approximately quarter million people, 133,417 were living on 133 reservations in twenty states and territories. They and another 56,030 Indians, described as living in New York State and Oklahoma, or confined in prisons, were not taxed. The rest of the quarter million, 58,806,were making their way off reservations in the white man's society and economy and, as citizens in various stages of assimilation, were liable for taxes.

The quarter million figure of Indians in 1890 had a significance as another dot on a graph line that for a long time had been curving gradually downward. It confirmed the belief that the Indian was a "vanishing American." In 1492, for instance, the best estimates are that the Indian population in what are now the forty-eight contiguous states of the United States had been at least 850,000 and possibly more—perhaps a million or a million and a quarter. . . . A high death rate among Indians, still exceeding their birth rate, seemed to ensure that the down curve on the graph would continue, and that the American Indian—at least as a separate ethnic entity in the population—would at length disappear. . . .

A new generalization could also be made about the American Indian from those statistics of 1890. He was now entirely pacified. But he had also lost his freedom and, because he was still unassimilated and so different from the rest of the population, he was helpless. As long as he existed, and remained in that state, he was a ward of the government, requiring—like a child, in the view of many whites—protection and special attention. . . . All unassimilated Indians could be categorized alike: they had to be brought along as fast as possible toward the white man's way of life, until they became homogenized, like all other Americans, in the national melting pot. . . .

The Dawes Act

The archstone of federal Indian policy, enacted on February 8, 1887, and destined to remain in force during the first thirty-four years of the twentieth century, was the Dawes General Allotment Act, named for Senator Henry L. Dawes of Massachusetts, chairman of the Senate Committee on Indian Affairs. The legislation had been initiated and given its most vocal support by those who were most sympathetic to the Indians and who genuinely sought methods for hurrying their social and economic improvement. The act, as they saw it, would lead the way to rapid assimilation by giving each Indian his own private plot of land and encouraging him to become an industrious farmer or mechanic in the image of the white man. In brief, the law provided for the end of tribal organization and stipulated that reservations were to be surrendered and divided into family-size farms which would be allotted to each Indian. Each adult was to receive 160 acres and each minor child 80 acres. The allotted lands would be held in trust for twenty-five years by the government, after which the Indian would be granted outright ownership and thereafter could sell the land if he wished to do so. Meanwhile, whatever reservation acreage was left over after the allotments were made would be declared surplus and would be bought by the government and opened for sale to whites.

The Dawes Act reflected a coinciding of the aims of both those who wished to hasten the assimilation of the Indians and those who wished to get at the lands and resources still owned by the tribes. By making the Indians give up their old tribal ties and lifestyles and live and toil like whites, it was hoped that the native poeples would soon become like whites, whether they wished to or not. Eventually, they would see that the white man knew best what was right for them, and all would turn out well.

But . . . the Dawes Act hurt the Indians gravely. It failed to recognize that many Indians, particularly those who traditionally had been nomadic hunters and gatherers, could not or would not become farmers overnight; they had neither the cultural heritage for the new way of life, nor the necessary training. Moreover, much of the land allotted to them was too poor or arid to farm, and they received no financial credit, and almost no assistance of any other kind. In 1891 an amendment to the Dawes Act permitted Indians to lease their holdings, and in 1906 the government's trusteeship protection was removed from their allotments. Many Indians, totally estranged from non-Indian economic motivations and customs, leased or sold their lands to whites at bargain prices; others were swindled out of their property. . . .

In 1887 the tribes had owned some 138,000,000 acres. By 1932 approximately 90,000,000 of them had passed into white ownership, and a large portion of the remainder was leased out. Much of what the Indians still owned, moreover, was hopelessly entangled in huge heirship problems. As Indians had died, their holdings had been divided among their heirs, one generation after another, until by the mid-twentieth century individuals owned ridiculous fractions of allotments, scattered here and there, often so small in size that nothing could be done with any of them . . . .

Living Under the Dawes Act

Throughout the period of the Allotment Act, life was harsh for the Indians. The reservations did not disappear and the Indians—demonstrating that no people can be stripped involuntarily of their own culture—continued to be Indians. Under the unremitting pressures and influences of the white man, many of their cultural traits changed, particularly in material things. In numerous ways, they adopted and accommodated to aspects of the white man's civilization, and from one generation to another they were a little less like their fathers and a little more like the whites. But they neither became assimilated, nor did they disappear.

In the beginning they suffered all the stern hardships and punishments of a conquered people. Reservations were ruled like empires by agents who were given almost complete authority over the Indians. . . . Many knew nothing about the Indians, their history and cultures, and cared less. Missionaries, usually totally uninformed about the Indians, were on most reservations, and many were given a free hand over the Indians. . . . If trouble threatened, the agent could call on the military for assistance. All three—the agent, the missionary, and the soldier—were united in carrying out national policy—stopping the Indian from being an Indian and forcing him to become a white. Often they were helped by compliant Indians. . . .

Generally, the end of the nineteenth century and the first few decades of the twentieth century were the most desperate of times for the Indians. Now that the wars were over and Indians were no longer in the newspaper headlines, they were out of sight and out of mind to most Americans who thought that the government was gradually getting them assimilated and that one day soon the reservations would be ended and the last of the Indians would be moving happily into white society. Congress paid scant attention to Indian affairs, appropriating meager sums each year which . . . was just enough to keep the problems going and to maintain the Indians at a bare subsistence level—although sometimes there was not enough even for that, and Indians starved. Indian men, who had once been motivated as hunters and warriors, now worked for the army as scouts or joined wild west shows or circuses, or, if they stayed on the reservations — as most of them did—had nothing to do but rot, recognizing in their helplessness that their women and children were turning away from them. . . .

Meanwhile, the Indians had few freedoms. For a long time they were not permitted to leave the reservation without a pass from the agent. Their religions, rituals, and ceremonies were banned. . . . Old traditions, social dances, games, the telling of myths, legends, and folk tales, even the speaking of native languages, were frowned upon and frequently forbidden. Children were wrenched away physically from their families and friends and sent to far-distant boarding schools to be educated as whites. It was all a part of the deliberate process of stamping out and obliterating Indianness, but there was worse. Bereft of freedom and rights, the Indian had almost no defenses against aggrandizers and despoilers. . . . The Indians were not recognized by the white men's courts as having rights, and they could not testify against their tormentors. All their affairs were handled for them, for better or worse, honestly or dishonestly, by the agent. It was remarkable that any Indian during this period had the motivation to think and act for himself, which normally would be a first necessary step on the road to assimilation.

And yet the national Indian policy—summed up in the 1890 census report as "enforced education . . . enforced labor . . . enforced allotment" of land—was not questioned, for it was not generally recognized that force and lack of freedom had within them the self-defeating effect of *preventing* assimilation. . . .

In 1921 . . . the Board of Indian Commissioners, an independent body established originally by Congress in 1869 and composed of ten eminent citizens appointed by the President, decided to investigate the matter. It found that a scandalously high percentage of the Indians who had received fee patents had soon been parted from their lands. . . .

Soon afterward, an attempt to divest the Pueblo Indians of New Mexico of a large part of their lands turned further attention to the Indians. The Pueblos' appeals to American public opinion gained an audience in Washington and elsewhere, and throughout the nation supporters rallied to help the Pueblos defeat their opponents. By this time, enough had surfaced to make it clear that all was not well—in fact, was far from well—on other reservations. . . .

In 1924, almost as a sop to the new public interest in Indians, those first Americans were granted citizenship by the Snyder Act—in acknowledgment, so it was announced, of the nation's gratitude to the many thousands of Indians who,though not subject to military service, had enlisted voluntarily in World War I. This ironic gesture, if anything, only increased the nation's nervous curiosity about the condition of the Indian peoples,and in 1926 . . . Secretary of the Interior Hubert Work requested the Institute for Government Research,a privately endowed foundation, later known as the Brookings Institution, to conduct a thorough investigation of the Indians' situation. Financed by a grant from John D. Rockefeller, Jr., the investigation was carried out by a staff of specialists headed by Lewis Meriam. In 1928 the group issued a report titled *The Problem of Indian Administration* which thoroughly shocked the nation. Not only did it reveal that the Indians were still far from being assimilated, but more importantly it told the American people just how badly off the Indians were. Most of them, said the Meriam Report, were poor, extremely poor. Their health, education, and economic condition—all discussed in detail—constituted an American tragedy and a national scandal. The report did not specifically advocate ending the allotment policy, but it made it clear that the drastic reduction of their land and resources was one of the prime causes of their impoverishment and demoralization. In almost every facet of Indian affairs the report found need for fundamental reform, and it proposed a sweeping list of changes. . . .

Indian Reorganization Act

On June 18, 1934, under the Roosevelt administration, the Wheeler-Howard Act, better known as the Indian Reorganization Act, stemming from the Meriam survey . . . finally brought to an end the era of the allotment policy. The act encouraged tribal self-government by authorizing the incorporating of tribal institutions, the writing of tribal constitutions, and the election of tribal councils; it extended financial credit to the tribes, brought new improvements in educational and medical facilities, and restored freedom of religion for the Indians; and it promoted a revival of Indian cultures and cultural activities.

The Indian Reorganization Act was an admission that assimilation was still far off, but though it halted allotments as a self-defeating and disastrous policy, it substituted slower-acting and more considerate

107

methods that were still designed, ultimately, to achieve the national goal of Indian assimilation. At the same time, it attempted to confer on the tribes greater freedom to proceed toward assimilation at a rate of speed and under conditions of their own choosing. In confirming Indian self-government—although in the image of the way white men did things, which unhappily caused new problems for the Hopis and certain other tribes—it tried to return to the Indians the right to organize their own institutions and manage their own affairs, a hope that was not genuinely achieved, since the Department of the Interior in practice continued to keep an upper hand and veto power over most reservation details, including, most importantly, financial and legal matters. . . .

During the 1930s and early 1940s, also, the Bureau of Indian Affairs went through a number of internal reforms in line with suggestions made by the Meriam Report; co-operative agreements were made by the Bureau with other government agencies like the Soil Conservation Service; and many new services, carried out by specialists and technicians, were brought to the Indians on the reservations.

In general, the Indian response to the new rights, responsibilities, and opportunities was slow at first; after so many years of wardship, most tribes could not easily adjust to the new policy. Nevertheless, tribal governments were formed, Indian inhibitions and fears began to disappear, the initiative and energies of the people began to stir, and conditions started gradually to improve. With money borrowed from a new government revolving credit fund, many tribes began to reacquire lands they had previously sold or leased, increasing the acreage they themselves could farm or graze. From 1934 to 1947 the total Indian land base increased by 3,700,000 acres, the first increase since the Allotment Act was passed in 1887. In the same period Indian-owned livestock increased from 171,000 to 361,000 head, and the total agricultural income received by Indians grew from $1,850,000 to $49 million.

During World War II approximately twenty-five thousand Indians served in the armed forces of the United States. Most of them mixed in the non-Indian world for the first time and returned to their reservations anxious to bring more of the white man's technology to their own people. At the same time, some Indians who had served in the war, as well as others who had left the reservations to work in war plants and shipyards, preferred to continue living in the white men's cities, and many of them gradually became assimilated into non-Indian life, although they retained their Indian identity and their attachments to their people. In time, they formed the nucleus of what by 1970 had become a large urban Indian population, living in all the major cities of the United States and presenting new and special situations and needs of their own. . . .

By 1946 strong voices were being raised in Congress, suggesting that the time was approaching when the federal government should "withdraw" its relations with the various tribes, ending the treaties and the federal services guaranteed by the treaties, and turning over the reservations to the states.

Termination Policy

On August 13, 1946, the government established a special Indian Claims Commission, which was of positive benefit to many tribes. Its function was to bring to an end all Indian claims of unjust land dealings in the past by hearing whatever evidence the tribes wished to present and awarding payments where fairness demanded restitution for lands taken illegally or for less than proper payment. The tribes filed more than 580 claims, and by 1970 many millions of dollars had been awarded to them. The life of the commission has had to be extended a number of times by Congress, and many claims still remain to be heard and settled. . . . But as Congressional pressure for withdrawal—or, as it came to be known, termination—increased, the true underlying reason for the creation of the Claims Commission was revealed. It was established, said Dillon Myer, the Commissioner of Indian Affairs in 1952, to provide "the means of removing a major Indian objection to any move in the direction of Bureau withdrawal.". . .

In 1953, two measures—Public Law 280, authorizing states to assume jurisdiction over criminal and civil court cases on reservations without approval by the tribes, and House Concurrent Resolution 108, declaring Congress's intent to terminate federal relations with the tribes at the earliest possible time—were adopted by the Eighty-third Congress. The goal of both measures was, again, to speed the assimilation of Indians and break down the remaining tribal and cultural bonds that supposedly interfered with their economic progress and hindered their becoming like all other citizens. . . .

The new termination policy quickly proved to be a catastrophe for the Indians. . . . Federal programs were stopped, reversed, or re-designed to hasten the day of termination of each group. Indian cultures and pride in Indianness were again frowned upon as impediments to inte-gration. All tribes felt the renewed threat of forced assimilation and loss of lands and became immobilized; ready or not, they faced the dread pros-pect of being turned over to the states, most if not all of which could not or would not assume the protective responsibilities, services and other obligations that the federal government had originally assumed by treaties and various agreements in the past and that the tribes still urgently re-quired. . . .

The inadvisability of continuing with the implementation of the termina-tion policy finally became clear to Congress and the Eisenhower admin-istration, and on September 18, 1958, Secretary of the Interior Fred A. Seaton announced that no tribe thereafter would be terminated without its consent and that the thrust of federal Indian policy would be redirected toward the health, education, and economic development of the In-dians. . . .

Relocation

Termination was not the only failure of the Eisenhower administration in the field of Indian affairs. In the 1950s, also, the Indian Bureau, attempting in a second way to hasten· assimilation and, in addition, to improve the Indian's economic status, gave increased emphasis to a "re-location" program that moved Indians off the reservation and into cities, where homes and jobs were found for them The Indians were first inter-viewed on the reservations, and those who seemed to possess the best chance for adjustment to the white man's urban society were sent to cities like Denver, Albuquerque, Los Angeles, Chicago, and Minneapolis. Many Indians made the change successfully and have continued to live in white society as so-called urban Indians. But in numerous cases the government abandoned interest in the "relocated" Indians after they had been in the cities a short time. When they lost their jobs or housing, they became stranded persons in alien surroundings. . . . Although many "relocated" Indians returned to their reservations, the program was never formally abandoned. It tapered off after 1960, and under succeeding administrations greater efforts were made to help Indians relocate more successfully. The large number of Indians now in cities, in fact—a number estimated in 1970 to be several hundred thousand—has just begun to impress the federal government with the realization that the problems of urban Indians, many of them poor, unassimilated, unknowledgeable in the ways of the whites, and lacking the governmental services to which they were entitled while on the reservations, pose a new sphere of activity and responsibility for agencies dealing with Indians.

As a result of the opposition of the tribes, and the traumatic experiences of the Menominees and Klamaths, the termination policy—while continuing to be the ultimate intent of Congress—was sidestepped in the 1960s by the Kennedy and Johnson administrations, which concentrated, instead, on revitalizing the most beneficial aspects of the Indian Reorganization Act of 1934 as the best road along which the Indians could travel. To stave off Congressional pressure for a renewal of the termination policy, administration energies were directed toward fashioning fresh programs to hasten the development of the economic and human resources of the reservations and lift the standards of living of the Indians. . . .

In 1955 Indian medical care and health services had been transferred from the Bureau of Indian Affairs to the United States Public Health Service, and that agency of the Department of Health, Education and Welfare made great progress in meeting reservation health and sanitation problems. By 1960, all thought of the Indian as a "vanishing American" had long since disappeared. A rising birthrate had gradually overcome and passed a falling death rate, and before the 1950s it had become clear that the Indian population was increasing at a faster rate than the white population. By 1970 the first unofficial count of the national census revealed that there were almost as many Indians and Alaska natives in the United States as there had been in the same areas of the continent in 1492— 827,091, including 775,563 in the "lower 48" states, as against 248,253 in the same area in 1890—an increase of more than half a million Indians in eighty years.

Self-Determination

The mothballing of the termination policy in the 1960s was accompanied by the rise of a new force in Indian affairs. Throughout the long history of federal-Indian relations, Indian leaders had often pleaded that the Indians knew better than the white man what was best for the Indians. . . . In June, 1961, an historic gathering of 420 Indians from sixty-seven tribes at an "American Indian Chicago Conference" at the University of Chicago, drew up a "Declaration of Indian Purpose," which stated, "We believe that where programs have failed in the past, the reasons were lack

of Indian understanding, planning, participation, and approval."
. . . Pointing out that each tribe had a history and cultural background
that shaped its present-day requirements, and about which the white man
knew little, speakers at the conference urged that Indians be given the
right to participate in the decision-making process for all policies and
programs that would affect them.

Although the Kennedy and Johnson administrations paid scant heed to
the appeal, it was the start of an Indian demand that grew louder and
more insistent as the decade of the 1960s progressed. Many factors,
including the example of the blacks, pressure from young, educated, and
militant Indians, and the ferment of the times themselves throughout the
world, contributed to what became a resolute Indian drive for self-
determination and self-government. But the new force, also, reflected
changes taking place among the Indians themselves. The instant communication, increased mobility, and rapid technological advances of the
white man's world had penetrated the reservations, speeding up acculturation. New government programs and greater funds had raised
standards—though they were still appallingly low compared with the rest
of the nation—and, in turn, they had increased Indian demands. More
Indians than ever before were traveling through the white man's world,
becoming familiar with urban existence, going to high school, college, and
even graduate school, and mastering the techniques of the white man's
politics and industry. Under the impact of these and other influences twin
developments were occuring: increasing numbers of Indians were becoming sophisticated in the white man's terms, acculturated and even
assimilated, while at the same time becoming more nationalistic as
Indians, aware and proud of their own history, cultures, and ethnic
uniqueness in the United States. While tribal identity continued to be
important, a Pan-Indian spirit appeared and grew, uniting Indians of
different tribes behind common causes. . . . One of the liveliest of the new
organizations was the National Indian Youth Council, which emerged
early in the 1960s and was composed principally of young, educated
Indians. Under the leadership of dynamic, activist intellectuals, including
Clyde Warrior, a Ponca Indian from Oklahoma, and Melvin Thom, a
Northern Paiute from Nevada, it ridiculed the "Uncle Tomahawks" in the
leadership of the tribes, who had seemed willing through the years to let
the white man rule the reservations and control the affairs of the Indian
people. As the decade progressed, its pressure and influence on the reservations, as well as among urban Indians, stoked the fires of Indian
nationalism. By the end of the decade, Indians in many organizations
were forcing confrontations with whites in different states at places like
Alcatraz Island over injustices which the tribes had long borne in silence,
and were demanding Red Power, which meant freedom for the Indians to
make their own decisions and control their own affairs, as well as an end to
what they regarded as the "colonial" rule by the Bueau of Indian Affairs
over the tribes.

. . . A momentous breakthrough occurred in 1964. Following a large
Capital Conference on Indian Poverty in Washington in May of that year,
Indians were included as beneficiaries of the programs of the new Office of
Economic Opportunity. Once reservation poverty programs, suggested by

Indians, were approved, funds were given to the Indians who ran the programs themselves. It was the first time that Indians generally had been permitted to assume the full responsibility for the management of, and the use of funds for, programs on reservations, and, by and large, the Indians showed that they were able to carry out functions which, up to then, had been supervised for them by the Indian agents. Part of the success, it was pointed out, stemmed from the fact that the programs were ones which the Indians themselves wanted and planned according to the needs as they saw them.

The lesson was not lost on the Indians, and they increased their demands on the Bureau of Indian Affairs for the same opportunities in all their federal programs. . . . Gradually, the Johnson administration showed an awareness of the new winds blowing in Indian affairs. . . . On March 6, 1968, the President, by executive order, later endorsed by Congress, created a National Council on Indian Opportunity. Chaired by the Vice-President of the United States, it included a number of Indian leaders appointed by the President and those members of the President's cabinet whose agencies had reservation programs. Particularly during the first years of the Nixon administration, the NCIO, as it was known, developed into a new center of power in Indian affairs. . . . At the same time, the Bureau of Indian Affairs inaugurated a policy of making contracts with individual tribes to manage and control some or all of the federal programs on their reservations. . . .

Although it is premature to attempt to appraise what has occured since the advent of the Nixon administration, it may be said that a new era in federal-Indian relations definitely began in 1970. Wary of Indian memories of the disastrous termination policy of the last Republican administration in office, President Nixon in July, 1970, announced to Congress a new Indian policy of self-determination without termination. . . . The changes in thrust, direction, and substance in Indian affairs since then have been substantial. The tribes' management of, and control over, their own affairs are being accelerated with the encouragement of the new Commissioner of Indian Affairs, Louis R. Bruce, the son of a Mohawk and a Sioux. To an extent greater than ever before, Indian leaders are being given an opportunity to participate in the decision-making process in Washington and on the reservations. Policy-making jobs in the Bureau of Indian Affairs and other agencies with Indian programs are being filled by Indians. Vastly increased funds are going to the reservations, which today total 267—including small Indian colonies, communities, and California rancherias. In fiscal year 1971, the government will spend $625,845,000 on Indians, as against $455,363,000 three years ago. In 1890, it may be recalled, the total sum was slightly over seven million, and the anonymous author of the essay in that year's census report was warning the nation to hurry and end the Indian problem so that another $200 to 300 million would not have to be "doled out" over another fifty or one hundred years.

It is not the purpose of this study to deal with the question of where and when it will all end. . . . In trying to turn the Indian into a white man, while at the same time robbing him of his resources, the nation protracted what it called the "Indian problem," but which, with true perspective, must be viewed as "the white man's problem." Now, at last, the United States may be on the right course. Given freedom to acculturate and assimilate on his own terms, to manage and control his own affairs, and to govern himself the way the people of any township or county govern themselves—though with the added provision of trusteeship protection of his lands and the continued receipt of treaty-guaranteed services as long as he feels he needs them—the Indian has a better chance than ever before to solve the problems which have defied the white man. . . .

There are still many hardships, injustices, and problems on many reservations. One emerging difficulty is the disagreement over the industrialization of reservations; progressive Indians encourage anything that will give jobs and income to their people, while traditionalist Indians oppose all changes that undermine the traditional beliefs and ways of life of the people. There are also many conflicts between the Indians and whites to be settled. The Bureau of Reclamation, the Army Engineers, and various other federal, state, and local agencies have joined corporations and smaller groups of whites in continuing to whittle away at Indian land and resources. At Kinzua Dam, Pennsylvania; Pyramid Lake, Nevada; Black Mesa, Arizona; Puget Sound, Washington; Pit River, California; Blue Lake, New Mexico; in Alaska and elsewhere, Indians have had to continue fighting defensively for their land, water, and fishing and hunting rights. Often, it has been a case of survival, no different from the desperate situations that led to last stands by the warriors of the nineteenth century. Today, there is little publicity about the struggles. They are fought in the halls of Congress and in the law courts.

Whatever the end is, it will be a long time in coming. The Indians are still with us, contributing more than their share to the greatness and majesty of all that means the United States of America. Their freedom will benefit all the American people, for at last the white man will be willing to welcome them as equals and listen to them as mature citizens. They still have much to teach all mankind. But that is another subject.

Americans—
With a Chicano Outlook

Ruben Salazar

Americans of Mexican descent, numbering between five and seven million, form a minority in the United States second in size only to black Americans. Mexican and Spanish culture were established in the Southwest more than two centuries before Anglo-Americans entered the area. By the mid-nineteenth century, 75,000 Spanish-speaking persons were working as ranchers, miners, and farmers in the territory that the United States acquired from Mexico. But as white settlers poured into the area, the Mexican-Americans became a minority. Differing from the dominant culture in race, religion, and language, they were subject to discrimination and exploitation; ignorant of Anglo law, they were unable to protect their property and interests. Nevertheless, opportunities for work continued to attract Mexicans, and immigration into the Southwest grew rapidly during the twentieth century. As a group, the Mexican-Americans occupied the lowest rung of the economic, social, and political ladder, supplying the cheap labor for farm and factory that European immigrants provided elsewhere in the country.

By the mid 1960s, however, their resentment against their unequal treatment boiled over into a new militancy. Striking against the grape growers near Delano, California, Mexican-American farm workers proclaimed their determination to "seek our basic, God-given rights as human beings. . . . We want to be equal with all the working men in the nation; we want a just wage, better working conditions, a decent future for our children." The movement for "brown power" was paralleled by a Chicano cultural movement, led by young intellectuals. Ruben Salazar, a Chicano newspaper reporter for the Los Angeles Times *who was allegedly killed by police a few months after writing the following article, describes what it means to be a member of* La Raza—the Race.

A Chicano is a Mexican-American with a non-Anglo image of himself. He resents being told Columbus "discovered" America when the Chicano's

Ruben Salazar, "Who Is a Chicano? And What Is It the Chicanos Want?" *Los Angeles Times,* Feb. 6, 1970. Copyright 1970, Los Angeles Times. Reprinted by permission.

ancestors, the Mayans and the Aztecs, founded highly sophisticated civilizations centuries before Spain financed the Italian explorer's trip to the "New World."

Chicanos resent also Anglo pronouncements that Chicanos are "culturally deprived" or that the fact that they speak Spanish is a "problem."

Chicanos will tell you that their culture predates that of the Pilgrims and that Spanish was spoken in America before English and so the "problem" is not theirs but the Anglos' who don't speak Spanish.

Having told you that, the Chicano will then contend that Anglos are Spanish-oriented at the expense of Mexicans.

They will complain that when the governor dresses up as a Spanish nobleman for the Santa Barbara Fiesta he's insulting Mexicans because the Spanish conquered and exploited the Mexicans.

It's as if the governor dressed like an English Redcoat for a Fourth of July parade, Chicanos say.

When you think you know what Chicanos are getting at, a Mexican-American will tell you that Chicano is an insulting term and may even quote the Spanish Academy to prove that Chicano derives from chicanery.

A Chicano will scoff at this and say that such Mexican-Americans have been brainwashed by Anglos and that they're Tio Tacos (Uncle Toms) This type of Mexican-Americans, Chicanos will argue, don't like the word Chicano because it's abrasive to their Anglo-oriented minds.

These poor people are brown Anglos, Chicanos will smirk.

What, then, is a Chicano? Chicanos say that if you have to ask you'll never understand, much less become a Chicano.

Actually, the word Chicano is as difficult to define as "soul."

For those who like simplistic answers, Chicano can be defined as short for Mexicano. For those who prefer complicated answers, it has been suggested that Chicano may have come from the word Chihuahua—the name of a Mexican state bordering on the United States. Getting trickier, this version then contends that Mexicans who migrated to Texas call themselves Chicanos because having crossed into the United States from Chihuahua they adopted the first three letters of that state, Chi, and then added cano, for the latter part of Texano.

Such explanations, however, tend to miss the whole point as to why Mexican-American activists call themselves Chicanos.

Mexican-Americans, the second largest minority in the country and the largest in the Southwestern states (California, Texas, Arizona, New Mexico and Colorado), have always had difficulty making up their minds what to call themselves.

In New Mexico they call themselves Spanish-Americans. In other parts of the Southwest they call themselves Americans of Mexican descent, people with Spanish surnames or Hispanos.

Why, ask some Mexican-Americans, can't we just call ourselves Americans?

Chicanos are trying to explain why not. Mexican-Americans, though indigeneous to the Southwest, are on the lowest rung scholastically, economically, socially and politically. Chicanos feel cheated. They want to effect change. Now.

Mexican-Americans average eight years of schooling compared to the

Negroes' 10 years. Farm workers, most of whom are Mexican-American in the Southwest, are excluded from the National Labor Relations Act,unlike other workers. Also, Mexican-Americans often have to compete for low-paying jobs with their Mexican brothers from across the border who are willing to work for even less. Mexican-Americans have to live with the stinging fact that the word Mexican is the synonym for inferior in many parts of the Southwest.

That is why Mexican-American activists flaunt the barrio word Chicano—as an act of defiance and a badge of honor. Mexican-Americans, though large in numbers, are so politically impotent that in Los Angeles, where the country's largest single concentration of Spanish-speaking live, they have no one of their own on the City Council. This, in a city politically sophisticated enough to have three Negro councilmen.

Chicanos, then, are merely fighting to become "Americans." Yes, but with a Chicano outlook.

The Unblended Blacks

For *black Americans, the melting pot has never been an appropriate image of America. For them, America has long been a racist society in which blacks were set apart, first by slavery and then by custom and by law. (See C. Vann Woodward, "The Strange Career of Jim Crow," in Unit III.) The tenets of democracy that have united other Americans have been for black Americans a sham or, at best, a dream yet to be realized. The extent of the discrimination they suffered is commented upon by the poet Witter Bynner in "Defeat," reprinted below.*

Ironically, it was the closing of American doors to "nonassimilable" Europeans in the 1920s that opened new opportunities for America's own nonassimilated blacks. With the supply of European peasantry cut off, rural blacks from the South became the "immigrants within," moving into cities to occupy the least desirable positions in the job market. But they continued to face economic and social discrimination.

In recent years, however, black Americans have militantly demanded entry into the mainstream of the affluent society—on their own terms, as Americans with an African heritage. In the article following, Nathan Huggins, professor of history at Columbia University, explores the position of the Afro-American community within a "nation of nations."

Selection 1   Witter Bynner

DEFEAT

On a train in Texas German prisoners eat
With white American soldiers, seat by seat,
While black American soldiers sit apart.
The white men eating meat, the black men heart.
Now, with that other war a century done,
Not the live North but the dead South has won,
Not yet a riven nation comes awake.
Whom are we fighting this time, for God's sake?
Mark well the token of the separate seat.
It is again ourselves whom we defeat.

From *Take Away the Darkness*, by Witter Bynner. Copyright 1947 by Witter Bynner. Reprinted by permission of Alfred A. Knopf, Inc.

Selection 2   Nathan I. Huggins

Few Afro-Americans today would regard integration into American society as an ultimate objective. Most would at least insist on important qualifications to a goal which would presume the ultimate abandonment of racial identity and the general dispersion of the black population in order to be "blended in." Since the nineteen sixties, integrationism and assimilation have been used as terms of derision by many black spokesmen. While few would consider themselves nationalists or segregationists, most would insist on the existence of distinct ethnic values and the maintenance of racial integrity.

This shift in attitude is remarkable, coming on the heels of the victory for integration in the 1954 Brown decision of the Supreme Court.* Doubtless, disillusion resulted from the failure of the decision, even with the early victories of the civil-rights movement, to bring results. But black ethnocentrism seems to be a part of a broader pattern in American life which rejects the image of the melting pot and emphasizes cultural diversity.

The melting pot assumed a notion of a common American type. The peoples who came to America were to be "melted down," either to be blended into a new amalgam or poured into a mold of the preferred type. Either way, the ultimate goal was an American character, and the evidences of cultural distinctiveness were indications that the process was unfinished. The recent disenchantment with this model is due to its failure to reflect what was actually the experience of many Americans, white and black. Diversity and ethnocentrism have been more the rule than the exception. Furthermore, with the decline of WASP influence, there could no longer be a consensus as to an ideal type. Cultural diversity became a positive value, and pluralism the concept to describe the dynamics of American life.

The pluralist, in the words of Nelson Polsby,** describes American society as "fractured into a congeries of hundreds of small 'special-interest' groups, with incompletely overlapping memberships, widely differing power bases, and a multiple of techniques for exercising influence on decisions salient to them." These "memberships" are something more than ethnic. Rather, the pluralists generally imagine a diversity in numerous voluntary associations, which are organized to gain for their members a share in the common wealth. Conceivably, these associations might be multi-ethnic. They are all competitive. But since none can get what it wants on its own, they operate through alliances and coalitions, sharing power among themselves. . . .

In the pluralists' model, as in the model of the laissez-faire economist, how the pie is cut depends on the weight of the competitors and the shrewdness each brings to the "market," not on considerations of abstract justice or equitable distribution of wealth or power.

As much as Afro-Americans may have found the melting pot an unsatisfactory metaphor for their experience, and as much as they may be

---

*Ed. note: See below, p. 268.
**Ed. note: Political scientist at University of California, Berkeley

From Nathan I. Huggins, "Afro-Americans: National Character and Community," *The Center Magazine*, July/August 1974, pp. 51-56. Copyright © 1974 by Nathan Huggins. Reprinted by permission of the author.

contributing to the current vogue in cultural diversity, they will find the pluralists' model just as problematic. There are two reasons. Pluralists, with their emphasis on voluntary associations, do not give adequate weight to the importance of ethnic divisions within interest groups. Secondly, particularly from the point of view of Afro-Americans, they do not appreciate the limits that race places on coalitions. The second of these problems is of special significance as one considers major patterns of black political behavior.

From the point of view of most Afro-Americans, however one defines "voluntary associations," the ultimate division in the United States has been between black and white. History and experience seem to support that view. Despite shared class, occupational, regional, or political interests, blacks have tended to find that their alliances with whites have crumbled when there was an appeal to racial interest. Poor whites in the South and poor white ethnics in Northern cities have seemed to prefer to languish in poverty rather than to join blacks in effective coalitions. If race interests are more important than bread and butter, the pluralist model can work for all except those racial minorities who can never expect to marshal power to overcome the white phalanx arrayed against them.

Politics

It is this perception that has caused black intellectuals, no matter what their other differences, sooner or later to consider the color line as the fundamental division in American life. Even in the politics of the Left, theoretical accord has often foundered in the mire of race. Such committed Socialists as W. E. B. Du Bois and A. Philip Randolph found the Socialist Party unprepared to confront race as distinct from the class issue. Blacks always risked the charge of racial chauvinism when they insisted that they had special problems in the American society, not the least of which was the ethnocentrism of the working class. Nor was the experience of blacks in the Communist Party any different. And the sometimes acrimonious debates about the importance of black votes in the leadership of the moderate National Association for the Advancement of Colored People suggests the pervasiveness of an assumption that the goals and tactics of Afro-Americans could best be determined by white men and women of good will.

This view of the intractability of race has sound basis in practical political life. Recent studies of New York politics have shown the general unwillingness of city bosses to exploit fully the black vote, even when it might have meant a difference in the election. It seems that whites hoped to win without depending on black voters, and that soliciting these votes too eagerly was somehow beneath acceptable practice.

Whatever may be said about race as a limit to coalition politics, however, the Afro-American style of politics has not been suited to the kind of give-and-take and competition implied by pluralism. The "typical" black spokesman of the nineteenth and early twentieth centuries followed the style of WASP, mugwump politics. They were "progressives" in sentiment, with a central preoccupation with race relations. Generally speaking, they were not interested in the kind of precinct organizations and vote grabbing that would produce the kind of solid constituencies needed for urban machines. Without such organization and such political work, black politicians could have little weight to throw into the balance.

Indeed, from Reconstruction to the New Deal, the black style of political leadership was determined by a reliance on the moral obligation that patrons and national leaders could be made to feel about the race issue. . . . Booker T. Washington was the most adept of all these black men of influence, and he neither asked for not got more than a voice in the symbolic appointments of blacks to office.

W. E. B. Du Bois, Monroe Trotter, and others often called for an independent black vote. From time to time they threatened to lead black voters away from the Republican Party (or, in 1916, away from Woodrow Wilson). But these were empty gestures since these men could not control the vote of blacks. Their style was publicity and moral suasion. They had no political base, and their only influence was through their journalism. So, while they dreamed of a black vote that could swing between the major parties, supporting candidates who promised to serve the interests of the race, they were not inclined to create the kind of political organizations that could make that dream a reality.

There were exceptions to this mugwump style in black political leadership. . . . Marcus Garvey . . . had a remarkable ability to mobilize and organize blacks at the grass roots across the country. But because his objectives were escape and expatriation, his effect in national and local politics was limited.

In general, however, black political leadership, below the level of national spokesmen such as Du Bois, simply tried to sell their influence to white patrons in political office. . . . The pattern is significant when one considers the assumptions of pluralism because, without a political base, blacks could not be full competitors.

Pluralism has also failed to hold out much hope for social mobility for Afro-Americans. Here, too, it can be argued that social mobility has been largely ethnically determined and that the losers, in time, find themselves struggling against accumulated odds. Stephan Thernstrom, in *Poverty and Progress,* has noted that various ethnics have shown different values in their concepts of social mobility. The interplay of values, opportunity, and expectation has caused a distinctive Afro-American approach to mobility. Individuals have generally chosen the professions (teaching, medicine, law, the ministry, and undertaking), and entertaining (including sports). Like other ethnics, blacks have found crime an important means for capital accumulation. But, in crime, America also has its ethnic boundaries, and blacks have been restricted even there. Except for West Indians, few Afro-Americans have persisted as petty merchants and peddlers in Northern cities. Relatively few blacks have found their way up through the city services and the blue-collar trades as represented in organized labor. . . .

Organized Labor and Coalitions

Ironically, after World War II, when blacks were numerous enough in cities to command a place in these [city] services, the terms of entry had been so changed by civil service reform that those ethnics who had found their places in the police and fire departments, the public schools, etc., were entrenched and could use the instruments of reform to hold their places against the pressure from this new quarter.

Furthermore, the unionization of city services has often given ethnics a way to maintain places of power. In fact, most of the progressive reforms of the nineteenth and twentieth centuries have worked to keep blacks and other "newcomers" from using the same avenues and instruments to power and mobility that white ethnics used before them. So, as it has worked out, white ethnics entrenched in urban bureaucracies and protecting their positions, seem aligned against all nonwhite ethnics rather than invited to find coalitions with them.

Generally speaking, the effort of blacks to find their way into organized labor has also been met with what appears to be a determined "rear guard" of white ethnics protecting their places of power. . . .

Except for some trades and industries—notably the mine workers—blacks were excluded from organized labor. While this condition changed with the industrial organization under the C.I.O., it was not until after World War II that important racial breakthroughs were made in the ranks of labor.

American craft unions, governed by principles of "business unionism," attempted to control the labor supply rather than to organize all working men. Thus, the basis of such unionism was exclusiveness, and blacks were the most convenient to exclude. . . . Race has posed a barrier in American labor history that has been more important than class; and, in many instances, ethnically organized unions, now at the height of their power and protective of their "job control," are closed as avenues for blacks to move upward.

'The failure to define class identification sharply in America—reflected in the inability of American unions to organize in terms of a working class—has deprived both black and white workers of an interest that would transcend ethos. Rather, it appears that ethnicity has replaced class interest as the basis of loyalty. Nathan Glazer goes even further; he says that "ethnicity has become a more effective form [than class] for the pursuit of interest . . . and one reason is that in some way ethnicity is more closely linked to affect"—that is, it is more closely related to feeling and emotion than is class loyalty.

The seeming failure of class and group interests to obliterate race identification has dissuaded some blacks from playing the game of coalitions. When the chips are down, they say, white men will protect their whiteness rather than their economic interests. Or, to put it another way, in American history whiteness is an element of one's economic and social interest. Thus, race has become a part of any equation, and it would be naive to assume that an "invisible hand" of pluralism and coalition politics can whisk it away.

While race may form an intractable limit to the play of the pluralists' model, few would argue that some gains for blacks could not be won by coalitions. The ability of Afro-Americans to participate effectively is determined by limitations imposed on the group by its historical circumstance and characteristic behavior developed over time.

A concentration of blacks was necessary in places where they were free to act politically before they could compete in pluralistic terms. Such concentration has been a fact of Northern urban life for some years, and it has been becoming so in the South, starting in the nineteen-sixties. But North or South, sophisticated political organization of blacks has been a recent phenomenon. There have been some remarkable victories of black politicians in local elections. It remains to be seen how much such political organization can affect the major parties and national policy.

Coalition politics demands an ethnic consciousness and discipline that would urge group interests over self-interest. In recent years, there appears to have been a strong development of such race consciousness, race solidarity, and race pride among Afro-Americans. The emergence of African nations in the postwar years has rekindled an affinity to the motherland and African culture. All suggests greater race solidarity than was evident in the past. In this connection, the black-power emphasis that marked the end of the civil-rights movement seems to have been an effort to elevate race interests over other loyalties. Some of the substance beneath the black-power rhetoric recognized that black people needed an ethnic sense and the determination to act as a group if coalitions were to work.

Yet, these very features of race solidarity make coalitions difficult to maintain. Appeals to race pride and race loyalty make compromise impossible. The give-and-take necessary for coalitions can hardly thrive in an atmosphere of absolute loyalties and non-negotiable objectives.

Associations based on ethnocentric loyalties work against coalition politics in another way. Coalitions are best used when groups can promote programs proportioned at available resources, serving an actual need, reasonable in terms of a recognized problem, and administratively practicable. Such programs must appeal across group lines if alliances are to make sense. The tendency of ethonocentric groups to demand something as "their right" and "their share" works against the spirit that would make such programs possible. For black groups, however, it is precisely the sense of futility in coalitions that has made their style of confrontation the apparent practical alternative.

Community

The notion of pluralism, with its dynamics of competition and cooperation, assumes that community interests will be served naturally. Like the model of laissez-faire economics, it is as if by an "invisible hand" that the collective interest will be formed out of the struggle for self-interest. But it is just the absence of a sense of larger community that has made pluralism a compelling concept. Where a sense of broad community does not exist, it becomes useful to reduce the whole to its parts. The result can seem like a collection of groups and interests grabbing whatever they can get, producing little sense of commonwealth.

Insofar as pluralism and ethnocentrism are responses to the lack of an American character that defines all in common and a lack of community that can transcend all ethnic loyalties, they beg rather than answer the question: Who is this American, the new man? For if Americans share only a condition of diversity, and are unified only in their competition, the fundamental question of nationality and national character are open to debate.

Is there something about Americans that sets them off even from their old-world kinsmen? Is there some cohesion in the American setting that calls men to a loyalty beyond particular ethos? When Carl Bridenbaugh delivered his presidential address to the American Historical Association in 1963, he complained that what had been a common American history encompassing a national experience had become, in the hands of historians with ethnocentric biases, a history of special and parochial interests. The problem was that the common history in the tradition of George Bancroft was not, in fact, the history of Americans. Thus, the urgency of focusing on the ethnic experience. Yet, the question remains: Can a common history emerge from such great diversity as has been the story of the United States?

Some would say that the immigrant experience is the American experience. There is much to be said for that since, in one way or another, all Americans (except Indians) have been products of the same drama of separation from the old and reestablishment in the New World. Afro-

122

Americans too, despite the important difference of their history, fit the context of the whole.

When Gerald Mullin*discussed the reaction of eighteenth-century blacks to slavery in Virginia, he sketched a pattern of assimilation of Africans into New World life that might have been a model for all immigrants. Briefly, he described "outlandish Africans," still tied to old-world ways, lacking fluency in English as well as sense of the territory, inclined to seek group ways to react to their condition. Mullin also described "New Negroes" who had acquired some English but not a fluency, who had learned to adapt themselves to the particular work system of the plantation, who were still unfamiliar with the territory away from their immediate location, and who thus resisted slavery by truancy from the plantation, inefficiency, sabotage, and theft. Finally, Mullin refers to the "assimilated" type who had a fluency in English, occupational skills that could be of use anywhere, a knowledge of the country far beyond their master's place and of how to get around. The assimilated blacks' style of resistance was to run away, most often by themselves, relying on their individual wit and skills.

Mullin restricted his style to eighteenth-century blacks, but it also applies to other immigrant groups. The suggested similarity of adaptarion and the similar characterization of the ultimate Americanization process points to the possible definition of a national character shared by all who have been molded by this experience.

Ethnic pluralism creates multiple refuges where persons can find a common identity when broader community is in doubt. But these retreats are ultimately narrow and fail to lift the person to participation in a higher unity of nation. There is a need to share in a general community—to look in the face of a fellow who is not of one's own ancestry or religion and to acknowledge shared assumptions and values, to anticipate behavior and feeling. Ethnic pluralism does not provide ways to such brotherhood.

The need for such community—the sense that one participates in the whole—explains the persistent appeal of ethnic humor and television situation comedy. One feels a pleasure as one's own argot and special characteristics become a part of (or actually define) a national humor. Thus, TV becomes a means (as did vaudeville and radio before it) for the individual American to become part of the whole. But such pleasure is limited. Ethnic culture broadcast to the nation is necessarily diluted and distorted: Porgy and Bess at the best, "Amos n' Andy" at the worst. Or, as in the case of Abie's Irish Rose and its parody on television, "Bridget and Bernie," they reduce important matters of ethnic tension to banalities.

More is needed. Is there a "new man" in America? Is there an essentially common American experience which can become the point of identity serving all ethnic particulars? Is there a community beyond ethos which can support such a personality and which can command a loyalty and a service above particularism? The melting-pot image assumed that such a character and such a community existed, or at least could exist. Can that image be abandoned—as it must—without losing the sense of oneness that was assumed? And, most important, can any such community be realized without the black American being part of it?

---

*Ed. note: Historian at California State University at Sacramento, author of Flight and Rebellion: Slave Resistance in Eighteenth-Century Virginia (1972).

The Migrant Experience

At this moment when the cultural diversity and ethnocentrism of America are being stressed, it is useful to redefine what common qualities there might be in American life. For, whatever the virtues of pluralistic visions, they seem to result from the failure of those centripetal elements that have formerly provided a sense of national order and purpose.

There are, I suspect, qualities of common experience and character that make us more like one another than like the peoples in the lands of our forebears. Despite what they may suspect, an Afro-American and the grandson of a Polish immigrant will be better able to take things for granted between themselves than the former could with a Nigerian or the latter with a Warsaw worker. They, like all other Americans except Indians, are sons of a migrant experience in the New World. Theirs has been a rather harsh, bitter, and strained relationship, but it has existed and has been a central element in their consciousness.

I have stressed the migrating experience as the central metaphor since it invokes a shared experience as well as common qualities of American character. This is much preferred to the assumption—especially as it applies to blacks and non-Europeans—that Americanization was a process of adopting a particular set of European characteristics. The truly important qualities of Americanness were no more part of traditional Europe than of traditional Africa. Individuality, mobility, risk-taking for opportunity, uneasiness with institutions, ambivalence about community are products of the shared experience of migration and settlement. To assume the abandonment of the familiar ways of living and working as well as habits of mind, to be exchanged for some European varieties, is a distortion. Neither the African nor the European immigrant was a *tabula rasa* on which an Anglo-Saxon culture was impressed. Rather, there was *a priori* "knowledge" which shaped experience in its own terms, manifested not simply in ethnic artifacts or Africanisms but in subjective areas of belief, myth, style, art, and imagination. As a subterranean influence, ethnic culture participated in standard American mass culture, defining it and losing its exclusiveness and distinctiveness in the process.

★ ★ ★

UNIT TWO
THE LAND OF PLENTY

★ ★ ★

*England Town, by Sumner C. Powell, by permission of
Wesleyan University Press*

Sudbury, Massachusetts:
The Village Center,
showing common fields
and distribution of land
among town inhabitants.
Each member of the
town (assigned a
number for this map)
was granted a house lot
of four acres, and strips
of meadowland and
upland. *"These men have
power to give and grant
out lands,. . . giving them
such an ample portion, both
of Medow and Upland, as
their present and future
stock of cattel and hands
were like to improve."*
—Johnson

Collection, Washington University, St. Louis

Daniel Boone Escorting Settlers through the Cumberland Gap. Painting by George Caleb
Bingham, 1851-2.

*"Most of the earlier American pioneers of the Mississippi Valley . . . came on foot and horseback
across the Cumberlands and Alleghenies, usually to settle for a while . . . and thence to move
on."*—Sauer

Dalzell's Clearing One Mile South West of Piqua, Ohio, 1831. By Thomas Kelah Wharton.

"The sounds of the axe were ceaseless, while the falling of the trees was like a distant cannonading, and the daylight broke into the depths of the woods with the suddenness of a winter morning."—Cooper

Sod Dugout, Custer County, Nebraska, 1892.

"Our neighbors lived in sod houses and dugouts—comfortable, but not very roomy."—Cather

Kentucky Farm, 1930s

"The family farm apprenticed youth well for life . . . and it enriched the quality of American life. It will be missed."—Sauer

THE RUN FOR HOMES IN OKLAHOMA.

The Run for Homes in Oklahoma, 1889.

"The public domain attracted people who . . . could only try to get there first and grab the most from areas to which they had no attachment. . . . Those who attempted to stay and improve their surroundings found it difficult to do so."—Dasmann

Open Pit Mining at Mahoning Mine, Minnesota, 1899.

"The intestines of our mountains are gorged with precious ore to plethora."—Twain

Tractored Out, 1938.

"And the dispossessed, the migrants, flowed into California. . . . Behind them new tractors were going on the land and the tenants were being forced off."—Steinbeck

Aerial View of Freeway, Los Angeles

"The current American way of life is founded not just on motor transportation but on the religion of the motor car."—Mumford

Pickwick Landing Dam, Tennessee—Tennessee Valley Authority creates a navigation channel, a reservoir, and electric power potential.

"For the first time in the history of the nation, the resources of a river . . . were to be developed in that unity with which nature herself regards her resources."—Lilienthal

New World
—New People

Thomas Jefferson Wertenbaker

In recent years there has been public alarm over the impact of human society on the natural environment. But the environment has also had an important impact on the development of the American nation.

The historian Frederick Jackson Turner was the most influential (though not the first) of those who called attention to the importance of natural resources in shaping the nation's history. Writing in 1893, he stated that "the existence of an area of free land, its continual recession, and the advance of American settlement westward explain American development." Subsequent generations of historians were to show that the "Turner thesis" was greatly oversimplified; nevertheless, environmental factors did play a highly significant role. The cultures of the earliest peoples in North America were adaptations to the various conditions of climate and soil they encountered. (See above, p. 38) Similarly, the earliest European settlers had to adjust to the wilderness conditions of the New World. In the following selection, the late historian Thomas Wertenbaker argued that the geography of the region in which the English colonies were planted determined their fate and transformed English men and women into the "first Americans."

When the English people first planted themselves in the New World, they had very definite ideas as to the cháracter of the industrial and social life which they were to establish there. . . . These plans envisaged the creation of industrial communities to supply England with various commodities which she herself could not produce, to create a market for English manufactures and to provide a stimulus for English shipping.

But in attempting to devise in advance a workable social and industrial scheme for far-off colonies, . . . publicists had set themselves an impossible task. They might propose what they would, but in the end the character of their colonies would be determined largely by geographic conditions, by the location of their settlements, the configuration of the country, its climate and its soil. To understand the history of the English in America, one must study those great natural features which the mother country could neither change nor fully reconcile with what became her fixed colonial policies.

The determining factors in the life of the English colonies were the Atlantic Ocean, the character of the coastline from Maine to Florida, the great coastal plain and the Appalachian range. All-important was it to the Englishmen who settled on the banks of the James or the shores of Massachusetts Bay that three thousand miles of water lay between them and Europe. Despite their sentiments of loyalty this made it impossible for them to remain Englishmen; slowly, but inevitably, it transformed them into Americans. Before the seventeenth century had drawn to a close Virginia and New England had developed types of men distinctly their own, with occupations, manners, dialect, interests and outlook upon life different from those of Englishmen. The government at London awoke gradually to the fact that England after all had not been extended to the shores of the New World, but that her settlements there were things apart, with separate economic and, therefore, with separate political and social interests. . . .

It was this fact which made the American Revolution inevitable. . . .

The Atlantic

In the present age, with its swift ocean steamers, its submarine cable and its wireless, it is difficult to realize the degree of isolation entailed by migrating to America in the seventeenth century. The only means of communication was the crude sailing vessel of the day. Not only did it require from four to eight weeks to make the voyage from England, but one might have to wait for months before finding a ship bound for his place of destination. The merchantmen trading to the Chesapeake Bay colonies usually made one trip a year, sailing from England in September and October, and returning after they had taken on their cargoes of tobacco. So general was this custom that an impression prevailed that a voyage of six or eight months was required to reach America. . . .

It was impossible for the mother country to offset the lack of common interests by the strictness of her control. The all-powerful arm of Britain became weak and nerveless when extended across the Atlantic. The local assemblies took advantage of their isolation and resorted to a policy of delay in their struggle with the crown. . . .

As the years passed, England and her colonies drifted apart. The American community grew as family after family was established. Despite the common heritage of blood, language, political institutions and traditions, the line of development for each led in different directions. After the lapse of a century and a half England awoke to the realization that she was trying to govern a foreign people, that the British child had grown into the American man.

It must be remembered, however, that though the Atlantic separated mother country and colony, it also served as the only highway between them, the highway over which passed immigrants and merchandise and all communications of whatever character. It was vital, then, that the settlements should be made upon or near its shores. For decades after Jamestown was founded the colonies were but infants, requiring the support of the Old World for nourishment and protection.

It was fortunate that the eastern shore of North America from the Gulf of Mexico to the Gulf of St. Lawrence should be so admirably suited for a seafaring people. At every point its lines are broken by sounds, bays and wide river mouths, large enough to harbor the greatest fleets. . . . Had it not been for this fact, it is probable that the English would have failed in their attempt to colonize this region. . . . Virginia and Maryland sent out their tobacco fleet each year and received in return the manufactured products of England; New York sold her furs in the European market; and New England found her prosperity in the carrying trade, shipbuilding and fishing.

The Rivers

The navigators of that day did not always cast anchor at the coast ports, for the rivers with which the country abounds gave them ready access to the interior. The Connecticut, the Hudson, the Raritan, the Delaware, the Susquehanna, the Potomac, the Rappahannock, the York, the James, the Roanoke, the Santee were all navigable for many miles for the ocean-going vessels of the day. The Dutch masters often took on their cargoes of furs at Fort Orange, where Albany now stands, while the tobacco traders ascended the great tributaries of Chesapeake Bay and tied up at the private wharves of the planters. And above the fall line were long stretches of river, deep enough for the shallop or the canoe, which served as avenues of approach to deep water. Had man himself planned this system of waterways, it could hardly have been better suited for the needs of foreign trade.

It was inevitable that the settlements should first group themselves around the bays and push up the river valleys. . . .

. . . In the eighteenth century came a remarkable growth of population and wealth, which made it possible for them to break in part this dependence on Europe and for the first time to turn their faces westward. In another hundred and fifty years they were destined to push out three thousand miles until they had covered the central parts of the continent and had reached the Pacific Ocean.

It is misleading to say that the colonists, during this first century, were prevented from spreading into the interior by the great mountain chain which extended from Maine to Alabama. Except in New York and New England, their settlements in no place approached the mountains, while in the South they were still hundreds of miles away. The colonists did not move westward in this their formative period, because there were no great rivers leading in that direction which they could follow without getting out of touch with the Old World. . . .

The French, in marked contrast to the English, placed their seventeenth-century colony on the one waterway which leads westward into the heart of the continent. The St. Lawrence, together with the Great Lakes, constitutes a vast highway, which could not fail to shape the life of the colony which was planted on its banks. . . .

Having a position of advantage for the traffic with the Indians in furs, the French made the most of it. They established their posts far out in the wilderness and attracted to Montreal and Quebec the trade of the northwest for a radius of a thousand miles. . . .

The far-flung line of the French colonies was a source of great weakness.

The century in which the English remained on the shore gave them an unshakable grip upon that region, a grip which made it possible for them later to strike out irresistibly to the west. The French settlements, on the other hand, stretching out for many hundreds of miles into the wilderness, were at all points loosely held. . . . In a very real sense, the collapse of French civilization in North America was the result of the chance which led the French discoverer Jacques Cartier into the mouth of the far-penetrating St. Lawrence.

The Coastal Plain

Not less important than the Atlantic and the river systems in shaping the destinies of the English colonies in America was the great coastal plain which stretches from northern New England to the Gulf of Mexico. Here the settlers, their children and their children's children were to remain and make their homes. This plain presents in its different portions wide divergences in configuration, soil and climate. In New England the belt of lowland is narrow, varying in width from fifty to eighty miles; in New Jersey, Delaware and Pennsylvania it widens to a hundred miles or more; while in the Carolinas the mountains recede a full two hundred miles from the shore.

The New England soil is largely of glacial origin, most of it boulder clay, not infertile, but difficult to cultivate. . . . With a small agricultural area, a stubborn soil and a harsh climate, the region is not well adapted to farming. . . . Although the Puritan settlers succeeded in producing food in abundance, New England was not intended to be a great agricultural region and their utmost efforts could not make it so. For commerce, however, there were splendid opportunities. Harbors abounded. In the extreme north, it is true, the lack of fertile back country and the extremely high tides offered serious obstacles to trade, and Maine and New Hampshire were slow in filling up. But Massachusetts, Connecticut and Rhode Island, because of their great protected bays, had every facility for commerce.

The settlers found the forests growing to the very edge of the shore, and the combination of cheap timber and excellent harbors offered an inviting outlook for ship-building. This industry gained an early start in New England. . . .

In the Middle colonies the wider plain presented a more inviting prospect for agriculture than in New England. The area of arable land was larger, there were fewer stones, the fertility was greater. . . . The Middle colonies found no staple comparable to tobacco or sugar, but they produced wheat, rye, barley and oats in considerable quantities. Fruit trees bore well, while cattle and sheep throve on the native grasses.

The rivers, although less numerous, were wider and deeper, and led further inland. . . . On the other hand, the long unbroken expanse of the Jersey Coast from Sandy Hook to Cape May, in contrast to the jagged New England shore, tended to keep the people of the region from turning to the sea. The Middle colonies were destined in the main to become an agricultural rather than a commercial section.

South of Pennsylvania, where the coastal plain widens, the summers are hot and the period of cultivation long, it was inevitable that extensive farming should absorb the attention of the settlers. The region around Chesapeake Bay proved especially suited to the cultivation of tobacco, and this plant became the staple, almost the only, product. Natural facilities for other things were not lacking. Wheat, barley, oats, Indian corn and many kinds of fruits grew in abundance; the timber was suitable both for shipbuilding and for smelting; the harbors afforded ample facilities for commerce. But in all these concerns Maryland and Virginia would have faced the sharpest competition, whereas in tobacco they could undersell the world. For a century and a half the history of the tidewater region from the mouth of the Susquehanna to Albemarle Sound was shaped by the needs of the Indian plant.

Since tobacco was a product which sought, almost demanded, a world market, it was fortunate that facilities for transportation were excellent. Chesapeake Bay stretched north and south like a vast natural boulevard, while to the westward were a number of connecting rivers that served as cross streets. . . .

Geography as Shaper of Revolution

England, when she secured a foothold in America, was far from understanding the irresistible force exercised by geography and climate upon the life of the inhabitants. She was intent on securing one great natural resource—the resource which she herself lacked and which she considered vital to her industrial life. This was wood. Three centuries ago the forests played a role in industrial life comparable with that of iron and coal today. For England wood was necessary for three great industries: shipbuilding, smelting and the manufacture of woolens. . . .

By the end of the Tudor period the country was face to face with the alternative of securing new territory in which woodland abounded or of sinking into a position of economic dependence. . . . Thus, years before the London Company received its charter from James I, Englishmen had learned to regard America as the land of promise which was to put new vigor into their drooping industrial life.

The settlements of Virginia and New England were mere incidents in the story of English expansion, an expansion impelled chiefly by economic necessity. . . . There were other motives in the English settlement of America—the desire to check the power of the king of Spain, the prospect of discovering a new route to the Orient, the hope of converting the Indians. But one need only read the letters and broadsides of the statesmen and economists of the day to realize that their minds dwelt long and hopefully upon the economic phases of the great undertaking. . . .

British America. . . was to produce—indeed it was founded chiefly for the purpose of producing—the raw materials which the mother country sorely needed. Had the original wishes of England been fulfilled, the Chesapeake Bay colonies would never have been covered with tobacco plantations, and New England would not have turned to farming, shipbuilding, fishing and trading. She had expected to people the forests of the New World with smelters of iron and copper, with glass makers, with workers in potash, pitch and tar, with rope makers. . . .

. . . In these first permanent English colonies on the mainland, Virginia and Plymouth, the colonists were regarded as servants of the English traders; for a time they worked under company direction and piled up their products in company storehouses, not their own. The colony existed for the benefit of the mother country, not for the benefit of the colonists.

There is no more interesting experiment in the history of colonization than this attempt by England to establish a prearranged economic system in her new possessions. Had she succeeded and the British America of her plans become the British America of reality, the course of events through succeeding centuries would have been entirely different. . . . But the experiment was foredoomed to failure. It was the geography of the region selected for settlement which was destined to shape its economic life, not the designs of the London Company, nor even the efforts of the British nation. . . .

. . . Virginia lacked skilled labor, especially such as would work at a reasonable wage. . . . Virginia found that she could not compete with the Baltic nations in producing ship stores, potash and iron, and was forced to devote herself almost exclusively to tobacco for which her soil and climate were so wonderfully suited.

The results in New England were even more disappointing. The Massachusetts Bay Company . . . would have been glad to produce the materials needed by the old country, had it been profitable to do so, but it had no idea of repeating the costly experiments which had been made on the James. The first concern of the Puritan settlers was to insure an ample food supply, and for a number of years agriculture absorbed much of their interest. In after years, when they actually turned to the production of masts, timber, pitch and cordage, it was more to supply their own shipbuilders than those of England. New England never assumed the place intended for her in the British colonial system, and so far from supplementing and aiding English industries, to a large degree paralleled and competed with them.

Though the ambition of England to plant colonies in North America was gratified, though the foundations of her empire were securely laid, she failed in her chief end. The colonies eventually proved for her a means to prosperity and wealth—they absorbed her manufactured goods, stimulated her carrying trade, aided the royal revenue and supplied her with articles for foreign export—but for many decades they failed to furnish the raw stuffs she needed to free her from dependence upon foreign imports. As for the economic and social structures of the various colonies, so far from following the plans mapped out for them in advance of their settlement, they were shaped by their own peculiar conditions of climate, soil and geography.

The New England Way: Puritan Town–Builders

Edward Johnson

Perhaps in few other places in America was the sense of community as strong as it was among the Puritans of New England. Writing aboard the ship that brought him to America, John Winthrop, the first governor of Massachusetts Bay Colony and its dominant figure during its first twenty years, described the Puritans as "a Company professing ourselves fellow members of Christ. . . knit together by this bond of love. . . . It is by a mutual consent. . . [that we] seek out a place of Cohabitation and Consortship under a due form of Government both civil and ecclesiastical. . . . The case of the public must oversway all private respects."

This sense of community helped shape the pattern of settlement in New England. Land was granted in townships by the General Court, the governing body in Massachusetts, to groups of settlers—usually congregations—rather than to individuals. The leaders of the group then decided on the layout of the town, which included a site for the meetinghouse and the village common. Each family was given a town lot as well as lots in the outlying areas for farming, grazing, and woodcutting. The size and location of these lots depended on the size and social status of the family. The New Englander, from the start, was a villager.

As the population grew and the generation of the founders was succeeded by those with less resolve, the bonds that had tied the community together began to dissolve, and the more venturesome began a westward exodus. But the New England town, with its participatory town government, left its mark on the nation and remains a viable institution today.

The Puritan land system is described in the following article by Edward Johnson, who helped establish the community of Woburn, Massachusetts.

But to begin, this Town, as all others, had its bounds fixed by the General Court, to the contenese [contents] of four miles square, (beginning at the end of Charles Town bounds). The grant is to seven men of good and honest report, upon condition, that within two year they erect houses for habitation

From Edward Johnson, *Wonder-Working Providence, 1628–1651*, ed., J. Franklin Jameson (New York: Charles Scribner's Sons, 1910).

thereon, and so go on to make a Town thereof, upon the Act of Court; these seven men have power to give and grant out lands unto any persons who are willing to take up their dwellings within the said precinct, and to be admitted to al common priviledges of the said Town, giving them such an ample portion, both of Medow and Upland, as their present and future stock of cattel and hands were like to improve, with eye had to others that might after come to populate the said Town; this they did without any respect of persons, yet such as were exorbitant, and of a turbulent spirit, unfit for a civil society, they would reject, till they come to mend their manners; such came not to enjoy any freehold. These seven men ordered and disposed of the streets of the Town, as might be best for improvement of the Land, and yet civil and religious society maintained; to which end those that had land neerest the place for Sabbath Assembly, had a lesser quantity at home, and more farther off to improve for corn, of all kinds; they refused not men for their poverty, but according to their ability were helpful to the poorest sort, in building their houses, and distributed to them land accordingly; the poorest had six or seven acres of Medow, and twenty five of Upland, or thereabouts. Thus was this Town populated, to the number of sixty families, or thereabout, and after this manner are the Towns of New England peopled. The scituation of this Town is in the highest part of the yet peopled land, neere upon the headsprings of many considerable rivers, or their branches, as the first rise of Ipswitch river, and the rise of Shashin river, one of the most considerable branches of Merrimeck, as also the first rise of Mistick river and ponds, it is very full of pleasant springs, and great variety of very good water, which the Summers heat causeth to be more cooler, and the Winters cold maketh more warmer; their Medows are not large, but lye in divers places to particular dwellings, the like doth their Springs; their Land is very fruitful in many places, although they have no great quantity of plain land in any one place, yet doth their Rocks and Swamps yeeld very good food for cattel; as also they have Mast and Tar for shipping, but the distance of place by land causeth them as yet to be unprofitable; they have great store of iron ore; their meeting-house stands in a small Plain, where four streets meet; the people are very laborious, if not exceeding some of them.

Now to declare how this people proceeded in religious matters, and so consequently all the Churches of Christ planted in New England, when they came once to hopes of being such a competent number of people, as might be able to maintain a Minister, they then surely seated themselves, and not before, it being as unnatural for a right N. E. man to live without an able Ministery, as for a Smith to work his iron without a fire. . . .

Advertising the
Southern Frontier

Thomas Nairne

*In contrast to Puritan New England, in the southern colonies
land was granted to individuals rather than to groups.   A
staple export crop—tobacco in Virginia and Maryland, indigo
and rice in South Carolina—was the basis of the economy and,
consequently, of the pattern of settlement.   Systems of land
tenure in the South varied, to some degree, with the origins of
the colonies, but they all led to widely dispersed settlement.*

*In Virginia as early as 1618 the Virginia Company, chartered
by the Crown, established a policy of granting a "headright"
of fifty acres to anyone who paid for the passage of a man
(himself or someone else) to the colony. In return, the holder
of the headright paid a "quitrent" of one shilling a year to the
company. Large tracts of land suitable for tobacco cultivation
thus fell into the hands of wealthy investors, who used
indentured servants or slaves to work the land. The death rate
among the servants was high, but those who survived could,
upon the expiration of their terms of servitude, acquire land of
their own. Taking up land along the coast and the navigable
streams, the settlers soon became widely scattered, living on
isolated farms and plantations.   Such community life as they
had was centered about the county seat, often a day's ride
away.*

*Maryland was established as a proprietary grant to Lord
Baltimore, who in turn granted large semifeudal estates to
others and collected rents from the settlers.*

*The system of land disposal in Carolina is described, perhaps
in somewhat ideal terms, in the following excerpt from a
promotional tract written in 1710 by Thomas Nairne, a Swiss.*

Nothing can be more reasonable than the Price of Lands in this Province;
we must do their Lordships the Justice to say, they have always, in that
Respect, dealt with great Favour and Gentleness. The first twenty Years they
got little or nothing at all, and since not much more than is barely sufficient

---

From Thomas Nairne, *A Letter from South Carolina* (London, 1710), pp. 46–51.

to support the necessary Charges of the Government. By this Conduct the Proprietors have advanc'd the Interest of the *English* Nation to their own present Loss. For if their Lordships had not remitted many Years Arrears of Rent, if they had not waited a great while for Money due for Lands, and suffer'd the People to supply themselves with Slaves, before they paid it; if they had not sold their Lands, and established their Rents, at so moderate a Rate; the Country had not been in Circumstances to purchase all the Effects brought yearly from *Great Britain,* in 22 Sail of Ships, as they now do.

The Method has hitherto often been for Men to settle themselves upon a Piece of Ground, improve it, build, raise stock, plant Orchards, and make such Commodities, which being sold, procur'd them Slaves, Horses, Houshold-Goods, and the like Conveniences; and after this was done, in seven or eight Years they might begin to think it Time to pay the Lords something for their Land.

Free and common Soccage* is the Tenure by which Lands are held, a small Quit-Rent being paid annually to the Proprietors, as Lords of the Fee, in lieu of all Services, Perquisites, and Demands whatsoever. There are two Ways of taking out Titles; one is by Purchase, at twenty Pounds a thousand Acres, paid to the Lords Reciever, the Grant whereof reserves to their Lordships an annual Rent of a Shilling for each hundred Acres; the other is without any Purchase money paid down, but by taking out a Patent, upon Condition to pay yearly to the Lords Proprietors a Penny for each Acre. Every one is at Liberty to choose which of these Methods he will, tho' the former, being much preferable, is most common.

The Tenour of the Grants of Lands from the Proprietors, runs to this Purpose: First their Lordships Title by a Charter from K. Charles II is recited; then in Consideration of so much Money there acknowledg'd to be received, they, sell, alienate, and make over unto *A. B.* his Heirs, &c. a Plantation, containing so many Acres of Land, situate and being in such a County, and having such a Form and Marks, as appear by the Plan of it annex'd, he or they paying for the same, the Sum of one Shilling yearly, for each hundred Acres, in lieu of all Dues or Demands whatsoever.

When a Person would take up Land, (as we term it) he first views the Place, and satisfies himself that no other has any Property there, and then goes to the Secretary, and takes out a Warrant for the Quantity he desires. Warrants ready sign'd by the Governour are left with proper Blanks in the Secretaries Office, and directed to the Surveyor, impowering him to measure and lay out such a Number of Acres for such a Person, and to return a Plan and Certificate thereof into the Secretaries Office. Then the Secretary files the Certificates, and writes a Grant (the Form where of is settled by Act of Assembly) which he annexes to the Plan, and carries it next Council Day, into the Council, to be sign'd by the Governour, and such of the Council as are Trustees for the Sale of Lands, and sealed with the publick Seal of the Colony. If the Grant is to be for Lands purchas'd, a Record of the Receipt of the Purchase-Money by the Lords Reciever, must be produced, as a Warrant for signing the Patent.

If any one designs to make a Plantation, in this Province, out of the Woods, the first thing to be done is, after having cutt down a few Trees, to

---

Ed. Note: A form of land tenure in which the tenant performed specified services or paid rent. No military service was required.

split Palissades, or Clapboards, and therewith make small Houses or Huts, to shelter the Slaves. After that, while some Servants are clearing the Land, others are to be employed in squaring or sawing Wallplats, Posts, Rafters, Boards and Shingles, for a small House for the Family, which usually serves for a Kitchin afterwards, when they are in better Circumstances to build a larger. During the Time of this Preparation, the Master Overseer, or white Servants, go every Evening to the next Neighbour's House, where they are lodg'd and entertain'd kindly, without any Charges. And if the Person have any Wife or Children, they are commonly left in some Friend's House, till a suitable dwelling Place and Conveniencies are provided, fit for them to live decently.

The properst Time to begin a Settlement is in *September,* or, at farthest, before the first of *December.* The Time between that and the first of *March* is spent in cutting down and burning the Trees, out of the Ground, design'd to be sowed that Year, splitting Rails, and making Fences round the Corn Ground, and Pasture. The smallest Computation usually made is, that each labouring Person will, in this Time, clear three Acres fit for Sowing.

In the second Fall, or Winter, after a Plantation is settled, they make Gardens, plant Orchards, build Barns, and other convenient Houses. The third or fourth Winter, Persons of any Substance provide Brick, Lime, or other Materials, in order to build a good House. The Lime here is all made of Oister-shells, burnt with Wood; of these there is great Plenty lying in and by all Creeks and Rivers, in great Heaps or Beds, where large Boats are loaden at low Water.

Our Cows graze in the Forests, and the Calves being separated from them, and kept in Pastures, fenced in, they return home at Night to suckle them. They are first milk'd, then shut up in a Fold all Night, milk'd again in the Morning, and then turn'd out into the Woods. Hogs rove several Miles over the Forests, eating such Nuts and Ground-Roots as they can find; but having a Shelter made at home to keep them warm, and something given them to eat, they generally return every Evening.

. . . In this Province as little will serve to put a Person into a Way of living comfortably, as in any Place whatever, and perhaps less. . . .

Missionaries and Indians:
The Spanish Frontier

Alexander Forbes

A continent away from the villages of New England and the plantations of the South, the Spanish were extending their frontier from Mexico into what is now the southwestern United States. From the late seventeenth to the early nineteenth century, the mission station was the principal institution for Spanish expansion. Friars, usually accompanied by a small group of soldiers, established missions among the Indians, teaching them husbandry and crafts skills in addition to Christianity. Like the New England towns, the missions were carefully laid out around a central plaza and were surrounded by farms and grazing lands; like the plantations of the South, the missions depended upon a more or less servile population to work the land.

The mission system reached its peak in California. By 1820, just before the Mexicans overthrew the Spanish rulers, a chain of twenty-one missions stretched from San Diego to the San Francisco Bay area. In 1833, when their lands were opened to settlers by the Mexican government, the missions had extensive herds of 400,000 head of cattle, 60,000 horses, and 300,000 sheep and swine, while wheat, grapes, and other produce flourished in irrigated fields.

The mission system at the height of its power is described by Alexander Forbes, a British visitor, in the following selection.

Each mission has allotted to it, in the first instance, a tract of land of about fifteen miles square, which is generally fertile and well suited for husbandry. This land is set apart for the general uses of the mission, part being cultivated, and part left in its natural condition and occupied as grazing ground. The buildings of the mission are, like the Presidio, all on the same general plan, but are varied according to the locality and number of the inhabitants. Most of the missionary villages or residences are surrounded by a high wall enclosing the whole; others have no such protection but consist of open rows of streets of little huts built of bricks: some of these are tiled and whitewashed and look neat and comfortable; others are dirty and

Excerpted from Alexander Forbes, *California, A History of Upper and Lower California from Their First Discovery to the Present Time* (London: Smith Elder & Co., 1839), pp. 210–216.

in disrepair and in every way uncomfortable. In the mission of Santa Clara, which in several respects excels the others, the houses of the Indians form five rows or streets, which compared with the old straw huts must be considered really comfortable: and this is the greatest improvement that has taken place in the domestic civilization of these people at the missions. The buildings are generally built in the form of a square or part of a square, the church usually forming a portion of the elevation. The apartments of the fathers, which are often spacious, the granaries and work-shops compose the remainder. The Indian population generally live in huts at about two hundred yards distant from the principal edifices; these huts are sometimes made of *adobes,* but the Indians are often left to raise them on their own plan; viz. of rough poles erected into a conical figure, of about four yards in circumference at the base, covered with dry grass and a small aperture for the entrance. When the huts decay, they set them on fire, and erect new ones; which is only the work of a day. In these huts the married part of the community live, the unmarried of both sexes being kept, each sex separate, in large barn-like apartments, where they work under strict supervision. The storehouses and workshops, at some of the larger missions, are of great extent and variety. There may be seen a place for melting tallow, one for making soap, workshops for smiths, carpenters, &c., storehouses for the articles manufactured, and the produce of the farms: viz. stores for tallow, soap, butter, salt, wool, hides, wheat, peas, beans, &c. &c. &c. Four or five soldiers have their residence a few yards further off, and are meant to watch the Indians, and to keep order; but they are generally lazy, idle fellows; and often give the missionary more trouble than all his Indians; and instead of rendering assistance increase his troubles. But in all Spanish countries, nothing can possibly be done without soldiers, and the idea of having any public establishment without a guard of soldiers would appear quite ridiculous.

The church, is of course, the main object of attraction at all the missions. . . .

Brute Action:
The Destructiveness
of Man

James Fenimore Cooper

The process of constructing communities and farms inevit-ably involved the destruction of the wilderness. As the popu-lation of the Atlantic seaboard area increased, so did the numbers of people moving westward in search of new lands. In the vanguard of this movement were the hunters and woodsmen, more dependent on their rifles than on farming implements, and usually content with a crude cabin in a small clearing. But the pioneer farmers who followed them regarded the seemingly endless woodlands as an obstacle to be destroyed. Although the practice of girdling trees to kill them was widely used for clearing farmland, the initial clearings in the woods were made with the axe.

In the following passage, James Fenimore Cooper, author of the Leatherstocking *series, graphically portrays the brute action of a woodcutter in western New York at the close of the eighteenth century.*

. . . The chief speaker was the man who had been mentioned by Natty as Billy Kirby. This fellow, whose occupation, when he did labor, was that of clearing lands, or chopping jobs, was of great stature, and carried, in his very air, the index of his character. He was a noisy, boisterous, reckless lad, whose good-natured eye contradicted the bluntness and bullying tenor of his speech. For weeks he would lounge around the taverns of the county, in a state of perfect idleness, or doing small jobs for his liquor and his meals, and cavilling with applicants about the prices of his labor; frequently preferring idleness to an abatement of a tittle of his independence, or a cent in his wages. But when these embarrassing points were satisfactorily arranged, he would shoulder his axe and his rifle, slip his arms through the straps of his pack, and enter the woods with the tread of a Hercules. His first object was to learn his limits, round which he would pace, occasionally freshening, with a blow of his axe, the marks on the boundary trees; and then he would proceed with an air of great deliberation, to the centre of his premises, and,

From James Fenimore Cooper, *The Pioneers* (1823; New York: D. Appleton & Co., 1901).

throwing aside his superfluous garments, measure, with a knowing eye, one or two of the nearest trees that were towering apparently into the very clouds as he gazed upwards. Commonly selecting one of the most noble for the first trial of his power, he would approach it with a listless air, whistling a low tune; and wielding his axe with a certain flourish, not unlike the salutes of a fencing master, he would strike a light blow into the bark, and measure his distance. The pause that followed was ominous of the fall of the forest which had flourished there for centuries. The heavy and brisk blows that he struck were soon succeeded by the thundering report of the tree, as it came, first cracking and threatening, with the separation of its own last ligaments, then threshing and tearing with its branches the tops of its surrounding brethren, and finally meeting the ground with a shock but little inferior to an earthquake. From that moment the sounds of the axe were ceaseless, while the falling of the trees was like a distant cannonading; and the daylight broke into the depths of the woods with the suddenness of a winter morning.

For days, weeks, nay months, Billy Kirby would toil with an ardor that evinced his native spirit, and with an effect that seemed magical, until, his chopping being ended, his stentorian lungs could be heard emitting sounds, as he called to his patient oxen, which rang through the hills like the cries of an alarm. He had been often heard, on a mild summer's evening, a long mile across the vale of Templeton; when the echoes from the mountains would take up his cries, until they died away in feeble sounds from the distant rocks that overhung the lake. His piles, or to use the language of the country, his logging, ended with a despatch that could only accompany his dexterity and Herculean strength, the jobber would collect together his implements of labor, light the heaps of timber, and march away under the blaze of the prostrate forest, like the conqueror of some city, who, having first prevailed over his adversary, applies the torch as the finishing blow to his conquest. For a long time Billy Kirby would then be seen, sauntering around the taverns, the rider of scrub-races, the bully of cock-fights, and not unfrequently the hero of such sports as the one in hand . . . .

Homesteading on the Middle Border

Carl O. Sauer

For almost three centuries, the availability of land was the magnet that lured millions of people to America. Each of the colonies had developed its own system of land grants, but the new national government was faced with the problem of developing a unified policy for disposal of the public lands. The government had two basic, and often conflicting, goals: to encourage settlement and to produce revenue. The Homestead Law of 1862 was the culmination of almost ninety years of changing land policy.

The basic pattern of the rectangular survey was established by the Ordinance of 1785, which provided that the Northwest Territory—the area lying east of the Mississippi and north of the Ohio River—be surveyed into townships six miles square along lines running north-south and east-west. Each township was subdivided into thirty-six lots, or sections, of one mile square (640 acres). Land was initially put up at auction; a section was the smallest unit for sale and one dollar per acre the lowest price accepted. Few small farmers could afford $640, and large tracts of land fell into the hands of speculators. Subsequent legislation reduced the minimum amount of land that could be purchased, and in 1820 it was set at eighty acres, at a price of $1.25 per acre.

Throughout the colonial and early national period, many of the settlers moving westward were squatters who occupied the land without establishing title to it. The Pre-emption Act of 1841 permitted these settlers to purchase their land at the minimum price, free from competitive bid. But as long as the land law failed to set limits on the amount of land that could be acquired and did not require actual settlement on the land by purchasers, speculation continued.

Finally, in 1862, Congress passed the Homestead Act, designed to encourage the small, independent farmer. It provided that a citizen or an alien who intended to become a citizen could obtain title to a quarter-section of land (160 acres) if he or she lived on the land for five years and improved it.

From Carl O. Sauer, "Homestead and Community on the Middle Border," in Howard W. Ottoson, ed., *Land Use Policy and Problems in the United States* (Lincoln, Nebraska: University of Nebraska Press, 1963). Copyright © 1963 by the University of Nebraska Press. Reprinted by permission of the author and the publisher.

There were widespread abuses of the law, and the 160-acre unit often proved inappropriate to much of the western region where it was applied. Of the public lands that passed into private hands between 1862 and 1900, only about one-sixth was settled by homesteaders. Nevertheless, those who succeeded in homesteading established a pattern of life that was to characterize Midwestern settlement until World War I. The historical geographer Carl Sauer describes that pattern in the following article.

A public anniversary* in the present American mood is likely to consider the date as a determinate point between the past and the future. The past thus is of interest chiefly because it shows what change has taken place and what its direction has been. The present is the base from which we project the future. Perhaps more than any other people, or at any other time, we are committed to living in a mundane future, confident we shall control it by anticipation, that is, by planning the march of the material progress desired.

The immediate instrument of change is provided by the spiraling advance of technics that appear to put limitless material possibilities in our hands, and it is of these that we think primarily. What we have gained, at least for the present, is the ability to produce many more goods of more kinds for more people. We not only think to hold the horn of plenty but we believe we can and should pass it on to the rest of the world. Capacity to produce and capacity to consume form a reciprocating system that we desire to expand without end. Growth in material wants and in the ability to satisfy them and so to stimulate new wants is what we are agreed is progress. We measure progress by such things as gross national product, income per capita, standard of living (a term we have introduced to the world; perhaps it is the most widely known of all American phrases), level of employment, new construction, and other quantitative indices of an expanding economy. The system, insofar as we have seen it work, depends on continued acceleration and perhaps on being kept jogged by the stimuli of debt and taxes as well as of consumption and obsolescence. . . .

Output grows with input and so on, requiring more and more engagement of expert technicians. The objective of growth necessitates making and carrying out more and more decision about public policy, which becomes an increasingly limited and coveted prerogative. For the individual and the community the choice as to how one would live becomes more restricted in the interest of the will and authority of what is proposed as the commonweal. Reducing the risks of livelihood we also diminish the diversity of purposes and ends of individual living, once richly present in rural America.

On this occasion we call to remembrance an event of a hundred years ago when American life differed greatly from the present in mode, mood, and meaning. We may take a look back over a formative span of our history which lasted for several generations, a long time as our history goes.

---

*Ed. note: This article was originally presented at a Homestead Centennial Symposium, marking the one-hundredth anniversary of the signing of the Homestead Act, at the Nebraska Center for Continuing Education, June, 1962.

In its first part we were a rural nation, the first major shift to city living coming as the result of the Civil War and its industrial mobilization. Thereafter, population flowed more and more from country to city but the ways and values of rural living continued for two more generations to have much the accustomed meaning and content. We are here in fact taking part in an Old Settlers Reunion, as descendants of those who left their previous places and conditions of life to take part in making a new West, the Promised Land which a chosen people came to possess. There was an Old Testament sense of fulfillment in the western migration which should not be forgotten.

The Homestead National Monument, situated where wooded valley met upland prairie, is a model geographic expression of the manner in which the West was settled. This first homestead as taken under the act lies well out into the farther and later part of the Midwest. Its specific location records still the original pioneer requirement of a living site with wood and water, requisites that the building of railroads soon made unnecessary. When this tract was taken up, only three young and raw towns were in the Territory of Nebraska, all of them on the Missouri River. Through them emigrant trails led to Oregon and California, bearing westward over prairie and wooded stream, in a land still ranged over by Indian, buffalo, antelope, and deer. In very short order the wild land was brought into cultivation and fully settled. By mid-century, the westward course of homesteading had begun to cross the Missouri line at the west, to be halted later by dryness farther on. In simple outline, I should like to direct attention to the peopling of that part of the interior we know as the Corn Belt. The Wheat Belt is another, though derivative, story. What sort of rural living was established on the Middle Border; what were its attainments and satisfactions, its lacks and failures?

The Homestead Act

The date of the Homestead Act marks conveniently for our recall a moment of significance in the mainstream of American history, the great westward movement of families seeking land to cultivate and own. This movement began from states of the eastern seaboard, swelled to surges across the wide basin of the Mississippi-Missouri and ebbed away in the High Plains. To the south and north there were other westward movements sufficiently different in kind and route as to be left out of present consideration. The Middle Border, as it has been named appropriately, was the wide, advancing wave of settlement that spread over the plains south of the Great Lakes and north of the Ohio River, making use of both waterways as approaches. Its advances made Cleveland, Toledo, and Chicago northern gateways. At the south it gave rise to border cities on rivers, such as Cincinnati on the Ohio, St. Louis at the crossing of the Mississippi, and Kansas City on the great bend of the Missouri. The Mississippi was crossed in force in the 1830's, the Missouri River into Kansas in the border troubles prior to the Civil War. Although it did not begin as such this became the peopling of the prairies, the founding and forming of the actual Midwest.

The Homestead Act came pretty late in the settlement of the interior. Land had been given free of cost to many. . . .

It had been sold at nominal prices and on easy terms by public land offices and by canal and railroad companies. The squatter who settled without title was generously protected by preemption rights and practices that grew stronger. Many millions of acres had been deeded as homesteads before the act and many more continued to be acquired by other means afterwards. Land was long available in great abundance. The price in money of the wild land was the least cost of making it into a farm. Public land offices were set up to get land into private hands quickly, simply, and cheaply. Under the Graduation Act lands were reduced in price according to the length of time they had been on the market, the last cut being to twelve and one-half cents an acre. Canal and railroad lands were priced to sell. The railroads were well aware that revenue from farm traffic would be their largest return. The land seeker was induced to buy railroad land because he knew that he was given facility of transportation. The theme that land was a commodity for speculation is certainly true, yet it may be overstressed and oversimplified. The settler knew that the price of the farm was mainly in the work of all the family, in making out or doing without, in minimizing wants and spending. Largely our farms could not be reproduced from wild land at present prices, wages, and standards.

Advantage of location was of first importance in selecting the home site. The original entry of a tract was because of its immediate suitability as a homestead rather than because it would continue to be most desirable; locational advantages change as might productive capacity. Settlers were in process of regrouping themselves in neighborhoods of their liking. The drawbacks of one place having been experienced, a better location might be sought farther on. Property passed from one hand to another at a price reflecting, perhaps, the improvements made more than rise in land value. The term land speculation is not fully adequate or appropriate. The relinquisher was paid for the worth he had put in, the purchaser received a partially improved farm. The early succession of owners largely was a passing from weaker to stronger hands financially. The border was pretty fluid in its first years. Those who moved on are forgotten, or appear only as names of patentees and first conveyors of title. Those who remained and took root became the Old Settlers. There were various kinds and conditions of people who moved into or across the Middle Border, the restless and the sedentary, the overflow from older settlements farther east and the immigrants from Europe for whom this was a first opportunity to live on land of their own.

The Turner Thesis

The famous frontier thesis of Professor Turner was adapted from a theory of social evolution that was popular late in the nineteenth century. According to it, mankind everywhere has gone through the same series of stages of progress from simpler to more advanced skills and societies. . . . Turner picked up the general idea and thought to reproduce the whole supposed history of human experience in the short span of the American frontier. Thus he saw our frontier as a "field for comparative study of social development," beginning (1) with Indian and white hunter, followed by (2) the "disintegration of savagery by the entrance of the trader, the pathfinder of civilization," then by (3) the pastoral stage

(4) the raising of unrotated crops of corn and wheat in sparsely settled farming communities (5) intensive agriculture, and finally (6) the industrial society. He saw each stage present "in the march toward the West, impelled by an irresistible attraction. Each passed in successive waves across the continent." This plot of a westward-moving pageant in six scenes was good drama but was not our history.

As corollary to this theory of cultural succession he proposed one of cultural regression, namely that whoever entered a new scene or stage reverted from his former ways to accept those of the "stage" he was joining. Thus, the wilderness "takes him from the railroad car and puts him in the birch canoe and arrays him in the hunting shirt and moccasin. . . ." A half truth. Every migrant group loses some of the elements of its previous culture in fitting itself into a new environment, whether wilderness or city. It may also introduce some traits of its own. . . .

The first three stages or waves of Turner did not exist in the Middle Border. The next two were not stages but the entry of differing cultures.

The Indian Legacy

The American settler acquired learning that was important for his survival and well-being from the Indian, mainly as to agricultural ways. The settler was still a European in culture who had the good sense to make use of what was serviceable to him in the knowledge of the Indians of the eastern woodlands. This learning began at Jamestown and Plymouth and was pretty well completed before the Appalachians were crossed. It contributed Indian corn, along with beans and squash, as the basis of frontier sustenance. . . . The settler took over Indian ways of woodland clearing and planting. . . . He brought with him the Indian art of dressing buckskins and making apparel. These were new learnings. . . .

Little seems to have passed from the Indians of the interior to the settlers. The Indian culture west of the Appalachians was still significantly based on cultivation, more largely so than is thought popularly to have been the case.

The American entry into the Mississippi Valley encountered the Indian tribes in an advanced condition of disturbance, dislodgement, and dissolution. In most of our early accounts they are described in terms of disdain, deprecation, and disgust, without awareness that what was being witnessed was the breakdown of a native society. . . . The remnants of a score of tribes were piled west beyond the Missouri line, some from as far east as Pennsylvania and New York. In the territories that were to become Kansas and Nebraska they were given reservations between the native Osages, Kansas, and Pawnees until most of them in a last remove were taken into the Indian Territory. (The original Kansas City, Kansas, was named Wyandot and began as a village of those Indians.)

Dispossessed of title to home, deprived of their economy and losing hope that there might be another start, many Indians were reduced to beggary or lived as pariahs about the white settlements. Their debauch was completed by alcohol, a thing wholly foreign to their ways, which became for them a last escape. Objects of despair to each other, and of contempt and annoyance to the whites, the time was missed when the two races might have learned from each other and lived together.

The French settlements, nearly all in river villages, were the meager reality of a vast colonial design of a New France that was planned to reach from the St. Lawrence to the Gulf of Mexico. The French habitants contributed little to the ways of the Middle Border. . . .

The Wave from the South

Most of the earlier American pioneers of the Mississippi Valley came by a southerly approach. They were known as Virginians and Carolinians, later as Kentuckians and Tennesseeans, and in final attenuation as Missourians. They came on foot and horseback across the Cumberlands and Alleghenies, usually to settle for a while in Kentucky or Tennessee and thence to move on by land or river and cross the Ohio and Mississippi rivers. The relocations of the Lincoln and Boone families are familiar examples. Turner's stages are not properly descriptive of the order or manner of their coming. By his scheme they would need to be distributed through his four first stages, least apparent in the second. Actually, they do not sort out as such separate waves.

The border had an element that came in for unfavorable comment in almost every early account, of persons who had taken to the backwoods because they did not fit into an ordered society, because of their indolence, perhaps for some misdemeanor or crime. They were the shiftless and the reckless, sometimes called drifters in the language of the West, the flotsam carried on the advancing wave of settlement, but not the first, nor a distinct wave. . . . Largely they drifted on into the farther Southwest and Far West. Some got stranded on the overflow lands of the Missouri and Mississippi, others in the "hollers" of the hill lands adjacent. They were early in the history of settlement and chose to live segregated from the rest, usually marrying among their own kind. Of all settlers these were the most fully self-sufficient. A patch of cleared ground was in the woman's care; a litter of hogs ranged free. The men fished and hunted and loafed and kept hound dogs. In the steamboat days money could be had by cutting and loading firewood. When the railroads came there were ties to be hacked. They would work to sell something when they wanted money, employment they avoided. They were indifferent to increasing their income or to owning property. Some were defectors from civilization; I knew two of the most famous names of Virginia among them. They were considered to be predominantly a farther fringe of the Southern poor whites, usually bearing English surnames, in part a residue from the least fit part of those shipped to the Colonies. I do not think that Turner's view of cultural regression on the frontier applies; the frontier gave room for antisocial elements as well as for the builders of society.

The main contingent of pioneer settlers were a different breed. Theodore Roosevelt hailed them as Scotch-Irish, Mencken stressed their Celtic tone and temperament, Ellen Semple saw them as Anglo-Saxons of the Appalachians. Whatever their origins, and they were multiple, those were the backwoodsmen who brought and developed the American frontier way of life. They were woodland farmers, hunters, and raisers of livestock in combination, and very skilled in the use of axe and rifle. Trees were raw material for their log cabins and worm fences, and also an encumbrance of the ground, to be deadened, burned, or felled. The

150

planting ground was enclosed by a rail fence, the livestock ranged free in wood or prairie. When the New Englander Albert Richardson reported life in eastern Kansas in the time of border troubles (*Beyond the Mississippi*) he said he could tell the home of a settler from Missouri by three things: The (log) house had the chimney built on the outside and at the end of the house; the house was located by a spring which served for keeping food in place of a cellar, and one was given buttermilk to drink. He might have added that there would be corn whiskey on hand and that if the family was really Southern the corn bread would be white.

This colonization was early and massive, beginning by 1800 and having the new West almost to itself until into the 1830's. At the time of the Louisiana Purchase, American settlers already held Spanish titles to a million acres in Missouri alone, mainly along the Mississippi and lower Missouri rivers. Their homes and fields were confined to wooded valleys, their stock pastured on the upland prairies. Nebraska alone of the mid-continent remained almost wholly beyond the limits of their settlement.

Viewed ecologically, their occupation of the land was indifferent to permanence. Trees were gotten rid of by any means, the grasslands were overgrazed, game was hunted out. They were farmers after the Indian fashion of woods deadening, clearing, and planting, and made little and late use of plow or wagon. The impression is that they gave more heed to animal husbandry than to the care of their fields or to the improvement of crops. Central and northwest Missouri, for example, the best flowering of this "Southern" frontier, developed the Missouri mule early in the Santa Fe trade, and later bred saddle and trotting horses and beef cattle. I do not know that it contributed anything to crop improvement, unless it was in bluegrass pastures.

There was self-sufficiency of food to this frontier but also there was a well-marked commercial side. It had things to sell or exchange for merchandise, above all tobacco, not a little corn whiskey, hogs on the hoof, in some cases hemp or cotton, all items that could be put on boat or horseback or driven to more or less distant markets. . . .

Corn and tobacco were the two crops planted in the new clearings in the woods, and they continued to be grown on the same land so long as its fertility lasted. Several acres of tobacco gave the needed purchasing power to the small farmer. Tobacco growing also attracted slave-owning planters north across the Ohio and especially west across the Mississippi, beginning with the Spanish government that freely granted land and sanction of slavery. From the beginning, the backwoods farmer, the hunter of the long rifle, and the slave-holding planter mingled in this stream of American Colonists; they might indeed be the same individuals. . . .

This migration of the early nineteenth century came without benefit of constructed facilities of transportation, of public or private capital, or of most of the products of the newly begun machine age, except for the river steamboat. The people came in bands of kindred and friendship to settle in contiguity that was less than close clustering and more than wide dispersal. Their locations bore the name of a "settlement" quite properly, identified perhaps by the name of the leader, or of the stream along which their homesteads were strung. . . . The lonely family cabin, removed far from and isolated from its neighbors is mostly a myth, even as to Daniel

Boone himself. Sociability, not aloofness, was the quality of life sought. Much of the work was done by mutual aid; leisure time was time for meeting, a word of special meaning in the vernacular of the frontier. Such were the people and the life that Mark Twain knew so well and portrayed with affection. They enjoyed discourse in all forms and on all occasions, respected those who excelled in it, and produced an able lot of politicians, lawyers, ministers of the gospel, and schoolteachers.

The Wave from the North

The great northern immigration set in in the 1830's and depended from the beginning on improved transportation: the Erie Canal, steamships on the Great Lakes, stout and capacious wagons. It continued to demand "internal improvements," the term of the time for public aid to communication, first canals and soon railroads, only rarely constructed, and surfaced roads. Wagon transport, however, was important and a wagon-making industry sprang up in the hardwoods south of the Great Lakes. It may be recalled that the automobile industry later took form in the same centers and by using the same skills and organization of distribution. Canals, most significantly the Illinois and Michigan Canal completed in 1848, linked the Great Lakes to rivers of the Mississippi system for shipping farm products to the East. Railroads were first projected as feeder lines to navigable waters. The first important construction, that of the Illinois Central, was chartered in 1850 to build a railroad from Cairo at the junction of the Ohio and Mississippi rivers to La Salle on the Illinois and Michigan Canal and on the Illinois River. It was given a grant by Congress of two million acres of land.

This last great movement of land settlement was out on to the prairies and it differed largely in manner of life and kind of people from the settlement of the woodlands. It depended on industry and capital for the provision of transportation. It was based from the start on plow-farming—cast-iron or steel plows to cut and turn the sod, plows that needed stout draft animals, either oxen or heavy horses. By 1850 agricultural machinery had been developed for cultivating corn and harvesting small grains, and was responsible for the gradual replacement of oxen by horses as motive power.

The prairie homestead differed from that of the woodlands, in the first instance by depending on plow, draft animals, and wagon. It, too, grew corn as the most important crop, in part for work stock but largely to be converted into pork and lard by new, large breeds developed in the West that were penned and fed. Fences were needed, not to fence stock out of the fields but to confine it. The livestock was provided with feed and housing. The farm was subdivided into fields, alternately planted to corn, wheat, oats, clover, and grass, arranged in a rotation that grew the feed for the work animals and for the stock to be marketed. A barn was necessary for storage and stabling. This mixed economy, its cash income from animals and wheat, spread the work time through the seasons and maintained the fertility of the land. It was a self-sustaining ecologic system, capable of continuing and improving indefinitely, and it was established by the process of prairie settlement. There was no stage of extractive or exhaustive cultivation.

By the time of the Civil War—in a span of twenty years or so—the prairie country east of the Mississippi, the eastern half of Iowa, and northern

Missouri were well settled. Some counties had reached their highest population by then. My native Missouri county had twice its current population in 1860. More people were needed to improve the land and to build the houses and barns than it took to keep the farms going. Some of the surplus sought new lands farther west, much of it went into building up the cities. These people who settled the prairies were farmers, born and reared, out of the Northeast or from overseas, first, and in largest number, Germans and thereafter Scandinavians. They knew how to plow and work the soil to keep it in good tilth, how to care for livestock, how to arrange and fill their working time. They needed money for their houses and barns, which were not log but frame structures with board siding. The lumber was mainly white pine shipped in from the Great Lakes, long the main inbound freight. They needed money as well as their own labor to dig wells and drain fields. The price of the land, again, was the lesser part of the cost of acquiring a farm. The hard pull was to get enough capital to improve and equip the homestead, and this was done by hard labor and iron thrift. This is a sufficient explanation of the work ethic and thrift habits of the Midwest, often stressed in disparagement of its farm life. In order to have and hold the good land, it was necessary to keep to a discipline of work and to defer the satisfactions of ease and comforts. The price seemed reasonable to the first generation who had wrested a living from scant acres in New England or to those who had come from Europe where land of one's own was out of reach.

The End of the Village

Dispersed living, the isolated family home, became most characteristic of the "Northern" folk on the frontier. In Europe nearly everyone had lived in a village or town; in this country the rural village disappeared or never existed. Our farmers lived in the "country" and went to "town" on business or pleasure. The word "village," like "brook," was one that poets might use; it was strange to our western language. Land was available to the individual over here in tracts of a size beyond any holdings he might ever have had overseas. The village pattern was retained almost only where religious bonds or social planning prescribed living in close congregation.

Normally the land holding was the place where the family lived, and this identification became recognized in the establishment of title. The act of living on the land occupied was part of the process of gaining possession. As time went on, prior occupation and improvement of a tract gave more and more weight to pre-emption rights; living on the land protected against eviction and gave a first right to purchase or contract for warranty of ownership. The Homestead Act was a late extension of the much earlier codes of pre-emption, by which possession by residence on the land and improvement could be used to secure full and unrestricted title.

The General Land Survey established the rectangular pattern of land description and subdivision for the public domain. Rural land holdings took the form of a square or sums of squares, in fractions or multiples of the mile-square section of land. The quarter section gradually came into greatest favor as the desired size of a farm and became the standard unit for the family farm in the Homestead Act. Thus four families per square mile, a score or so of persons, were thought to give a desirable density of rural population. The reservation of one school section out of the thirty-six in a township, for the support of primary public schools, provided an incentive for the only kind of public building contemplated in the disposal of public lands. Four homes to the square mile, and about four schools to the six-mile square township, gave the simple general pattern for the rural geography of the Midwest. The pattern was most faithfully put into effect on the smooth upland prairies. Here the roads followed section lines and therefore ran either north-south or east-west, and the farmsteads were strung at nearly equal intervals upon one or the other strand of the grid. It is curious that this monotony was so generally accepted, even a clustering of homes at the four corners where the sections met (and giving the same density) being exceptional. . . .

The logistics of home location is an attractive and hardly investigated field of study, as is indeed the whole question of the rural landscape and its changes. The location of house and farm buildings involved conservation of energy in the work on the farm, cultural preferences of different colonizing groups, microclimatic adjustments, and esthetic satisfactions. The relation of water, drainage, and sanitation was unrecognized, the toll paid in typhoid and "summer complaint."

Building was starkly utilitarian and unadorned. Neither the log cabin of the woodlands nor the box-shaped farm house of the prairies, nor yet the sod house of the trans-Missouri country (made possible by the sod-cutting plow) was more than compact and economical shelter, varying but little in each form. Ready-cut houses, of standard and simple pattern, were already offered by railroads to buyers of their land, an early form of tract housing. Quality of house and quality of land seem to be in no relation. The embellishment of the home and the planting of the yard were left mostly to the second generation, for country town as well as farm . . . .

The Self-sufficient Family

The economy, from its beginnings, was based on marketing products, but it also maintained a high measure of self-sufficiency. Smokehouse, cellar, and pantry stored the food that was produced and processed on the farm. The farm acquired its own potato patch, orchard, berry and vegetable garden, diversified as to kind from early to late maturity, for different flavors and uses, selected for qualities other than shipping or precocious bearing. The farm orchards now are largely gone, and the gardens are going. Many varieties of fruits that were familiar and appreciated have been lost. A family orchard was stocked with diverse sorts of apple trees for early and midsummer applesauce, for making apple butter and cider in the fall, for laying down in cool bins in the cellar to be used, one kind after another, until the russets closed out the season late in winter. The agricultural bulletins and yearbooks of the past century invited attention to new kinds of fruits and vegetables that might be added to the home orchard and garden, with diversification, not standardization in view. Exhibits in the county and state fairs similarly stressed excellence in the variety of things grown, as well as giving a prize for the fattest hog and the largest pumpkin.

The Mason jar became a major facility by which fruit and vegetables were "put up" for home use in time of abundance against winter or a possible season of failure in a later year. The well-found home kept itself insured against want of food at all times by producing its own and storing a lot of it.

The family, of ample size and age gradation, was able to provide most of the skills and services for self-sufficiency by maintaining diversified production and well-knit social organization. This competence and unity was maintained long after the necessity had disappeared. As time is measured in American history, the life of this society, and its vitality, were extraordinary.

Looking back from the ease of the present, these elder days may seem to have been a time of lonely and hard isolation. It was only toward the end of the period that the telephone and rural delivery were added. The prairie lacked wet-weather roads. In the hill sections, ridge roads might be passable at most times; on the plains, winter was likely to be the season of easiest travel, spring that of immobilization by mud. The country doctor was expected to, and did, rise above any emergency of weather. Life was so arranged that one did not need to go to town at any particular time. When the weather was bad the activities of the family took place indoors or about the farmyard. In our retrospect of the family farm as it was, we may incline to overstress its isolation. The American farmstead did not have the sociability of rural villages of Europe or of Latin America, but the entire family had duties to learn and perform, and times of rest and diversion. It depended on a work morale and competence, in which all participated and in which its members found satisfaction. Perhaps it suffered fewer social tensions and disruptions than any other part of our society.

The Community

Though living dispersed, the farm families were part of a larger community, which might be a contiguous neighborhood or one of wider association. The community in some cases got started on the Boone pattern of a settlement of kith and kin. A sense of belonging together was present to begin with, or it soon developed. The start may have been as a closed community; it was likely to continue in gradual admission of others by some manner of acceptance. Consanguinity, common customs, faith, or speech were such bonds that formed and maintained viable communities through good times and bad. The Mennonite colonies are outstanding examples. The absence of such qualities of cooption is shown in the Cherokee strip, opened as a random aggregation of strangers.

The bond of common customs and language showed up strongly in the German settlements made between 1830 and the Civil War, and in the Scandinavian settlements of somewhat later origin. Both were attracted to districts where some of their people had chanced to locate and tended to increase about such nuclei. This clustering, a partial segregation, gave protection from cultural alienation and loss and afforded time to adjust and contribute to the common ways of life. . . .

The country church played a leading part in social communication, differing again according to the particular confession. Catholic and Lutheran communicants perhaps had more of their social life determined by their church than did the others. Their priests and pastors were most likely to remain in one community and to exercise and merit influence on it. Parochial schools extended the social connections. Church festivals were numerous and attractive. Sunday observance was less austere. The Methodist church on the other hand shifted its ministers, usually every two years. In a half century of service my grandfather was moved through a score of charges in five states. The high periods of the Methodist year were the winter revival meetings and the camp meetings in summer after the corn was laid by. For some, these were religious experiences, for others, especially for the young people, they were sociable times, particularly the camp meeting, held in an attractive, wooded campground where one lived in cabins or tents on an extended picnic. Almost everyone belonged to some church and in them found a wide range of social contacts and satisfaction.

The churches also pioneered higher education, founding colleges and academies across the Middle West from Ohio into Kansas before the Civil War and before the Morrill Act fathered the tax supported colleges. These church-supported small colleges, about fifty of which still exist, first afforded education in the liberal arts to the youth of the prairie states and they did so by coeducation. Their students were drawn by their church affiliations, not only from nearby but from distant places. In these colleges, humane learning was cultivated and disseminated. Their campuses today are the Midwest's most gracious early monuments of the civilization aspired to by its pioneers.

Country and town were interdependent, of the same way of life, and mostly of the same people. By a tradition that may go back to the town markets of Europe, Saturday was the weekday for coming to town to transact business (note the pioneer implications in the term "to trade") and to visit. The town provided the services, goods, and entertainment that the farm family required. In time, it also became home for the retired farmer. Farmstead and its particular town were linked in community by factors beyond the one of economy of distance. When the railroads were building across the prairie, they laid out what seemed a most rational spacing of town sites for shipping and trading centers. Some grew, some withered away, and some never got started. Quantitative measurement of radius of trade never has been enough. The choice of direction and destination in going to town had other reasons than economy of energy expended. One liked it better in one town than in another, a matter of social values and affinities which are ponderable but not measurable.

Decline of the Middle Border

The era of the Middle Border ended with World War I. Hamlin Garland introduced the name in 1917 in his *A Son of the Middle Border,* a retrospect he made in middle age. Willa Cather, growing up on its westernmost fringes in Nebraska, drew its life in quiet appreciation in her two books written before the war, and then saw her world swept away. Some of us have lived in its Indian Summer, and almost no one was aware how soon and suddenly it was to end. A quarter section was still a good size for a family farm, and the farm was still engaged in provisioning itself as well as in shipping grain and livestock. It was still growing a good crop of lusty off-spring. The place of the family in the community was not significantly determined by its income, nor had we heard of standard of living.

The outbreak of the war in 1914 brought rapidly rising demand and prices for supplies to the Allies and to American industry. Our intervention in 1917 urged the farmer to still more production: "Food Will Win the War" that was to end all wars. He made more money than ever before, he had less help, he was encouraged to buy more equipment and more land. The end of the war saw a strongly industrialized country that continued to draw labor from the rural sections. Improved roads, cars, tractors, and trucks made the horse unnecessary, and thereby the old crop rotation broke down. Farming became less a way of life and more a highly competitive business for which the agricultural colleges trained specialists as engineers, chemists, economists, to aid fewer and fewer farmers to produce more market goods, to widen their incomes against the rising cost of labor, taxes, and capital needs. This became known as "freeing people from the land," so that now we have about a tenth of our population living on farms (among the lowest ratios in the world), and these are not reproducing themselves.

The Middle Border now belongs to a lost past, a past in which different ways and ends of life went on side by side. We have since defined the common welfare in terms of a society organized for directed material progress. For the present, at the least, we control the means to produce goods at will. We have not learned how to find equivalent satisfactions in jobs well done by simple means and by independent judgment that gave competence and dignity to rural work. The family farm apprenticed youth well for life there or elsewhere, and it enriched the quality of American life. It will be missed.

Settling the Prairie

Willa Cather

The prairies and plains were destined to become one of the most productive agricultural regions of the world. But for the individuals—many of them immigrants—pioneering this area, it often seemed as if nature would triumph over human endurance. Blizzards and subzero temperatures in the winter gave way to spring floods and summer droughts; plagues of grasshoppers stripped the fields of crops; prairie fires and dust storms threatened human and beast alike. And always the unbroken plains stretched unendingly to the horizon, leaving individual families with a profound sense of aloneness.

This treeless landscape required new adaptations, and thus was born the sodhouse frontier. Built of slabs of turf, the sodhouse sometimes was constructed with four walls and a roof supported with branches hauled from distant groves; often the house was little more than a dugout cut in the side of a bank. The sodhouse was designed as a temporary shelter until the farmer could acquire sufficient capital for a frame house.

The strength and determination of the prairie pioneers inspired many novels, including those of Ole Rølvaag and Willa Cather. In the following excerpt from My Antonia, *Miss Cather, who moved to Nebraska in 1883 at the age of ten, tells of both the beauty and loneliness of the land and of the hardships of the immigrant Bohemian family, the Shimerdas.*

Early the next morning I ran out-of-doors to look about me. I had been told that ours was the only wooden house west of Black Hawk—until you came to the Norwegian settlement, where there were several. Our neighbours lived in sod houses and dugouts—comfortable, but not very roomy. Our white frame house, with a storey and half-storey above the basement, stood at the east end of what I might call the farmyard, with the windmill close by the kitchen door. From the windmill the ground sloped westward, down to the barns and granaries and pig-yards. This slope was trampled hard and bare, and washed out in winding gullies by the rain. Beyond the corn-cribs, at the bottom of the shallow draw, was a muddy little pond, with rusty willow bushes growing about it. The road from the post-office came directly by our door, crossed the farmyard, and curved round this little pond, beyond which it began to climb the gentle swell of unbroken prairie to the west. There, along the western sky-line it skirted a great cornfield, much larger than any field I had ever seen. This cornfield, and the sorghum patch behind the barn, were the only broken land in sight. Everywhere, as far as the eye could reach, there was nothing but rough, shaggy, red grass, most of it as tall as I.

North of the house, inside the ploughed fire-breaks, grew a thick-set strip of box-elder trees, low and bushy, their leaves already turning yellow. This hedge was nearly a quarter of a mile long, but I had to look very hard to see it at all. The little trees were insignificant against the grass. It seemed as if the grass were about to run over them, and over the plum-patch behind the sod chicken-house.

As I looked about me I felt that the grass was the country, as the water is the sea. The red of the grass made all the great prairie the colour of wine-stains, or of certain seaweeds when they are first washed up. And there was so much motion in it; the whole country seemed, somehow, to be running. . . .

I can remember exactly how the country looked to me as I walked beside my grandmother along the faint wagon-tracks on that early September morning. Perhaps the glide of long railway travel was still with me, for more than anything else I felt motion in the landscape; in the fresh, easy-blowing morning wind, and in the earth itself, as if the shaggy grass were a sort of loose hide, and underneath it herds of wild buffalo were galloping, galloping . . .

Alone, I should never have found the garden—except, perhaps, for the big yellow pumpkins that lay about unprotected by their withering vines—and I felt very little interest in it when I got there. I wanted to walk straight on through the red grass and over the edge of the world, which could not be very far away. The light air about me told me that the world ended here: only the ground and sun and sky were left and if one went a little farther there would be only sun and sky, and one would float off into them, like the tawny hawks which sailed over our heads making slow shadows on the grass. . . .

I sat down in the middle of the garden, where snakes could scarcely approach unseen, and leaned my back against a warm yellow pumpkin. There were some ground-cherry bushes growing along the furrows, full of fruit. I turned back the papery triangular sheaths that protected the berries and ate a few. All about me giant grasshoppers, twice as big as any I had ever seen, were doing acrobatic feats among the dried vines. The gophers scurried up and down the ploughed ground. There in the sheltered draw-bottom the wind did not blow very hard, but I could hear it singing its humming tune up on the level, and I could see the tall grasses wave. The earth was warm under me, and warm as I crumbled it through my fingers. . . . I kept as still as I could. Nothing happened. I did not expect anything to happen. I was something that lay under the sun and felt it, like the pumpkins, and I did not want to be anything more. I was entirely happy. Perhaps we feel like that when we die and become a part of something entire, whether it is sun and air, or goodness and knowledge. At any rate, that is happiness; to be dissolved into something complete and great. When it comes to one, it comes as naturally as sleep. . . .

On Sunday morning Otto Fuchs was to drive us over to make the acquaintance of our new Bohemian neighbours. We were taking them some provisions, as they had come to live on a wild place where there was no garden or chicken-house, and very little broken land . . . .

I could hardly wait to see what lay beyond that cornfield; but there was only red grass like ours, and nothing else, though from the high wagon-seat one could look off a long way. The road ran about like a wild thing, avoiding the deep draws, crossing them where they were wide and shallow. And all along it, wherever it looped or ran, the sunflowers grew. . . .

The Bohemian family, grandmother told me as we drove along, had bought the homestead of a fellow countryman, Peter Krajiek, and had paid him more than it was worth. Their agreement with him was made before they left the old country, through a cousin of his, who was also a relative of Mrs. Shimerda. The Shimerdas were the first Bohemian family to come to this part of the country. Krajiek was their only interpreter, and could tell them anything he chose. . . .

"If they're nice people, I hate to think of them spending the winter in that cave of Krajiek's," said grandmother. "It's no better than a badger hole; no proper dugout at all." . . .

The land was growing rougher; I was told that we were approaching Squaw Creek, which cut up the west half of the Shimerdas' place and made the land of little value for farming. Soon we could see the broken, grassy clay cliffs which indicated the windings of the stream, and the glittering tops of the cottonwoods and ash trees that grew down in the ravine. Some of the cottonwoods had already turned, and the yellow leaves and shining white bark made them look like the gold and silver trees in fairy tales.

As we approached the Shimerdas' dwelling, I could still see nothing but rough red hillocks, and draws with shelving banks and long roots hanging out where the earth had crumbled away. Presently, against one of those banks, I saw a sort of shed, thatched with the same wine-coloured grass that grew everywhere. Near it tilted a shattered windmill frame, that had no wheel. We drove up to this skeleton to tie our horses, and then I saw a door and window sunk deep in the drawbank . . . .

Mrs. Shimerda opened the door before we knocked and seized grandmother's hand. She did not say "How do!" as usual, but at once began to cry, talking very fast in her own language, pointing to her feet which were tied up in rags, and looking about accusingly at everyone.

The old man was sitting on a stump behind the stove, crouching over as if he were trying to hide from us. Yulka was on the floor at his feet, her kitten in her lap. She peeped out at me and smiled, but, glancing up at her mother, hid again. Antonia was washing pans and dishes in a dark corner. The crazy boy lay under the only window, stretched on a gunny-sack stuffed with straw. As soon as we entered, he threw a grain-sack over the crack at the bottom of the door. The air in the cave was stifling, and it was very dark, too. A lighted lantern, hung over the stove, threw out a feeble yellow glimmer. . . .

Grandmother went on talking in her polite Virginia way. . . .

"Haven't you got any sort of cave or cellar outside, Antonia? This is no place to keep vegetables. How did your potatoes get frozen?"

"We get from Mr. Bushy, at the post-office—what he throw out. We got no potatoes, Mrs. Burden," Tony admitted mournfully.

When Jake went out, Marek crawled along the floor and stuffed up the door-crack again. Then, quietly as a shadow, Mr. Shimerda came out from behind the stove. He stood brushing his hand over his smooth grey hair, as if he were trying to clear away a fog about his head. He was clean and neat as usual, with his green neckcloth and his coral pin. He took grandmother's arm and led her behind the stove, to the back of the room. In the rear wall was another little cave; a round hole, not much bigger than an oil barrel, scooped out in the black earth. When I got up on one of the stools and peered into it, I saw some quilts and a pile of straw. The old man held the lantern. "Yulka," he said in a low, despairing voice, "Yulka; my Antonia!"

Grandmother drew back. "You mean they sleep in there—your girls?" He bowed his head.

Tony slipped under his arm. "It is very cold on the floor, and this is warm like the badger hole. I like for sleep there," she insisted eagerly. "My *mamenka* have nice bed, with pillows from our own geese in Bohemie. See, Jim?" She pointed to the narrow bunk which Krajiek had built against the wall for himself before the Shimerdas came.

Grandmother sighed, "Sure enough, where *would* you sleep, dear! I don't doubt you're warm there. You'll have a better house after while, Antonia, and then you will forget these hard times.". . .

"Amber Waves of Grain"

C. C. Coffin

*Individual homesteaders were not alone in developing agri-
culture on the Great Plains. In the Dakotas and Minnesota,
the railroads sold large tracts of the land that had been granted
to them as a subsidy by the state and federal governments.
Individual investors and land companies acquired holdings of
thousands of acres, and bonanza wheat farming—an early form
of agribusiness—became well established in the area in the late
1870s.*

*This large-scale farming represented the application to agri-
culture of big business techniques that were being applied in
the industrial sector of the economy: large capital investment,
absentee ownership, professional management, specialized
production, and mechanization. The bonanza farms of the
northern plains were usually subdivided, with a local foreman
responsible for each subdivision. Transient laborers were employed during planting, harvesting, and threshing time;
skeleton crews were retained year-round to care for the
livestock.*

*The following article by C. C. Coffin, a correspondent for
Harper's New Monthly Magazine, describes the bonanza farms
during one of their peak years. Articles such as this did much
to publicize the Dakota area and increase land values there, but
the success reported by Coffin was probably the exception
rather than the rule. Such problems as fluctuating market
prices, variable weather, and crop damage from insects often
resulted in insufficient income to carry the heavy capital outlay
of large-scale organization. In many cases the bonanza farms
resorted to selling land to small-scale farmers, whose crops were
more diversified and operating costs far lower than those of the
single-crop wheat farmers.*

Ride over these fertile acres of Dakota, and behold the working of this
latest triumph of American genius. You are in a sea of wheat. On the farms
managed by Oliver Dalrymple are 13,000 acres in one field. There are other
farmers who cultivate from 160 to 6000 acres. The railroad train rolls
through an ocean of grain. Pleasant the music of the rippling waves as the
west wind sweeps over the expanse. We encounter a squadron of war chariots, not such as once swept over the Delta of the Nile in pursuit of an

From C. C. Coffin, "Dakota Wheat Fields," *Harper's New Monthly Magazine,* LX:533–535
(March, 1880).

army of fugitive Israelites, not such as the warriors of Rome were wont to drive, with glittering knives projecting from the axles to mow a swath through the ranks of an enemy, to drench the ground with blood, to cut down the human race, as if men were noxious weeds, but chariots of peace, doing the work of human hands for the sustenance of men. There are twenty-five of them in this one brigade of the grand army of 115, under the marshalship of this Dakota farmer. A superintendent upon a superb horse, like a brigadier directing his forces, rides along the line, accompanied by his staff of two on horseback. They are fully armed and equipped, not with swords, but the implements of peace—wrenches, hammers, chisels. They are surgeons in waiting, with nuts and screws, or whatever may be needed.

This brigade of horse artillery sweeps by in echelon—in close order, reaper following reaper. There is a sound of wheels. The grain disappears an instant, then reappears; iron arms clasp it, hold it a moment in their embrace, wind it with wire, then toss it disdainfully at your feet. You hear in the rattling of the wheels the mechanism saying to itself, ''See how easy I can do it!''

An army of ''shockers'' follow the reapers, setting up the bundles to ripen before threshing. The reaping must ordinarily all be done in fifteen days, else the grain becomes too ripe. The first fields harvested, therefore, are cut before the ripening is complete. Each reaper averages about fifteen acres per day, and is drawn by three horses or mules.

The reaping ended, threshing begins. Again memory goes back to early years, to the pounding out of the grain upon the threshing-floor with the flail—the slow, tedious work of the winter days. Poets no more will rehearse the music of the flail. The picture for February in the old *Farmer's Almanac* is obsolete. September is the month for threshing, the thresher doing its 600 or 700 bushels per day, driven by a steam-engine of sixteen horse-power. Remorseless that sharp-toothed devourer, swallowing its food as fast as two men can cut the wire bands, requiring six teams to supply its demands! And what a cataract of grain pours from its spout, faster than two men can bag it!

The latest triumph of invention in this direction is a straw-burning engine, utilizing the stalks of the grain for fuel.

The cost of raising wheat per bushel is from thirty-five to forty cents; the average yield, from twenty to twenty-five bushels per acre. The nearness of these lands to Lake Superior, and the rates established by the railroad—fifteen cents per bushel from any point between Bismarck and Duluth—give the Dakota farmers a wide margin of profit.

Since the first furrow was turned in the Red River Valley, in 1870, there has been no failure of crops from drought, excessive rains, blight, mildew, rust, or other influence of climatology. The chinch-bug has not made its appearance; the grasshoppers alone have troubled the farmers, but they have disappeared, and the fields are smiling with bounty. With good tilth, the farmer may count upon a net return of from eight to ten dollars per acre per annum. The employment of capital has accomplished a beneficent end, by demonstrating that the region, instead of being incapable of settlement, is one of the fairest sections of the continent. Nor is it a wonder that the land-offices are besieged by emigrants making entries, or that the surveyors find the lands ''squatted'' upon before they can survey them; that hotels are crowded; that on every hand there is activity. During the months of May, June, and July, 1879, the sales of government land were nearly 700,000 acres, and the entries for the year will probably aggregate 1,500,000, taken in homestead, pre-emption, and tree claims. There are other millions of acres, as fair and fertile, yet to be occupied.

Silver Fever

Mark Twain

The search for wealth had inspired most of the European voyages of exploration from the fifteenth to seventeenth century, but only the Spanish Conquistadores had found the sudden riches of precious metals in the New World. The territory that is now the United States yielded her riches more slowly—in the form of pelts, timber, and farm products—until 1848. With the discovery that year of gold in California, the dream of sudden wealth was revived. Some 80,000 forty-niners poured into California from all over the United States, and from Europe, Asia, Latin America, and Australia as well. Within the decade, the California gold fields had yielded $555 million. From 1848 until 1874, the year of the last strike in South Dakota, the scene of the gold rush was repeated all along the mining frontier: in Nevada, Colorado, Arizona, Wyoming, Montana, Idaho, Washington, and South Dakota. Within these thirty years, most of the area west of the farmer's frontier had been penetrated.

As the surface metals were quickly extracted in each area, most of the prospectors moved on in search of new strikes of gold and silver. Ironically, they left behind the great bulk of the precious metals, which remained embedded in rock; heavy equipment and capital were needed to extract them, and the mining frontier of the individual soon gave way to the corporate frontier of big business.

During its heyday, the mining camp was populated by some of the most colorful, lawless elements in American history. Relatively few struck it rich; some realized modest returns after months of hard work; and many went broke. But gold and silver fever were catching, as Mark Twain points out in the following selection, and those who were smitten could not resist.

By and by I was smitten with the silver fever. "Prospecting parties" were leaving for the mountains every day, and discovering and taking possession of rich silver-bearing lodes and ledges of quartz. Plainly this was the road to fortune. The great "Gould and Curry" mine was held at three or four

From Mark Twain, *Roughing It* (Hartford, Conn.: American Publishing Co., 1872).

hundred dollars a foot when we arrived; but in two months it had sprung up to eight hundred. The "Ophir" had been worth only a mere trifle, a year gone by, and now it was selling at nearly *four thousand dollars a foot!* Not a mine could be named that had not experienced an astonishing advance in value within a short time. Everybody was talking about these marvels. Go where you would, you heard nothing else, from morning till far into the night. Tom So-and-So had sold out of the "Amanda Smith" for $40,000—hadn't a cent when he "took up" the ledge six months ago. John Jones had sold half his interest in the "Bald Eagle and Mary Ann" for $65,000, gold coin, and gone to the States for his family. The widow Brewster had "struck it rich" in the "Golden Fleece" and sold ten feet for $18,000—hadn't money enough to buy a crape bonnet when Sing-Sing Tommy killed her husband at Baldy Johnson's wake last spring. The "Last Chance" had found a "clay casing" and knew they were "right on the ledge"— consequence, "feet" that went begging yesterday were worth a brick house apiece to-day, and seedy owners who could not get trusted for a drink at any bar in the country yesterday were roaring drunk on champagne today and had hosts of warm personal friends in a town where they had forgotten how to bow or shake hands from long-continued want of practice. . . . And so on—day in and day out the talk pelted our ears and the excitement waxed hotter and hotter around us.

I would have been more or less than human if I had not gone mad like the rest. Cart-loads of solid silver bricks, as large as pigs of lead, were arriving from the mills every day, and such sights as that gave substance to the wild talk about me. I succumbed and grew as frenzied as the craziest.

Every few days news would come of the discovery of a brand-new mining region; immediately the papers would teem with accounts of its richness, and away the surplus population would scamper to take possession. By the time I was fairly inoculated with the disease, "Esmeralda" had just had a run and "Humboldt" was beginning to shriek for attention. "Humboldt! Humboldt!" was the new cry. . . . That the reader may see what moved me, and what would as surely have moved him had he been there, I insert here one of the newspaper letters of the day . . . just as it appeared in the *Daily Territorial Enterprise:*

> But what about our mines? I shall be candid with you. I shall express an honest opinion, based upon a thorough examination. Humboldt County is the richest mineral region upon God's foot-stool. Each mountain range is gorged with the precious ores. Humboldt is the true Golconda.
>
> The other day an assay of mere *croppings* yielded exceeding *four thousand dollars to the ton.* A week or two ago an assay of just such surface developments made returns of *seven thousand* dollars to the ton. Our mountains are full of rambling prospectors. Each day and almost every hour reveals new and more startling evidences of the profuse and intensified wealth of our favored county. The metal is not silver alone. There are distinct ledges of auriferous ore. A late discovery plainly evinces cinnabar. The coarser metals are in gross abundance. Lately evidences of bituminous coal have been detected. . . . Have no fears of the mineral resources of Humboldt County. They are immense— incalculable.

Let me state one or two things which will help the reader to better comprehend certain items in the above. At this time, our near neighbor, Gold Hill, was the most successful silver-mining locality in Nevada. It was from there that more than half the daily shipments of silver bricks came. "Very rich" (and scarce) Gold Hill ore yielded from $100 to $400 to the ton; but the usual yield was only $20 to $40 per ton—that is to say, each hundred pounds of ore yielded from one dollar to two dollars. But the reader will perceive by the above extract, that in Humboldt from one-fourth to nearly half the mass was silver! That is to say, every one hundred pounds of the ore had from *two hundred* dollars up to about *three hundred and fifty* in it. Some days later this same correspondent wrote:

> I have spoken of the vast and almost fabulous wealth of this region—it is incredible. The intestines of our mountains are gorged with precious ore to plethora. I have said that nature has so shaped our mountains as to furnish most excellent facilities for the working of our mines. I have also told you that the country about here is pregnant with the finest mill sites in the world. . . .
>
> A very common calculation is that many of our mines will yield five hundred dollars to the ton. Such fecundity throws the Gould & Curry, the Ophir and the Mexican, of your neighborhood, in the darkest shadow. I have given you the estimate of the value of a single developed mine. Its richness is indexed by its market valuation. The people of Humboldt County are *feet* crazy. As I write, our towns are near deserted. They look as languid as a consumptive girl. What has become of our sinewy and athletic fellow-citizens? They are coursing through ravines and over mountain-tops. Their tracks are visible in every direction. Occasionally a horseman will dash among us. His steed betrays hard usage. He alights before his adobe dwelling, hastily exchanges courtesies with his townsmen, hurries to an assay office and from thence to the District Recorder's. In the morning, having renewed his provisional supplies, he is off again on his wild and unbeaten route. Why, the fellow numbers already his feet by the thousands. He is the horse-leech. He has the craving stomach of the shark or anaconda. He would conquer metallic worlds.

This was enough. The instant we had finished reading the above article, four of us decided to go to Humboldt. We commenced getting ready at once. And we also commenced upbraiding ourselves for not deciding sooner—for we were in terror lest all the rich mines would be found and secured before we got there, and we might have to put up with ledges that would not yield more than two or three hundred dollars a ton, maybe. . . .

*   *   *

Hurry, was the word! We wasted no time. Our party consisted of four persons—a blacksmith sixty years of age, two young lawyers, and myself. We bought a wagon and two miserable old horses. We put eighteen hundred pounds of provisions and mining-tools in the wagon and drove out of Carson on a chilly December afternoon. . . . Within the hour, we found that it would not only be better, but was absolutely necessary, that we four, taking turns, two at a time, should put our hands against the end of the wagon and push it through the sand, leaving the feeble horses little to do but keep out of the way and hold up the tongue. . . .

We were fifteen days making the trip—two hundred miles; thirteen, rather, for we lay by a couple of days, in one place, to let the horses rest. . . .

It was a hard, wearing, toilsome journey, but it had its bright side; for after each day was done and our wolfish hunger appeased with a hot supper of fried bacon, bread, molasses, and black coffee, the pipe-smoking, song-singing, and yarn-spinning around the evening camp-fire in the still solitudes of the desert was a happy, care-free sort of recreation that seemed the very summit and culmination of earthly luxury. It is a kind of life that has a potent charm for all men, whether city or country bred. . . .

*   *   *

After leaving the Sink, we traveled along the Humboldt River a little way. People accustomed to the monster, mile-wide Mississippi, grow accustomed to associating the term "river" with a high degree of watery grandeur. Consequently, such people feel rather disappointed when they stand on the shores of the Humboldt or the Carson and find that a "river" in Nevada is a sickly rivulet which is just the counterpart of the Erie canal in all respects save that the canal is twice as long and four times as deep. One of the pleasantest and most invigorating exercises one can contrive is to run and jump across the Humboldt River till he is overheated, and then drink it dry.

On the fifteenth day we completed our march of two hundred miles and entered Unionville, Humboldt County, in the midst of a driving snowstorm. Unionville consisted of eleven cabins and a liberty pole. Six of the cabins were strung along one side of a deep cañon, and the other five faced them. The rest of the landscape was made up of bleak mountain walls that rose so high into the sky from both sides of the cañon that the village was left, as it were, far down in the bottom of a crevice. It was always daylight on the mountain-tops a long time before the darkness lifted and revealed Unionville.

We built a small, rude cabin in the side of the crevice and roofed it with canvas, leaving a corner open to serve as a chimney, through which the cattle used to tumble occasionally, at night, and mash our furniture and interrupt our sleep. It was very cold weather and fuel was scarce. Indians brought brush and bushes several miles on their backs; and when we could catch a laden Indian it was well—and when we could not (which was the rule, not the exception), we shivered and bore it.

I confess, without shame, that I expected to find masses of silver lying all about the ground. I expected to see it glittering in the sun on the mountain summits. I said nothing about this, for some instinct told me that I might possibly have an exaggerated idea about it, and so if I betrayed my thought I might bring derision upon myself. Yet I was as perfectly satisfied in my own mind as I could be of anything, that I was going to gather up, in a day or two, or at furthest a week or two, silver enough to make me satisfactorily wealthy—and so my fancy was already busy with plans for spending this money. The first opportunity that offered, . . . I began my search with a feverish excitement that was brimful of expectation—almost of certainty. I crawled about the ground, seizing and examining bits of stone, blowing the dust from them or rubbing them on my clothes, and then peering at them with anxious hope. Presently I found a bright fragment and my heart bounded! . . . Up and down the rugged mountainside I searched, with always increasing interest and always augmenting gratitude that I had come to Humboldt and come in time. Of all the experiences of my life, this secret search among the hidden treasures of silver-land was the nearest to unmarred ecstasy. It was a delirious revel. By and by, in the bed of a shallow rivulet, I found a deposit of shining yellow scales, and my breath almost forsook me! A gold-mine, and in my simplicity I had been content with vulgar silver! I was so excited that I half believed my overwrought imagination was deceiving me. Then a fear came upon me that people might be observing me and would guess my secret. Moved by this thought, I made a circuit of the place, and ascended a knoll to reconnoiter. Solitude. . . . At last the descending sun warned me to give up the quest, and I turned homeward laden with wealth. As I walked along I could not help smiling at the thought of my being so excited over my fragment of silver when a nobler metal was almost under my nose. In this little time the former had so fallen in my estimation that once or twice I was on the point of throwing it away.

The boys were as hungry as usual, but I could eat nothing. Neither could I talk. I was full of dreams and far away. . . . It was hard to resist the impulse to burst out with exultation and reveal everything; but I did resist. I said within myself that I would filter the great news through my lips calmly and be serene as a summer morning while I watched its effect in their faces. I said:

"Where have you all been?"

"Prospecting."

"What did you find?"

"Nothing."

"Nothing? What do you think of the country?"

"Can't tell, yet," said Mr. Ballou, who was an old gold-miner, and had likewise had considerable experience among the silver-mines. . . . "It's fair enough here, maybe, but overrated. Seven-thousand-dollar ledges are scarce, though. That Sheba may be rich enough, but we don't own it; and, besides, the rock is so full of base metals that all the science in the world can't work it. We'll not starve, here, but we'll not get rich, I'm afraid."

"So you think the prospect is pretty poor?"

"No name for it!"

"Well, we'd better go back, hadn't we?"

"Oh, not yet—of course not. We'll try it a riffle, first." . . .

". . . But just for the sake of argument, suppose—in a kind of general way—suppose some person were to tell you that two-thousand-dollar ledges were simply contemptible—contemptible, understand—and that right yonder in sight of this very cabin there were piles of pure gold and pure silver—oceans of it—enough to make you all rich in twenty-four hours! Come!"

"I should say he was as crazy as a loon!" said old Ballou, but wild with excitement, nevertheless.

"Gentlemen," said I, "I don't say anything—I haven't been around, you know, and of course don't know anything—but all I ask of you is to cast your eye on *that*, for instance, and tell me what you think of it!" and I tossed my treasure before them.

There was an eager scrabble for it, and a closing of heads together over it under the candle-light. Then old Ballou said:

"Think of it? I think it is nothing but a lot of granite rubbish and nasty glittering mica that isn't worth ten cents an acre!"

So vanished my dream. So melted my wealth away. So toppled my airy castle to the earth and left me stricken and forlorn.

Moralizing, I observed, then, that "all that glitters is not gold."

Mr. Ballou said I could go further than that, and lay it up among my treasures of knowledge, that *nothing* that glitters is gold. So I learned then, once for all, that gold in its native state is but dull, unornamental stuff, and that only low-born metals excite the admiration of the ignorant with an ostentatious glitter. However, like the rest of the world, I still go on underrating men of gold and glorifying men of mica. Commonplace human nature cannot rise above that.

*   *   *

True knowledge of the nature of silver-mining came fast enough. We went out "prospecting" with Mr. Ballou. We climbed the mountainsides, and clambered among sage-brush, rocks, and snow till we were ready to drop with exhaustion, but found no silver—nor yet any gold. Day after day we did this. Now and then we came upon holes burrowed a few feet into the declivities and apparently abandoned; and now and then we found one or two listless men still burrowing. But there was no appearance of silver. These holes were the beginnings of tunnels, and the purpose was to drive them hundreds of feet into the mountain, and some day tap the hidden ledge where the silver was. Some day! It seemed far enough away, and very hopeless and dreary. Day after day we toiled, and climbed, and searched, and we younger partners grew sicker and still sicker of the promiseless toil. At last we halted under a bettling rampart of rock which projected from the earth high upon the mountain. Mr. Ballou broke off some fragments with a hammer, and examined them long and attentively with a small eyeglass; threw them away and broke off more; said this rock was quartz, and quartz was the sort of rock that contained silver. *Contained* it! I had thought that at least it would be caked on the outside of it like a kind of veneering. He still broke off pieces and critically examined them, now and then wetting the piece with his tongue and applying the glass. At last he exclaimed:

"We've got it!"

We were full of anxiety in a moment. The rock was clean and white, where it was broken, and across it ran a ragged thread of blue. He said that that little thread had silver in it, mixed with base metals, such as lead and antimony, and other rubbish, and that there was a speck or two of gold visible. After a great deal of effort we managed to discern some little fine yellow specks, and judged that a couple of tons of them massed together might make a gold dollar, possibly. We were not jubilant, but Mr. Ballou said there were worse ledges in the world than that. He saved what he called the "richest" piece of the rock, in order to determine its value by the process called the "fire-assay." Then we named the mine "Monarch of the

Mountains'' (modesty of nomenclature is not a prominent feature in the mines), and Mr. Ballou wrote out and stuck up the following "notice," preserving a copy to be entered upon the books in the mining recorder's office in the town.

NOTICE
We the undersigned claim three claims, of three hundred feet each (and one for discovery), on this silver-bearing quartz lead or lode, extending north and south from this notice, with all its dips, spurs, and angles, variations and sinuosities, together with fifty feet of ground on either side for working the same.

We put our names to it and tried to feel that our fortunes were made. But when we talked the matter all over with Mr. Ballou, we felt depressed and dubious. He said that this surface quartz was not all there was of our mine; but that the wall or ledge of rock called the "Monarch of the Mountains" extended down hundreds and hundreds of feet into the earth. . . . And he said that down in the great depths of the ledge was its richness, and the deeper it went the richer it grew. Therefore, instead of working here on the surface, we must either bore down into the rock with a shaft till we came to where it was rich—say a hundred feet or so—or else we must go down into the valley and bore a long tunnel into the mountainside and tap the ledge far under the earth. To do either was plainly the labor of months; for we could blast and bore only a few feet a day—some five or six. But this was not all. He said that after we got the ore out it must be hauled in wagons to a distant silver-mill, ground up, and the silver extracted by a tedious and costly process. Our fortune seemed a century away!

But we went to work. We decided to sink a shaft. So, for a week we climbed the mountain, laden with picks, drills, gads, crowbars, shovels, cans of blasting-powder and coils of fuse, and strove with might and main. At first the rock was broken and loose, and we dug it up with picks and threw it out with shovels, and the hole progressed very well. But the rock became more compact, presently, and gads and crowbars came into play. But shortly nothing could make an impression but blasting-powder. That was the weariest work! One of us held the iron drill in its place and another would strike with an eight-pound sledge—it was like driving nails on a large scale. In the course of an hour or two the drill would reach a depth of two or three feet, making a hole a couple of inches in diameter. We would put in a charge of powder, insert half a yard of fuse, pour in sand and gravel and ram it down, then light the fuse and run. When the explosion came and the rocks and smoke shot into the air, we would go back and find about a bushel of that hard, rebellious quartz jolted out. Nothing more. One week of this satisfied me. I resigned. Claggett and Oliphant followed. Our shaft was only twelve feet deep. We decided that a tunnel was the thing we wanted.

So we went down the mountainside and worked a week; at the end of which time we had blasted a tunnel about deep enough to hide a hogshead in, and judged that about nine hundred feet more of it would reach the ledge. I resigned again, and the other boys only held out one day longer. We decided that a tunnel was not what we wanted. We wanted a ledge that was already "developed." There were none in the camp.

We dropped the "Monarch" for the time being. Meantime the camp was filling up with people, and there was a constantly growing excitement about our Humboldt mines. We fell victims to the epidemic and strained every nerve to acquire more "feet." We prospected and took up new claims, put "notices" on them, and gave them grandiloquent names. We traded some of our "feet" for "feet" in other people's claims. In a little while we owned largely in the "Gray Eagle," the "Columbiana," the "Branch Mint," the "Maria Jane," the "Universe," the "Root-Hog-or-Die," the "Samson and Delilah," the "Treasure Trove," the "Golconda," the "Sultana," the "Boomerang," the "Great Republic," the "Grand Mogul," and fifty other "mines" that had never been molested by a shovel or scratched with a pick. We had not less than thirty thousand "feet" apiece in the "richest mines on earth" as the frenzied cant phrased it—and were in debt to the butcher. We were stark mad with excitement—drunk with happiness—smothered under mountains of prospective wealth—arrogantly compassionate toward the plodding millions who knew not our marvelous cañon—but our credit was not good at the grocer's.

It was the strangest phase of life one can imagine. It was a beggars' revel. There was nothing doing in the district—no mining—no milling—no productive effort—no income—and not enough money in the entire camp to buy a corner lot in an eastern village, hardly; and yet a stranger would have supposed he was walking among bloated millionaires. Prospecting parties swarmed out of town with the first flush of dawn, and swarmed in again at nightfall laden with spoil—rocks. Nothing but rocks. Every man's pockets were full of them; the floor of his cabin was littered with them; they were disposed in labeled rows on his shelves.

Paper Farmers
and Hungry Hordes

John Steinbeck

Almost ninety years after the gold rush of '49, California was again the destination of a westward rush—"a gold rush for work," as the novelist John Steinbeck has called it. The migrants came by the hundreds of thousands, trekking overland in jalopies heaped high with household possessions and children. Most came from Arkansas, Texas, Missouri, and Oklahoma, driven out by dust storms or "tractored out" from their tenant farms when the South, under the impact of New Deal farm policies, turned toward the mechanization of agriculture—long after it had been applied in other parts of the country.

In California, large-scale agriculture had prevailed ever since the 1850s and 1860s, when huge Mexican land claims and railroad land grants had been acquired by wealthy individuals and corporate enterprises. Americans grazed large herds of cattle on ranchos; the bonanza wheat fields of Minnesota and the Dakotas had their counterpart in California; the citrus industry became so successful that the California Fruit Growers Exchange was formed in 1905 to market the increasing crop; and by the early twentieth century the widespread use of irrigation was leading to greatly expanded fruit and vegetable yields. California therefore had little to offer the dispossessed farmers of the 1930s. Many became agricultural laborers; countless others went on the relief rolls.

The story of the migrants' journey to California has been immortalized by John Steinbeck in The Grapes of Wrath. *In the excerpt below, he contrasts the attitudes toward the land of the "Arkies and Okies," for whom the soil meant life and food, with those of the large corporate owners, for whom it was an impersonal source of profit.*

Once California belonged to Mexico and its land to Mexicans; and a horde of tattered feverish Americans poured in. And such was their hunger for land that they took the land—stole Sutter's land, Guerrero's land, took the grants and broke them up and growled and quarreled over them, those frantic hungry men; and they guarded with guns the land they had stolen. They put up houses and barns, they turned the earth and planted crops. And these things were possession, and possession was ownership.

The Mexicans were weak and fled. They could not resist, because they wanted nothing in the world as frantically as the Americans wanted land.

Then, with time, the squatters were no longer squatters, but owners; and their children grew up and had children on the land. And the hunger was gone from them, the feral hunger, the gnawing, tearing hunger for land, for water and earth and the good sky over it, for the green thrusting grass, for the swelling roots. They had these things so completely that they did not know about them any more. They had no more the stomach-tearing lust for a rich acre and a shining blade to plow it, for seed and a windmill beating its wings in the air. They arose in the dark no more to hear the sleepy birds' first chittering, and the morning wind around the house while they waited for the first light to go out to the dear acres. These things were lost, and crops were reckoned in dollars, and land was valued by principal plus interest, and crops were bought and sold before they were planted. Then crop failure, drought, and flood were no longer little deaths within life, but simple losses of money. And all their love was thinned with money, and all their fierceness dribbled away in interest until they were no longer farmers at all, but little shopkeepers of crops, little manufacturers who must sell before they can make. Then those farmers who were not good shopkeepers lost their land to good shopkeepers. No matter how clever, how loving a man might be with earth and growing things, he could not survive if he were not also a good shopkeeper. And as time went on, the business men had the farms, and the farms grew larger, but there were fewer of them.

Now farming became industry, and the owners followed Rome, although they did not know it. They imported slaves, although they did not call them slaves: Chinese, Japanese, Mexicans, Filipinos. They live on rice and beans, the business men said. They don't need much. They wouldn't know what to do with good wages. Why, look how they live. Why, look what they eat. And if they get funny—deport them.

And all the time the farms grew larger and the owners fewer. And there were pitifully few farmers on the land any more. And the imported serfs were beaten and frightened and starved until some went home again, and some grew fierce and were killed or driven from the country. And the farms grew larger and the owners fewer.

And the crops changed. Fruit trees took the place of grain fields, and vegetables to feed the world spread out on the bottoms: lettuce, cauliflower, artichokes, potatoes—stoop crops. A man may stand to use a scythe, a plow, a pitchfork; but he must crawl like a bug between the rows of lettuce, he must bend his back and pull his long bag between the cotton rows, he must go on his knees like a penitent across a cauliflower patch.

And it came about that owners no longer worked on their farms. They farmed on paper; and they forgot the land, the smell, the feel of it, and remembered only that they owned it, remembered only what they gained and lost by it. And some of the farms grew so large that one man could not even conceive of them any more, so large that it took batteries of bookkeepers to keep track of interest and gain and loss; chemists to test the soil, to replenish; straw bosses to see that the stooping men were moving along the rows as swiftly as the material of their bodies could stand. Then such a farmer really became a storekeeper, and kept a store. He paid the men, and sold them food, and took the money back. And after a while he did not pay the men at all, and saved bookkeeping. These farms gave food on credit. A man might work and feed himself; and when the work was done, he might find that he owed money to the company. And the owners not only did not work the farms any more, many of them had never seen the farms they owned.

And then the dispossessed were drawn west—from Kansas, Oklahoma, Texas, New Mexico; from Nevada and Arkansas families, tribes, dusted out, tractored out. Carloads, caravans, homeless and hungry; twenty thousand and fifty thousand and a hundred thousand and two hundred thousand. They streamed over the mountains, hungry and restless—restless as ants, scurrying to find work to do—to lift, to push, to pull, to pick, to cut—anything, any burden to bear, for food. The kids are hungry. We got no place to live. Like ants scurrying for work, for food, and most of all for land.

We ain't foreign. Seven generations back Americans, and beyond that Irish, Scotch, English, German. One of our folks in the Revolution, an' they was lots of our folks in the Civil War—both sides. Americans.

They were hungry, and they were fierce. And they had hoped to find a home, and they found only hatred. Okies—the owners hated them because the owners knew they were soft and the Okies strong, that they were fed and the Okies hungry; and perhaps the owners had heard from their grandfathers how easy it is to steal land from a soft man if you are fierce and hungry and armed. The owners hated them. And in the towns, the storekeepers hated them because they had no money to spend. There is no shorter path to a storekeeper's contempt, and all his admirations are exactly opposite. The town men, little bankers, hated Okies because there was nothing to gain from them. They had nothing. And the laboring people hated Okies because a hungry man must work, and if he must work, if he has to work, the wage payer automatically gives him less for his work; and then no one can get more.

And the dispossessed, the migrants, flowed into California, two hundred and fifty thousand, and three hundred thousand. Behind them new tractors were going on the land and the tenants were being forced off. And new waves were on the way, new waves of the dispossessed and the homeless, hardened, intent, and dangerous.

And while the Californians wanted many things, accumulation, social success, amusement, luxury, and a curious banking security, the new barbarians wanted only two things—land and food; and to them the two were one. And whereas the wants of the Californians were nebulous and undefined, the wants of the Okies were beside the roads, lying there to be seen and coveted: the good fields with water to be dug for, the good green fields, earth to crumble experimentally in the hand, grass to smell, oaten stalks to chew until the sharp sweetness was in the throat. A man might look at a fallow field and know, and see in his mind that his own bending back and his own straining arms would bring the cabbages into the light, and the golden eating corn, the turnips and carrots.

And a homeless hungry man, driving the roads with his wife beside him and his thin children in the back seat, could look at the fallow fields which might produce food but not profit, and that man could know how a fallow field is a sin and the unused land a crime against the thin children. And such a man drove along the roads and knew temptation at every field, and knew the lust to take these fields and make them grow strength for his children and a little comfort for his wife. The temptation was before him always. The fields goaded him, and the company ditches with good water flowing were a goad to him.

And in the south he saw the golden oranges hanging on the trees, the little golden oranges on the dark green trees; and guards with shotguns patrolling the lines so a man might not pick an orange for a thin child, oranges to be dumped if the price was low.

He drove his car into a town. He scoured the farms for work. Where can we sleep the night?

Well, there's Hooverville on the edge of the river. There's a whole raft of Okies there.

He drove his old car to Hooverville. He never asked again, for there was a Hooverville on the edge of every town.

The rag town lay close to water; and the houses were tents, and weed-thatched enclosures, paper houses, a great junk pile. The man drove his family in and became a citizen of Hooverville—always they were called Hooverville. The man put up his own tent as near to water as he could get; or if he had no tent, he went to the city dump and brought back cartons and built a house of corrugated paper. And when the rains came the house melted and washed away. He settled in Hooverville and he scoured the countryside for work, and the little money he had went for gasoline to look for work. In the evening the men gathered and talked together. Squatting on their hams they talked of the land they had seen.

There's thirty thousan' acres, out west of here. Layin' there. Jesus, what I could do with that, with five acres of that! Why, hell, I'd have ever' thing to eat.

Notice one thing? They ain't no vegetables nor chickens nor pigs at the farms. They raise one thing—cotton, say, or peaches, or lettuce. 'Nother place'll be all chickens. They buy the stuff they could raise in the dooryard.

Jesus, what I could do with a couple pigs!

Well, it ain't yourn, an' it aint' gonna be yourn.

What we gonna do? The kids can't grow up this way.

In the camps the word would come whispering, There's work at Shafter. And the cars would be loaded in the night, the highways crowded—a gold rush for work. At Shafter the people would pile up, five times too many to do the work. A gold rush for work. They stole away in the night, frantic for work. And along the roads lay the temptations, the fields that could bear food.

That's owned. That ain't our'n.

Well, maybe we could get a little piece of her. Maybe—a little piece. Right down there—a patch. Jimson weed now. Christ, I could git enough potatoes off'n that little patch to feed my whole family!

It ain't our'n. It got to have Jimson weeds.

Now and then a man tried; crept on the land and cleared a piece, trying like a thief to steal a little richness from the earth. Secret gardens hidden in the weeds. A package of carrot seeds and a few turnips. Planted potato skins, crept out in the evening secretly to hoe in the stolen earth.

Leave the weeds around the edge—then nobody can see what we're a-doin'. Leave some weeds, big tall ones, in the middle.

Secret gardening in the evenings, and water carried in a rusty can.

And then one day a deputy sheriff: Well, what you think you're doin'?

I ain't doin' no harm.

I had my eye on you. This ain't your land. You're trespassing.

The land ain't plowed, an' I ain't hurtin' it none.

You goddamned squatters. Pretty soon you'd think you owned it. You'd be sore as hell. Think you owned it. Get off now.

And the little green carrot tops were kicked off and the turnip greens trampled. And then the Jimson weed moved back in. But the cop was right. A crop raised—why, that makes ownership. Land hoed and the carrots eaten—a man might fight for land hes taken food from. Get him off quick! He'll think he owns it. He might even die fighting for the little plot among the Jimson weeds. . . .

Patterns of Space

John Brinckerhoff Jackson

The grid pattern of land surveys that had been superimposed on the natural landscape since 1785 proved ill-adapted to the semi-arid terrain of the High Plains and to the kinds of agriculture that developed there and in California: cattle and sheep ranching and large-scale wheat farming. Ranchers accustomed to grazing their livestock on the public domain were unable to keep their herds on 160-acre homesteads. Nor could the new agricultural machines be economically applied to small-scale farming. In the years following the Civil War, therefore, Americans began to develop new methods of organizing space. Congress passed several laws modifying the Homestead Act and permitting individuals to acquire land, free or at low prices, beyond the 160-acre quarter section. And land that could not be acquired legally to make up a large holding was frequently obtained by fraudulent claims.

The demand for increasingly efficient agriculture was stimulated by an increasingly industrialized and urbanized population. Yet as John B. Jackson, long-time editor of Landscape *magazine, points out in the following article, the growth of urban and suburban communities also required new ways of thinking about the land. The efforts of landscape architects to plan for small suburban lots were in striking contrast to the efforts of ranchers and farmers to expand their holdings; but both elements contributed to the changing organizaion of the American environment.*

The tendency of certain forms and spaces to increase in size, either by expansion or consolidation, accounted for many of the changes in the American landscape in the postwar* years. Another tendency, closely related to it but distinct in origin, was also at work: the defining (or redefining) of spaces in terms of "natural" boundaries. It manifested itself in two widely separated fields of spatial organization: in the design of parks and gardens and suburbs, and in the layout of farms and ranches in the West.

Ed. note: The author is referring to the Civil War.

The selection (pp. 25–30) is reprinted from *American Space: The Centennial Years; 1865–1876*, by John Brinckerhoff Jackson, with the permission of the publisher, W. W. Norton & Company, Inc. Copyright © 1972 by W. W. Norton & Company, Inc.

The preference for "natural" boundaries ran counter to the well-established American tradition of artificial or man-made boundaries. West of the Appalachians almost every boundary had been determined by the grid: that pattern of sections, townships, ranges imposed by the Land Survey of 1785. The great majority of the states, territories, counties, and townships—to say nothing of individual holdings—were defined by survey lines running due north and south, east and west. A map of any large section of the United States, even today, resembles an immense composition of squares and rectangles, regardless of the nature of the terrain or the type of exploitation.

The grid system of land subdivision is unpopular with many contemporary Americans, chiefly for esthetic reasons; yet it possessed and still possesses important virtues, political as well as economic, and in the early years of Western (and Midwestern) settlement it served the nation well; it expressed very clearly the general belief in equality of opportunity, and in the possession of land as one of the bases of citizenship. But that was in the day of the independent, more or less self-sufficient farm, and as settlement after the Civil War pushed into the Great Plains and beyond, and as farming became more of a commercial enterprise, the disregard of topography, the assumption that all pieces of land of the same size had the same value, became totally unrealistic.

This was especially true when farming invaded the relatively dry and treeless region west of the 100th meridian, which cuts through the western half of the Dakotas, Nebraska, and Kansas. Beyond that fateful line the climate changes radically; land without the presence or availability of surface water to supplement rainfall is unfit for agriculture, and the possession of a homestead as such means nothing. The square of 160 acres, so reassuring in the more humid East, has no fixed value on the Plains; often it does not suffice to feed a half dozen cows.

So it was water in one form or another that determined the size and location of a viable unit, whatever Washington supposed; it was topography that made land profitable or worthless. In the seventies a number of "colonies," of which Greeley was the largest and most successful, established themselves in eastern Colorado. The location which each of them chose was in a valley with a river, where irrigation could be practiced. The communities adapted themselves to the terrain, leaving the higher surrounding plains, in Horace Greeley's words, "to the half-savage herdsmen who rear cattle and sheep." They were defining their holdings in terms of physical characteristics, that is to say; and where those characteristics ceased, there they fixed their line of demarcation. Instead of all spaces being potentially equal, they fell into classifications based on natural features and natural boundaries.

Cattlemen defined their holdings in the same manner. A writer on Colorado as a prospective home for settlers in the 1870s explained the word "ranch" as "a term for a spring of water and some rude buildings, and an indefinite amount of grazing land."

So obvious was it that the old system of land subdivision did not suit the West that even the government began to see the need for classifying land in a different, more topographical way. It no longer served any useful purpose to lump all (or most) of the public domain under the heading of agricultural land, to be divided into rectangular holdings of 160 acres. Tentatively, and even reluctantly, Washington, beginning in 1866, undertook to classify lands according to physical characteristics, in terms of suitability for mining, farming, grazing, and so on.

It was not until 1909—more than a half century later—that a Land Classification Board was established, with the Geological Survey doing the field work. But the intervening steps, ineffectual though they may have been, serve to illustrate the growth of what was then a new concept of how to organize space. First it was the mining lands which were officially recognized as possessing distinct characteristics of their own; then it was land suited to irrigation, then forests, until much of the American landscape became a composition not only of political units but of natural environments. And was it not this new kind of definition of land that inspired the creation in 1872 of Yellowstone National Park? It was an environment with spectacular natural characteristics, and for that reason Congress set it aside as "a public park or pleasuring ground for the benefit and enjoyment of the people."

The man who most clearly formulated the new doctrine was Major John Wesley Powell. The first white man to descend the Colorado River, he was recognized as an authority on the geography of the desert Southwest and the culture of its Indian inhabitants. In 1870 he was commissioned by the Department of the Interior to undertake a Geographical and Geological Survey of the Rocky Mountain Region, and for the next seven years he and his small party explored and mapped the little-known Plateau region surrounding the Grand Canyon. In 1878 he finally submitted his report. Despite the fact that all the recommendations it contained were rejected by Congress and that many of his judgments were bitterly resented by Western publishers and politicians, Powell's *Report on the Arid Region of the United States* remains a document of exceptional importance, and it has been called "one of the most significant and seminal books ever written about the West."

It is neither long nor impressively erudite; it is a straightforward discussion of the climatic peculiarities of the desert Southwest and of the possibilities for agriculture in the region. Nowhere does Powell express any interest in its natural beauties or their preservation. Agriculture would be possible, he declared, under certain very restricted conditions: that the inhabitants practice a combination of ranching and irrigation farming on a limited scale, that they organize irrigation districts and form small communities or neighborhoods, and that they organize for the communal use of the range. He further stipulated that every rancher-farmer possess at least 2560 acres—or four square miles—most of which would be part of the community pasturelands.

. . . He rejected not only the traditional homestead of 160 acres but the rectilinear survey as well. The holdings were to be defined by the physical characteristics of the land: by the availability of water and range. Two points were repeatedly made: "The division of these lands should be controlled by topographic features," and "The people settling on these lands. . . should not be hampered with the present arbitrary system of dividing lands into rectangular tracts."

A minor point in Powell's proposals but an interesting one was his aversion to fencing the communal pastureland, on the somewhat implausible ground that it would cost too much. But Powell after all belonged to his generation, and along with many contemporaries he undoubtedly objected to the artificial boundary, the man-made definition of space. Across the continent, among the farmers of the Midwest and East, the same desire for innovation in the layout of fields was already apparent: mechanization had not only eliminated many walls and fences, it was also demanding its own special terrain. "The general use of the mowing machine," observed a contributor to *Rural Affairs* in 1865, "will, we trust, make for a great improvement in the external appearance of farms. Stumps, bushes, stone heaps, and obtruding rocks must disappear." And so they did in the course of time, setting the smooth mowed fields apart from the hillsides with their rocks and stumps; and with the planting of trees on the rough terrain the contrast between the physical characteristics of the various sections of the farm became all the greater.

The effect of a landscape of fields all conforming to the topography of the farm, none of them rigidly confined within straight lines, struck many as a great improvement over the former system of rectangular divisions. Somewhat diffidently a landscape architect suggested to the readers of a rural magazine that farms be laid out in an ornamental, not to say picturesque, manner: fields of an irregular shape, bounded by hedges or rows of trees, with gently curving carriage roads leading to the house and its neighboring barn. But the farm had to evolve in its own way, without benefit of advice from landscape architects. A countryside far more hospitable to their ideas was the new suburb. The challenge here was unmistakable: the average developer laid out the land in rectangular, more or less uniform lots with a grid pattern of streets. To transform this depressing spatial artificiality into a series of "natural" environments called for art and ingenuity. The first traditional element to be eliminated from the plan of the suburban property was the fence or wall; both had fallen into great disfavor among landscape architects and their prosperous clients. In the 1840s Emerson had quoted with approval the old New England dictum that good fences made good neighbors. A generation later the wall was seen not only as distinctly *un*-neighborly but even un-Christian. The most cherished feature of the suburban domain was not (as with the farm) its crops, but its privacy, its integrity as a domestic environment. Fences therefore played a different role: polite indications that a property line existed and was not to be casually crossed. "That kind of fence," said one landscape architect, "is best which is least seen and best seen through"— but which still suggested exclusion.

Frank Scott . . . wrote a book on *Suburban Home Grounds* in 1870, in which he discussed the landscaping problems of the commuter, "the man who must leave his home after an early breakfast to attend to his office or store business," and who had built a home on a suburban lot. Urging the suburbanite to eschew all pretensions of having a parklike estate with a vegetable garden, Scott offered as the ideal a composition of trees and lawn —trees as a tactful and natural-appearing boundary, lawn as a private and sheltered environment. . . . "The speculative habit of cutting up suburban lands into narrow city lots 25 x 100 feet," Scott declared, "or but little more, destroys all chance of making true suburban improvements. Such lots will only sell to citizens who are either too poor, too cockneyish, or too ignorant of their own needs to insist on something more."

The spatial reorganization underway on the farms and ranches of America, and proposed by Powell, was impressive because of the vast dimensions involved and the struggle for survival on the part of the hard-pressed men who urged it. By contrast the contribution of landscape architects, fussily detailed and inevitably influenced by fashion, seemed trivial. Nevertheless the new American landscape was the creation of many elements in society: farmers, ranchers, engineers; architects and landscape architects; and innumerable men and women working for urban and rural improvement. The spirit behind the new kind of space—expansive, free of the past, more and more involved with the transformation of the natural environment—derived from workaday America, but it was the artist who gave it form and meaning.

Stretching the City

Daniel J. Boorstin

"The United States was born in the country and has moved to the city," the historian Richard Hofstadter once observed. When the first census was taken in 1790, only 3.35 percent of the population lived in towns of 8,000 or more. But by 1890 ten times that percentage, or one third of the total population, lived in such urban communities. Cities had increased both in numbers and in size, and by 1900 there were six American cities of half a million or more. Urbanization was experienced in the industrialized nations of Western Europe as well as in the United States, but the rate of urban growth in America was greater. Most of the increase in the nineteenth century took place in the decades following the Civil War, and it was the result of two migrations: one from Europe to America, and one from the country to the city.

Urbanization was largely the outgrowth of industrialization. The factory system required large concentrations of workers, and the mechanization of agriculture made it possible for millions of people to leave their farms for the cities. Among the factors that made possible the growth of large cities was the transportation revolution. The development of the streetcar, as historian Daniel Boorstin points out in the following selection, was "the beginning of the end of the walking city."

But the expansion and growth of urban space, facilities, and services were seldom able to keep pace with the growth in urban population. By the middle of the twentieth century, the host of urban ills seemed incurable, and many residents sought escape. The development of the suburb, and its relation to traditional American values, is the subject of the following excerpt from Daniel Boorstin's The Americans: The Democratic Experience.

The circumstances of city founding, in the days before the automobile, tended to shape each American city into a clear, coherent form. Cities of the colonial age were (in the phrase of the architect Kevin Lynch) delightfully "legible." Their districts and pathways were easily identified, leaving little doubt of where to find the city center. Yet each offered its own unique visual image, reminding the visitor where he was, giving the resident a sense of being at home. The needs of defense, together with the need for access to waterways, had tended both to keep the city together and to keep it in focus. . . .

The American opportunity to build new towns across the continent in the late eighteenth and early nineteenth centuries offered the temptation, too, to simplify, schematize, and stereotype the visual form of a city. And just as the unmapped countryside of the West was checkerboarded into arbitrary neat rectangles for sale, so many new cities of the West were given a repetitive schematic geometry which ignored their varying landscape. . . .

In the long run a scheme so repetitive, which showed so little respect for varied terrain, even if it provided an orderly street plan, prevented many an American city from acquiring a distinctive visual image. Everywhere— on the prairies, in the desert, up and down the mountainside, and in the city—appeared the checkerboard.

The checkerboard pattern did not provide an obvious visual center, but in the growing cities of the West during the mid-nineteenth century and later, new forms of transportation tended to provide a focus of arrival and activity. In the age of the railroad, a few speedy lines had brought people to the city center. Partly for that reason, manufacturing and wholesaling were commonly focused there. The city's busy, impressive railway depot, a kind of inland harbor, had been a measure of its commerce and its vitality. The meeting points of railroad lines were natural city centers, and "the other side of the railroad tracks" was the natural dividing line within the city.

Trolleys, Trams, and Streetcars

But within the city at first there was no public transportation at all. In the early nineteenth century, Paris set an example with its *voiture omnibus*, or "vehicle for all," which supplied the English word "omnibus," soon shortened to "bus." . . . An obvious improvement . . . was to lay rails, like those already used inside coal mines, and shape the wagon wheels to conform to the rails. These omnibuses on rails were still, of course, drawn by horses. "Streetcar," an Americanism, came into use about the time of the Civil War. Now it became possible for someone who could not afford a private carriage to work in the city and live outside.

The rails of streetcars, like those of the steam railroads, tended to keep the city in focus. Streetcars which ran to the center of the city . . . brought customers for department stores, visitors to museums, and audiences to theatres, and so built "downtown." And with the rise of suburbs, the rails kept the suburb, too, in focus, for the rails commonly led to a central station in each suburb; and the rail lines had determined the location of the new developments outside Philadelphia, Chicago, Los Angeles, or the areas first settled in Florida. But the steam railroad, driven by a locomotive that was cumbersome, noisy, and a fire hazard, was not well suited for shorter runs and frequent stops. Nor was it suited at all for running inside a city.

The suburb required a different kind of transportation, and some of the first suburbs were a kind of by-product of the streetcar. "Streetcar suburbs" (as historian Sam B. Warner, Jr., calls them) stretched the city. Before the coming of the streetcar, a city's natural boundaries had extended only to the distance that a man could walk from the center in about an hour. For among city dwellers, horses and carriages were mostly for the rich. The steam railroad which went to a central station had enlarged the trading area of the city but did not provide transportation for short distances, and so did not change the patterns of daily life. The streetcar was another story. While it did not take the city out of focus, it was the beginning of the end of the walking city. . . .

An American street railway, some call it the first anywhere, was built for the New York & Harlem Railway in 1832 by an Irish immigrant, John Stephenson. His design for a huge horse-drawn omnibus mounted on four flange wheels made him the leading manufacturer of streetcars in their heyday after the mid-century.

One of the most effective of the streetcar pioneers was Stephen Dudley Field. . . . Importing the latest Siemens electric motors from Germany, he collaborated with Thomas A. Edison to provide an electric railway at the Chicago Railway Exposition in 1883.

Still there was the grave problem of how to transmit the electricity from a central power station to the moving streetcar without endangering the lives of people on the streets. Accidents with live rails and underground conduits led to the overhead trolley system, which, because of its safety, became the usual source of streetcar power. . . . "Trolley," displacing the English "tram," referring not to the wire but to the vehicle, was an Americanism in common use by the 1890s. . . .

The electric streetcar naturally widened the reach of the city. And the spread of other services helped. By 1920 a new device, the single-residence septic tank, had come into use for houses out of reach of city sewage systems. Improved techniques of well drilling had made it easier for an unattached residence to have its own water supply. Now new techniques extended the reach of electricity. At first, under Edison's favored system of direct current, electric power could be conveniently sent out only for a mile or two. The shift to alternating current and George Westinghouse's improvements in the transformer simplified and cheapened the sending of electricity for long distances. By the early twentieth century there were practical and economical systems for distributing electricity to widely dispersed households.

Even before the opening of the new century, promoters of streetcar-suburbs proclaimed the importance of suburban life for widening home ownership and so strengthening the roots of American democracy.

Henry M. Whitney, a steamship operator who made a fortune out of his Boston street-railway monopoly, propagandized for the uniform five-cent fare by contrasting the congested, tenant-ridden cities of Europe with the new promise of suburbia. In the United States, now, he said, the city workingman could own his own home on a plot of his own. As late as 1900 only one fourth of Boston suburban dwellers owned their own homes. But this American ideal of the independent home owner, a latter-day form of the Old World sturdy independent "yeoman," helped inspire the nationwide growth of suburbs, and promised to democratize the "Old World" luxuries of country living. The very names of the new suburbs were faintly redolent of manorial establishments, while the promotional literature and the architecture of even the smallest houses conjured up for middle-class urban Americans seductive visions of "gracious living" in mini-manors and micro-palaces.

The Growth of Suburbs

Out from cities in all directions the new electrified street railways reached. Occasionally they went to where the people were, but more often they went where real estate developers wanted the people to come. Streetcars had become necessary for the promotion of new suburbs. Just as, a half-century earlier, railroad builders had made fortunes by attracting the people to the railroads, so now it was with the streetcar builders. . . .

Two canons of the new suburbs were: Romanticize and Stratify. Landscape architects bent their efforts to creating a rural, deliberately random, countryfied character. But to reassure settlers that their cash and their prejudices were safe, residential zoning (which the suburbs helped create) separated families according to income, race, and religion. The suburbs promised homogeneous islands, where those who could afford it and did not suffer the stigma of the wrong race or religion, could hope to live an artificial, antiseptic idyl, untroubled by any not of their own "kind".

The new suburbs would provide a ladder of consumption in housing like that which General Motors was offering in automobiles. Both provided visible, reachable goals. The newness of the suburbs and the visibility of their place in the consumption scale helped Americans who were uncomfortably but optimistically vague about their social class to locate themselves in the social scheme. One of the last legacies of the New World emptiness was this new geography of status. And while the new suburbs professed to sharpen and define, they also did much to blur the situation of Americans.

The changing profile of the American city appeared in the shifting definitions used by the United States Bureau of the Census. In 1870 the census officially distinguished the nation's "urban" from its "rural" population for the first time. "Urban population" was defined as persons living in towns of 8,000 inhabitants or more. But after 1900 an "urban" person meant one living in an incorporated place having 2,500 or more inhabitants.

Then, in 1950 the Census Bureau radically changed its definition of "urban" to take account of the new vagueness of city boundaries. In addition to persons living in incorporated units of 2,500 or more, the census now included those who lived in *un*incorporated units of that size, and also all persons living in "the densely settled urban fringe, including both incorporated and unincorporated areas, around cities of 50,000 inhabitants or more." Each such new unit, conceived as "an integrated economic and social unit with a large population nucleus," was christened a "Standard Metropolitan Statistical Area"(SMSA).

Each SMSA would contain at least "(a) one central city with 50,000 inhabitants or more, or (b) two cities having contiguous boundaries and constituting, for general economic and social purpose, a single community with a combined population of at least 50,000, the smaller of which must have a population of at least 15,000." Such an area included "the county in which the central city is located, and adjacent counties that are found to be metropolitan in character and economically and socially integrated with

186

the county of the central city." By 1970, about two thirds of the population of the United States was living in these urbanized areas, and of that figure more than half were living *outside* the central cities. . . .

The Automobile: An Anywhere Vehicle

While many forces had been at work to befuzz and disperse the metropolis, the most effective was the automobile. . . . The predominant visual image of the city was no longer of an urban center but of highways. And they might lead anyplace. . . .

Now, when almost anybody's own high-speed-powered vehicle could go anywhere, the old city center ceased to be the natural destination of transportation from the fringes. For the automobile, unlike the railroad or the streetcar, was an anywhere-vehicle, ideally suited for the age of the everywhere community. . . .

The paving of city streets and the building of intracity, intercity, and interstate highways diffused and interfused "urban" and "rural" activities as never before. . . .

The airplane, when it became, second to the automobile, the principal means of intercity passenger transport, diffused the city still farther. . . . Improvements in the airplane, from the propeller plane to the jet to the jumbo jet to the supersonic transport, pushed big-city airports farther and farther out to the countryside so that when the visitor "arrived" on the ground he might not even see the city to which he had come.

Cities Without a Function

The new spatial vagueness of the city brought with it countless functional vaguenesses. Just as in the nineteenth century the life of a city might depend on the coming of the canal or the railroad (which had received federal and state subsidies), so, in the twentieth century, a city's prosperity might depend on federal and state aid to highways and airports. Each federal unit—national, state, county, and municipal—from the beginning expected some contribution from all the others for its everyday services like water supply, sewage disposal, firefighting, and police protection. . . . In a metropolitan region only an unusually well informed citizen knew which of the numerous agencies of government was responsible for each of the public services for which he was taxed or was paying fees.

In cities all over the nation, the need to go downtown for culture and for spectacular entertainment declined with the coming of motion pictures and the rise of the neighborhood movie houses. Then television made it possible for the citizen to see everything he wanted to see (as well as much he did not want to see) without going outside his living room.

Another institution, described in the Americanism "shopping center," came into being in the 1920s and further confused Americans about where and what their city was. . . . The design of shopping centers became a new architectural specialty. By 1940, about one quarter of the nation's retail-trade volume in metropolitan regions was dispersed into suburban shopping centers; by 1950 the amount was about one third, and it increased with the decades. By 1955, some eighteen hundred shopping centers had been built in the outskirt business districts of metropolitan regions, and as many more were being planned.

At the same time, an increasing proportion of the population of the metropolitan regions worked at jobs outside the old central city. With the passing decades, as retailing, banking, professional centers for lawyers, doctors, and others, and factories were dispersed, a smaller proportion of the inhabitants of a metropolitan region had a clear dependent relationship to the core of the great city.

Suburbia

The vagueness of the city compounded ancient problems and led Americans at first to search for remedies, then to reach for anitdotes. Some tried importing Old World schemes of paternalist utopia. Others hoped that old ills could be cured by renewal, by trying to erase what was there and begin all over again. But by mid-century the future seemed to lie with refugees from the city, who were finding new ways to make suburbs into communities. . . .

. . . The movement to the suburbs in the early decades of the twentieth century was an internal migration which for speed was without precedent in American life. Between 1950 and 1960 the suburban population of the United States increased by about 17 million. More that 12 million of these had actually moved to a suburb, either from some central city or from a farm. The census of 1910 showed less than half as many Americans (12 percent) living in suburbs as lived in central cities (26 percent). But the census of 1960 showed almost exactly as many Americans (31 percent) living in suburbs as lived in central cities (32 percent), and the suburban population was leaping ahead. While the proportion of population both in central cities and on the farm steadily declined, the proportion in the suburbs grew, and by the late '60s already exceeded that in the central cities. Unless the trend changed sharply, by the end of the twentieth century most Americans would be suburbanites. . . .

In the early twentieth century a new American genre, the "subdivider" (the word in this sense appears to be an Americanism) or suburban "developer" came into being on the urban penumbra. An enterprising promoter would buy acreage on the edge of a promising town, "subdivide" it into lots, build streets and lay sewers, bring in electricity and water, and then advertise for buyers.

The real estate go-getter's techniques improved. From a high-pressure salesman he became a long-range planner, enlisting all the expertise of the new social scientists. After World War II, when returning veterans and expanding birth rates increased the demand for housing, speculative building enlarged real estate enterprises to a scale reminiscent of the late-eighteenth century and early-nineteenth-century Western land companies. Abraham Levitt, son of poor Russian-Jewish immigrants, pioneered in the mass production of suburban housing. Using experience acquired in building houses for the Navy during the war, Levitt and Sons began building suburban towns. The first Levittown, on Long Island, begun in 1947, was a whole new community, with houses (most appliances included) around village greens, where there were shops, a playgound, and a swimming pool. . . . Similar "development" cities, like Park Forest outside Chicago, or Bowie outside Washington, D.C., appeared in other parts of the country.

Suburbs, upstart towns in a new pattern, brought a revival of active, small-town political life. . . . Suburbs, with their problems of creating new school systems, new recreational facilities, and new units of government, relived the conditions which accounted for may of the virtues which American historians had found in the "Frontier" community. . . . Just as new states and counties and upstart cities had offered new arenas for political democracy in the nineteenth century, so thousands of new suburbs with myriad local problems awakened the interests and political energies of mid-twentieth-century Americans.

In other respects, too, suburbs revived the spirit of an earlier age. Despite the rising divorce rate and other widely advertised forces which loosed the marriage bond, the suburbs, a bastion of the free-standing single-family residence, strengthened home and family. If, as was often observed, the cosmopolitan city enticed the family outside the family residence, the small town in its suburban reincarnation reinforced the home as center. The homogeneity and compatibility which characterized much small-town life in its heyday was found once again in the suburb. . . .

But there was a price. . . . In large developments where the developer had a plan, and even in the smaller developments, there was a new kind of paternalism: . . . It was the paternalism of the marketplace. The suburban developer, unlike the small-town booster, seldom intended to live in the community he was building. For him community was a commodity, a product to be sold at a profit. And the suburban home owner often moved into a whole town which had been shaped in advance by a shrewd developer's sense of the market.

The suburb was the Upstart Town, twentieth-century model, in a world where newer was better. . . . The suburb was a world of brand names, of shopping centers, of franchised outlets, and of repeatable experience. . . .

The suburb was a new version, too, of the American transient community. Instead of the wagon train, where people leaned on one another as they moved across the continent, Americans in suburbs leaned on one another as they moved rapidly about the country and up the ladder of consumption. A small town was a place where a man settled. A suburb was a place to or from which a person moved. Except in a few of the most costly (and speedily disappearing) suburbs outside a few cities, suburbanites did not think of building their town for their children or their grandchildren. They expected their children to live elsewhere. And even before their children grew up, they themselves hoped to have moved to a more "exclusive" suburb. The quest to make suburbs more comfortable, more convenient, and more attractive made them more and more interchangeable.

In the late twentieth century, to move from almost any suburb to almost any other of comparable class anywhere else in the United States was like moving from one part of a neighborhood to another. With few exceptions, the products and services available, and the residence itself were only slightly different. With the addition of air conditioning to central heating as common amenities, soon to become "necessities" for middle-class Americans, even climate had less and less effect on the comfort of daily life. When they moved from the vast vague city to their very own home in the perfect suburb of their choice, they might feel that they were joining not a community of 10,000, but a community of 10 million American suburbanites living everywhere.

Our Motorized Mistress

Lewis Mumford

Although Daniel Boorstin attributes the development of the earliest suburbs to the streetcar, the modern suburbs would not, of course, be possible without the automobile and the modern highway. Perhaps few other inventions in history have had as pervasive an impact on American society as the gasoline-powered automobile. The first workable automobile in the United States was built by Ransom Olds in 1890; Henry Ford's first car followed five years later. By 1900, about 8,000 cars had been manufactured, but only three decades later some twenty million American families owned automobiles. Quite apart from its effect on the steel, rubber, and oil industries, the automobile changed both the landscape and life-styles of America. Roads were improved and highways built; horses virtually disappeared from city streets; millions of Americans moved out of cities and into the suburbs; and one-room schoolhouses gave way to consolidated school districts.

For the individual, the automobile meant freedom, adventure, and status. It was little wonder that the automobile became the object of a religion. But the worship of the motorcar also had negative and dangerous consequences, as social critic and historian Lewis Mumford points out in his now-classic essay, "The Highway and the City." Writing in 1958, Mr. Mumford showed amazing foresight in predicting the impact of the federal highway program. In 1955, there were 52 million automobiles registered in the United States; by 1969 the figure stood at more than 87 million, an increase of two-thirds within fifteen years, and the automobile bid fair to become "Our Motorized Mistress."

The God on Wheels

When the American people, through their Congress, voted last year for a twenty-six-billion-dollar highway program, the most charitable thing to

From Lewis Mumford, "The Highway and the City," *Architectural Record*, CXXIII, No. 4 (April 1958), 179–86. Copyright © 1958 by Lewis Mumford. This article also appears in Mumford's book, *The Highway and the City* (New York: Harcourt, Brace & World, Inc. 1963) and will be reprinted in a collection of Mumford's articles for *Architectural Record*, 1931–1963, honoring his eightieth birthday in 1975.

assume about this action is that they hadn't the faintest notion of what they were doing. Within the next fifteen years they will doubtless find out; but by that time it will be too late to correct all the damage to our cities and our countryside, to say nothing of the efficient organization of industry and transportation, that this ill-conceived and absurdly unbalanced program will have wrought. Yet if someone had foretold these consequences before this vast sum of money was pushed through Congress, under the specious guise of a national defense measure, it is doubtful whether our countrymen would have listened long enough to understand; or would even have been able to change their minds if they did understand. For the current American way of life is founded not just on motor transportation but on the religion of the motor car, and the sacrifices that people are prepared to make for this religion stand outside the realm of rational criticism. Perhaps the only thing that could bring Americans to their senses would be a clear demonstration of the fact that their highway program will, eventually, wipe out the very area of freedom that the private motor car promised to retain for them.

Our Motorized Mistress

As long as motor cars were few in number, he who had one was a king; he could go where he pleased and halt where he pleased; and this machine itself appeared as a compensatory device for enlarging an ego which had been shrunken by our very success in mechanization. That sense of freedom and power remains a fact today only in low-density areas, in the open country; the popularity of this method of escape has ruined the promise it once held forth. In using the car to flee from the metropolis the motorist finds that he has merely transferred congestion to the highway; and when he reaches his destination, in a distant suburb, he finds that the countryside he sought has disappeared: beyond him, thanks to the motorway, lies only another suburb, just as dull as his own. To have a minimum amount of communication and sociability in this spread-out life, his wife becomes a taxi-driver by daily occupation, and the amount of money it costs to keep this whole system running leaves him with shamefully overtaxed schools, inadequate police, poorly staffed hospitals, overcrowded recreation areas, ill-supported libraries.

In short, the American has sacrificed his life as a whole to the motor car, like someone who, demented with passion, wrecks his home in order to lavish his income on a capricious mistress who promises delights he can only occasionally enjoy.

Delusions of Progress

For most Americans, progress means accepting what is new because it is new, and discarding what is old because it is old. This may be good for a rapid turnover in business, but it is bad for continuity and stability in life. Progress, in an organic sense, should be cumulative, and though a certain amount of rubbish-clearing is always necessary, we lose part of the gain offered by a new invention if we automatically discard all the still valuable inventions that preceded it. In transportation, unfortunately, the old-fashioned linear notion of progress prevails. Now that motor cars are becoming universal, many people take for granted that pedestrian movement will disappear and that the railroad system will in time be abandoned. . . . The result is that we have actually crippled the motor car, by placing on this single means of transportation the burden for every kind of travel. Neither our cars nor our highways can take such a load. This overconcentration, moreover, is rapidly destroying our cities, without leaving anything half as good in their place.

What's Transportation For?

This is a question that highway engineers apparently never ask themselves: probably because they take for granted the belief that transportation exists for the purpose of providing suitable outlets for the motor car industry. To increase the number of cars, to enable motorists to go longer distances, to more places, at higher speeds has become an end in itself. Does this over-employment of the motor car not consume ever larger quantities of gas, oil, concrete, rubber, and steel, and so provide the very groundwork for an expanding economy? Certainly, but none of these make up the essential purpose of transportation, which is to bring people or goods to places where they are needed, and to concentrate the greatest variety of goods and people within a limited area, in order to widen the possibility of choice without making it necessary to travel. A good transportation system minimizes unnecessary transportation; and in any event, it offers a change of speed and mode to fit a diversity of human purposes.

Diffusion and concentration are the two poles of transportation: the first demands a closely articulated network of roads—ranging from a footpath to a six-lane expressway and a transcontinental railroad system. The second demands a city. Our major highway systems are conceived, in the interests of speed, as linear organizations, that is to say as arteries. That conception would be a sound one, provided the major arteries were not over-developed to the exclusion of all the minor elements of transportation. Highway planners have yet to realize that these arteries must not be thrust into the delicate tissue of our cities; the blood they circulate must rather enter through an elaborate network of minor blood vessels and capillaries. As early as 1929 Benton MacKaye worked out the rationale of sound highway development, in his conception of the Townless Highway; and this had as its corollary the Highwayless Town. In the quarter century since, all the elements of MacKaye's conception have been carried out, except the last— certainly not the least.

The Highway as a Work of Art

In many ways, our highways are not merely masterpieces of engineering, but consummate works of art: a few of them, like the Taconic State Parkway in New York, stand on a par with our highest creations in other fields. Not every highway, it is true, runs through country that offers such superb opportunities to an imaginative highway builder as this does; but then not every engineer rises to his opportunities as the planners of this highway did, routing the well-separated roads along the ridgeways, following the contours, and thus, by this single stratagem, both avoiding towns and villages and opening up great views across country, enhanced by a lavish planting of flowering bushes along the borders. If this standard of comeliness and beauty were kept generally in view, highway engineers would not so often lapse into the brutal assaults against the landscape and against urban order that they actually give way to when they aim solely at speed and volume of traffic, and bulldoze and blast their way across country to shorten their route by a few miles without making the total journey any less depressing.

Perhaps our age will be known to the future historian as the age of the bulldozer and the exterminator; and in many parts of the country the building of a highway has about the same result upon vegetation and human structures as the passage of a tornado or the blast of an atom bomb. Nowhere is this bulldozing habit of mind so disastrous as in the approach to the city. Since the engineer regards his own work as more important than the other human functions it serves, he does not hesitate to lay waste to woods, streams, parks and human neighborhoods in order to carry his roads straight to their supposed destination.

The Need for a Transportation System

The fatal mistake we have been making is to sacrifice every other form of transportation to the private motor car—and to offer as the only long-distance alternative the airplane. But the fact is that each type of transportation has its special use; and a good transportation policy must seek to improve each type and make the most of it. This cannot be achieved by aiming at high speed or continuous flow alone. If you wish casual opportunities for meeting your neighbors, and for profiting by chance contacts with acquaintances and colleagues, a stroll at two miles an hour in a relatively concentrated area, free from vehicles, will alone meet your need. But if you wish to rush a surgeon to a patient a thousand miles away, the fastest motorway is too slow. And again, if you wish to be sure to keep a lecture engagement in winter, railroad transportation offers surer speed and better insurance against being held up than the airplane. There is no one ideal mode or speed: human purpose should govern the choice of the means of transportation. That is why we need a better transportation *system*, not just more highways . . . .

The Traffic Pyramids

In order to overcome the fatal stagnation of traffic in and around our cities, our highway engineers have come up with a remedy that actually expands the evil it is meant to overcome. They create new expressways to serve cities that are already overcrowded within, thus tempting people who had been using public transportation to reach the urban centers to use these new private facilities. Almost before the first day's tolls on these expressways have been counted, the new roads themselves are overcrowded. So a clamor arises to create other similar arteries and to provide more parking garages in the center of our metropolises; and the generous provision of these facilities expands the cycle of congestion, without any promise of relief until that terminal point when all the business and industry that originally gave rise to the congestion move out of the city, to escape strangulation, leaving a waste of expressways and garages behind them. This is pyramid building with a vengeance: a tomb of concrete roads and ramps covering the dead corpse of a city.

But before our cities reach this terminal point, they will suffer, as they now do, from a continued erosion of their social facilities. . . . Unfortunately, highway engineers, if one is to judge by their usual performance, lack both historic insight and social memory: accordingly, they have been repeating, with the audacity of confident ignorance, all the mistakes in urban planning committed by their predecessors who designed our railroads. The wide swathes of land devoted to cloverleaves and expressways, to parking lots and parking garages, in the very heart of the city, butcher up precious urban space in exactly the same way that freight yards and marshalling yards did when the railroads dumped their passengers and freight inside the city. These new arteries choke off the natural routes of circulation and limit the use of abutting properties, while at the points where they disgorge their traffic, they create inevitable clots of congestion, which effectively cancel out such speed as they achieve in approaching these bottlenecks.

. . . Arterial roads, ideally speaking, should engirdle the metropolitan area and define where its greenbelt begins; and since American cities are still too impoverished and too improvident to acquire greenbelts, they should be planned to go through the zone where relatively high-density building gives way to low-density building. On this perimeter, through traffic will bypass the city, while cars that are headed for the center will drop off at the point closest to their destination. . . . It is on relatively cheap land, on the edge of the city, that we should be building parking areas and garages: with free parking privileges, to tempt the commuter to leave his car and finish his daily journey on the public transportation system. The public officials who have been planning our highway system on just the opposite principle are likewise planning to make the central areas of our cities unworkable and uninhabitable. Route 128 in Boston is a belated effort to provide such a circular feeder highway; but its purpose is cancelled by current plans for arterial roads gouging into the center of the city.

Down and Up with the Elevated

Just as highway engineers know too little about city planning to correct the mistakes made in introducing the early railroad systems into our cities, so, too, they have curiously forgotten our experience with the elevated railroad—and unfortunately most municipal authorities have been equally forgetful. In the middle of the nineteenth century the elevated seemed the most facile and up-to-date method of introducing a new kind of rapid transportation system into the city; and in America, New York led the way in creating four such lines on Manhattan Island alone. The noise of the trains and the overshadowing of the structure lowered the value of the abutting properties even for commercial purposes; and the supporting columns constituted a dangerous obstacle to surface transportation. So unsatisfactory was elevated transportation even in cities like Berlin, where the structures were, in contrast to New York, Philadelphia, and Chicago, rather handsome works of engineering, that by popular consent subway building replaced elevated railroad building in all big cities, even though no one could pretend that riding in a tunnel was nearly as pleasant to the rider as was travel in the open air. The destruction of the old elevated railroads in New York was, ironically, hailed as a triumph of progress precisely at the moment that a new series of elevated highways were being built, to repeat on a more colossal scale the same errors.

Highway Robbery

Like the railroad, again, the motorway has repeatedly taken possession of the most valuable recreation space the city possesses, not merely by thieving land once dedicated to park uses, but by cutting off easy access to the waterfront parks, and lowering their value for refreshment and repose by introducing the roar of traffic and the bad odor of exhausts, though both noise and carbon monoxide are inimical to health. . . . Even when the people who submit to these annexations and spoliations are dimly aware of what they are losing, they submit without more than a murmur of protest. What they do not understand is that they are trading a permanent good for a very temporary advantage, since until we subordinate highway expansion to the more permanent requirements of regional planning, the flood of motor traffic will clog new channels. What they further fail to realize is that the vast sums of money that go into such enterprises drain necessary public monies from other functions of the city, and make it socially if not financially bankrupt.

The Cart Before the Horse

Neither the highway engineer nor the urban planner can, beyond a certain point, plan his facilities to accommodate an expanding population. . . . But there can be no sound planning anywhere until we understand the necessity for erecting norms, or ideal limits, for density of population. Most of our congested metropolises need a lower density of population, with more parks and open spaces, if they are to be attractive enough physically to retain even a portion of their population for day-and-night living; but most of our suburban and exurban communities must replan large areas at perhaps double their present densities in order to have the social, educational, recreational, and industrial facilities they need closer at hand. Both suburb and metropolis need a regional form of government, working in private organizations as well as public forms, to reapportion their resources and facilities, so as to benefit the whole area.

To say this is to say that both metropolitan congestion and suburban scattering are obsolete. This means that good planning must work to produce a radically new pattern for urban growth. On this matter, public policy in the United States is both contradictory and self-defeating. Instead of lowering central area densities, most urban renewal schemes, not least those aimed at housing the groups that must be subsidized, either maintain old levels of congestion, or create higher levels than existed in the slums they replaced. But the Home Loan agencies, on the other hand, have been subsidizing the wasteful, ill-planned, single-family house, on cheap land, ever remoter from the center of our cities; a policy that has done as much to promote the suburban drift as the ubiquitous motor car. In order to cement these errors in the most solid way possible, our highway policy maximizes congestion at the center and expands the area of suburban dispersion—what one might call the metropolitan "fall-out." The three public agencies concerned have no official connections with each other: but the total result of their efforts proves, once again, that chaos does not have to be planned. . . .

The Place of the Pedestrian

If we want to make the most of our New Highway program, we must keep most of the proposed expressways in abeyance until we have done two other things. We must replan the inner city for pedestrian circulation, and we must rebuild and extend our public forms of mass transportation. In our entrancement with the motor car, we have forgotten how much more efficient and how much more flexible the footwalker is. Before there was any public transportation in London, something like 50,000 people an hour used to pass over London Bridge on their way to work: a single artery. Mass public transportation can bring from forty to sixty thousand people per hour, along a single route, whereas our best expressways, using far more space, cannot move more than four to six thousand cars, and even if the average occupancy were more than one and a half passengers, as at present, this is obviously the most costly and inefficient means of handling the peak hours of traffic. . . . For open spaces, long distances and low densities, the car is now essential; for urban space, short distances and high densities, the pedestrian.

Every urban transportation plan should, accordingly, put the pedestrian at the center of all its proposals, if only to facilitate wheeled traffic. But to bring the pedestrian back into the picture, one must treat him with the respect and honor we now accord only to the automobile: we should provide him with pleasant walks, insulated from traffic, to take him to his destination, once he enters a business precinct or residential quarter. . . . The legs will come into their own again, as the ideal means of neighborhood transportation, once some provision is made for their exercise. . . . But if we are to make walking attractive, we must not only provide trees and wide pavements and benches, beds of flowers and outdoor cafes, as they do in Rotterdam; we must scrap the monotonous uniformities of American zoning practice,, which turns vast areas, too spread out for pedestrian movement, into single-district zones, for commerce, industry, or residential purpose. . . .

Why should anyone have to take a car and drive a couple of miles to get a package of cigarettes or a loaf of bread, as one must often do in a suburb? Why, on the other hand, should a growing minority of people not be able again to walk to work, by living in the interior of the city, or, for that matter, be able to walk home from the theater or the concert hall? . . . Nothing would do more to give life back to our blighted urban cores than to reinstate the pedestrian, in malls and pleasances designed to make circulation a delight. And what an opportunity for architecture!

The Case for Mass Transportation

While federal funds and subsidies pour without stint into highway improvements, the two most important modes of transportation for cities—the railroad for long distances and mass transportation, and subway for shorter journeys—are permitted to languish and even to disappear. . . .

If we could overcome the irrational drives that are now at work, promoting shortsighted decisions, the rational case for rebuilding the mass transportation system in our cities would be overwhelming. The current objection to mass transportation comes chiefly from the fact that it has been allowed to decay: this lapse itself reflects the general blight of the central areas. . . . Yet mass transportation, with far less acreage in roadbeds and rights of way, can deliver at least ten times more people per hour than the private motor car. This means that if such means were allowed to lapse in our metropolitan centers—as the interurban electric trolley system, that beautiful and efficient network, was allowed to disappear in the nineteen twenties—we should require probably five to ten times the existing number of arterial highways to bring the present number of commuters into the city, and at least ten times the existing parking space to accomodate them.

This reduces a one-dimensional transportation system, by motor car alone, to a calamitous absurdity. . . . The notion that the private motor car can be substituted for mass transportation should be put forward only by those who desire to see the city itself disappear, and with it the complex, many-sided civilization that the city makes possible.

Brakes and Accelerations

There is no purely engineering solution to the problems of transportation in our age: nothing like a stable solution is possible without giving due weight to all the necessary elements in transportation—private motor cars, railroads, airplanes and helicopters, mass transportation services by trolley and bus, even ferryboats, and finally, not least, the pedestrian. To achieve the necessary overall pattern, not merely must there be effective city and regional planning, before new routes or services are planned; we also need eventually—and the sooner the better—an adequate system of federated metropolitan government. Until these necessary tools of control have been created, most of our planning will be empirical and blundering; and the more we do, on our present premises, the more disastrous will be the results. . . . We cannot have an efficient form for our transportation system until we can envisage a better permanent structure for our cities.

"A Very Large City"

Jean Gottmann

Among the effects of the automobile was a breakdown in traditional city boundaries. The Census Bureau recognized this change by creating the Standard Metropolitan Statistical Area [See above, p.186]. But not even the SMSA could adequately describe the confused and congested regions in the Northeastern United States, where the suburbs of New York, Newark, Philadelphia, and Trenton merge and overlap. Throughout American history, this region has had the heaviest concentration of population; today, it forms an almost continuous stretch of urban and suburban areas.

Is "Megalopolis," with its new patterns of intense living, the wave of the future, or does it contain elements that will lead to self-destruction? Is such concentration a malignancy or a benign growth? These and other crucial questions about urban growth are discussed by Jean Gottmann, professor of geography at Oxford University, in Megalopolis, *excerpted below.*

The Northeastern seaboard of the United States is today the site of a remarkable development—an almost continuous stretch of urban and suburban areas from southern New Hampshire to northern Virginia and from the Atlantic shore to the Appalachian foothills. The processes of urbanization, rooted deep in the American past, have worked steadily here, endowing the region with unique ways of life and of land use. No other section of the United States has such a large concentration of population, with such a high average density, spread over such a large area. And no other section has a comparable role within the nation or a comparable importance in the world. Here has been developed a kind of supremacy, in politics, in economics, and possibly even in cultural activities, seldom before attained by an area of this size.

A Very Special Region: Megalopolis

This region has indeed a "personality" of its own, which for some three centuries past has been changing and evolving, constantly creating new problems for its inhabitants and exerting a deep influence on the general organization of society. The modern trends in its development and its present degree of crowding provides both examples and warnings for other

From Jean Gottmann, *Megalopolis: The Urbanized Northeastern Seaboard of the United States,* pp. 3–16. © 1961 by The Twentieth Century Fund, New York. First published November, 1961. First MIT Press Paperback Edition, February, 1964.

less urbanized areas in America and abroad and call for a profound revision of many old concepts, such as the usually accepted distinctions between city and country. . . .

Great, then, is the importance and significance of this section of the United States and of the processes now at work within it. And yet it is difficult to single this area out from surrounding areas, for its limits cut across established historical divisions, such as New England and the Middle Atlantic states, and across political entities, since it includes some states entirely and others only partially. A special name is needed, therefore, to identify this special geographical area.

This particular type of region is new, but it is the result of age-old processes, such as the growth of cities, the division of labor within a civilized society, the development of world resources. The name applied to it should, therefore, be new as a place name but old as a symbol of the long tradition of human aspirations and endeavor underlying the situations and problems now found here. Hence the choice of the term *Megalopolis*, used in this study.

Some two thousand years before the first European settlers landed on the shores of the James River, Massachusetts Bay, and Manhattan Island, a group of ancient people, planning a new city-state in the Peloponnesus in Greece, called it *Megalopolis,* for they dreamed of a great future for it and hoped it would become the largest of the Greek cities. Their hopes did not materialize. . . . Through the centuries the word *Megalopolis* has been used in many senses by various people, and it has even found its way into Webster's dictionary, which defines it as "a very large city." Its use, however, has not become so common that it could not be applied in a new sense, as a geographical place name for the unique cluster of metropolitan areas of the Northeastern seaboard of the United States. There, if anywhere in our times, the dream of those ancient Greeks has come true.

An Urbanized Area with a Nebulous Structure

As one follows the main highways or railroads between Boston and Washington, D.C., one hardly loses sight of built-up areas, tightly woven residential communities, or powerful concentrations of manufacturing plants. Flying this same route one discovers, on the other hand, that behind the ribbons of densely occupied land along the principal arteries of traffic, and in between the clusters of suburbs around the old urban centers, there still remain large areas covered with woods and brush alternating with some carefully cultivated patches of farmland. These green spaces, however, when inspected at closer range, appear stuffed with a loose but immense scattering of buildings, most of them residential but some of industrial character. That is, many of these sections that look rural actually function largely as suburbs in the orbit of some city's downtown. Even the farms, which occupy the larger tilled patches, are seldom worked by people whose only occupation and income are properly agricultural. And yet these farm areas produce large quantities of farm goods!

Thus the old distinctions between rural and urban do not apply here any more. Even a quick look at the vast area of Megalopolis reveals a revolution in land use. Most of the people living in the so-called rural areas, and still classified as "rural population" by recent censuses, have very little, if anything, to do with agriculture. In terms of their interests and work they are what used to be classified as "city folks," but their way of life and the landscapes around their residences do not fit the old meaning of urban.

In this area, then, we must abandon the idea of the city as a tightly settled and organized unit in which people, activities, and riches are crowded into a very small area clearly separated from its nonurban surroundings. Every city in this region spreads out far and wide around its original nucleus; it grows amidst an irregularly colloidal mixture of rural and suburban landscapes; it melts on broad fronts with other mixtures, of somewhat similar though different texture, belonging to the suburban neighborhoods of other cities. Such coalescence can be observed, for example, along the main lines of traffic that link New York City and Philadelphia. Here there are many communities that might be classified as belonging to more than one orbit. It is hard to say whether they are suburbs, or "satellites," of Philadelphia or New York, Newark, New Brunswick, or Trenton. The latter three cities themselves have been reduced to the role of suburbs of New York City in many respects, although Trenton belongs also to the orbit of Philadelphia. . . .

Thus an almost continuous system of deeply interwoven urban and suburban areas, with a total population of about 37 million people in 1960, has been erected along the Northeastern Atlantic seaboard. It straddles state boundaries, stretches across wide estuaries and bays, and encompasses many regional differences. In fact, the landscapes of Megalopolis offer such variety that the average observer may well doubt the unity of the region. And it may seem to him that the main urban nuclei of the seaboard are little related to one another. Six of its great cities would be great individual metropolises in their own right if they were located elsewhere. This region indeed reminds one of Aristotle's saying that cities such as Babylon had "the compass of a nation rather than a city."

Megapolis—Main Street and Crossroads of the Nation

There are many other large metropolitan areas and even clusters of them in various parts of the United States, but none of them is yet comparable to Megalopolis in size of population, density of population, or density of activities, be these expressed in terms of transportation, communications, banking operations, or political conferences. Megalopolis provides the whole of America with so many essential services, of the sort a community used to obtain in its "downtown" section, that it may well deserve the nickname of "Main Street of the nation." And for three centuries it has performed this role, though the transcontinental march of settlement has developed along east-west axes perpendicular to this section of the Atlantic seaboard.

In recent times Megalopolis has had concentrated within it more of the Main Street type of functions than ever, and it does not yet seem prepared to relinquish any of them. Witness, for example, the impact of the Federal government in Washington, D.C., as it tightens up over many aspects of national life; the continued crowding of financial and managerial operations into Manhattan; New York's dominance of the national market for mass communication media, which resists all attempts at erosion; and the pre-eminent influence of the universities and cultural centers of Megalopolis on American thinking and policy-making. Megalopolis is also the country's chief facade toward the rest of the world. From it, as from the Main Street of a city, local people leave for distant travel, and to it arriving strangers come. For immigrants it has always served as the chief debarkation wharf. And just as passing visitors often see little of a city except a few blocks of its Main Street, so most foreign visitors see only a part of Megalopolis on their sojourns in the United States.

Just as Main Street lives for and prospers because of the functions of the whole city, rather than because of any purely local advantages of its own, so is Megalopolis related to the whole United States and its rich resources. In general, Megalopolis itself was blessed only moderately by nature. . . . But it does excel in locational advantages—deep harbors of a drowned shoreline, on which its principal cities were early established, and a connecting-link relationship between the rich heart of the continent and the rest of the world. By hard work man has made the most of these locational resources. . . . It is now the most active crossroads on earth, for people, ideas, and goods, extending its influence far beyond the national borders, and only as such a crossroads could it have achieved its present economic pre-eminence.

Megapolis as a Laboratory of Urban Growth

Modern technology and social evolution provide increasing opportunity in urban pursuits on the one hand, and on the other steadily improving means of producing more agricultural goods with less manpower. The forces at work in our time, coupled with the growth in population, are, therefore, bound to channel a rising flow of people toward urban-type occupations and ways of life. As this tide reaches more and more cities they will burst out of old bounds to expand and scatter all over the landscape, taking new forms like those already observable throughout Megalopolis. This region serves thus as a laboratory in which we may study the new evolution reshaping both the meaning of our traditional vocabulary and the whole material structure of our way of life. . . .

. . . The modern urban revolution, so apparent already in the affluent society of Megalopolis, devours time and space as well as food and industrial goods, and the fulfilling of these needs requires many types of movements.

These various tidal movements involve a reshaping of land use. Much agricultural land has been taken over by residential and industrial development. On the remaining farms a new specialized type of agriculture is developing, which requires less space than did the old system of farming. Woods have spread over much of the land abandoned by the farms, and this expansion of forests calls for new methods and concepts of forestry management, to provide for recreational and other suburban needs and for a better conservation of the landscape and of wildlife. Simultaneously the old city cores or "downtowns" are evolving toward decline or renewal, while uptowns, suburbs, and outer suburbia are becoming interlocked in a new and still constantly changing web of relationships. Regional integration is taking on forms unknown a generation or two ago, and the old system of local, state, and national authorities and jurisdictions, which has changed little, is poorly suited to present needs.

New *patterns of intense living* that have become normal in Megalopolis affect not only land use. They also exert a strong influence on the economic and social foundations of society. . . . The density of activities and of movement of all kinds is certainly the most extraordinary feature of Megalopolis, more characteristic even than the density of population and of skyscrapers. It has become a means of maintaining economic growth and stabilizing society; but how far can it go without destroying itself? For example, the growth of Megalopolis owes much to the automobile, but highway traffic jams are beginning to strangle city activities and to take the pleasure and efficiency out of driving a car. At the same time cars contribute to the ruination of other means of transportation, made more necessary than ever by the massive tidal currents of people and goods. The self-defeating effect of dense concentrations may be observed also in other fields than transportations. Many industries, for example, are now aiming at decentralization. The intense living of Megalopolis, makes a great deal of waste inescapable, waste of space and time as well as of materials. . . .

The many millions of people who find themselves *neighbors in Megalopolis,* even though they live in different states and hundreds of miles from one another, are barely becoming aware of the imperatives of such a "neighborhood.". . . Responsible public opinion is becoming conscious of the problems involved, and the struggle to find solutions has started. It is especially difficult because no one problem can be tackled without affecting the others. Transportation, land use, water supply, cultural activities, use and development of resources, government and politics—all are interrelated.

Today it is essential that solutions be found to save this area from decay and to reassure the nation and the world about the kind of life modern urbanization trends presage for the future. Megalopolis has been built and often reshaped by its people. These people are now wealthier, better educated, and better endowed with technological means than ever. They ought to be able to find ways of avoiding decline of the area.

For the Better of for the Worse?

. . . Modern urban sprawl is viewed by many as a threat to progress and general welfare. What is happening in Megalopolis today has been described as a pathological phenomenon, a sickness, a cancer. Such views are held by distinguished and respectable citizens of the area. . . .

Urban growth in general has been discussed and condemned on moral grounds for a long time. Such debate is expectable and desirable, but on the whole history has shown the condemnation to be unjust, as can be seen by a brief review of some of the consequences of crowding.

. . . In contrast to the more conservative "open" country, the "closed-in" city offers a more dynamic environment, socially and economically. . . .

Crowding of population within a small area creates shortages of various resources, and most of the crowded people are bound to suffer in some ways because of the shortages. To alleviate them, to make crowding more bearable and the population happier, ways and means of constantly better distribution must be found. Otherwise no lasting growth can develop, and the whole enterprise will soon be doomed. From the struggle against such shortages have come some of mankind's most important advances. . . . Everywhere, the more crowded people have become in cities the more they have craved both security and freedom. Modern political life and its concepts of liberty, self-government, and democracy are the products of urban growth, the inheritance of cities in process of growth and development—places such as Jerusalem, Athens, Rome, Bruges, Florence, Paris, London, to mention only those that have been most studied by historians. And the same places, or similar urban centers, have contributed most of our scientific and technological developments, either because people there were struggling to solve pressing problems or because urban societies make possible a leisurely enough elite, some of whose members can devote themselves to disinterested research and a search for a better understanding of the universe.

Thus urban crowding and the slums and mobs characteristic of it may be considered growing pains in the endless process of civilization.

In the same way, the picture of Megalopolis is not as dark as the outspoken pessimists and frequent protests would seem to paint it. Crowded within its limits is an extremely distinguished population. It is, *on the average,* the richest, best educated, best housed, and best serviced group of similar size (i.e., in the 25-to-40-million-people range) in the world. The area is still a focus of attraction for successful or adventurous people from all over America and beyond. It is true that many of its sections have seen pretty rural landscapes replaced by ugly industrial agglomerations or drab and monstrous residential developments; it is true in many parts of Megalopolis the air is not clean any more, the noise is disturbing day and night, the water is not as pure as one would wish, and transportation at times becomes a nightmare. Many of these problems reflect the revolutionary change that has taken place as cities have burst out of their narrow bounds to scatter over the "open" countryside. In some ways this suburban sprawl may have alleviated a crowding that had threatened to become unbearable, for residential densities of population per square mile have decreased. But new problems have arisen because of the new densities of activities and of traffic in the central cities and because the formerly rural areas or small towns have been unprepared to cope with the new demands made upon their resources. New programs are needed to conserve the natural beauty of the landscape and to assure the health, prosperity, and freedom of the people. In spite of these problems, however, available statistics demonstrate that in Megalopolis the population is on the average healthier, the consumption of goods higher, and the opportunity for advancement greater than in any other region of comparable extent. . . .

Working With Nature

Landing in America in 1620, William Bradford described New England as "a hideous and desolate wilderness. . . full of wild beasts and wild men." For almost 250 years, most Americans, with the exception of the Indians, regarded the wilderness as an enemy to be conquered in the name of progress. Nature was to be subjected to humans, who were free to exploit the land for their own profit. They felled the forests, planted the soil year after year with a single cash crop, stripped the land to obtain its mineral wealth, and grazed their livestock until the natural grass cover was destroyed. In a country of seemingly endless resources, little thought was given to conservation.

Prior to the 1860s, only a few isolated voices had been raised in defense of preserving the wilderness. George Catlin, the artist who chronicled the North American Indians, urged in 1832 that the government preserve "in their pristine beauty and wildness, in a magnificent park, where the world could see for ages to come, the native Indian in his classic attire . . . amid the fleeting herds of elk and buffaloes." The philosopher and essayist Henry David Thoreau, who regarded nature as necessary to man's spiritual well-being, also called for preservation of the wilderness.

But it remained for George Perkins Marsh, writing in 1864, to warn of the dire consequences that would result from man's misuse of the land. He urged the need to work in harmony with nature. His Man and Nature, or Physical Geography as Modified by Human Action, *excerpted below, was published in Europe as well as in America and was extremely influential in stimulating a conservationist movement in the late nineteenth century.*

With great foresight, Marsh had speculated on a time when people might actually regenerate or reclaim the natural resources that they had destroyed. The Tennessee Valley Authority, created in 1933, was designed for such reclamation on a region-wide basis. For centuries engineers had harnessed nature for humans' uses, but the TVA represented the first attempt at a planned recovery and development program for an entire area—affecting three million people in parts of seven states. David Lilienthal, who served on the TVA board from its creation until 1946, describes this unique experiment in the selection reprinted below.

Selection 1 George Perkins Marsh

In fine, in countries untrodden by man, the proportions and relative positions of land and water, the atmospheric precipitation and evaporation, the thermometric mean, and the distribution of vegetable and animal life, are subject to change only from geological influences so slow in their operation that the geographical conditions may be regarded as constant and immutable. These arrangements of nature it is, in most cases, highly desirable substantially to maintain, when such regions become the seat of organized commonwealths. It is, therefore, a matter of the first importance that, in commencing the process of fitting them for permanent civilized occupation, the transforming operations should be so conducted as not unnecessarily to derange and destroy what, in too many cases, it is beyond the power of man to rectify or restore. . . .

Destructiveness of Man

Man has too long forgotten that the earth was given to him for usufruct alone, not for consumption, still less for profligate waste. Nature has provided against the absolute destruction of any of her elementary matter, the raw material of her works; the thunderbolt and the tornado, the most convulsive throes of even the volcano and the earthquake, being only phenomena of decomposition and recomposition. But she has left it within the power of man irreparably to derange the combinations of inorganic matter and of organic life, which through the night of aeons she had been proportioning and balancing, to prepare the earth for his habitation, when, in the fulness of time, his Creator should call him forth to enter into its possession.

Apart from the hostile influence of man, the organic and the inorganic world are . . . bound together by such mutual relations and adaptations as secure, if not the absolute permanence and equilibrium of both, a long continuance of the established conditions of each at any given time and place, or at least, a very slow and gradual succession of changes in those conditions. But man is everywhere a disturbing agent. Wherever he plants his food, the harmonies of nature are turned to discords. The proportions and accommodations which insured the stability of existing arrangements are overthrown. Indigenous vegetable and animal species are extirpated, and supplanted by others of foreign origin, spontaneous production is forbidden or restricted, and the face of the earth is either laid bare or covered with a new and reluctant growth of vegetable forms, and with alien tribes of animal life. These intentional changes and substitutions constitute, indeed, great revolutions; but vast as is their magnitude and importance, they are . . . insignificant in comparison with the contingent and unsought results which have flowed from them.

The fact that, of all organic beings, man alone is to be regarded as

From George Perkins Marsh, *Man and Nature; or Physical Geography as Modified by Human Action* (New York, Charles Scribner, 1864) pp. 35–44.

essentially a destructive power, and that he wields energies to resist which, nature—that nature whom all material life and all inorganic substance obey—is wholly impotent, tends to prove that, though living in physical nature, he is not of her, that he is of more exalted parentage, and belongs to a higher order of existences than those born of her womb and submissive to her dictates.

There are, indeed, brute destroyers, beasts and birds and insects of prey—all animal life feeds upon, and, of course, destroys other life,—but this destruction is balanced by compensations. It is, in fact, the very means by which the existence of one tribe of animals or of vegetables is secured against being smothered by the encroachments of another; and the reproductive powers of species, which serve as the food of others, are always proportioned to the demand they are destined to supply. Man pursues his victims with reckless destructiveness; and, while the sacrifice of life by the lower animals is limited by the cravings of appetite, he unsparingly persecutes, even to extirpation, thousands of organic forms which he cannot consume.

The earth was not, in its natural condition, completely adapted to the use of man, but only to the sustenance of wild animals and wild vegetation. . . .

But man, the domestic animals that serve him, the field and garden plants the products of which supply him with food and clothing, cannot subsist and rise to the full development of their higher properties, unless brute and unconscious nature be effectually combated, and, in a great degree, vanquished by human art. Hence, a certain measure of transformation of terrestrial surface, of suppression of natural, and stimulation of artificially modified productivity becomes necessary. This measure man has unfortunately exceeded. He has felled the forests whose network of fibrous roots bound the mould to the rocky skeleton of the earth; but had he allowed here and there a belt of woodland to reproduce itself by spontaneous propagation, most of the mischiefs which his reckless destruction of the natural protection of the soil has occasioned would have been averted. He has broken up the mountain reservoirs, the percolation of whose waters through unseen channels supplied the fountains that refreshed his cattle and fertilized his fields; but he has neglected to maintain the cisterns and the canals of irrigation which a wise antiquity had constructed to neutralize the consequences of its own imprudence. While he has torn the thin glebe which confined the light earth of extensive plains, and has destroyed the fringe of semi-aquatic plants which skirted the coast and checked the drifting of the sea sand, he has failed to prevent the spreading of the dunes by clothing them with artificially propagated vegetation. He has ruthlessly warred on all the tribes of animated nature whose spoil he could convert to his own uses, and he has not protected the birds which prey on the insects most destructive to his own harvests.

. . . The destructive agency of man becomes more and more energetic and unsparing as he advances in civilization, until the impoverishment, with which his exhaustion of the natural resources of the soil is threatening him, at last awakens him to the necessity of preserving what is left, if not of restoring what has been wantonly wasted. . . .

Physical Improvement

True, there is a partial reverse to this picture. On narrow theatres, new forests have been planted; inundations of flowing streams restrained by heavy walls of masonry and other constructions; . . . swamps and even lakes have been drained, and their beds brought within the domain of agricultural industry; drifting coast dunes have been checked and made productive by plantation; seas and inland waters have been repeopled with fish. . . . These achievements are more glorious than the proudest triumphs of war, but, thus far, they give but faint hope that we shall yet make full atonement for our spendthrift waste of the bounties of nature.

It is, on the one hand, rash and unphilosophical to attempt to set limits to the ultimate power of man over inorganic nature, and it is unprofitable, on the other, to speculate on what may be accomplished by the discovery of now unknown and unimagined natural forces, or even by the invention of new arts and new processes. But . . . it is hard to restrain the imagination from wandering forward a couple of generations to an epoch when our descendants shall have advanced as far beyond us in physical conquest, as we have marched beyond the trophies erected by our grandfathers.

Selection 2 David E. Lilienthal

This is the story of a great change. It is an account of what has happened in this [Tennessee] valley since 1933 when Congress set the Tennessee Valley Authority to the task of developing the resources of this region. It is a tale of a wandering and inconstant river now become a chain of broad and lovely lakes which people enjoy, and on which they can depend, in all seasons, for the movement of the barges of commerce that now nourish their business enterprises. It is a story of how waters once wasted and destructive have been controlled and now work, night and day, creating electric energy to lighten the burden of human drudgery. Here is a tale of fields grown old and barren with the years, which now are vigorous with new fertility, lying green to the sun; of forests that were hacked and despoiled, now protected and refreshed with strong young trees just starting on their slow road to maturity. It is a story of the people and how they have worked to create a new valley.

One Valley—and a Thousand

I write of the Tennessee Valley, but all this could have happened in almost any of a thousand other valleys where rivers run from the hills to the sea. . . . In those thousand valleys, live men of a hundred different tongues and many racial strains. . . . But the things the people live by are the same; the soil and the water, the rivers in their valleys, the minerals within the earth. It is upon these everywhere that men must build, in California or Morocco, the Ukraine or Tennessee. These are the things they dig for and hew and process and contrive. These are the foundation of all their hopes for relief from hunger, from cold, from drudgery, for an end to want and constant insecurity. . . .

Today it is builders and technicians that we turn to: men armed not with the ax, rifle, and bowie knife, but with the Diesel engine, the bull-

Abridged from pp. 1–7, 51–61 in *TVA: Democracy on the March* by David E. Lilienthal. Copyright © 1944, 1953 by David E. Lilienthal. By permission of Harper & Row, Publishers.

dozer, the giant electric shovel, the retort—and most of all, with an emerging kind of skill, a modern knack of organization and execution. When these men have imagination and faith, they can move mountains; out of their skills they can create new jobs, relieve human drudgery, give new life and fruitfulness to worn-out lands, put yokes upon the streams, and transmute the minerals of the earth and the plants of the field into machines of wizardry to spin out the stuff of a way of life new to this world. . . .

Here is the central fact with which today's statesmanship must contend. The political promises that will be made and the great popular movements that have come into being deal with the demands of people for the ever larger harvest that science and nature, devoted to a common purpose, can be made to yield. The terms under which the people of the world receive the products of technical advance, such as those that have come to this valley, are at the vortex of the cyclonic forces of our century. . . .

The physical achievements that science and technology now make possible *may bring no benefits,* may indeed be evil, unless they have a moral purpose, unless they are conceived and carried out for the benefit of the people themselves. Without such a purpose, advances in technology may be disastrous to the human spirit; the industrialization of a raw material area may bring to the average man only a new kind of slavery and the destruction of democratic institutions.

But such a moral purpose alone is not enough to insure that resource development will be a blessing and not a curse. Out of TVA experience in this valley I am persuaded that to make such a purpose effective two other principles are essential.

First, that resource development must be governed by the unity of nature herself.

Second, that the people must participate actively in that development.

The physical job is going to be done; of that I think we can be sure. But if, in the doing, the unity of nature's resources is disregarded, the price will be paid in exhausted land, butchered forests, polluted streams, and industrial ugliness. And, if the people are denied an active part in this great task, then they may be poor or they may be prosperous but they will not be free. . . .

. . . The TVA experiment has been carried on under the existing rules of the game of American life. It required no change in the Constitution of the United States. Congress has maintained full control. Property rights and social institutions have undergone no drastic amendment. In short, the valley's change has gone forward under typical and traditional American conditions, rather than under non-existent "ideal" conditions that would not or could not be duplicated. . . .

A New Way—An Old Task

A new chapter in American public policy was written when Congress in May of 1933 passed the law creating the TVA. For the first time since the trees fell before the settlers' ax, America set out to command nature not by defying her, as in that wasteful past, but by understanding and acting upon her first law—the oneness of men and natural resources, the unity that binds together land, streams, forests, minerals, farming, industry, mankind.

This, of course, is not what the creation of TVA meant to most people who read in their newspapers of the action of Congress. For TVA was then ordinarily thought of simply as a "power" project, a venture in public ownership of hydro-electricity. . . .

For fifteen years before TVA came into being Congressional and public debate centered largely on a single potential resource of the Tennessee River, hydro-electric power. For long years there had been determined efforts to dispose of the government dam and power plant at Muscle Shoals in Alabama, built with public funds for World War I. . . . How those power facilities were to be used was the major question which attracted public discussion down the years. That question was settled by the passage of the Act creating TVA. But in the end it was not settled on the narrow issue of "public ownership" of power. The message of President Roosevelt urging approval of the Norris bill (which became a law with his signature on May 18, 1933) boldly proposed a new and fundamental change in the development of our country's resources. . . .

It is clear [the message read] that the Muscle Shoals development is but a small part of the potential public usefulness of the entire Tennessee River. Such use, if envisioned in its entirety, transcends mere power development: it enters the wide fields of flood control, soil erosion, afforestation, elimination from agricultural use of marginal lands, and distribution and diversification of industry. In short, this power development of war days leads logically to national planning for a complete river watershed involving many states and the future lives and welfare of millions. It touches and gives life to all forms of human concerns.

The President then suggested

legislation to create a Tennessee Valley Authority—a corporation clothed with the power of government but possessed of the flexibility and initiative of a private enterprise. It should be charged with the broadest duty of planning for the proper use, conservation, and development of the natural resources of the Tennessee River drainage basin and its adjoining territory for the general social and economic welfare of the Nation. This authority should also be clothed with the necessary power to carry these plans into effect. . . .

Many hard lessons have taught us the human waste that results from lack of planning. Here and there a few wise cities and counties have looked ahead and planned. But our Nation has "just grown." It is time to extend planning to a wider field, in this instance comprehending in one great project many States directly concerned with the basin of one of our greatest rivers.

The TVA Act was nothing inadvertent or impromptu. It was rather the deliberate and well-considered creation of a new national policy. For the first time in the history of the nation, the resources of a river were not only to be "envisioned in their entirety"; they were to be developed *in that unity with which nature herself regards her resources*—the waters, the land, and the forests together, a "seamless web." . . . Under this new policy, the opportunity of creating wealth for the people from the resources of their valley was to be faced as a single problem. To help integrate the many parts of that problem into a unified whole was to be the responsibility of one agency. . . .

"Envisioned in its entirety" this river, like every river in the world, had many potential assets. It could yield hydro-electric power for the comfort of the people in their homes, could promote prosperity on their farms and foster the development of industry. But the same river by the very same dams, if they were wisely designed, could be made to provide a channel for navigation. The river could also be made to provide fun for fishermen, and fish for food, pleasure from boating and swimming, a water supply for homes and factories. But the river also presented an account of liabilities. It threatened the welfare of the people by its recurrent floods; pollution from industrial wastes and public sewage diminished its value as a source of water supply and for recreation; its current carried to the sea the soil of the hills and fields to be lost there to men forever.

To a single agency, the TVA, the planning for the greatest sum total of these potentialities of the river for good and evil were entrusted. But the river was to be seen as part of the larger pattern of the region, one asset of the many that in nature are interwoven: the land, the minerals, the waters, the forests—and all of these as one—in their relation to the lives of the valley's people. It was the total benefit to all that was to be the common goal and the new agency's responsibility. . . .

Through the long years there has been a continuing disregard of nature's truth: that in any valley of the world what happens on the *river* is largely determined by what happens on the *land*—by the kind of crops that farmers plant and harvest, by the type of machines they use, by the number of trees they cut down. The full benefits of stream and of soil cannot be realized by the people if the water and the land are not developed in harmony.

If the soil is exposed, unprotected from the rains by cover and by roots, the people will be poor and the river will be muddy, heavy with the best soil of the fields. . . . Industries and railroads will be interrupted, farms flooded out, towns and villages destroyed, while heavy silt deposits fill the power reservoirs and stop up the channels of navigation.

It is otherwise where land is covered with sod or trees, and cultivated each season with the purpose of holding the rain where it falls. Such land literally serves as a water reservoir, a part of a system of flood control and river development, quite as directly as dams that stretch from bank to bank to hold the waters back. . . .

As the river is not separable from the land, so the land is inseparable from the forests and minerals, from the factories and shops, from the people making their living from their resources. . . .

Because they sinned against the unity of nature, because they developed some one resource without regard to its relation to every other resource in the life of man, ancient civilizations have fallen into decay and lie buried in oblivion. Everywhere in the world the trail of unbalanced resource development is marked by poverty, where prosperity seemed assured; by ugliness and desolation, with towns now dying that once were thriving; by land that once supported gracious living now eroded and bare, and over wide areas the chill of death to the ambitions of the enterprising young and to the security of the mature.

How industry came to Ducktown in the mountains of eastern Tennessee a generation ago is one such story. Copper ore was discovered; mining began; a smeltery was built. One of the resources of this remote region was being developed; it meant new jobs, income to supplement farming and forestry. But the developers had only copper in their plans. The magnificent hardwood forests to a distance of seven miles were cut and burned as fuel for the smelter's roasting ovens. The sulphur fumes from the stacks destroyed the thin cover that remained; not only the trees but every sign of living vegetation was killed and the soil became poison to life. The dead land, shorn of its cover of grass and trees was torn mercilessly by the rains; and the once lovely and fruitful earth was cut into deep gullies that widened into desolate canyons twenty and more feet deep. No one can look upon this horror as it still is today without a shudder. . . .

The fumes from Ducktown's copper smelteries are harmless now. Indeed, in the hands of a successor company a new technical process that makes the fumes harmless yields a by-product—sulphuric acid—now more valuable than the copper itself. The copper company itself is co-operating actively with the TVA in an extensive reforestation program on the area the fumes destroyed. What it has already cost and what it ultimately will cost, in manpower, materials, and the dollars of taxpayers, because copper was developed rather than the resources of Ducktown as a unity, has never been calculated. But the bill will be high.

This case seems to be extreme only because the accounting came quickly and was so clearly evident to the eye. . . .

There is no security or safety for us anywhere if nature's resources are exhausted. This day of machines and increasing populations multiplies our jeopardy. For this we must remember: Unless nature's laws of restoration are observed, modern technology can compress a once gradual process of resource exhaustion into the quick cycle of a generation or two. . . .

Great energies are now being released in the development of many parts of the world. But unless a new way of thinking and acting wins support, this period of "development" may duplicate for every continent and every region the stories of modern Ducktown and of ancient Mesopotamia. . . .

Controlling Growth: Future Environments

Raymond F. Dasmann

By the end of the nineteenth century, American settlement stretched across the entire continent. The natural landscape of America had almost everywhere been transformed into a landscape created by humans. And almost everywhere the environment had been modified to suit the purposes of individual profit and economic growth.

Until recent years, few people questioned the possibility or the wisdom of continued growth. But by the 1960s it was becoming increasingly apparent that the environment was not infinitely malleable and that the nation's population could not continue to expand without encountering high social costs.

In the following article, Raymond Dasmann, senior ecologist with the International Union for the Conservation of Nature in Morges, Switzerland, examines the implication of America's traditional individualism and "bulldozer mentality" for the future of our environment.

To discuss man in North America, it is necessary to generalize. This is always done at the risk of losing sight of the complexity of reality. . . . Our knowledge of those natural environments that once existed in North America is imperfect. We do not know enough about the changes that have been caused by man's activities. We have not even a clear picture of what is taking place around us today in the various processes of environmental change. Only with hesitancy, therefore, should we dare predict the future.

We do know that man found in North America a rich and varied land with a marvelously complex biota. We know that in a few centuries European man has reduced this variety and complexity. Save for the differences forced by geography, he has tended to create everywhere an environment marked by uniformity. There is a likelihood that this process will continue. The first of the Europeans found in America a wilderness, a place that frightened the timid and challenged the adventurous. The new settlers set forth to tame the wilds and seek their fortunes. However, for most of the span that man has been in America the wilderness has been

---

there with him. It was always beyond the settlements, or over the far horizon, and thus a factor in life and an influence upon the outlook of men. Regardless of one's opinion of it the wilderness was a reality, a place to retreat to, a possible refuge from injustice or tyranny. It could be a home for landless men, a hiding place for outlaws or simply space for those who were tired of associating with their fellow man. Today, however, the old wilderness has forever gone and the fragments we have saved are but souvenirs of a past journey. They can bring back memories or create the atmosphere of past days, but they are not the reality. Thus the new generations of Americans are growing up in a tamed land with no wild frontiers. They may well be a different breed from those of the past. It is difficult to foresee their attitudes toward their lands or environment.

Social Responsibility Versus Individualism

One can see in the story of man in relation to his North American environment an interplay between two contrasting social attitudes. Since these attitudes were often dominant at different times within the same individual, this was not a conflict between exploiter and the conservationist, between the good guys and the bad guys, but rather between the conflicting interests of man. One attitude is that of social responsibility involving the presence of a social conscience. With this the individual having knowledge or power assumes responsibility for those who may lack either, and for the lands and environment in which those without adequate knowledge, or power to influence their circumstances, must live. Running at times counter to this has been the individualistic tradition, so much extolled in America, in which each is considered responsible for his own welfare. In the pioneer history of America the scramble of individuals for personal wealth, power, prestige, or simply a place in the sun has been dominant, and responsible at times and in places for grave crimes against the environment. Accompanying it, however, has always been the social conscience, working to prevent, alleviate, or repair the damage. This attitude of concern for the welfare of the environment in which man must live, and consequently for human welfare, has been well exemplified in the words and deeds of such past American Presidents as Thomas Jefferson, the Roosevelts, and John F. Kennedy. It has been responsible for some of the major accomplishments in preservation of the American land as a place fit for men to dwell.

Today there is some evidence that the social conscience is becoming more active, and at times developing into . . . [a] kind of ecological conscience. . . . A spread of the attitude of social responsibility is exemplified today in diverse ways such as the drive toward urban renewal and the successful attempt to preserve the remaining wilderness areas of the United States. But there is always an ambiguity in the workings of the social conscience, arising in part from failure to understand fully the consequences of one's actions, and in part from conflict with individualistic motives. Thus its effectiveness is limited.

Action in the individualistic tradition is not always contrary to the public interest nor necessarily adverse in its effects upon the natural environment. There is nothing wrong in the individual seeking first to secure his own well-being. Indeed it has been part of our social philosophy that "enlightened self-interest" can serve the good of the whole. The important

214

element is that of enlightenment. Too often a lack of enlightenment about nature and land has been destructive both to the natural resources of America and to man's welfare.

Actions guided by feelings of social responsibility and directed toward care for the natural environment are not always above reproach. Many who act strongly for conservation in America are most concerned with measures designed to take effect far from their own back yards. It was easy for the easterner in the period from 1870 to 1910 to vote for national parks and forests in the distant West. . . . There is . . . reflected the desire to maintain the East as an area where economic development could be carried out without undue restraint. Today it is easier to pass a wilderness preservation act that affects areas where votes are few than it is to preserve the natural scene in lands near our urban centers where money is to be made and votes are numerous.

The ambiguity that exists in our feelings of responsibility toward preserving the natural beauty of our land is important in any consideration of the future. The individual naturally prefers those measures that add to his pleasure but cost him nothing. . . . Consequently the Supreme Court decision calling for the apportionment of political power in our states on the basis of population rather than region will have important implications toward preservation of the natural environment. With shifting of greater political power to urban populations we can expect a fuller exercise of the social conscience by cityfolk toward distant rural areas about which they may be poorly informed. That this will bring feelings of desperation to those who seek to wring a livelihood from these rural areas can be foreseen. It is likely, however, that in the future the rural hinterlands of America will be shaped to a degree previously unknown to suit the needs and wishes of those who dwell in urban centers. Local economies and local governments may well be crippled in this process.

Americans as Transient Exploiters

Those who set forth in their individual pursuits of wealth and happiness to conquer the American continent have in general lacked those attitudes toward the land that have in other countries characterized the peasantry. A sense of belonging or attachment to the land has not been characteristic of most Americans. Admittedly, the peasant tradition was carried to America by some groups of farmer-colonists, but over much of the country it has been absent. In its place has been the attitude of the transient exploiter who seeks to gain wealth by use of the land or exploitation of its resources, but feels that his true home is elsewhere and hopes to return with his wealth to some urbane and settled place. This attitude of transient exploitation was behind the activities of the hunters and trappers, miners and lumbermen, livestock producers and those farmers who planted their tobacco or cotton in the cleared forests of the South, or their wheat in the dry Great Plains. The rawness and ugliness of large areas, particularly in the West, is evidence of the passing or the presence of the transient exploiter, and of the absence of those who feel a sense of belonging to the land.

Transient exploitation was encouraged in the western United States by the manner in which the public domain was handled. Through a failure to establish any early control over its use, and through inept provisions for its disposal, the government favored the transient, nomadic use of federal lands. The public domain attracted people who had no hope of achieving any tenure, who could only try to get there first and grab the most from areas to which they had no attachment and in which they could plan no future. Those who attempted to stay and improve their surroundings found it difficult to do so. The West still carries the scars.

The attitude of the transient exploiter is with us today and is encouraged in some places by the nature of the American economy and the ecology of some of our biotic resources. Thus livestock ranching in much of the American West is an enterprise in which the margin of profit is often small and the return on an investment in land and capital equipment is less than could be expected from a similar investment in other activities. It is easier in many places to overstock, overgraze, sell when prices are high, and get out than it is to attempt to stay and build the land and its grazing resources. Similarly the prospects for long-term sustained-yield forest management are not bright in many private lands. The temptation to liquidate a forest resource quickly and use the profit for other enterprise is difficult to resist. . . .

An attitude of transcience and nonattachment toward the land or the social community is further encouraged by the way of life forced upon people in urban areas by the dispersed nature of the modern city and suburb. Many are forced to live in one place, work in another many miles distant, play in still a different area, and consequently feel no particular attachment or commitment toward any. Furthermore the extreme mobility, both spatial and social, of the American people makes it difficult to arouse their concern for the local problems of an area in which they may live for only a few years before advancement or transfer moves them to a different job in a different region.

The absence of that respect for the land characteristic of those regions in which cultures have grown up in place has had one further effect upon American attitudes. Americans have always shown a greater willingness to shape the land to suit their enterprise than to adapt their enterprise to the shape of the land. Of all past attitudes this is the one most conspicuously present and active today and has been referred to as our "bulldozer mentality." The engineer, not the ecologist, sets the tone for public debate. We locate our centers of population in arid lands and demand that water be brought to them. We chop out a forest or bulldoze off a hill to locate a suburb, rather than adapt our roads and buildings to the vegetation or topography. Exceptions to this rule among our suburbs are high in price. We prefer and find it cheaper in the short run to subdue nature rather than cooperate with it.

The preparation of this paper was slowed by a catastrophe that struck the region in which I live, northwestern California. The economy of the area was shattered by devastating river floods of a severity not before experienced in the history of the region. These floods and their consequent damage, however, have helped to illustrate the attitude of man toward his natural environment in America. . . .

Floods are not new in the valleys of the Eel, the Klamath, the Trinity, or the Mad rivers. Yet people have built their homes, towns, railroads, and highways on the floodplains or in the river canyons and have hoped that

216

the floods would not affect them. . . . In the winter of 1955, floods of a magnitude rated by the experts as unlikely to occur more often than once in a century hit this region and did great damage. But when the waters receded, the people believed the statistical odds and moved back into the same areas to put up more expensive buildings, lay out grander highways and construct wider bridges. . . . But this year the flood was of a magnitude rated as unlikely to occur more than once in a thousand years. The fine new highways were crumpled, the bridges tossed aside, the towns obliterated. I fear, however, that many of the people will still move back; indeed they are already doing so. They will build larger towns and wider freeways in the same places. . . . This is not a purely American behavior pattern. People all over the world live on active volcanoes or are drowned on floodplains. But no other group of people manages such colossal mistakes with the help of advice from so highly trained a group of experts. . . .

. . . We do not believe in adapting to environmental necessities; we demand that they be removed. This outlook admittedly had contributed to our rapid material progress. But our gains are made at the risk of high personal losses and always with the destruction of much that could have enriched our lives in other ways. . . .

Although optimistic by nature, I often find it difficult to look forward with much optimism to the future of man in North America. It seems strange to me to read accounts by those who believe that the greatest problem in our future will be the question of how best to use our leisure time. In a world dominated by human misery and ignorance such an outlook seems incredible. . . . America cannot live in isolation from the rest of the world. If we continue to think that leisure will be our greatest future problem, we may well spend that leisure defending our fat land against the hungry majority of mankind.

But apart from the possible effects of international developments upon our future, it is still difficult to be highly optimistic about the fate of our natural environments or about the kind of world we are building in North America. Admittedly, my outlook is influenced by my living in California. My home state, like all of North America, was unusually well endowed with natural beauty and resource wealth. But we have been busy destroying its beauty and perhaps will not desist until only fragments are left. . . .

California: A Harbinger for America?

The cities of California have grown and continue to grow into sprawling, formless conurbations, and their suburbs have caused Wood and Heller to add the new word "slurb" to the English language to describe them. The highways of the state grow wider by the day and probe into previously undisturbed quarters. The search for water is endless, since people are encouraged to settle in greatest numbers in the more arid regions. Through the massive California state water plan we propose to dam and capture every river, move water any distance without much regard for cost in dollars or damage to the natural environment. We continue to pave over our best farmlands, but compensate by creating their replacements in vast, expensive irrigation projects in our driest regions. We behave as though we were in a desperate war for survival, and we are, but our only enemy is our own unwillingness to adapt our pattern of living to the shape of our environment. . . .

It is madness to assume that population growth can be unending. . . . We know that eventually growth must cease, for resources all have some limits. It would be wise to limit growth while the land was still worth living in. . . .

We would like to preserve the beauty of the American land, but we are tied to the dynamics of an expanding economy. We are unwilling to face a future in which property will not increase in value because of increased demand, in which business or industry cannot grow and expand, in which opportunities for promotion or advancement become limited, and profits will find a plateau. We have grown accustomed to dependence on the economic horn of plenty for an unending and ever-increasing supply of material goods. So we vote for measures to preserve the environment only in those areas where our segment of the expanding economy will not be affected.

Hope for maintaining the richness and variety in life that come with open space, wild animal life, wilderness, or just slightly wild country lies in our facing the necessity for curtailment of population growth, and for slowing down the expansion of those segments of our economy that demand vital space or are destructive to scarce resources. California today presents an extreme example of this problem, but all of America is in the same predicament. It is difficult, however, to believe that we will take the necessary action. It seems more likely that we will restrict growth and expansion only at that time when lessened returns in material advantages result. . . . By then it may well be too late to save more than token pieces of our natural environment.

I am taking this pessimistic view despite the success of the conservation movement in America. Conservation has been successful because we are still a rich country, and population growth has not done its most serious damage. We are able to set aside new parks and reserves and to some degree improve the care given to existing ones because these actions still do not involve much cost or sacrifice on the part of most people. . . . But when space becomes more scarce the picture can change. Even today when any serious conflict develops between those who would preserve the natural scene and those who speak for the expanding economy, it is usually the former who give way. The great water-development plans in the West take precedence over attempts to preserve or maintain wild areas. It is virtually impossible to prevent the economic exploitation of areas that conceal valuable minerals. Highway commissions retain the power to shatter communities or slice apart state parks. Suburbs still spread over farmlands despite efforts to zone them out. The individual's quest for economic advancement still rides over his social conscience and smothers the development of any true ecological conscience.

The Future

It is a temptation to end this paper on this pessimistic note, but it would be unfair not to present other evidence. In answering questions about probable trends, or in making predictions of the future, it is necessary to ask the basic philosophical question regarding free will and determinism.

To what extent are we actually free to make choices concerning our future? Most conservationists act on the premise that we have a high degree of freedom of choice. Many Americans, however, and perhaps the great majority, accept an economic determinism as a rule of life, and believe that the very nature of our economic and social system forces a pattern for the future upon us whether we will it or not. Rachel Carson has noted this feeling with her question in *Silent Spring*: "Have we fallen into a mesmerized state that makes us accept as inevitable that which is inferior, as though having lost the will or the vision to demand that which is good?"

My hopes for the future are based on the belief that people are free to determine the course they will follow, and that when faced with alternatives they will select the one most favorable to their survival. . . .

Yet there are reasons for some optimism. Economic considerations do not provide our only drives. The great and successful mass movements that have changed the world for better or for worse have seldom had purely materialistic goals. The religious leaders that changed the face and spirit of the Western world did not promise an additional crust of bread to their followers. As the pressure of our materialistic civilization becomes more restrictive to the human spirit there are increased stirrings against purely material progress.

One of the most effective conservation books of recent years is the novel *The Roots of Heaven*, by Romain Gary; although I doubt that the author intended it to be such. Morel, the hero or perhaps antihero, of the novel, who waged a war to save the elephants, represents a misdirected mass striving toward a more meaningful world. He and those who attempted to understand him in the novel ask the question that many of us in conservation fields have also raised: "Are we no longer capable of respecting nature, or defending a living beauty that has no earning power, no utility, no object except to let itself be seen from time to time? Liberty, too, is a natural splendor on its way to becoming extinct.". . .

Today more than before leaders with an appreciation of our natural heritage and the value of wild things are appearing in America, often in fields once thought to be far removed from the traditional area of conservation. In consequence we are seeing some surprising happenings. The population problem has crept into the daily newspapers and receives serious attention at all levels of national life. In places the blighting suburban spread is being halted, the omnipotent freeway builders have been turned aside by some communities, a massive federal program for breathing new life into the dying hearts of our old central cities is underway, and books such as *Silent Spring* become national best-sellers. These are stirrings, but strong ones, and suggest that pathways of understanding are being built more rapidly today, and that the losses in the quality of our living are being noticed soon enough to be remedied. If so, then there is hope that we can save those unique environments that once composed the wild lands of America. Adding to this hope is the recreative power of living organisms and natural communities. With assistance even the most battered landscape can be brought back to life. If we can save the pieces, the whole can someday be reconstituted.

[1]Wood, Samuel E., and Heller, Alfred E. 1962. *California Going, Going.* California Tomorrow, Sacramento, Calif.

Communist Demonstration in Union Square, New York City, 1932.

"Congress shall make no law . . . abridging the freedom of speech."—U.S. Constitution

UPI-COMPIX

"YOU MEAN THESE APPLY TO THE
RIFFRAFF TOO?"

6/14/66

"YOU MEAN THESE APPLY TO THE RIFFRAFF TOO?" from *The Herblock Gallery* (Simon & Schuster, 1968)

*"Both the individual and society are entitled
to 'due process' of law. . . . The Supreme
Court has come under heavy fire because of
its tightening of due process concepts,
particularly in the field of criminal justice.
Has the Court gone too far—or not far enough?"*
—**Abraham**

"THERE'S SOMETHING WRONG ABOUT THIS."

2/7/71

"THERE'S SOMETHING WRONG ABOUT THIS" from *Herblock's State of the Union* (Simon & Schuster, 1972)

Classroom in Kentucky.

"In the field of public education, the doctrine of 'separate but equal' has no place. Separate educational facilities are inherently unequal."
—Brown v. Board of Education of Topeka

Jacques Lowe

Suffragette Parade, Washington, 1913.

"The inferior status of women is a venerable tradition in Anglo-American law."—Cary

Library of Congress

The United States Supreme Court, 1967
Left to right, seated: Associate Justices John M. Harlan, Hugo L. Black, Chief Justice Earl Warren, Associate Justices William O. Douglas, William J. Brennan, Jr. Standing: Abe Fortas, Potter Stewart, Byron White, and Thurgood Marshall.

"The Constitution is what the judges say it is."—Charles Evans Hughes, quoted in Kilpatrick

UPI-COMPIX

Essential Afterthoughts: The Bill of Rights

The Constitution of the United States, ratified in 1789, did not originally contain a Bill of Rights. This fact alarmed many Americans, who were accustomed to the specific restraints on government contained in the British Magna Charta. Among those expressing concern was Thomas Jefferson, who wrote: "What I disapproved from the first moment. . . was the want of a bill of rights to guard liberty against the legislative as well as executive branches of the government, that is to say to secure freedom in religion, freedom of the press, freedom from monopolies, freedom from unlawful imprisonment, freedom from a permanent military, and a trial by jury in all cases determinable by the laws of the land."

In response to those who shared these fears, the first Congress proposed and in 1791 the states ratified the first ten amendments to the Constitution.

Following the Civil War, in an attempt to protect the free status of former slaves, Congress and the states adopted the Fourteenth Amendment, securing personal rights against invasion by the states. These amendments, limiting both Federal and state power, became the most important sources for judicial protection of individual liberty.

CONSTITUTION OF THE UNITED STATES

Articles in addition to, and amendment of, the Constitution of the United States of America, proposed by Congress, and ratified by the several States, pursuant to the Fifth Article of the original Constitution.

AMENDMENT I

Congress shall make no law respecting an establishment of religion, or prohibiting the free exercise thereof; or abridging the freedom of speech, or of the press; or the right of the people peaceably to assemble, and to petition the Government for a redress of grievances.

AMENDMENT II

A well regulated Militia, being necessary to the security of a free State, the right of the people to keep and bear Arms, shall not be infringed.

AMENDMENT III

No Soldier shall, in time of peace be quartered in any house, without the consent of the Owner, nor in time of war, but in a manner to be prescribed by law.

AMENDMENT IV

The right of the people to be secure in their persons, houses, papers, and effects, against unreasonable searches and seizures, shall not be violated, and no Warrants shall issue, but upon probable cause, supported by Oath or affirmation, and particularly describing the place to be searched, and the persons or things to be seized.

AMENDMENT V

No person shall be held to answer for a capital, or otherwise infamous crime, unless on a presentment or indictment of a Grand Jury, except in cases arising in the land or naval forces, or in the Militia, when in actual service in time of War or public danger; nor shall any person be subject for the same offence to be twice put in jeopardy of life or limb; nor shall be compelled in any criminal case to be a witness against himself, nor be deprived of life, liberty, or property, without due process of law; nor shall private property be taken for public use, without just compensation.

AMENDMENT VI

In all criminal prosecutions, the accused shall enjoy the right to a speedy and public trial, by an impartial jury of the State and district wherein the crime shall have been committed, which district shall have been previously ascertained by law, and to be informed of the nature and cause of the accusation; to be confronted with the witnesses against him; to have compulsory process for obtaining witnesses in his favor, and to have the Assistance of Counsel for his defence.

AMENDMENT VII

In Suits at common law, where the value in controversy shall exceed twenty dollars, the right of trial by jury shall be preserved, and no fact tried by a jury, shall be otherwise re-examined in any Court of the United States, than according to the rules of the common law.

AMENDMENT VIII

Excessive bail shall not be required, nor excessive fines imposed, nor cruel and unusual punishments inflicted.

AMENDMENT IX

The enumeration in the Constitution, of certain rights, shall not be construed to deny or disparage others retained by the people.

AMENDMENT X

The powers not delegated to the United States by the Constitution, nor prohibited by it to the States, are reserved to the States respectively, or to the people.

AMENDMENT XIV
(Adopted July 28, 1868)

SECTION 1. All persons born or naturalized in the United States and subject to the jurisdiction thereof, are citizens of the United States and of the State wherein they reside. No State shall make or enforce any law which shall abridge the privileges or immunities of citizens of the United States; nor shall any State deprive any person of life, liberty, or property, without due process of law.; nor deny to any person within its jurisdiction the equal protection of the laws. . . .

SECTION 5. The Congress shall have the power to enforce, by appropriate legislation, the provisions of this article.

Guardians of
the Constitution

Alexander Hamilton

Americans quickly discovered that the Bill of Rights did not automatically prevent governments from seeking to restrain speech, assembly, and press. In 1798, for example, Congress adopted the Alien and Sedition Acts, which the administration of John Adams believed necessary to prevent domestic subversion during the many diplomatic crises produced by the French Revolution. Although the judicial branch did not definitely pass upon the validity of these early laws, it seemed clear even in the 1790s that the courts, particularly the Supreme Court, would become the principal bulwarks against legislative and executive violations of the Constitution and the Bill of Rights.

The most brilliant defense of the courts' role in the Constitutional scheme had been made by Alexander Hamilton during the debates over ratification of the Constitution. In The Federalist No. 78, one of a series of essays written by Hamilton, James Madison, and John Jay, he argued that the courts, "the least dangerous" branch of the government, should function as guardians of the Constitution by means of judicial review.

. . . Whoever attentively considers the different departments of power must perceive, that, in a government in which they are separated from each other, the judiciary, from the nature of its functions, will always be the least dangerous to the political rights of the Constitution; because it will be least in a capacity to annoy or injure them. The Executive not only dispenses the honors, but holds the sword of the community. The legislature not only commands the purse, but prescribes the rules by which the duties and rights of every citizen are to be regulated. The judiciary, on the contrary, has no influence over either the sword or the purse; no direction either of the strength or the wealth of the society; and can take no active resolution whatever. It may truly be said to have neither *force* nor *will*, but merely judgment; and must ultimately depend upon the aid of the executive arm even for the efficacy of its judgments.

From *The Federalist No. 78*

This simple view of the matter suggests several important consequences. It proves incontestably, that the judiciary is beyond comparison the weakest of the three departments of power; that it can never attack with success either of the other two; and that all possible care is requisite to enable it to defend itself against their attacks. It equally proves, that though individual oppression may now and then proceed from the courts of justice, the general liberty of the people can never be endangered from that quarter; I mean so long as the judiciary remains truly distinct from both the legislature and the Executive. For I agree, that "there is no liberty, if the power of judging be not separated from the legislative and executive powers.". . .

The complete independence of the courts of justice is peculiarly essential in a limited Constitution. By a limited Constitution, I understand one which contains specified exceptions to the legislative authority; such, for instance, as that it shall pass no bills of attainder, no *ex-post-facto* laws, and the like. Limitations of this kind can be preserved in practice no other way than through the medium of courts of justice, whose duty it must be to declare all acts contrary to the manifest tenor of the Constitution void. Without this, all the reservations of particular rights or privileges would amount to nothing.

Some perplexity respecting the rights of the courts to pronounce legislative acts void, because contrary to the constitution, has arisen from an imagination that the doctrine would imply a superiority of the judiciary to the legislative power. It is urged that the authority which can declare the acts of another void, must necessarily be superior to the one whose acts may be declared void. As this doctrine is of great importance in all the American constitutions, a brief discussion of the ground on which it rests cannot be unacceptable.

There is no position which depends on clearer principles, than that every act of a delegated authority, contrary to the tenor of the commission under which it is exercised, is void. No legislative act, therefore, contrary to the Constitution, can be valid. To deny this, would be to affirm, that the deputy is greater than his principal; that the servant is above his master; that the representatives of the people are superior to the people themselves; that men acting by virtue of powers, may do not only what their powers do not authorize, but what they forbid.

If it be said that the legislative body are themselves the constitutional judges of their own powers, and that the construction they put upon them is conclusive upon the other departments, it may be answered, that this cannot be the natural presumption, where it is not to be collected from any particular provisions in the Constitution. It is not otherwise to be supposed, that the Constitution could intend to enable the representatives of the people to substitute their *will* to that of their constituents. It is far more rational to suppose, that the courts were designed to be an intermediate body between the people and the legislature, in order, among other things, to keep the latter within the limits assigned to their authority. The interpretation of the laws is the proper and peculiar province of the courts. A constitution is, in fact, and must be regarded by the judges, as a fundamental law. It therefore belongs to them to ascertain its meaning, as well as the meaning of any particular act proceeding from the legislative body. If there should happen to be an irreconcilable variance between the two, that which has the superior obligation and validity ought, of course, to be preferred; or, in other words, the Constitution ought to be preferred to the statute, the intention of the people to the intention of their agents.

Nor does this conclusion by any means suppose a superiority of the judicial to the legislative power. It only supposes that the power of the people is superior to both; and that where the will of the legislature, declared in its statutes, stands in opposition to that of the people, declared in the Constitution, the judges ought to be governed by the latter rather than the former. They ought to regulate their decisions by the fundamental laws, rather than by those which are not fundamental. . . .

If, then, the courts of justice are to be considered as the bulwarks of a limited Constitution against legislative encroachments, this consideration will afford a strong argument for the permanent tenure of judicial offices, since nothing will contribute so much as this to that independent spirit in the judges which must be essential to the faithful performance of so arduous a duty.

This independence of the judges is equally requisite to guard the Constitution and the rights of individuals from the effects of those ill humors, which the arts of designing men, or the influence of particular conjunctures, sometimes disseminate among the people themselves, and which, though they speedily give place to better information, and more deliberate reflection, have a tendency, in the meantime, to occasion dangerous innovations in the government, and serious oppressions of the minor party in the community. . . .

"Liberty of Speech and Silence"

Leo Pfeffer

How should the courts interpret the First Amendment when faced with legislative or executive attempts to curtail speech, assembly, and press? Were all forms of speech to be protected, or only those that involved political expression? Did the guarantees apply in times of war or other national emergencies? In searching for answers to these and other questions about the First Amendment, the courts often turned to history: what had the framers intended? As Leo Pfeffer points out in the following selection, the generation of the Founding Fathers was itself divided over the very questions that later perplexed the courts.

The First Amendment and Sedition

For practical purposes, the issue of freedom of speech today is largely the issue of freedom of political speech. The struggle for religious freedom has been won. So too has the struggle for freedom of artistic expression and freedom of scientific inquiry. It cannot, however, be said that the struggle for freedom of political expression has been successfully concluded. Of all our liberties, the liberty of political dissent is in the most precarious position. Full freedom of political expression yet remains to be won.

When the fathers of the Bill of Rights proclaimed in the First Amendment that "Congress shall make no law. . . abridging the freedom of speech or of the press" they were thinking primarily in terms of political speech. This guarantee of freedom of speech grew out of the struggle against the severities of the English law of sedition and seditious libel. Originally sedition was the equivalent of treason and was punishable by death. . . . By the seventeenth century seditious libel had achieved a distinct and lesser status as a crime, and it was no longer punishable as treason to say of King Charles I that he was unwise and no more fit to be a king than was a simple shepherd. By the time the First Amendment was written into our Constitution the crime of seditious libel was clearly recognized in English law as "the intentional publication, without lawful excuse or justification, of written blame of any public man, or of the law, or of any institution established by law."

Contemporaneously with the struggle against the severities of punishment for sedition was the struggle against censorship of books and the press. . . . The status of the law of England as stated by Blackstone (an authority well known in the United States in 1791) was somewhat as follows:

Liberty of the press, essential as it is to the nature of a free state, consists in laying no previous restraints upon publications, but not in freedom from punishment for publishing what is criminal. Every person has an undoubted right to express publicly whatever sentiments he pleases, but if he publishes what is improper, mischievous, or illegal he must take the consequences. The punishment of dangerous and offensive writings, which, when published, are found by a fair and impartial jury to be of a pernicious tendency, is necessary for the preservation of peace and good order.

Hamiltonian and Jeffersonian Views of Free Speech

This was the state of the English law at the time the Constitution was amended to prohibit laws abridging the freedom of speech. The First Amendment does not spell out what is intended by the term "freedom of speech." The Amendment speaks in terms of the absolute; it prohibits any law abridging freedom of speech. Yet the fathers of the Bill of Rights could not have intended that the right to speak should be absolute and subject to no punishment irrespective of the nature of the speech and its consequences. They could not have intended that a person who during wartime discloses to the enemy the positions, strengths, and planned movements of our armed forces should be immune from punishment.

If, then, the Amendment is not to be construed literally as conferring an absolute right to say anything, anywhere, anytime, how is it to be construed? There are some who contend that the fathers of the Bill of Rights meant to do no more than crystallize and formalize the English law as expressed by Blackstone. According to this view, the basic purpose of the Amendment was to guarantee the right not to be prevented in advance from saying whatever one wants to say—but this does not guarantee him any right to immunity from punishment after he has his say. . . . The government's discretion in what utterances should be made punishable is quite broad. If it reasonably finds that a particular type of speech may have, to use Blackstone's phrase, a "pernicious tendency," the government may make it punishable—although the government may not in advance prevent its publication.

This was the view of a number of the Federalist judges appointed by Washington upon the establishment of the republic. . . . They interpreted the freedom-of-speech guarantee of the First Amendment to mean only that Congress might not penalize utterances which were not then seditious under the English common law. Since common-law sedition then included criticism of the government even without any incitement to illegal action, it is clear that under this view the Amendment granted an extremely limited protection to free speech.

This was also the view taken by the Federalist Congress in 1798 when it sought to destroy the Republican opposition by enacting the Alien and Sedition Acts. The Alien Act empowered President Adams to imprison or deport aliens if he deemed such action necessary for public safety. The Sedition Act, which concerns us here, made it a criminal act, punishable by fines and imprisonment, to utter or publish false, scandalous, and malicious sentiments tending to bring the government of the United States or its officers into disrepute or to excite the hatred of the people. The Act, applied with vigor by the Federalist judges, resulted in fines and prison sentences not only for editors of anti-Federalist newspapers but even for bystanders at political meetings who were overheard to make contemptuous remarks against President Adams or others in the government.

The underlying philosophy of this approach to freedom of speech is simple. It is that people are inherently evil and must be restrained by their rulers, who by nature are and ought to be their superiors. The people, Hamilton said, is a beast. . . . Since the purpose of government is to protect the wealthy and wise from the predatory instincts of the people, it would be disastrous if the people were permitted to speak ill of the government.

This was the underlying philosophy of the English common law of sedition and of the Sedition Act of 1798. Hamilton and John Marshall, who concurred in this philosophy, were nevertheless too astute politically not to realize that its implementation through rigorous enforcement of the Sedition Act would not be accepted by a people who had only a short time before waged a bloody and successful revolution against a government that sought to implement that philosophy even less harshly than the Federalist judges. Accordingly they cautioned restraint; but in vain. The Federalist judges would not be restrained. The resentment against them, the Act, and the Federalist Party intensified to a degree bordering upon revolutionary fervor. It was probably the fortunate intervention of the election of 1800, enabling the people to throw the Federalists out of office, repeal the Alien and Sedition Acts, and destroy the Federalist Party through peaceful means, that prevented forceful defiance and armed resistance.

. . . The Declaration of Independence had sprung from a diametrically opposite philosophy: from the philosophy that man was born good not evil; that government was established by the people in order to secure the people's inalienable rights; that government was therefore the servant, not the master, of the people; that government had to be watched carefully lest it usurp powers not conferred upon it by the social contract and thus become a tyranny and a despotism. Under such a philosophy, public discussion of public issues is not merely a right but a duty, and criticism of government and its officials is desirable so that they will keep within the bounds of their conferred powers.

These conflicting philosophies lead to conflicting approaches to political speech. Significantly, the classic expression of each approach was made by the leading advocate of each philosophy, Hamilton for the one and Jefferson for the other. Under the common-law-sedition or Federalist approach, political speech is looked upon with suspicion, and political speech critical of the government is *prima facie* wrong and can escape merited punishment only if it be justified. According to Hamilton, liberty of political expression "is the right to publish with impunity, truth with good motives, for justifiable ends though reflecting on government, magistracy, or individuals." In other words, to justify saying anything critical of the government and its officials, one must be able to prove that he has spoken only the truth, that his motives were good, and that his aims were acceptable. In effect this means little more than that constitutional liberty to speak means that one may say what one would most likely not be prevented or punished for saying were there no First Amendment.

The opposite approach assumes full liberty of expression as the norm and scrutinizes with suspicion any governmental restriction upon that liberty. It is governmental restriction upon speech, not speech critical of government, that is *prima facie* wrong and must be justified. This approach was expressed by Jefferson in his Virginia Statute for Religious Liberty, which, though addressed primarily to religious expression, articulates a philosophy intended to encompass discussion of all public issues. Said Jefferson:

> To suffer the civil magistrate to intrude his powers into the field of opinion, and to restrain the profession or propagation of principles on supposition of their ill tendency is a dangerous fallacy, which at once destroys all religious liberty, because he being of course judge of that tendency will make his opinions the rule of judgment, and approve or condemn the sentiments of others only as they shall square with or differ from his own; *it is time enough for the rightful purposes of civil government for its officers to interfere when principles break out into overt acts against peace and good order;* truth is great and will prevail if left to herself; she is the proper and sufficient antagonist to error and has nothing to fear from the conflict unless by human interposition disarmed of her natural weapons, free argument and debate. (Italics added.)

This approach is thus based upon the romantic faith in the inherent goodness and wisdom of the people. If truth and error are permitted to struggle without the interposition of force on one side or the other, truth will win out. The people, in short, can be trusted. It may be an oversimplification, yet it is not far from the truth to suggest that the extent to which the expression of political opinion has been allowed or restricted by the courts reflects the extent to which the courts have judged that the people can or cannot be trusted.

What Is Meant by Speech?

Both the Hamiltonian and Jeffersonian approaches recognize the social interest in free speech. The Hamiltonian approach, by exempting from punishment truthful speech published with good motives for justifiable ends, implicitly recognizes that such speech serves a useful and beneficial social purpose. The Jeffersonian approach goes further and finds a useful and beneficial purpose in all speech since only by competition in the free and open market of ideas can truth be distinguished from falsehood and error. While the Jeffersonian view also considers speech as an inherent right of human beings, the exercise of which is essential to the individual's happiness, nevertheless it agrees that if such exercise were detrimental rather than beneficial to the public welfare, the state would have a right to restrain or suppress it.

Since the key to the issue of free speech is the communal interest in what is said, it follows that the First Amendment is concerned primarily not with the articulation of sound but with the expression of ideas or the communication of thoughts. The degree to which speech is protected by the Amendment is directly proportionate to the degree to which it constitutes communication of ideas. Not everything which is said is "speech" within the purview of the Amendment.

This is well illustrated by the 1942 case of *Chaplinsky v. New Hampshire.* A man named Chaplinsky, one of the Jehovah's Witnesses, while being brought to a police station in the town of Rochester, New Hampshire, after complaints about his tactics in distributing the sect's literature, was met by a city police official at whom Chaplinsky shouted: "You are a God-damned racketeer and a damned Fascist, and the whole government of Rochester are Fascists or agents of Fascists." Chaplinsky was prosecuted and convicted under a statute making it a crime to address "any offensive, derisive or annoying word" to any other person in a public place.

The conviction was sustained by the Supreme Court. It was not the purpose of the First Amendment, said the Court, to protect insulting or "fighting" words. Such utterances are no essential part of any exposition of ideas, and are of such slight social value in the quest for truth that any benefit that might be derived from them is clearly outweighed by the social interest in order and morality. . . .

"Fighting words" are not "speech" as contemplated by the Amendment; or at best they are such a low grade of speech as to be easily expendable. . . .

In the same category is the lewd, the obscene, or the profane. To call someone by a dirty name in public is hardly an essential part of any exposition of ideas, and the social benefit from such a verbal act is negligible. In a similar, though not identical, category is the fraudulent and the libelous. . . . The social interest in fraudulent misrepresentations made for a venal purpose is so slight that it is clearly outweighed by the social interest in preventing fraud and protecting the fool and his money.

The same is true of defamatory statements. These are frequently made in anger, and like insulting or fighting words their purpose is not primarily to communicate ideas but to hurt the person defamed. . . . If I fall out with my neighbor and go around telling everybody he is a thief or a rapist, little social purpose is served by my statements, and the spirit of the First Amendment is not offended if I am held legally accountable for the injury I thus cause my neighbor.

The case is not so clear where my neighbor happens to be running for public office. Here there is a clear social interest served by allowing free discussion of his character. This fact is generally recognized by the courts, which usually will allow fairly severe attacks upon the character of candidates for public office, provided the speaker is not motivated by a special malice against the individual defamed. But this is a matter of general libel law and not of the constitutional law of free speech. . . .

Nor is the case clear where the defamation is aimed not at a single person but at a large group, particularly a racial or religious group, such as Negroes or Jews or Catholics. At common law and today in most States the concept of group libel is not recognized. To write in a newspaper that a particular person is a rapist or a Communist may subject the writer to civil and criminal liability, but there is no penalty for writing that all Negroes are rapists and all Jews Communist. . . .

While, therefore, not all verbal articulations constitute speech within the protection of the freedom-of-speech guarantee, conversely the term "speech" may encompass expression completely unrelated to the vocal organs or even to silent reading. In *Stromberg v. California* the Supreme Court, in 1931, upset a conviction of the operator of a children's camp who each day raised a camp-made reproduction of the red flag of Soviet Russia, which was also the flag of the Communist Party of the United States. The defendant had been indicted under a State statute making it a felony to display a red flag "as a sign, symbol or emblem of opposition to organized government." The Court held that exhibition of the flag is a part of political discussion within the guarantee of freedom of speech. The display of a symbol may communicate ideas no less than the articulation of words.

Moreover, the term "speech" in the First Amendment may include silence, and freedom of speech may encompass freedom not to speak. . . .

Finally, freedom of speech may include freedom not to listen. . . . Captive audiences, so familiar in totalitarian societies, are offensive to American democratic concepts. . . .

Can Speech Be Absolutely Free?

If particular verbal articulation is found to be truly a communication of ideas on a matter of public concern, the unqualified language of the First Amendment would seem to guarantee its complete freedom no matter what consequences might flow from the communicated thoughts. The Amendment would appear to secure the right to say anything on a matter of public interest, at least so long as no obscenities or fighting words are used and no person or ethnic group is defamed.

This broad and even unrestricted view of the right of speech represents the thinking of the Jeffersonians. To them government could legitimately concern itself with deeds, not words. . . . "We have," Jefferson said, "nothing to fear from the demoralizing reasonings of some, if others are left free to demonstrate their errors and especially when the law stands ready to punish the first criminal act produced by the false reasonings; these are safer corrections than the conscience of the judge."

It requires a courageous, perhaps even a foolhardy government—one with an unbounding faith in the good judgment of people—to accept and practice fully the Jeffersonian principle of free speech. . . . When presented with the Jeffersonian principle that the government can rightfully punish only the unlawful act and not the speech that evoked it, Lincoln asked bitterly: "Must I shoot a simple soldier boy who deserts, while I must not touch a hair of a wily agitator who induces him to desert?"

Our government, obviously, will not go to this extreme; nor can it realistically be expected to. Words which directly incite riot or the desertion of soldiers during war will be punished, and it would be quixotic to expect the Supreme Court to interpret the freedom-of-speech guarantee as precluding such punishment.

Evil Mind and Evil Tendency

If, then, the Constitution does not exempt from punishment all communication of ideas, what does the principle of free speech protect? According to the Hamiltonians, it protects the communication of truthful ideas

233

which have no evil tendency and which are uttered for a good motive. It does not exempt from punishment the utterance with evil intent of words having an evil tendency. . . . To the Jeffersonian argument that the rulers will judge evil tendency and evil intent according to their own opinions, the Hamiltonians reply that the only safeguard is the right to a jury trial. If the Jeffersonians argue that this means that speech is only so free as a cross-section of the people, reflected in a jury, will allow it to be, the Hamiltonians will answer, along with Madison, that it is unrealistic to expect a "parchment barrier" to protect the people from themselves and that it is inevitable that expression will be only as free as the people will allow it to be. . . .

"A Clear and Present Danger"

. . . During the first century of our republic's existence . . . the expanding frontier, the spirit of American individualism, the tradition of suspicion of government inherited from Locke, Rousseau, and the anti-Federalists—all combined to assure among the people generally and juries particularly a robust tolerance for heretical views and a decent respect for freedom of speech.

However, with the industrialization of America, the disappearance of the frontier, the intensification of nationalism, the rise of international Marxism with its threat to a wealthy capitalist society growing ever wealthier, the tolerance of juries could no longer be relied upon. The Hamiltonian approach proved wanting in the eyes of the enlightened conscience of the community. Such an approach makes of the Constitution little more than a parchment barrier, and of the First Amendment an almost meaningless exhortation to be tolerant. It makes the Judiciary merely the referee in an uneven battle between an enraged and fear-ridden majority and a weak, defenseless, and detested minority (rather than the protector of that minority, as Madison believed its role would be).

This was not what Justices Holmes and Brandeis, and later Justices Stone, Murphy, Rutledge, Black, and Douglas, envisaged as the true function either of the Constitution or of the Court. Out of their disaffection with the Hamiltonian philosophy came the "clear and present danger" approach, an approach that seeks a satisfactory reconciliation of the competing demands of national security and personal liberty. Briefly, the following is the "clear and present danger" theory.

As in all constitutional problems concerning the liberties of Americans, the question is the proper weighing of competing interests. On the one hand is the interest the community has in communication of thoughts so that in the free market place of ideas truth will prevail and the community benefit thereby. On the other hand is the need to prevent internal violence and external aggression. The fulfillment of this need may sometimes require the restriction of the free communication of ideas, as when the idea communicated is that the government should be overthrown by force or violence or that able-bodied men should not volunteer for military service.

The ultimate responsibility of reconciling these competing claims and of marking the boundary between the areas properly belonging to each rests upon the Federal Judiciary. . . .

In evaluating the claims of freedom of expression as against the other social interests whose promotion is asserted to justify a particular restriction on freedom of expression, the Court must consider the high estate held in our democratic scheme of things by the rights secured in the First Amendment. . . . Only if the Court is convinced that the interest threatened by the speech sought to be restricted is truly superior in importance will it uphold the restriction. . . .

Finally, the threat to the superior interest must be immediate and certain, not remote and speculative. It is not sufficient that the words used may have a tendency to bring on evil consequences at some time in the remote future. In other words, the danger must be *clear and present*. . . .

"Free Trade in Ideas"

Abrams v. United States

In a series of cases decided during and after World War 1, the Supreme Court attempted to define the contours of the First Amendment. It rejected a literal interpretation— that the right to freedom of speech is absolute and cannot be infringed—by upholding the power of Congress to punish spoken or written communications that disrupted the war effort. Writing for a unanimous Court in the case of Schenck v. United States *(1919), Justice Oliver Wendell Holmes affirmed the defendant's conviction under the Espionage Act. Schenck and others had distributed literature outside draft board offices urging young men to resist induction into the military. Holmes argued that Schenck's activities represented "a clear and present danger" of bringing about "a substantive evil," draft evasion, which Congress had a right to prevent.*

But having established the "clear and present danger" test, the Court proceeded to ignore it, reverting instead to the older doctrine of "evil mind and evil tendency." Thus in the case of Abrams v. United States, *heard later that year, the Court upheld a conviction under the Espionage Act for distributing pamphlets that glorified the Russian Revolution, denounced American military intervention against the Bolsheviks, and urged a general strike among munitions workers. Holmes, joined by Justice Louis Brandeis, dissented. Such advocacy, Holmes said, did not meet the* Schenck *test of "a clear and present danger."*

Justice Holmes dissenting

I do not doubt for a moment that by the same reasoning that would justify punishing persuasion to murder, the United States constitutionally may punish speech that produces or is intended to produce a clear and imminent danger that it will bring about forthwith certain substantive evils that the United States constitutionally may seek to prevent. The power undoubtedly is greater in time of war than in time of peace because war opens dangers that do not exist at other times.

But as against dangers peculiar to war, as against others, the principle of the right to free speech is always the same. It is only the present danger of immediate evil or an intent to bring it about that warrants Congress in

From *Abrams* v. *United States*, 250 U.S. 616 (1919)

setting a limit to the expression of opinion where private rights are not concerned. Congress certainly cannot forbid all effort to change the mind of the country. Now nobody can suppose that the surreptitious publishing of a silly leaflet by an unknown man, without more, would present any immediate danger that its opinions would hinder the success of the government arms or have any appreciable tendency to do so. . . .

I do not see how anyone can find the intent required by the statute in any of the defendants' words. The second leaflet is the only one that affords even a foundation for the charge, and there, without invoking the hatred of German militarism expressed in the former one, it is evident from the beginning to the end that the only object of the paper is to help Russia and stop American intervention there against the popular government—not to impede the United States in the war that it was carrying on. To say that two phrases taken literally might import a suggestion of conduct that would have interference with the war as an indirect and probably undesired effect seems to me by no means enough to show an attempt to produce that effect. . . .

Persecution for the expression of opinions seems to me perfectly logical. If you have no doubt of your premises or your power and want a certain result with all your heart you naturally express your wishes in law and sweep away all opposition. To allow opposition by speech seems to indicate that you think the speech impotent, as when a man says that he has squared the circle, or that you do not care whole-heartedly for the result, or that you doubt either your power or your premises. But when men have realized that time has upset many fighting faiths, they may come to believe even more than they believe the very foundations of their own conduct that the ultimate good desired is better reached by free trade in ideas—that the best test of truth is the power of the thought to get itself accepted in the competition of the market, and that truth is the only ground upon which their wishes safely can be carried out. That at any rate is the theory of our Constitution. It is an experiment, as all life is an experiment. Every year if not every day we have to wager our salvation upon some prophecy based upon imperfect knowledge. While that experiment is part of our system I think that we should be eternally vigilant against attempts to check the expression of opinions that we loathe and believe to be fraught with death, unless they so imminently threaten immediate interference with the lawful and pressing purposes of the law that an immediate check is required to save the country. I wholly disagree with the argument of the Government that the First Amendment left the common law as to seditious libel in force. History seems to me against the notion. I had conceived that the United States through many years had shown its repentance for the Sedition Act of 1798, by repaying fines that it imposed. Only the emergency that makes it immediately dangerous to leave the correction of evil counsels to time warrants making any exception to the sweeping command, "Congress shall make no law. . . abridging the freedom of speech." Of course I am speaking only of expressions of opinion and exhortations, which were all that were uttered here, but I regret that I cannot put into more impressive words my belief that in their conviction upon this indictment the defendants were deprived of their rights under the Constitution of the United States.

Protecting Unpopular Thought

Brandenburg v. Ohio

Justice Holmes's "clear and present danger" test had a checkered career over the next decades as the Supreme Court permitted Congress and the state legislatures frequently to define the "substantive evils" to be prevented. Membership in certain organizations, such as the Communist Party, or advocacy of violent revolution became "substantive evils" that the legislatures could forbid, even if freedom of speech, assembly, and press were thereby curtailed.

On the one hand, the Supreme Court upheld state syndicalism laws (Whitney v. California, 1927) *during the 1920s, and in the period of the Cold War it found the Smith Act* (Dennis v. United States, 1951) *also constitutional. Both the syndicalism statutes and the Smith Act punished membership in organizations advocating or teaching revolution. On the other hand, the Supreme Court adhered to the "clear and present danger" test in numerous decisions of the late 1930s and early 1940s, overturning the convictions of individuals who had been sentenced to prison for radical or subversive speech. During the years of the Cold War, anticommunism, and Senator McCarthy, however, the "clear and present danger" test again went into eclipse. It became the dominant position on the Court during the final years of Earl Warren's Chief Justiceship, as the following decision in* Brandenburg v. Ohio *(1969) indicates.*

Per Curiam *

The appellant, a leader of a Ku Klux Klan group, was convicted under the Ohio Criminal Syndicalism statute of "advocat(ing) . . . the duty, necessity, or propriety of crime, sabotage, violence, or unlawful methods of terrorism as a means of accomplishing industrial or political reform" and of "voluntarily assembl(ing) with any society, group or assemblage of persons formed to teach or advocate the doctrines of criminal syndicalism." Ohio Rev. Code 2923.13.

Ed. note: By the court.

From *Brandenburg* v. *Ohio,* 395 U.S. 444 (1969).

He was fined $1,000 and sentenced to one to 10 years' imprisonment. The appellant challenged the constitutionality of the criminal syndicalism statute under the First and Fourteenth Amendments to the United States Constitution, but the intermediate appellate court of Ohio affirmed his conviction without opinion. The Supreme Court of Ohio dismissed his appeal, . . . "for the reason that no substantial constitutional question exists herein." . . . We reverse.

The record shows that a man, identified at trial as the appellant, telephoned an announcer-reporter on the staff of a Cincinnati television station and invited him to come to a Ku Klux Klan "rally" to be held at a farm in Hamilton County. With the cooperation of the organizers, the reporter and a cameraman attended the meeting and filmed the events. Portions of the films were later broadcast on the local station and on a national network.

The prosecution's case rested on the films and on testimony identifying the appellant as the person who communicated with the reporter and who spoke at the rally. The State also introduced into evidence several articles appearing in the film, including a pistol, a rifle, a shotgun, ammunition, a Bible, and a red hood worn by the speaker in the films.

One film showed 12 hooded figures, some of whom carried firearms. They were gathered around a large wooden cross, which they burned. No one was present other than the participants and the newsmen who made the film. Most of the words uttered during the scene were incomprehensible when the film was projected, but scattered phrases could be understood that were derogatory of Negroes and, in one instance, of Jews. Another scene on the same film showed the appellant, in Klan regalia, making a speech. The speech, in full, was as follows:

> This is an organizers' meeting. We have had quite a few members here today which are—we have hundreds, hundreds of members throughout the State of Ohio. I can quote from a newspaper clipping from the Columbus Ohio Dispatch, five weeks ago Sunday morning. The Klan has more members in the State of Ohio than does any other organization. We're not a revengent organization, but if our President, our Congress, our Supreme Court, continues to suppress the white, Caucasian race, it's possible that there might have to be some revengence taken.
>
> We are marching on Congress July the Fourth, four hundred thousand strong. From there we are dividing into two groups, one group to march on St. Augustine, Florida, the othe group to march into Mississippi. Thank you.

The second film showed six hooded figures, one of whom, later identified as the appellant, repeated a speech very similar to that recorded on the first film. The reference to the possibility of "revengence" was omitted, and one sentence was added: "Personally, I believe the nigger should be returned to Africa, the Jew returned to Israel." Though some of the figures in the films carried weapons, the speaker did not.

The Ohio Criminal Syndicalism Statute was enacted in 1919. From 1917 to 1920, identical or quite similar laws were adopted by 20 States and two territories. . . . In 1927, this Court sustained the constitutionality of California's Criminal Syndicalism Act, the text of which is quite similar to that of the laws of Ohio. Whitney v. California, 274 U.S. 357 (1927). The Court upheld the statute on the ground that, without more, "advocating" violent means to effect political and economic change involves such danger to the security of the State that the State may outlaw it. . . . But Whitney has been thoroughly discredited by later decisions. . . . These later decisions have fashioned the principle that the constitutional guarantees of free speech and free press do not permit a State to forbid or proscribe advocacy of the use of force or of law violation except where such advocacy is directed to inciting or producing imminent lawless action and is likely to incite or produce such action. . . .

Measured by this test, Ohio's Criminal Syndicalism Act cannot be sustained. The Act punishes persons who "advocate or teach the duty, necessity, or propriety" of violence "as a means of accomplishing industrial or political reform"; or who publish or circulate or display any book or paper containing such advocacy; or who "justify" the commission of violent acts "with intent to exemplify, spread or advocate the propriety of the doctrines of criminal syndicalism"; or who "voluntarily assemble" with a group formed "to teach or advocate the doctrines of criminal syndicalism.". . .

Accordingly, we are here confronted with a statute which, by its own words and as applied, purports to punish mere advocacy and to forbid, on pain of criminal punishment, assembly with others merely to advocate the described type of action. Such a statute falls within the condemnation of the First and Fourteenth Amendments. . . .

Reversed

Serving the Governed: Freedom of the Press

New York Times Co. *v.* United States

Although the Supreme Court has adopted a flexible standard in some areas covered by the First Amendment, it has consistently rejected government attempts to censor materials before publication. A dramatic confrontation between the First Amendment and the government took place in 1971, when the United States government sought to prevent the Washington Post *and the* New York Times *from printing the contents of a classified study on the history of American policy in Vietnam, the so-called Pentagon Papers. Publication of these documents, the government argued, would jeopardize national security by hampering diplomatic negotiations with the enemy and endangering the lives of military personnel in Vietnam.*

Rejecting the government's contentions, the Supreme Court, in New York Times Co. v. United States, *refused to enjoin publication. "Any system of prior restraints of expression," the Court said, "comes . . . bearing a heavy presumption against its constitutional validity." Justices Black and Douglas, joining the Court's opinion, wrote the following eloquent defense of freedom of the press.*

Mr. Justice Black, with whom
Mr. Justice Douglas joins, concurring.

I adhere to the view that the Government's case against the Washington Post should have been dismissed and that the injunction against the New York Times should have been vacated without oral argument when the cases were first presented to this Court. I believe that every moment's continuance of the injunctions against these newspapers amounts to a flagrant, indefensible, and continuing violation of the First Amendment. . . . In my view it is unfortunate that some of my Brethren are apparently willing to hold that the publication of news may sometimes be enjoined. Such a holding would make a shambles of the First Amendment.

Our Government was launched in 1789 with the adoption of the Constitution. The Bill of Rights, including the First Amendment, followed in 1791. Now, for the first time in the 182 years since the founding of the Republic, the federal courts are asked to hold that the First Amendment

From *New York Times Co.* v. *United States*, 403 U.S. 713 (1971).

does not mean what it says, but rather means that the Government can halt the publication of current news of vital importance to the people of this country.

In seeking injunctions against these newspapers and in its presentation to the Court, the Executive Branch seems to have forgotten the essential purpose and history of the First Amendment. When the Constitution was adopted, many people strongly opposed it because the document contained no Bill of Rights to safeguard certain basic freedoms. They especially feared that the new powers granted to a central government might be interpreted to permit the government to curtail freedom of religion, press, assembly, and speech. In response to an overwhelming public clamor, James Madison offered a series of amendments to satisfy citizens that these great liberties would remain safe and beyond the power of government to abridge. Madison proposed what later became the First Amendment in three parts, two of which are set out below, and one of which proclaimed: "The people shall not be deprived or abridged of their right to speak, to write, or to publish their sentiments; *and the freedom of the press, as one of the great bulwarks of liberty, shall be inviolable."* (Emphasis added.) The amendments were offered to *curtail* and *restrict* the general powers granted to the Executive, Legislative, and Judicial Branches two years before in the original Constitution. The Bill of Rights changed the original Constitution into a new charter under which no branch of government could abridge the people's freedoms of press, speech, religion, and assembly. Yet the Solicitor General argues and some members of the Court appear to agree that the general powers of the Government adopted in the original Constitution should be interpreted to limit and restrict the specific and emphatic guarantees of the Bill of Rights adopted later. I can imagine no greater perversion of history. Madison and the other Framers of the First Amendment, able men that they were, wrote in language they earnestly believed could never be misunderstood: "Congress shall make no law . . . abridging the freedoms . . . of the press. . . . "|Both the history and language of the First Amendment support the view that the press must be left free to publish news, whatever the source, without censorship, injunctions, or prior restraints.

In the First Amendment the Founding Fathers gave the free press the protection it must have to fulfill its essential role in our democracy. The press was to serve the governed, not the governors. The Government's power to censor the press was abolished so that the press would remain forever free to censure the Government. The press was protected so that it could bare the secrets of government and inform the people. Only a free and unrestrained press can effectively expose deception in government. And paramount among the responsibilities of a free press is the duty to prevent any part of the government from deceiving the people and sending them off to distant lands to die of foreign fevers and foreign shot and shell. In my view, far from deserving condemnation for their courageous reporting, the New York Times, the Washington Post, and other newspapers should be commended for serving the purpose that the Founding Fathers saw so clearly. In revealing the workings of government that led to the Vietnam war, the newspapers nobly did precisely that which the Founders hoped and trusted they would do. . . .

The Government argues in its brief that in spite of the First Amendment, "(t)he authority of the Executive Department to protect the nation against publication of information whose disclosure would endanger the national security stems from two interrelated sources: the constitutional power of the President over the conduct of foreign affairs and his authority as Commander-in-Chief."

In other words, we are asked to hold that despite the First Amendment's emphatic command, the Executive Branch, the Congress, and the Judiciary can make laws enjoining publication of current news and abridging freedom of the press in the name of "national security." The Government does not even attempt to rely on any act of Congress. Instead it makes the bold and dangerously far-reaching contention that the courts should take it upon themselves to "make" a law abridging freedom of the press in the name of equity, presidential power and national security, even when the representatives of the people in Congress have adhered to the command of the First Amendment and refused to make such a law. . . . To find that the President has "inherent power" to halt the publication of news by resort to the courts would wipe out the First Amendment and destroy the fundamental liberty and security of the very people the Government hopes to make "secure." No one can read the history of the adoption of the First Amendment without being convinced beyond any doubt that it was injunctions like those sought here that Madison and his collaborators intended to outlaw in this Nation for all time.

The word "security" is a broad, vague generality whose contours should not be invoked to abrogate the fundamental law embodied in the First Amendment. The guarding of military and diplomatic secrets at the expense of informed representative government provides no real security for our Republic. The Framers of the First Amendment, fully aware of both the need to defend a new nation and the abuses of the English and Colonial governments, sought to give this new society strength and security by providing that freedom of speech, press, religion, and assembly should not be abridged.

"The Right of the People to be Secure"

Johnson *v.* United States

Before the American Revolution, no single practice of the British government generated more hatred among the colonists than the use of general search warrants, known as Writs of Assistance. Authorized by Parliament and valid for the lifetime of each British monarch, these writs seldom described a specific person or place to be searched. British colonial officials, however, eager to impose "law and order" upon the unruly Americans, believed that general warrants were necessary to stamp out smuggling and other illicit trading activities. John Adams, for one, believed that resistance to the writs in Massachusetts "was the first scene of the first act of opposition to the arbitrary claims of Great Britain. Then and there, the child Independence was born."

The Fourth Amendment's prohibition against "unreasonable searches and seizures," and its command that "no warrants shall issue" unless "particularly describing the place to be searched, and the persons or things to be seized," thus sprang from the Revolutionary generation's deep suspicion of such official conduct, which could jeopardize the liberty of innocent citizens. From the eighteenth century to the present, disputes over search and seizure have been marked by constant tension between the community's desire to control criminal actions and the value of individual security. Supreme Court Justice Robert Jackson provided a classic analysis of these tensions in the 1948 case of Johnson *v.* United States, *excerpted below.*

Mr. Justice Jackson delivered the opinion of the Court:

Petitioner was convicted on four counts charging violation of federal narcotic laws. The only question which brings the case here is whether it was lawful, without a warrant of any kind, to arrest petitioner and to search her living quarters.

Taking the Government's version of disputed events, decision would rest on these facts:

From *Johnson* v. *United States*, 333 U.S. 10 (1948).

At about 7:30 P.M. Detective Lieutenant Belland, an officer of the Seattle police force narcotic detail, received information from a confidential informer, who was also a known narcotic user, that unknown persons were smoking opium in the Europe Hotel. The informer was taken back to the hotel to interview the manager, but he returned at once saying he could smell burning opium in the hallway. Belland communicated with federal narcotic agents and between 8:30 and 9 o'clock went back to the hotel with four such agents. All were experienced in narcotic work and recognized at once a strong odor of burning opium which to them was distinctive and unmistakable. The odor led to Room 1. The officers did not know who was occupying that room. They knocked and a voice inside asked who was there. "Lieutenant Belland," was the reply. There was a slight delay, some "shuffling or noise" in the room and then the defendant opened the door. The officer said, "I want to talk to you a little bit." She then, as he described it, "stepped back acquiescently and admitted us." He said, "I want to talk to you about this opium smell in the room here." She denied that there was such a smell. Then he said, "I want you to consider yourself under arrest because we are going to search the room." The search turned up incriminating opium and smoking apparatus, the latter being warm, apparently from recent use. This evidence the District Court refused to suppress before trial and admitted over defendant's objection at the trial. Conviction resulted and the Circuit Court of Appeals affirmed.

The defendant challenged the search of her home as a violation of the rights secured to her, in common with others, by the Fourth Amendment to the Constitution. The Government defends the search as legally justifiable, more particularly as incident to what it urges was a lawful arrest of the person.

I

The Fourth Amendment to the Constitution of the United States provides:

"The right of the people to be secure in their persons, houses, papers, and effects, against unreasonable searches and seizures, shall not be violated, and no Warrants shall issue, but upon probable cause, supported by Oath or affirmation, and particularly describing the place to be searched, and the persons or things to be seized."

Entry to defendant's living quarters, which was the beginning of the search, was demanded under color of office. It was granted in submission to authority rather than as an understanding and intentional waiver of a constitutional right. . . .

At the time entry was demanded the officers were possessed of evidence which a magistrate might have found to be probable cause for issuing a search warrant. We cannot sustain defendant's contention, erroneously made . . . that odors cannot be evidence sufficient to constitute probable grounds for any search. . . . If the presence of odors is testified to before a magistrate and he finds the affiant qualified to know the odor, and it is one sufficiently distinctive to identify a forbidden substance, this Court has never held such a basis insufficient to justify issuance of a search warrant. Indeed it might very well be found to be evidence of most persuasive character.

The point of the Fourth Amendment, which often is not grasped by zealous officers, is not that it denies law enforcement the support of the usual inferences which reasonable men draw from evidence. Its protection consists in requiring that those inferences be drawn by a neutral and detached magistrate instead of being judged by the officer engaged in the often competitive enterprise of ferreting out crime. Any assumption that evidence sufficient to support a magistrate's disinterested determination to issue a search warrant will justify the officers in making a search without a warrant would reduce the Amendment to a nullity and leave the people's homes secure only in the discretion of police officers. Crime, even in the privacy of one's own quarters, is, of course, of grave concern to society, and the law allows such crime to be reached on proper showing. The right of officers to thrust themselves into a home is also a grave concern, not only to the individual but to a society which chooses to dwell in reasonable security and freedom from surveillance. When the right of privacy must reasonably yield to the right of search is, as a rule, to be decided by a judicial officer, not by a policeman or government enforcement agent.

There are exceptional circumstances in which, on balancing the need for effective law enforcement against the right of privacy, it may be contended that a magistrate's warrant for search may be dispensed with. But this is not such a case. No reason is offered for not obtaining a search warrant except the inconvenience to the officers and some slight delay necessary to prepare papers and present the evidence to a magistrate. These are never very convincing reasons and, in these circumstances, certainly are not enough to by-pass the constitutional requirement. No suspect was fleeing or likely to take flight. The search was of permanent permises, not of a movable vehicle. No evidence or contraband was threatened with removal or destruction, except perhaps the fumes which we suppose in time would disappear. But they were not capable at any time of being reduced to possession for presentation to court. The evidence of their existence before the search was adequate and the testimony of the officers to that effect would not perish from the delay of getting a warrant.

If the officers in this case were excused from the constitutional duty of presenting their evidence to a magistrate, it is difficult to think of a case in which it should be required.

II

The Government contends, however, that this search without warrant must be held valid because incident to an arrest. The alleged ground of validity requires examination of the facts to determine whether the arrest itself was lawful. Since it was without warrant, it could be valid only if for a crime committed in the presence of the arresting officer or for a felony of which he had reasonable cause to believe defendant guilty.

The Government, in effect, concedes that the arresting officer did not have probable cause to arrest petitioner until he had entered her room and found her to be the sole occupant. It points out specifically, referring to the time just before entry, "For at that time the agents did not know whether there was one or several persons in the room. It was reasonable to believe that the room might have been an opium smoking den." And it says, ". . . that when the agents were admitted into the room and found only petitioner present they had a reasonable basis for believing that she had been smoking opium and thus illicitly possessed the narcotic." Thus the

Government quite properly stakes the right to arrest, not on the informer's tip and the smell the officers recognized before entry, but on the knowledge that she was alone in the room, gained only after, and wholly by reason of, their entry of her home. It was therefore their observations inside of her quarters, after they had obtained admission under color of their police authority, on which they made the arrest.

Thus the Government is obliged to justify the arrest by the search and at the same time to justify the search by the arrest. This will not do. An officer gaining access to private living quarters under color of his office and of the law which he personifies must then have some valid basis in law for the intrusion. Any other rule would undermine "the right of the people to be secure in their persons, houses, papers, and effects," and would obliterate one of the most fundamental distinctions between our form of government, where officers are under the law, and the police-state where they are the law.

Reversed

The Chief Justice, Mr. Justice Black, Mr. Justice Reed and Mr. Justice Burton dissent.

Law, Criminals, and the Court

Henry J. Abraham

As the Johnson *case illustrates, the Fourth Amendment requires judges to walk a fine line between two competing social interests: the desire of the community to be secure against criminal activity and the equally intense desire to protect personal freedoms guaranteed to all citizens by the Bill of Rights.*

In Fourth Amendment cases, the line drawn by the Supreme Court has frequently been a jagged one, its direction depending upon the specific facts of each case and the composition of the Court itself. Justice Jackson's opinion in Johnson *argues that searches conducted without warrant, where opportunity had existed to secure a warrant, are always "unreasonable." Yet in subsequent cases, the "reasonableness" of the search itself, not the warrant requirement, became the standard of constitutionality. These and other issues relating to due process, the Fourth Amendment, and the criminal law are discussed by Henry J. Abraham in his book* Freedom and the Court, *from which this excerpt is drawn.*

No one challenges the basic contention that both the individual and society are entitled to "due process of law." The balance, however, has of late shifted to the side of the potential or actual lawbreaker—in the opinion of a good many observers. The Supreme Court has come under fire because of its tightening of due process concepts in recent decisions, particularly in the field of criminal justice. Has the Court gone too far—or not far enough? There is no answer that will please everyone but it is possible to consider some fundamental points.

"The Criminal Gets the Breaks"

This caption in an article in *The New York Times Magazine* late in 1964 was written by Dean Daniel Gutman of the New York Law School. . . . With unassailable statistics demonstrating a continued upward trend in crime, Dean Gutman warned that "we do not solve the

---

problem of dealing with those who make crime their business by providing procedural methods of escape for the guilty, to the detriment of the law-abiding who are victimized by the lawless." After reciting a number of the more controversial Supreme Court decisions "in favor of criminals" . . . the author called for a series of steps to be taken "within the framework of the Constitution and the Bill of Rights" to remedy the situation. Among them were (a) legislation to permit wiretapping, pursuant to court order, for evidence of major crimes; (b) "recodification" of procedural requirements for search and seizure, "which are distinctive for ancient strictures no longer valid"; (c) extension of the right to detain and interrogate, with due safeguards against coercion or other violation of constitutional rights; (d) classification of the "extent and application" of the concept of right to counsel; and (e) "relaxation of the rule excluding all evidence improperly obtained, so as to vest discretion as to admission in the trial judge." Such a list prompts recognition of the paradox that the administration of justice poses to thoughtful and committed Americans like Dean Gutman, the members of the Supreme Court, and their respective supporters and detractors. The basic issues are likely to remain unresolved—notwithstanding the valiant efforts of such qualified groups as the American Bar Association (which undertook a three-year $750,000 study and search for minimum standards of justice); the President's National Commission on the Causes and Prevention of Violence (the Milton Eisenhower Commission); or, for that matter, the feverish activity by Congress in the popular "law-and-order" realm (especially following the 1968 elections).

Has the Court Been Too Lenient?

It is entirely natural to ask—as Mr. Justice Lewis F. Powell, Jr., as the 1965 president of the American Bar Association, did—whether the Supreme Court of the United States has not in fact tipped the balance of justice in favor of the criminal to the detriment of the public? Given a rise in crime from 1958 to 1971 at a rate five times faster than the growth of America's population, it is understandable that professionals and laymen alike should be fond of quoting Mr. Justice Cardozo's well-known observation that "[J]ustice is due the accused, but it is also due the accuser." . . .

In insisting upon strict standards of decency and fairness in governmental law-making, law-enforcing, and prosecuting, the Court simply performs its historic function of protecting the rights of the individual against the alleged unlawful acts of government. . . .

But to devote some thought to certain of the specific attacks upon Supreme Court rulings, *just which* of the more recent controversial issues would we have the Court or—failing its acquiescence to a hearing—the legislative branches alter, if not negate? The famed *Gideon* decision that guaranteed counsel in state criminal proceedings for indigent defendants in all criminal cases? Or its subsequent extension to the preliminary hearing stage? Or its further extension to the interrogation stage following arrest? Can any member of a democratic society *honestly* argue the point that counsel in a criminal case is a luxury, that he who cannot afford it is not entitled to it? Or that, as in Danny Escobedo's situation, a request to consult with one's attorney prior to a police interrogation is somehow loading the dice against the government? * . . .

Of course, it is revolting to find obvious, confessed murderers go scot-free (indeed, the phrase "getting away with murder" applies here literally). . . . One may well ask why the State was not justified in utilizing *any* methods that would bring such a criminal to justice. The answer is simple: because of our civilized standards of decency, fair play, and due process, our Constitution simply and resolutely proscribes such methods. . . .

We have neither time nor space to survey each of the various contentious and difficult areas in which the lines of private and public rights converge. But one last illustration: the complex matter permissible of search and seizure—which may well be *the* most complex to analyze as well as to adjudicate. Under the Fourth Amendment, *unreasonable* searches and seizures are forbidden; out of this grew the so-called exclusionary rule applied to the federal government as of 1914 and . . . to the states as of 1961. The exclusionary rule now forbids the use of *any* illegally obtained evidence to convict an accused in court, although the as yet (fall 1971) untested Organized Crime Control Act of 1970 contains a provision of questionable constitutionality which sets a five-year statute of limitations on challenges by defendants of evidence from leads picked up by officers during *illegal* searches. The basic exclusionary rule also means that an otherwise illegal search is not rendered legal simply by what it turns up; *a fortiorari*, "fishing expeditions" on the part of police in search of evidence are thus out. Before asking for an arrest warrant, the police officer must convince the warrant-issuing magistrate of his "personal knowledge" of "probable cause." To obtain a search warrant, the place to be searched *and* the object(s) to be seized must be described "particularly." Warrants are not issuable for "general" searches.

But there are, because there must be, situations in which the search of a person or the *immediate* surroundings is lawful *if* it is "incidental" to a legal arrest—i.e. one authorized by an arrest warrant or on the basis of probable cause—but such an "incidental" search, to be considered "reasonable," must *really* be "confined to the immediate vicinity of the arrest . . . to the area within the arrestee's reach at the time of his arrest, the area from which he might gain possession of a weapon or destructible evidence." *Mere* "suspicion," without more, is never enough to meet the constitutional commands, but there are instances, other than the narrowly drawn "incidental" search rule, in which it *is* possible to search without a search warrant, *provided there is probable cause*. Some examples would be: to discover weapons and/or prevent the destruction of evidence; the

---

*Ed. note: Gideon v. Wainwright (1963) involved an indigent who claimed he was improperly convicted and fought his case to the Supreme Court from a prison in Florida. In Escobedo v. Illinois (1964), the Court held that a confession obtained from a defendant who had been denied permission to see his lawyer could not be used as evidence. In the 1966 case of Miranda v. Arizona, the Court held that prior to any questioning, a defendant must be informed of his constitutional rights, including the right to remain silent.

common-law right of an arresting police agent to search when he has reasonable grounds to believe that a crime is being committed or that an individual on the scene is "armed and dangerous"; and, again always assuming the presence of "probable cause," in the case of *moving* vehicles. Despite the stringent judicial requirements in the search-and-seizure field, however, the cards are still heavily stacked in favor of the agents of government—and perhaps they have to be. But here, too, frustrating as it may be, the constitutional rules must be observed.

The Case Study of Wiretapping

To illustrate further, wiretapping, one of the most vexatious of the due process problems, is *not* unconstitutional—or at least the Supreme Court has never so held it. The famous 5:4 *Olmstead* case of 1928 set the tone, Mr. Chief Justice Taft holding it *not* to be a Fourth Amendment violation because the telephonic messages at issue did not involve a physical intrusion on the defendant's premises, nor was any "material thing" seized. Mr. Justice Holmes's vigorous dissent that it is "dirty business," and Mr. Justice Brandeis's prophetic warning about the "progress" of science, also rendered in a separate dissenting opinion, failed to command a majority. The response to *Olmstead* was the Federal Communications Act of 1934 which (like state statutes) expressly forbade it; yet the F.B.I. successfully qualified it with the interpretation that mere "interception" is not a violation of the Act's famous Section 605 *unless there* is also *"divulgence"*—an interpretation which served as the agency's rationale for much of its wiretapping, despite the language of Section 605. Hence we had something that was proscribed yet went on constantly!

But does not wiretapping make the citizen prey to the very kind of "fishing expedition" which is theoretically forbidden under the Fourth Amendment? The modern scientific "advances" in the realm of detection, so perceptively predicted by Brandeis, are rapidly reducing privacy to a shibboleth. Thus, as was demonstrated in 1965 and 1966 to a subcommittee of the United States Senate's Committee on the Judiciary, headed by Senator Edward V. Long (D.—Mo.), we now have available such eavesdropping devices as tiny radio transmitters that can be concealed in a martini olive, with the toothpick serving as the antenna; in a woman's purse or her brassiere—even in the cavity of a tooth of an intimate associate! Then there is the laser, a device which can transmit a concentrated beam of light to a room several blocks away so as to reflect back a television picture of everything happening in the room, including the sound! Perhaps it was specters such as these that caused Mr. Justice Nathan R. Sobel of the New York State Supreme Court (Brooklyn Division) to declare unconstitutional on March 1, 1965, the New York State law that had authorized court-approved electronic eavesdropping on a suspect's private premises. In his 32-page opinion, Justice Sobel held the law invalid because the eavesdropping orders it authorized could not, in his judgment, meet the standards required for the issuance of search warrants under the Fourth Amendment. Just a year later, the Federal Communications Commission issued an order prohibiting private citizens from using radio devices to eavesdrop. Theoretically, the F.C.C. order made illegal such equipment as the tiny radio transmitters described above (unless everyone present knew the equipment was being used). Yet it did *not* affect the use of a miniature tape recorder directly connected to a small camouflaged microphone, since no radio transmission is involved—although the same kind of eavesdropping may take place. Nor did the ban affect law enforcement agencies, such as the F.B.I., the Internal Revenue Service, or state and local police and similar authorities. However, in July 1967 the then Attorney-General, Ramsey Clark, in a dramatic order going far beyond any previously issued governmental limitations in the wiretapping and eavesdropping field, issued sweeping new regulations forbidding all wiretapping and virtually all eavesdropping except in national security cases. The new rules generated considerable controversy and opposition among federal agents and prosecutors.

. . . It might well be asked, could not and should not the kind of search and seizure represented by wiretapping be authorized under our Constitution? Although wiretapping and electronic eavesdropping are clearcut invasions of the basic rights of privacy, perhaps they *are* necessary in cases of subversive activities, seditious conduct, espionage, kidnapping, and certain other major crimes. Perhaps a good case *can* be made for eavesdropping in the fields just mentioned when the act is duly requested *and judicially authorized before the fact,* notwithstanding the reprehensible nature of the incursions of privacy involved. However, it would be much harder to make a viable case for such intrusions on privacy in crimes like fraud, racketeering, prostitution, and gambling, or for the "investigation" of public and private employees in anything but highly secret positions. In the final analysis, our response must turn first on the constitutionality of any such proposed action and second on its wisdom. And even assuming the former, any thoughts on the wisdom of such action must confront the basic issues raised by Mr. Justice Brandeis in his memorable dissent in the *Olmstead* case, when he wrote:

> The makers of our Constitution undertook to secure conditions favorable to the pursuit of happiness. They recognized the significance of man's spiritual nature, of his feelings and of his intellect. They knew that only a part of the pain, pleasure and satisfactions of life are to be found in material things. They sought to protect Americans in their beliefs, their thoughts, their emotions and their sensations. They conferred, as against the Government, *the right to be let alone—the most comprehensive of rights and the right most valued by civilized men.* To protect that right, every unjustifiable intrusion by the Government upon the privacy of the individual, whatever the means employed, must be deemed a violation of the Fourth Amendment. . . .

The Court—the recipient of so many governmentally, especially legislatively, "passed bucks"—in its December 1967 catalystic *Katz* case seemed to take a long stride toward a possible solution of at least the eavesdropping ("bugging") aspect of the problem, and by implication, of the entire privacy/intrusion dilemma. In that decision, with a solo dissent by Mr. Justice Black—who consistently rejected the contention that the safeguards of the Fourth Amendment apply to eavesdropping—the Court *eased curbs* on "bugging" *while adding safeguards* against it! It made clear that the Constitution does not forbid electronic "bugging" by law enforcement officers *if* they first obtain warrants authorizing the eavesdropping—warrants being a basic requirement of the Fourth Amendment, of course. *But,* at the same time, the Court extended the reach of that Amendment by holding that the search warrant procedure must be followed by the police officers even when they plan to eavesdrop on persons in semi-public places, such as a phone booth. Moreover, and significantly, the Court threw out its old "physical trespass" test by ruling that the trespass *per se* was not the crucial point, that the Fourth Amendment "protects people not places," and thus in effect overruled both the "material things seized" rationale of the *Olmstead* holding and the "physical intrusion" distinction of the *Goldman·* case (which had come midway between the *Olmstead* and *Katz* decisions). . . . What *Katz* did, then, was to enable the enactment of both wiretapping and eavesdropping ("bugging") statutes, *provided* the carefully delineated Fourth Amendment safeguards against unreasonable searches and seizures would be scrupulously observed by *all* branches of the government, both statutorily and procedurally.

Against the backdrop of the rising controversy of the "law and order" issue, Congress took the *Katz* cue, and enacted Title III of the Omnibus Crime Control and Safe Streets Act of 1968, headed "Wiretapping and Electronic Surveillance." It permits *court-approved* interceptions by both federal and state law enforcement officials in the investigation of a large number of listed crimes—there were 302 such court orders in 1969 and 597 in 1970 throughout the United States. Replete with procedural safeguards—with an eye toward *Katz*—the law has a contentious "exemption" section in the case of "an emergency situation exist[ing] with respect to conspiratorial activities threatening the national security interest or to conspiratorial activities characteristic of organized crime. . . ." Under its terms, and if the action at issue is so classified by either the U.S. Attorney-General or the principal prosecuting attorney of any state or its subdivisions, interception may proceed *without* court order, provided an application for an order is obtained and entered "within forty-eight hours after the interception has occurred or begins to occur." Here, then, is the loophole—which may, or may not be justifiable and constitutional. It is assuredly controversial, and there is little doubt that, sooner or later, the delicate issue will reach the Supreme Court.

A different, and perhaps even more significant test, however, did come in January 1971 when, breaking new ground in a surprisingly bold decision, United States District Judge Warren J. Ferguson ruled in Los Angeles that the federal government's "no-warrant-needed" national security wiretap policy, allegedly inherent in that section of the 1968 statute, which states that the law's provisions "do not restrict the constitutional powers of the President," was unconstitutional as applied to *domestic* cases (rather than foreign ones). As he put the issue:

> National security cannot be invoked to abridge basic rights. . . . To guarantee political freedom, our forefathers agreed to take certain risks which are inherent in a free democracy. It is unthinkable that we should now be required to sacrifice those freedoms in order to defend them.

A month later, Judge Ferguson's ruling was echoed in an even more strongly worded decision against the government's interpretation of its asserted authority under the 1968 Wiretapping Act by United States District Judge Damon J. Keith in a Detroit case. [*Plamondon* v. *Mitchell*]. The government appealed; lost 2:1 at the bar of the United States Court of Appeals for the Sixth Circuit in April, which held, *inter alia,* that there was not "one written phrase" in the Constitution or statutes to support the Administration's view that federal agents might legally wiretap radical domestic groups without court order; and took a further appeal to the Supreme Court, which granted review in June 1971 for the 1971-72 term of Court. Obviously, another attempt at line-drawing will have to be undertaken by the Supreme Court in this difficult and emotion-charged realm. But this time that line will be drawn by the Burger Court, a group of men evidently more cautious and more deferential to legislative wishes than its predecessor, assuredly in the criminal justice sector, if not in some of the others that we shall treat presently.

Law, Order, and Justice Reconsidered

Notwithstanding the great public outcry in the late 1960s and early 1970s, particularly, to do something about the alarmingly predictable annual 10 per cent rise in crime, there are no shortcuts in democratic society to regulation, prosecution, and conviction. But it would be sophistry to gainsay the genuine concern, both lay and professional, over the recent augmentation of judicial supervision in the realm of criminal justice and the resultant stringent new rules of procedure that have evolved. Given the increasing rate of crime, is there an alternative to "easy" or "shortcut" apprehensions, prosecutions, and convictions that either circumvent, dilute, or disregard basic constitutional guarantees? Since, according to the most authentic and reliable recent statistics, between 65 and 92 per cent of those booked on criminal charges were recidivists ("repeaters"), it seems reasonable to ask whether our courts might not be more severe in the type and length of sentences meted out to recidivists. The public has the right to be protected from habitual criminality; and perhaps longer, less readily commutable, and less easily parolable sentences may well be in order. It does seem that trial judges and parole officers have often been guilty of the kind of lenience in criminal cases involving "repeaters" that may be appropriate only for an *initial* offense. But there is another aspect to that suggestion.

254

Because "bigger and better" prison sentences will not solve the problem of crime, a plea for toughness in sentencing must join one for *much* more effective prison rehabilitation; for *much* more modern institutional facilities; and for *much* better trained professional personnel. Revelations in 1969 and 1970 of conditions in prisons, styled "universities of crime" by President Nixon, gave shocking proof of the state of America's prisons—of which six, still in use in 1971, were built in the eighteenth century, and four prior to George Washington's inauguration. Since 1967, four presidential commissions, dozens of legislative reports, and more than 500 books and articles have pleaded for prison reform. Although 1971 saw some *bona fide* groping for such reform, the future still looked bleak. Coordination and improvement of federal, state, and local systems are vital.

Of course, there is a limit to the type of rehabilitation that a prison can provide—but much more can be done than is done at present. The public, however, must be willing to foot the bill for such measures; insistence on more protection has been accompanied by opposition to paying for it.

Whether or not these suggestions might help us come to grips with important aspects of the problem and assuage the fears of the lay and professional public, or whether the Organized Crime Control Act of 1970, with its drastic provisions, has some answers, when it comes to the fundamental standards of due process of law under our Constitution, there can be no compromises, no shortcuts. "The interest of . . . [the government]," to quote . . . Mr. Justice Brennan, "is not that it shall win a case, but that justice shall be done." There is no reason why in our democratic society, well-trained, professional agents of the law cannot apprehend and convict alleged criminals without, in the process, becoming criminals themselves. As Arnold S. Trebach put it so well in his *The Rationing of Justice,* the argument *against* greater protection for the rights of the accused "reduces itself to an argument *for* violation of the law in order to enforce it. It is a crime to violate the rights of *any* person," whether he be a criminal or a saint. Under our system, in the words of Mr. Chief Justice Warren to Anthony Lewis, the prosecutor "is not paid to convict people. He is there to protect the rights of the people in our community and to see that when there is a violation of the law, it is vindicated by trial and prosecution under fair judicial standards."

As he did so frequently, Mr. Justice Brandeis went to the heart of the matter in his dissent in the *Olmstead* case in 1928:

Decency, security, and liberty alike demand that government officials shall be subjected to the same rules of conduct that are commands to the citizen. In a government of laws, existence of the government will be imperilled if it fails to observe the law scrupulously. Our government is the potent, the omnipresent teacher. For good or for ill, it teaches the whole people by example. Crime is contagious. If the government becomes a lawbreaker, it breeds contempt for law; it invites every man to become a law unto himself; it invites anarchy. *To declare that in the administration of the criminal law the end justifies the means—to declare that the government may commit crimes in order to secure the conviction of a private criminal—would bring terrible retribution.* Against that pernicious doctrine this court should resolutely set its face.

In the main the Supreme Court has for some time now been setting its face "against that pernicious doctrine," and it has done so regardless of criticism.

The Right to Privacy

Barry M. Goldwater, Jr.

The Fourth Amendment defines an area of personal privacy where government may intrude only for the most compelling reasons of public safety and welfare. For example, the Supreme Court has become increasingly sensitive over the past half century to governmental invasions of privacy that occur by means of electronic equipment or "bugging" devices used in criminal investigations. "We cannot forgive the requirements of the Fourth Amendment in the name of law enforcement," the Court said in Lopez v. *United States (1963). "Few threats to liberty exist which are greater than that posed by the use of eavesdropping devices." So, too, did the Court attempt to define, in* Griswold v. *Connecticut, a zone of marital privacy that government could not regulate by prohibiting the distribution and use of birth control devices.*

As the technological capacity of American society has increased, the ability of both governmental and nongovernmental institutions to collect and catalog information about individual citizens has mushroomed. In the future world of computers and other advanced surveillance equipment, it is likely that privacy will become even more difficult to protect. Barry M. Goldwater, Jr., a member of Congress from California since 1968 and co-sponsor of an Omnibus Privacy Bill, analyzes some of these issues in the following selection.

There is a popular notion that privacy rights are in the exclusive domain of liberals. To my mind, such conventional wisdom is absurd. The issue of personal privacy does not belong to any one philosophy, tradition, or partisan position. Privacy is an essential element of every individual's right to life, liberty, and the pursuit of happiness. When a person's privacy is abridged, his freedom is not diminished—it ceases to exist. No precept is more fundamental—or more conservative—than that.

Only recently have Americans begun to wake up to the fact that their privacy is being imperiled by two related developments of modern society: computers and social security cards. For most of us, both of these are benign, even useful, things. After all, many current information-gathering practices utilizing computers have been of benefit to the average citizen. By giving out personal information, Americans have been able to receive many services from both government and private industry. Today, a person almost anywhere in the United States can conduct credit transactions thousands of miles away in a matter of seconds; when he moves, his records follow without much difficulty. The wide use of computerized credit has also led to the development of a multimillion dollar industry.

A Short History of Record Keeping

The inventors of computer technology probably never imagined that their creations would enter into so many aspects of American life—and so quickly. There were several reasons for this rapid development and for the privacy problem it has engendered. The Great Depression of the 1930s, followed by World War II, ushered in an era of social, political, and economic uncertainty in the United States. New defense needs were mainly responsible for great technological developments that are still taking place. To solve our continuing problems, the government assumed more and more power, in the mistaken belief that increased liberty and personal freedom would result. Government always likes to believe, of course, that it acts only in the citizen's best interests.

In 1943, in an unrelated and seemingly innocuous move, President Franklin Roosevelt issued an executive order directing the federal government to use the social security number as the indexing device for the employment records of all federal employees. In wartime the number of federal employees was growing fast, and the nine-digit SS number was a convenient and efficient numerical identifier. However, the order was never rescinded or qualified, and soon the practice came into use in the private sector as well.

It was never much doubted in those days that the application of scientific development to society's difficulties would bring automatic benefits, or that science would eventually solve most of our problems. Technocracy, or the application of science by technicians, is especially appealing to bureaucrats. It stresses utility, convenience, and precision. Unfortunately it often does so at the expense of human considerations.

All this has led to the collection of more and more information and the massive use, and subsequent misuse, of record keeping. The government was in the process from the beginning. Since only the *advantages* of data collection through technology were publicized, the loss of our privacy has often seemed quite palatable.

Beneficial as the computer has been in some ways, its uncontrolled use is seriously compromising our freedom. But it is not merely the computer that is responsible for the erosion of privacy. Our society has become so habituated to record keeping of all kinds that its citizens are not even aware it takes place or that it may be pernicious. Most people assume that when they give an organization vital information, it will be protected. They do not realize that all future rights to and control over personal information have been severed as soon as it is given. Only later does one discover that information collected for a specific purpose has been used for other purposes. Since one is often denied access to files, challenging their accuracy or the propriety of their use or prohibiting the transfer of information to another file system or user is impossible. Occasionally, personal information is sold without one's permission or benefit. Objecting too strenuously can lead to a loss of benefits or services.

The use of the social security number is now pervasive; a citizen must reveal it to register to vote, receive a driver's license, purchase firearms, open a bank account, obtain insurance, apply for a marriage license, enroll in public and private schools. The number is used almost everywhere. Often you are not required by law to give it, but through force of habit--and sometimes mild coercion--you are pressured into revealing it. The problem is that the SS number can be used to track a person from cradle to grave. I am no alarmist, and this is no flight of fancy. There are already proposals circulating in the government that call for the creation of a national data bank using the SS number as the indexer. I am utterly opposed to such indiscriminate use of the SS number. It has already engendered a chilling depersonalization of the individual and encouraged the secret use of information about him. The implications of these new proposals are Orwellian, and I find no comfort in that.

The Need for Action

Considering the proliferating use of the SS number, and that there will be twice as many computers in operation by 1985 as there are today, the need to take action to regulate all forms of record keeping now is urgent.

In the past, most congressional legislative approaches to this problem have followed traditional partisan lines, with liberals and conservatives often behaving as if collaboration would diminish the virtuousness of their respective proposals—if not their reputations. Partisan considerations contributed to the legislative failure to set limits on the kinds of questions asked in the censuses of 1960 and 1970. I did not want to repeat this failure, and neither did a liberal congressman from New York, Edward Koch. We decided to demonstrate that liberals and conservatives together could do something to muster a coalition that would act to protect the privacy of individuals.

The results of our efforts have been cheering. A congressional commitment to privacy has been discovered and encouraged. A special discussion of the subject was held in the House of Representatives on April 2, 1974. Sixty members of Congress participated, and by Capitol Hill standards that is a substantial demonstration of interest. Subsequently, Congressman Koch and I introduced H.R. 14163, the Omnibus Privacy Bill.

We have three general objectives:

1. To prohibit the use of the social security number or any other number as an identifier in all instances in which it is not specifically required by law;

2. To establish safeguards that protect the individual from the misuse of personal information;

3. To establish a set of procedures that provide continuing control over the collection of personal information.

More specifically, we are seeking to have the following principles and practices become matters of law:

• There should be no personal information system whose very existence is secret.

• Information should be collected only when a clearly established need has been demonstrated, and the information should be appropriate and relevant to the purpose for which it is collected.

• There should be a clearly prescribed procedure for an individual to learn what information about him is being stored, the purpose for which it has been recorded, and the purpose of its use and dissemination.

• There should be a clearly prescribed procedure for an individual to challenge information as to its timeliness, pertinence, and accuracy, and to be able to correct, eradicate, or amend it.

• Personal information collected for one purpose could be used for another purpose only if specifically authorized by the individual or by Congress. There should be a clearly prescribed procedure for an individual to prevent any unauthorized use.

• A bipartisan privacy board of five members to be appointed by the president with the advice and consent of the Senate should be brought into existence and charged with oversight of information-collection practices and privacy safeguards. Its powers would be modest by normal standards, yet its impact would be great. The citizen would be given the opportunity to help himself; failing that, he would have recourse to government, since the Congress would have recovered its control over federal and private information practices.

We are encouraged by the discussions taking place between the House and Senate concerning omnibus privacy legislation. Senator Sam J. Ervin, who has long been a privacy advocate, recently introduced a bill that embodies proposals similar to the ones we have set forth. There is every reason to believe that the Senate and House can amicably move to pass bipartisan measures to protect privacy. *

I believe opposition to these proposals will come from several segments of both government and private industry. Some of the proposals strike directly at bureaucratic sacred cows, and some curtail the discretion both government and industry have long enjoyed.

Clearly, there are expenses involved, and there will be opposition to that. However, freedom and liberty cannot be measured in dollars; the problem will only increase, and subsequent solutions will cost far more—if solutions in the future can be had at all.

Personal privacy has a close parallel in private property. Each is an essential element in the maintenance of liberty. Each is a direct extension of the person. Each is so basic to free human existence that to infringe upon it compromises a person's individuality, integrity, and independence. The theme of individual initiative and responsibility is central in the Omnibus Privacy Bill, and this theme is the key to successful restoration of personal privacy. Human rights have value and meaning only because of the efforts each person is willing to make to protect and nurture them.

I have always presumed that not only would a person rather help himself, but that he will, if given an even chance. My role as a citizen legislator is to assist us all in preserving the opportunity for positive action by the individual. However, my colleagues and I can only do so much alone. We now have the opportunity to confine and control unbridled personal information practices by government and industry. The Congress, the president, and the

---

Ed. note: Many of the provisions of this bill, as they applied to the Federal government, were included in the Freedom of Information Act of 1974. Rep. Goldwater's bill has been reintroduced as H. R. 1984, The Comprehensive Right to Privacy Act, which would apply to state and local governments and to private enterprise.

people are at last developing a commitment to personal privacy. We have decided the time has come to summon the record keepers for an accounting, and to establish standards of conduct to restore our privacy. I am optimistic that Congress can pass some privacy legislation before the fall elections, but the effort will not succeed without public support.

The Strange Career
of Jim Crow

C. Vann Woodward

*Black slaves, declared a majority of the Supreme Court in
1857, were not citizens of the United States entitled to Constitutional protection. Nor could Congress, in the Court's
opinion, forbid slave owners from bringing their human
property into the western territories. That decision, rendered
in* Dred Scott v. Sandford, *intensified the sectional crisis
leading to Civil War. At the time, Northern hostility to* Dred
Scott *focused chiefly upon the territorial issue, but in the
aftermath of the war and because of emancipation, the constitutional status of the Negro assumed much greater importance.*

Laying Dred Scott *finally to rest, the Fourteenth Amendment of 1868 affirmed that "all persons born or naturalized in
the United States . . . are citizens of the United States and of
the State wherein they reside. No state shall make or enforce
any law which shall abridge the privileges or immunities of
citizens of the United States; nor shall any State deprive any
person of life, liberty, or property, without due process of law;
nor deny to any person . . . the equal protection of the laws."*

*Despite passage of the Fourteenth Amendment, numerous
Civil Rights laws, and the Fifteenth Amendment, which guaranteed that the right to vote "shall not be denied or abridged
. . . by any State on account of race, color, or previous condition of servitude," the legal, political, and social condition of
American blacks deteriorated by the end of the nineteenth century. In the following selection, the distinguished Yale
historian, C. Vann Woodward, analyzes how racial segregation
and denial to blacks of the right to vote came about in the
South.*

The South's adoption of extreme racism was due not so much to a con-
version as it was to a relaxation of the opposition. All the elements of fear,
jealousy, proscription, hatred, and fanaticism had long been present, as they
are present in various degrees of intensity in any society. What enabled them

to rise to dominance was not so much cleverness or ingenuity as it was a general weakening and discrediting of the numerous forces that had hitherto kept them in check. The restraining forces included not only Northern liberal opinion in the press, the courts, and the government, but also internal checks imposed by the prestige and influence of the Southern conservatives, as well as by the idealism and zeal of the Southern radicals. What happened toward the end of the century was an almost simultaneous— and sometimes not unrelated—decline in the effectiveness of restraint that had been exercised by all three forces: Northern liberalism, Southern conservatism, and Southern radicalism.

The acquiescence of Northern liberalism in the Compromise of 1877* defined the beginning, but not the ultimate extent, of the liberal retreat on the race issue. The Compromise merely left the freedman to the custody of the conservative Redeemers**upon their pledge that they would protect him in his constitutional rights. But as these pledges were forgotten or violated and the South veered toward proscription and extremism, Northern opinion shifted to the right, keeping pace with the South, conceding point after point, so that at no time were the sections very far apart on race policy. . . . It was quite common in the 'eighties and 'nineties to find in the *Nation, Harper's Weekly,* the *North American Review,* or the *Atlantic Monthly* Northern liberals and former abolitionists mouthing the shibboleths of white supremacy regarding the Negro's innate inferiority, shiftlessness, and hopeless unfitness for full participation in the white man's civilization. Such expressions doubtless did much to add to the reconciliation of North and South, but they did so at the expense of the Negro. Just as the Negro gained his emancipation and new rights through a falling out between white men, he now stood to lose his rights through the reconciliation of white men.

The cumulative weakening of resistance to racism was expressed also in a succession of decisions by the United States Supreme Court between 1873 and 1898. . . . In the *Slaughter House Cases* of 1873 and in *United States* v. *Reese* and *United States* v. *Cruikshank* in 1876, the court drastically curtailed the privileges and immunities recognized as being under federal protection. It continued the trend in its decision on the *Civil Rights Cases* of 1883 by virtually nullifying the restrictive parts of the Civil Rights Act. By a species of what Justice Harlan in his dissent described as "subtle and ingenious verbal criticism," the court held that the Fourteenth Amendment gave Congress power to restrain states but not individuals from acts of racial discrimination and segregation. The court, like the liberals, was engaged in a bit of reconciliation—reconciliation between federal and state jurisdiction, as well as between North and South, reconciliation also achieved at the Negro's expense. Having ruled in a previous case (*Hall* v. *de Cuir,* 1877) that a state could not *prohibit* segregation on a common carrier, the Court in 1890 (*Louisville, New Orleans, and Texas Railroad* v. *Mississippi*) ruled that a state could constitutionally *require* segregation on carriers. In *Plessy* v. *Ferguson,* decided in 1896, the Court subscribed to the doctrine that "legislation is powerless to eradicate racial instincts" and laid down the

---

*Ed. note: To gain the support of Southern conservatives following the contested election of 1876, Hayes and the Republicans promised to end federal efforts to enforce the political and civil rights of blacks. (They also promised economic benefits to the South.)

**Ed. note: The southern political leaders who came into power following Reconstruction, claiming to have "redeemed" the South from carpetbaggers and foreign rule.

"separate but equal" rule for the justification of segregation. Two years later, in 1898, in *Williams v. Mississippi* the Court completed the opening of the legal road to proscription, segregation, and disfranchisement by approving the Mississippi plan for depriving Negroes of the franchise....

Then, in the year 1898, the United States plunged into imperialistic adventures overseas under the leadership of the Republican party. These adventures in the Pacific and the Caribbean suddenly brought under the jurisdiction of the United States some eight million people of the colored races, "a varied assortment of inferior races," as the *Nation* described them, "which, of course, could not be allowed to vote." As America shouldered the White Man's Burden, she took up at the same time many Southern attitudes on the subject of race. . . . The doctrines of Anglo-Saxon superiority by which Professor John W. Burgess of Columbia University, Captain Alfred T. Mahan of the United States Navy, and Senator Albert Beveridge of Indiana justified and rationalized American imperialism in the Philippines, Hawaii, and Cuba differed in no essentials from the race theories by which Senator Benjamin R. Tillman of South Carolina and Senator James K. Vardaman of Mississippi justified white supremacy in the South. The Boston Evening *Transcript* of 14 January 1899, admitted that Southern race policy was "now the policy of the Administration of the very party which carried the country into and through a civil war to free the slave. . . .

At the dawn of the new century the wave of Southern racism came in as a swell upon a mounting tide of national sentiment and was very much a part of that sentiment. Had the tide been running the other way, the Southern wave would have been broken feebly instead of becoming a wave of the future. . . .

* * *

Having served as the national scapegoat in the reconciliation and reunion of North and South, the Negro was now pressed into service as a sectional scapegoat in the reconciliation of estranged white classes and the reunion of the Solid South. . . . The only formula powerful enough to accomplish that was the magical formula of white supremacy, applied without stint. . . .

The first step in applying the formula was the total disfranchisement of the Negro. In part this was presented as a guarantee that in the future neither of the white factions would violate the white man's peace by rallying the Negro's support against the other. . . .

The standard devices for accomplishing disfranchisement on a racial basis and evading the restrictions of the Constitution were invented by Mississippi, a pioneer of the movement. . . . Other states elaborated the original scheme and added devices of their own contriving, though there was a great deal of borrowing and interchange of ideas throughout the South. First of all, the plan set up certain barriers such as property or literacy qualifications for voting, and then cut certain loopholes in the barrier through which only white men could squeeze. The loopholes to appease (though not invariably accommodate) the underprivileged whites were the "understanding clause," the "grandfather clause," or the "good character clause." * Some variation of the scheme was incorporated into the constitutions

---

Ed. note: These clauses limited suffrage to those who could read and interpret the Constitution; to those whose fathers or grandfathers had the right to vote in 1867; and to those not convicted of any crimes.

of South Carolina in 1895, Louisiana in 1898, North Carolina in 1900, Alabama in 1901, Virginia in 1902, Georgia in 1908, and Oklahoma in 1910. The restrictions imposed by these devices were enormously effective in decimating the Negro vote, but in addition all these states as well as the remaining members of the old Confederacy—Florida, Tennessee, Arkansas, and Texas—adopted the poll tax. . . .

But if the Negroes did learn to read, or acquire sufficient property, and remember to pay the poll tax and to keep the receipt on file, they could even then be tripped by the final hurdle devised for them--the white primary. Another of the fateful paradoxes that seemed to dog the history of the progressive movement in the South, the primary system was undoubtedly an improvement over the old convention system and did much to democratize nominations and party control. But along with the progressively inspired primary system were adopted the oppositely inspired party rules, local regulations, and in some cases state laws excluding the minority race from participation and converting the primary into a white man's club. . . .

The effectiveness of disfranchisement is suggested by a comparison of the number of registered Negro voters in Louisiana in 1896, when there were 130,334 and in 1904, when there were 1,342. Between the two dates the literacy, property, and poll-tax qualifications were adopted. In 1896 Negro registrants were in a majority in twenty-six parishes—by 1900 in none.

In spite of the ultimate success of disfranchisement, the movement met with stout resistance and succeeded in some states by narrow margins or the use of fraud. In order to overcome the opposition and divert the suspicions of the poor and illiterate whites that they as well as the Negro were in danger of losing the franchise—a suspicion that often proved justified—the leaders of the movement resorted to an intensive propaganda of white supremacy, Negrophobia, and race chauvinism. . . .

Wide agreement prevailed in the early years of the [twentieth] century that there was less sympathy, tolerance, and understanding between the races than there had been during the Reconstruction period. . . .

*   *   *

Within this context of growing pessimism, mounting tension, and unleashed phobias the structure of segregation and discrimination was extended by the adoption of a great number of the Jim Crow type of laws. Up to 1900 the only law of this type adopted by the majority of Southern states was that applying to passengers aboard trains. And South Carolina did not adopt that until 1898, North Carolina in 1899, and Virginia, the last, in 1900. Only three states had required or authorized the Jim Crow waiting room in railway stations before 1899, but in the next decade nearly all of the other Southern states fell in line. The adoption of laws applying to new subjects tended to take place in waves of popularity. Street cars had been common in Southern cities since the 'eighties, but only Georgia had a segregation law applying to them before the end of the century. Then in quick succession North Carolina and Virginia adopted such a law in 1901, Louisiana in 1902, Arkansas, South Carolina, and Tennessee in 1903, Mississippi and Maryland in 1904, Florida in 1905, and Oklahoma in 1907. These laws referred to separation within cars, but a Montgomery city ordinance of 1906 was the first to require a completely separate Jim Crow street car. During these years the older seaboard states of the South also extended the segregation laws to steamboats.

The mushroom growth of discriminatory and segregation laws during the first two decades of this century piled up a huge bulk of legislation. Much of the code was contributed by city ordinances or by local regulations and rules enforced without the formality of laws. Only a sampling is possible here. For up and down the avenues and byways of Southern life appeared with increasing profusion the little signs: "Whites Only" or "Colored." Sometimes the law prescribed their dimensions in inches, and in one case the kind and color of paint. Many appeared without requirement by law— over entrances and exits, at theaters and boarding houses, toilets and water fountains, waiting rooms and ticket windows.

A large body of law grew up concerned with the segregation of employees and their working conditions. The South Carolina code of 1915, with subsequent elaborations, prohibited textile factories from permitting laborers of different races from working together in the same room, or using the same entrances, pay windows, exits, doorways, stairways, "or windows (sic)" at the same time, or the same "lavatories, toilets, drinking water buckets, pails, cups, dippers or glasses" at any time. . . . In most instances segregation in employment was established without the aid of statute. And in many crafts and trades the written or unwritten policies of Jim Crow unionism made segregation superfluous by excluding Negroes from employment.

State institutions for the care of the dependent or incapacitated were naturally the subject of more legislation than private institutions of the same sort, but ordinarily the latter followed pretty closely the segregation practices of the public institutions. . . . Segregation of the races in homes for the aged, the indigent, the orphans, the blind, the deaf, and the dumb was the subject of numerous state laws.

Much ingenuity and effort went into the separation of the races in their amusements, diversions, recreations, and sports. The Separate Park Law of Georgia, adopted in 1905, appears to have been the first venture of a state legislature into this field, though city ordinances and local custom were quite active in pushing the Negro out of the public parks. Circuses and tent shows, including side shows, fell under a law adopted by Louisiana in 1914, which required separate entrances, exits, ticket windows, and ticket sellers that would be kept at least twenty-five feet apart. The city of Birmingham applied the principle to "any room, hall, theatre, picture house, auditorium, yard, court, ball park, or other indoor or outdoor place" and specified that the races be "distinctly separated . . . by well defined physical barriers." North Carolina and Virginia interdicted all fraternal orders or societies that permitted members of both races to address each other as brother.

Residential segregation in cities, still rare in the older seaboard towns, developed along five different patterns in the second decade of the century. The type originating in Baltimore in 1910 designated all-white and all-Negro blocks in areas occupied by both races. . . . Virginia sought to legalize segregation by a state law that authorized city councils to divide territories into segregated districts and to prohibit either race from living in the other's district, a method adopted by Roanoke and Portsmouth, Virginia. The third method, invented by Richmond, designated blocks throughout the city black or white according to the majority of the residents and forbade any

266

person to live in any block "where the majority of residents on such streets are occupied by those with whom said person is forbidden to intermarry.". . . . A still more complicated law originated in Norfolk, which applied to both mixed and unmixed blocks and fixed the color status by ownership as well as occupancy. And finally New Orleans developed a law requiring a person of either race to secure consent of the majority of persons living in an area before establishing a residence therein. After these devices were frustrated by a Supreme Court decision in 1917, attempts continued to be made to circumvent the decision. Probably the most effective of these was the restrictive covenant, a private contract limiting the sale of property in an area to purchasers of the favored race.

The most prevalent and widespread segregation of living areas was accomplished without need for legal sanction. The black ghettos of the "Darktown" slums in every Southern city were the consequence mainly of the Negro's economic status, his relegation to the lowest rung of the ladder. . . .

The extremes to which caste penalties and separation were carried in parts of the South could hardly find a counterpart short of the latitudes of India and South Africa. In 1909 Mobile passed a curfew law applying exclusively to Negroes and requiring them to be off the streets by 10 p.m. The Oklahoma legislature in 1915 authorized its Corporation Commission to require telephone companies "to maintain separate booths for white and colored patrons." North Carolina and Florida required that textbooks used by the public-school children of one race be kept separate from those used by the other, and the Florida law specified separation even while the books were in storage. South Carolina for a time segregated a third caste by establishing separate schools for mulatto as well as for white and Negro children. A New Orleans ordinance segregated white and Negro prostitutes in separate districts. Ray Stannard Baker found Jim Crow Bibles for Negro witnesses in Atlanta courts and Jim Crow elevators for Negro passengers in Atlanta buildings. . . .

The Jim Crow laws, unlike feudal laws, did not assign the subordinate group a fixed status in society. They were constantly pushing the Negro farther down. In seeking to distinguish between the Southern white attitudes toward the Negro during Reconstruction and the era following and the attitudes later developed, Edgar Gardner Murphy in 1911 called the one "defensive" and "conservative" and the other "increasingly aggressive" and "destructive." "The new mood," he wrote, "makes few professions of conservatism. It does not claim to be necessary to the state's existence. . . . These new antipathies are not defensive, but assertive and combative . . . frankly and ruthlessly destructive." The movement had proceeded in mounting stages of aggression. "Its spirit is that of an all-absorbing autocracy of race, an animus of aggrandizement which makes, in the imagination of the white man, an absolute identification of the stronger race with the very being of the state.". . .

Separate Is Not Equal

Brown *v.* Board of Education of Topeka

*Segregation of blacks and depriving them of the right to vote
continued throughout the South until the 1950s and 1960s,
despite piecemeal decisions by the Supreme Court attacking
the white primary, discriminatory jury selections, and racial
covenants in housing. The doctrine of "separate but equal,"
announced in* Plessy v. *Ferguson (1896), governed application
of the Fourteenth Amendment's equal protection clause in
racial matters until the epochal decision of 1954 in* Brown v.
Board of Education of Topeka.*

The Brown *decision, declaring racially segregated public
schools unconstitutional, not only revitalized the equal protection clause and launched an expanded civil rights movement,
but also signaled the beginning of the Supreme Court's "activism"—a willingness to decide issues of basic social and
economic policy—under Chief Justice Earl Warren.*

Mr. Chief Justice Warren delivered the opinion of the Court

These cases come to us from the States of Kansas, South Carolina,
Virginia, and Delaware. They are premised on different facts and different
local conditions, but a common legal question justifies their consideration
together in this consolidated opinion.

In each of the cases, minors of the Negro race, through their legal
representatives, seek the aid of the courts in obtaining admission to the
public schools of their community on a nonsegregated basis. In each instance, they had been denied admission to schools attended by white
children under laws requiring or permitting segregation according to race.
This segregation was alleged to deprive the plaintiffs of the equal protection
of the laws under the Fourteenth Amendment. In each of the cases other
than the Delaware case, a three-judge federal district court denied relief to
the plaintiffs on the so-called "separate but equal" doctrine announced by
this Court in *Plessy* v. *Ferguson,* 163 U.S. 537. Under that doctrine,
equality of treatment is accorded when the races are provided substantially
equal facilities, even though these facilities be separate. In the Delaware
case, the Supreme Court of Delaware adhered to that doctrine, but ordered
that the plaintiffs be admitted to the white schools because of their
superiority to the Negro schools.

The plaintiffs contend that segregated public schools are not "equal" and

---

From *Brown* v. *Board of Education of Topeka,* 347 U.S. 483 (1954).

cannot be made "equal," and that hence they are deprived of the equal protection of the laws. Because of the obvious importance of the question presented, the Court took jurisdiction. Argument was heard in the 1952 Term, and reargument was heard this Term on certain questions propounded by the Court.

Reargument was largely devoted to the circumstances surrounding the adoption of the Fourteenth Amendment in 1868. It covered exhaustively consideration of the Amendment in Congress, ratification by the states, then existing practices in racial segregation, and the views of proponents and opponents of the Amendment. This discussion and our own investigation convince us that, although these sources cast some light, it is not enough to resolve the problem with which we are faced. At best, they are inconclusive. The most avid proponents of the post-War Amendments undoubtedly intended them to remove all legal distinctions among "all persons born or naturalized in the United States." Their opponents, just as certainly, were antagonistic to both the letter and the spirit of the Amendments and wished them to have the most limited effect. What others in Congress and the state legislatures had in mind cannot be determined with any degree of certainty.

An additional reason for the inconclusive nature of the Amendment's history, with respect to segregated schools, is the status of public education at that time. In the South, the movement toward free common schools, supported by general taxation, had not yet taken hold. Education of white children was largely in the hands of private groups. Education of Negroes was almost nonexistent, and practically all of the race were illiterate. In fact, any education of Negroes was forbidden by law in some states. Today, in contrast, many Negroes have achieved outstanding success in the arts and sciences as well as in the business and professional world. It is true that public school education at the time of the Amendment had advanced further in the North, but the effect of the Amendment on Northern States was generally ignored in the congressional debates. Even in the North, the conditions of public education did not approximate those existing today. The curriculum was usually rudimentary; ungraded schools were common in rural areas; the school term was but three months a year in many states; and compulsory school attendance was virtually unknown. As a consequence, it is not surprising that there should be so little in the history of the Fourteenth Amendment relating to its intended effect on public education.

In the first cases in this Court construing the Fourteenth Amendment, decided shortly after its adoption, the Court interpreted it as proscribing all state-imposed discriminations against the Negro race. The doctrine of "separate but equal" did not make its appearance in this Court until 1896 in the case of *Plessy* v. *Ferguson, supra,* involving not education but transportation. American courts have since labored with the doctrine for over half half a century. In this Court, there have been six cases involving the "separate but equal" doctrine in the field of public education. In *Cumming* v. *County Board of Education,* 175 U.S. 528, and *Gong Lum* v. *Rice,* 275 U.S. 78, the validity of the doctrine itself was not challenged. In more recent cases, all on the graduate school level, inequality was found in that specific benefits enjoyed by white students were denied to Negro students of the same educational qualifications. . . . In none of these cases was it necessary to re-examine the doctrine to grant relief to the Negro plaintiff.

And in *Sweatt* v. *Painter*. . . the Court expressly reserved decision on the question whether *Plessy* v. *Ferguson* should be held inapplicable to public education.

In the instant cases, that question is directly presented. Here, unlike *Sweatt* v. *Painter,* there are findings below that the Negro and white schools involved have been equalized, or are being equalized, with respect to buildings, curricula, qualifications and salaries of teachers, and other "tangible" factors. Our decision, therefore, cannot turn on merely a comparison of these tangible factors in the Negro and white schools involved in each of the cases. We must look instead to the effect of segregation itself on public education.

In approaching this problem, we cannot turn the clock back to 1868 when the Amendment was adopted, or even to 1896 when *Plessy* v. *Ferguson* was written. We must consider public education in the light of its full development and its present place in American life throughout the Nation. Only in this way can it be determined if segregation in public schools deprives these plaintiffs of the equal protection of the laws.

Today, education is perhaps the most important function of state and local governments. Compulsory school attendance laws and the great expenditures for education both demonstrate our recognition of the importance of education to our democratic society. It is required in the performance of our most basic public responsibilities, even service in the armed forces. It is the very foundation of good citizenship. Today it is a principal instrument in awakening the child to cultural values, in preparing him for later professional training, and in helping him to adjust normally to his environment. In these days, it is doubtful that any child may reasonably be expected to succeed in life if he is denied the opportunity of an education. Such an opportunity, where the state has undertaken to provide it, is a right which must be made available to all on equal terms.

We come then to the question presented: Does segregation of children in public schools solely on the basis of race, even though the physical facilities and other "tangible" factors may be equal, deprive the children of the minority group of equal educational opportunities? We believe that it does.

In *Sweatt* v. *Painter*, . . . in finding that a segregated law school for Negroes could not provide them equal educational opportunities, this Court relied in large part on "those qualities which are incapable of objective measurement but which make for greatness in a law school." In *McLaurin* v. *Oklahoma State Regents*, . . . the Court, in requiring that a Negro admitted to a white graduate school be treated like all other students, again resorted to intangible considerations: ". . . his ability to study, to engage in discussions and exchange views with other students, and, in general, to learn his profession." Such considerations apply with added force to children in grade and high schools. To separate them from others of similar age and qualifications solely because of their race generates a feeling of inferiority as to their status in the community that may affect their hearts and minds in a way unlikely ever to be undone. The effect of this separation on their educational opportunities was well stated by a finding in the Kansas case by a court which nevertheless felt compelled to rule against the Negro plaintiffs:

Segregation of white and colored children in public schools has a detrimental effect upon the colored children. The impact is greater when it has the sanction of the law; for the policy of separating the races is usually interpreted as denoting the inferiority of the negro group. A sense of inferiority affects the motivation of a child to learn. Segregation with the sanction of law, therefore, has a tendency to (retard) the educational and mental development of negro children and to deprive them of some of the benefits they would receive in a racial(ly) integrated school system.

Whatever may have been the extent of psychological knowledge at the time of *Plessy* v. *Ferguson,* this finding is amply supported by modern authority. Any language in *Plessy* v. *Ferguson* contrary to this finding is rejected.

We conclude that in the field of public education the doctrine of "separate but equal" has no place. Separate educational facilities are inherently unequal. Therefore, we hold that the plaintiffs and others similarly situated for whom the actions have been brought are, by reason of the segregation complained of, deprived of the equal protection of the laws guaranteed by the Fourteenth Amendment. This disposition makes unnecessary any discussion whether such segregation also violates the Due Process Clause of the Fourteenth Amendment. : . .

Pregnancy Without Penalty: Civil Rights of Women

Eve Cary

Racial minorities were not the only groups in American society who suffered discrimination through the legal system until the Supreme Court began to revitalize the equal protection clause of the Fourteenth Amendment in the 1960s and early 1970s. As Eve Cary points out in the following article, "the inferior status of women is a venerable tradition in Anglo-American law."

Until quite recently, sex discrimination was an accepted and little-challenged assumption of the American social order. Ms. Cary, a graduate of the New York University Law School and a staff attorney for the New York Civil Liberties Union, traces recent developments in this area of equal protection.

The inferior status of women is a venerable tradition in Anglo-American law. Until recently sex discrimination in virtually every sphere of human activity was legislated, upheld judicially, and taken for granted by the public at large. A woman's right to contract, to own property, to sue, to vote, to hold public office, to sit on juries, to travel, to establish residence, to work, to go to school, either did not exist or was closely circumscribed.

Legal sex discrimination was justified on the basis of accepted ideas about the Nature of Woman—her childlike character, refinement, lack of intelligence, and hypersensitivity—and the resulting assumption that God meant her to stay at home with children while men ran things out in the world. As the Supreme Court said in *Bradwell* v. *State of Illinois* (1873), upholding a law forbidding women to practice law:

> Man is, or should be, woman's protector and defender. The natural and proper timidity and delicacy which belongs to the female sex evidently unfits it for many of the occupations of civil life. The constitution of the family organization, which is founded in the divine ordinance, as well as in the nature of things, indicates the domestic sphere as that which properly belongs to the domain and functions of womanhood. . . . The paramount destiny and mission of woman are to fulfill the noble and benign offices of wife and mother. This is the law of the

Creator. And the rules of civil society must be adapted to the general constitution of things, and cannot be based upon exceptional cases.

Few courts today would dare cite the Will of God as a rationale for their decisions; thus in the past decade the more blatant forms of sex discrimination have been struck down in cases where no legally demonstrable difference between the sexes could be proven. Now we must grapple with the issue of discrimination in situations involving genuine sex differences, such as on the basis of child-bearing ability and pregnancy. And it is apparent that some of the same traditional attitudes as those held by the *Bradwell* court still prevail.

. . . When the Supreme Court issued its historic opinion upholding a woman's right to have an abortion, some feminists believed that a truly revolutionary blow had been struck for women's liberation. For the first time in history women would no longer be the slave of biology. Now that they could control childbearing, the remaining rationale for discrimination against them was destroyed and true equality with men was possible at last. But as the first glow of success wears off, women are beginning to realize that the abortion decision has not ended their fight for true sexual freedom and equality. In the words of one pregnant woman struggling to get herself off welfare, "Now I have the right to have an abortion but I don't have the right to be pregnant." And she was correct. In a society that considers child care to be the responsibility of mothers alone, women, and especially poor women, pay a heavy price for getting pregnant. . . .

Despite increasing judicial sensitivity to sex discrimination, some courts have not yet been willing to rule that discrimination against pregnant women and mothers is *ipso facto* sex discrimination. Instead they still accept the argument of employers and others that they are not discriminating because they would treat a man the same way if *he* got pregnant. Judge Clement T. Haynesworth recently defended just this view when he wrote the opinion of the Federal Court of Appeals for the Fourth Circuit in *Cohen* v. *Chesterfield County School Board* (1973), upholding the right of a public employer to force a pregnant woman to take an unpaid maternity leave:

> Only women become pregnant; only women become mothers. But [the] leap from those physical facts to the conclusion that any regulation of pregnancy and maternity is an invidious classification by sex is simplistic. The fact that only women experience pregnancy and motherhood removes all possibility of competition between the sexes in this area. No man-made law or regulation excludes males from those experiences and no such laws or regulations can relieve females from all the burdens which naturally accompany the joys and blessings of motherhood.

In other words, discrimination against pregnant women and mothers is justified because it follows the natural order of things. But while it may be true that no man-made law or regulation ordained that only women have children, it is equally true that God never ordered bank managers to refuse to give mortgages to women of childbearing age or ordained that the denial of the right to an education is one of those burdens, like getting fat, that naturally accompanies the joys and blessings of motherhood. . . .

Employment

Despite the popular myth, the fact is that many women have *not* found their places in the home; many women have always worked at paid jobs because they had to in order to live. Employers simply benefited from the image of women as weak, unintelligent, and suited only for domestic employment: no one would expect an employer to pay men's wages to such creatures. Many businesses, such as the garment industry, were run completely on female labor hired, as were children, at a fraction of the wages paid to men. Paying women less for doing the same work as men was so axiomatic that this assumption was used as an analogy in one early case in which the court upheld an employer's practice of paying black people less than whites. It is startling to realize that pay discrimination against women continued to be accepted and legal until 1961 when the Federal Equal Pay Act was passed.

While legislating equal pay for equal work was a great step forward, it did not end sex discrimination in employment once a woman could be shown to be different from a man—that is, when she became pregnant.

The idea that women have the right to be pregnant *and* to work and maintain job security while raising children is a new one. Up until the past few years no one questioned the right of an employer not only to fire a pregnant employee, but to refuse to hire a woman who has children or is of childbearing age. . . .

The major reason given by employers for discriminating against women who have or might have children is the assumption that a mother must take more time off from work than a father because of her children's sicknesses and other emergencies. This notion, while accepted as gospel by most employers, is not borne out by the facts. Overall sickness statistics compiled by the U.S. Department of Labor show that the absenteeism of women does not differ significantly from that of men.

In *Phillips* v. *Martin Marietta Corporation* (1971), the first sex discrimination case to be heard in recent years by the U.S. Supreme Court, it was shown that the practice of the company was to refuse to hire women with pre-school-age children. The Supreme Court declined to rule that the company had such a right and remanded the case to the trial court to determine whether evidence substantiated the proposition that mothers of pre-school-age children are demonstrably less able to perform their duties than are the fathers of such children. The case was eventually settled and no further judicial findings were made.

The fears of many employers that women will leave their jobs after a short time to have children and therefore not repay the time and money spent on their training often become self-fulfilling prophecies. The employer who discriminates against women in hiring is often the one who also imposes penalties on his employees when they become pregnant. This in turn increases the possibility that in fact they won't return to work after the birth of their children. . . .

274

The practice of firing a woman as soon as her pregnancy is discovered is becoming less prevalent. At least some of the more egregious discriminations have been struck down. For example, a lower federal court in 1971 held that when untenured teachers receive the same medical benefits as tenured teachers they cannot be denied maternity leave merely because they are untenured. Later that year another lower federal court ruled that a maternity leave cannot be denied a woman solely because she is unwed.

Usually the working woman today who gets pregnant is simply faced with unwelcome solicitude for her health by her employer in the form of a mandatory, unpaid maternity leave after the first months of her pregnancy. (Few "concerned" employers bother to consider that a woman's health may deteriorate if she's not eating regularly because she lost her job.) The following situation is typical. A pregnant woman called the New York Civil Liberties Union to say that she was being forced at the end of her sixth month to take an unpaid maternity leave from her job as a high school English teacher. She explained that she had planned very carefully so that her baby was due during her two-week Christmas vacation. She had accrued two weeks of sick leave, and school board rules entitled employees to borrow up to two weeks of sick leave from the following year. This would give her six weeks to give birth and recover, which she and her doctor agreed was ample. The school board, however, not only refused to permit her to use her accrued and future sick leave as paid maternity leave, but refused to permit her even to use her vacation. Her unpaid leave was to begin at the start of the vacation and she would not be paid from that date until she was permitted by the school board to return to work. This meant not only the loss of three to four months' salary during the school year and the interruption of her classes, but it further reduced her summer pay which was a percentage of the amount of money she earned during the year. She also would lose so many tenure credits during her leave (which she would not lose while on sick leave or vacation) that she would be prevented from getting tenure for another year. The board would have let her have cosmetic surgery during her six weeks of vacation and sick leave or, what is more relevant, she could have had an abortion. But she was not free to have a child.

The reason usually given for requiring women to take maternity leave is concern for their health and welfare and fear of possible lawsuits if "something should go wrong" on the job. . . .

Frequently the health-and-welfare and lawsuit arguments appear to be simply a coverup for the feeling that pregnant women are embarrassing. School boards often argue that students may be too immature to cope with a pregnant teacher. . . . In the rare situation where it might genuinely be difficult for a pregnant woman to carry out her job, employers tend to feel justified in firing her rather than attempting to accommodate her. American Airlines, for instance, fires pregnant stewardesses rather than transfer them to desk jobs. . . .

Once the baby is born, its would-be working mother's problems are not yet over. No matter how much time has gone by since the birth of the baby many employers require a woman to produce a doctor's certificate giving her permission to return to work despite the absence of such a requirement for employees recovering from surgery or disease. . . .

275

Just how entrenched is the traditional attitude toward childrearing is well illustrated by the experience of the New York couple, both teachers in the New York City school system, who decided after the birth of their first child that the husband would stay home to help care for the baby. Under Board of Education regulations the wife was entitled to an unpaid childrearing leave of absence for five years. When the couple explained to the board that they also wanted paternity leave for the father it was denied: mothers are the ones who take care of children. The case* is now being litigated by the New York Civil Liberties Union.

The requirement that pregnant women take unpaid leaves of absence from their jobs before and after giving birth is an issue that by now has received considerable attention in both state and federal courts. In *Struck* v. *Secretary of Defense* (1972) the Ninth Circuit Court of Appeals ruled that an unwed nurse who was planning to give her baby up for adoption could not keep her air force commission. Captain Struck was serving in a combat zone in Vietnam and the court, noting that the hospital in which she worked had been shelled, found that

> a not improbable consequence might have been that the Captain, as a result of injury or shock might have suffered a miscarriage, and become a patient instead of a nurse. As such, instead of being a useful soldier, she would have been a liability and a burden to the Air Force. . . . The fact that other personnel, males and non-pregnant females, might have been disabled and made useless in the attack is irrelevant. Those events would have been the result of the fortunes of war.

After the Supreme Court agreed to hear Struck's appeal the air force changed its mind and allowed her to keep her commission. She had her child, remains a career officer today, and at last report plans to go to flight school.

In *La Fleur* v. *Cleveland Board of Education* (1972), a case brought by Jane Picker of the Women's Law Fund in Cleveland, the Sixth Circuit Court ruled in favor of three schoolteachers who challenged the Cleveland school board's policy of forcing pregnant women to take maternity leave and not permitting them to return to work until the semester beginning at least three months after childbirth. The court found that the teachers' Fourteenth Amendment right to equal protection had been violated, pointing out that while only women require leave to have babies, men routinely were granted time off from work for medical disabilities. . . . The Tenth Circuit not only found a similar regulation invalid under the simple test used by the other courts of whether the rule could be considered rational, but went a long step further and required the state to show a compelling public interest in forcing pregnant women to go on maternity leave. The court reasoned that the right to bear a child is fundamental and only the greatest public need could justify requiring a teacher to choose between that right and the right to employment. . . .

Ed. note: Ackerman v. New York City Board of Education. The district court ruled in favor of the Ackermans, and the Board of Education was appealing the decision at the time this book went to press.

Unemployment Compensation

The pregnant woman who gets fired or forced to take an unpaid, unwanted maternity leave cannot easily turn to unemployment compensation benefits to sustain her until she can return to work. Just as their employers force them to leave jobs they are perfectly capable of performing, so too the majority of states concur that pregnant women are not able to work. Most states' unemployment compensation statutes specifically deny unemployment compensation to women who become unemployed while they are pregnant, regardless of their wish to continue working. . . . A few statutes of this kind have been found unconstitutional by state courts. . . . However, in most states, women still have no right under law to collect unemployment compensation if they have become unemployed while pregnant; in others where they have the right on paper it is often still denied them in practice.

Credit

The working world is not the only place in which women are constantly reminded of their second-class status. Women have always been considered bad credit risks for bank loans, credit cards, mortgages, and similar transactions, because they have rarely had any money of their own; until recently they usually were denied credit altogether. Today, however, when more women are employed and therefore making money, banks have begun at last to consider extending them the same credit as men. Well, almost the same: In figuring out how good a credit risk a woman is, especially when she is purchasing real estate, the likelihood of her getting pregnant is an important consideration.

Bankers simply presume, unless given proof to the contrary, that most young women will get pregnant, and if they get pregnant they will quit their jobs, and if they quit their jobs they will default on their loans—despite the fact that all the available statistics contradict these propositions. For example: In the last ten years the work force of young mothers aged twenty to twenty-four has almost doubled, from 18 percent to 33 percent of all working mothers. Participation in the labor force by mothers with children under three years increased by two-thirds from 1960 to 1971. Of all mothers with children under six, 44 percent were working at some time during 1969. Further, no study has produced any evidence that women, including those with children, are less reliable financially than men. . . .

Many banks refuse altogether to lend money to women of childbearing age. Others, moving slowly into the twentieth century, have become aware of advances in birth control. Thus, a woman who wants credit might inform her banker of the method of contraception she uses; if he approves, he may lend her money.

. . . A bank in a Virginia suburb of Washington, D.C., refused to consider the wife's income for a mortgage unless (1) she got a statement from her doctor that she was on the pill, *and* (2) she signed a statement that she would have an abortion if she got pregnant, *and* (3) the husband signed a statement that he would agree to an abortion, *and* (4) her husband would consider a vasectomy if the wife became unable to take the pill. . . .

In New York City a woman was told by bank officials that they would be happy to give her the mortgage for which she applied—all she had to do was get a hysterectomy.

When abortion was illegal a woman's agreement to remain childless could not be made a condition of receiving some other benefit. After the change in abortion laws the banking business was the first to come up with the requirement of childlessness. It also may be the last, for the requirement is unconstitutionally discriminatory both on the basis of sex, and, in the case of Catholics, whose religion prohibits contraception and abortion, on the basis of religion. It is also against public policy; just as a promise to marry or not to marry is not enforceable in courts because state involvement in such an intimate personal relationship would be intolerable, so must a promise not to have children also remain outside official compulsion. . . .

At this time, nothing in most states prevents any bank from simply requiring proof of sterility before granting women a mortgage or from refusing the mortgage altogether. In a society that runs on credit this is far from a minor penalty. Some relief may be in sight, however. Both the federal government and several states now are considering bills or have passed laws prohibiting sex discrimination in lending. While these do not deal directly with the question of childbearing ability, as courts increasingly recognize that pregnancy discrimination is sex discrimination they will almost certainly be interpreted as outlawing "baby" questions. . . .

The many lawsuits challenging the penalties imposed on pregnancy are evidence that women are no longer willing to live with the assumption that they should be singled out to bear all the costs of having children. . . .

Some of the costs of childbearing and childrearing are real, but this fact does not compel the conclusion that women should have the sole responsibility for shouldering them simply because it is they who give birth. Just as the nation as a whole has always borne the costs of educating its young in public schools, so must the burden of bearing children be distributed equally.

While sex discrimination may have a long history in American law, so does the acceptance of the fact that giving people their rights costs money. Minimum wage laws, for example, cost employers a lot of money, but the public has come to accept the idea that it is worthwhile to pay workers a wage that will give dignity and respect to their labor, and that, in the long run, society benefits if people are earning enough money to live decently. The laws prohibiting child labor fall into the same pattern; they cost employers money, but they were adopted to protect children from the rigors of factory life. The same holds true for sex discrimination. Providing daycare centers for working parents will cost money, but it will also help enable women to become independent and productive workers, which in the long run costs far less than the waste of the talents of half the population. . . .

True equal protection takes into account individual differences. It does not attempt to force one group of people to become just like another in order to get their rights. Society must recognize that as long as equality remains the prize of only those women willing to give up childbearing, equality will be an illusion.

What Price Equality?

While the Fourteenth Amendment to the Constitution prohibits the states from denying to women the "equal protection of the laws," many persons argue that the only way to abolish discrimination based on sex, such as that described by Eve Cary in the preceding article, is through the Equal Rights Amendment. Under the proposed amendment, now before the states for ratification, "Equality of rights under the law shall not be denied or abridged by the United States or by any state on account of sex." Such an amendment was first introduced into Congress in 1923. Although Congress voted overwhelmingly in its favor in 1972, it remains a highly controversial issue. There are sharp divisions of opinion, even among women, as to the desirability of "equality of rights under the law." The following excerpts from the Senate's consideration of the amendment—one by Senator Sam J. Ervin, Jr., and one by Myra K. Wolfgang, illuminate some of the problems that might result from trying to "legislate equality."

Selection 1
—Hon. Sam J. Ervin, Jr.,
United States Senator, North Carolina, Democrat*

"While I believe that any unfair discriminations which the law makes against women should be abolished by law, I have the abiding conviction that the law should make such distinctions between the sexes as are reasonably necessary for the protection of women and the existence and development of the race. . . .

"Congress and the legislatures of the various States have enacted certain laws based upon the conviction that the physiological and functional differences between men and women make it advisable to exempt or exclude women from certain arduous and hazardous activities in order to

---

*Sen. Ervin proposed several amendments to the House-passed Equal Rights Amendment as well as a substitute proposal which differed from the House version in several respects.

From an address by the Honorable Sam J. Ervin, Jr., on the floor of the U.S. Senate. *Congressional Record*, Vol. 116, part 22 (August 21, 1970), Washington, 1970.

protect their health and safety.

"Among Federal laws of this nature are the Selective Service Act which confines compulsory military service to men; the acts of Congress governing the voluntary enlistments in the Armed Forces of the Nation which restrict the right to enlist for combat service to men; and the acts establishing and governing the various service academies which provide for the admission and training of men only."

"Among the State laws of this kind are laws which limit hours during which women can work, and bar them from engaging in occupations particularly arduous and hazardous. . . .

"If the House-passed equal rights amendment should be interpreted by the Supreme Court to forbid any legal distinctions between men and women, all existing and future laws of this nature would be nullified.

"The common law and statutory law of the various States recognize the reality that many women are homemakers and mothers, and by reason of the duties imposed upon them in these capacities, are largely precluded from pursuing gainful occupations or making any provision for their financial security during their declining years. To enable women to do these things and thereby make the existence and development of the race possible, these State laws impose upon husbands the primary responsibility to provide homes and livelihoods for their wives and children, and make them criminally responsible to society and civilly responsible to their wives if they fail to perform this primary responsibility. Moreover, these State laws secure to wives dower and other rights in the property left by their husbands in the event their husbands predecease them in order that they may have some means of support in their declining years.

"If the House-passed equal rights amendment should be interpreted by the Supreme Court to forbid any legal distinctions between men and women, it would nullify all existing and all future laws of this kind.

"There are laws in many States which undertake to better the economic position of women. I shall cite only one class of them; namely, the laws which secure to women minimum wages in many employments in many States which have no minimum wage laws for men, and no other laws relating to the earnings of women.

"If the House-passed equal rights amendment should be interpreted by the Supreme Court to prohibit any legal distinction between men and women, it would nullify all existing and future laws of this kind. . . .

"There are laws in many States which undertake to better the economic

"I do not believe that the advocates of the House-passed equal rights amendment wish to nullify laws which are adopted for the protection of women and for the promotion of the highest interest of society. Moreover, I am unwilling to attribute any such motive to the Representatives who voted for the House-passed equal rights amendment, or to the Senators who have sponsored the Senate version of such amendment. I attribute to all of them the laudable desire of abolishing unfair discrimination against women without destroying laws reasonably designed to protect them, and without robbing Congress and the legislatures of the 50 States of the power to enact similar laws in the future."

Selection 2
—Myra K. Wolfgang
Vice President, Hotel and Restaurant Employees and
Bartenders International Union, AFL-CIO

"My concern with the Equal Rights Amendment is not an academic one. It embodies the problems that I work with day in and day out, year in and year out. My concern is for the widowed, divorced mother of children who is the head of her family and earns less than $3500.00 a year working as a maid, laundry worker, hospital cleaner or dishwasher. There are millions of such women in the work force. Now is as good a time as any to remind you that only one out of ten women in the work force have had four or more years of college, so I am not speaking of or representing the 'bird in the gilded cage.' I speak for 'Tillie the Toiler.'

"I am opposed to enactment of the Equal Rights Amendment to our Constitution. I recognize that the impetus for the passage of the Equal Rights Amendment is the result of a growing anger amongst women over job discrimination, social and political discrimination and many out-moded cultural habits of our way of life.

"The anger is justified, for certainly discrimination against women exists. I do not believe, however, that passage of the Equal Rights Amendment will satisfy, or is the solution to, the problem. The problem of discrimination against women will not be solved by an Equal Rights Amendment to the Constitution; conversely, the Amendment will create a whole new series of problems. It will not bring about equal pay for equal work, nor guarantee job promotion free from discrimination. The Equal Rights Amendment is a negative law with no positive or specific provisions to combat descrimination.

"The Amendment is excessively sweeping in scope, reaching into the work force, into family and social relationships and other institutions, in which 'equality' cannot always be achieved through 'identity.' Differences in laws are not necessarily discriminatory, nor should all laws containing different provisions for men and women be abolished.

"Opposed, as I am, to the Equal Rights Amendment, certainly does not mean that I am opposed to equality. . . .

"Representing women service workers gives me a special concern over the threat that a simple Equal Rights Amendment would present to minimum labor standards legislation, since such standards influence working conditions. Many such State laws apply only to women.

"Today, the 50 States, the District of Columbia and Puerto Rico, all have minimum labor standards laws applying to women. The principal subjects of regulations are: (1) minimum wage; (2) overtime compensation; (3) hours of work, meal and rest periods; (4) equal pay; (5) indus-

Statement by Mrs. Myra K. Wolfgang, Vice-President, Hotel and Restaurant Employees and Bartenders International Union, AFL-CIO, in behalf of Michigan Women's Commission. U.S. Senate, 91st Congress, 2nd Session. Committee on the Judiciary, Subcommittee on Constitutional Amendments. *Hearing on S. J. Res, 61 to amend the Constitution to Provide Equal Rights for Men and Women*, May 6, 1970. (Washington, D.C., 1970) pp. 321–24.

trial homework; (6) employment before and after childbirth; (7) occupational limitations; and (8) other standards, such as seating and washroom facilities and weightlifting limitations. It would be desirable for some of these laws to be extended to men, but the practical fact is that an Equal Rights Amendment is likely to destroy the laws altogether rather than bring about coverage for both sexes. . . .

"You will be hearing from many Feminists who will contend that there are no real differences between men and women, other than those enforced by culture. What nonsense!! Has culture created the differences in the size of the hands, in muscular mass, in respiratory capacity? Of course not, the differences are physical and biological. Nothing can alter that fact.

"One can take any cell from a human being and determine whether it came from a male or a female. This does not suggest superiority or inferiority among the sexes, it emphasizes the differences. Because of the physical and I emphasize physical differences between men and women, the question of protective legislation for women must be reviewed. In addition, the dual role of women in our modern society makes protective legislation a necessity.

"The working mother has no 'wife' to care for her or her children. She assumes the role of homemaker and worker and must perform both these roles in a 24-hour period. Even in the two-parent households, there is an unequal division of domestic chores. While much could be done to ease the burden of the working women by men assuming a fair and equal share of domestic chores, they are not prepared to do so. What is more, society as a whole is reluctant to expect this of men or to build child care centers to ease the burden of woman's dual role.

"If the community does not take action through protective legislation to enable women to work outside the home, then the expressed desire for equal rights is an empty promise and myth. The Equal Rights Amendment would make it unconstitutional to enact and would repeal legislation embodying this protection for working women. You must ask yourself the question. Should women workers be left without any legislation because of State Legislatures' failure and unwillingness to enact such legislation for men? Do we discard protective legislation for women if we are unable to get such legislation for men? The passage of the Equal Rights Amendment would do this, and it is wrong. . . .

"In this made whirl to 'equalize'—male, female—everyone, one question remains unanswered—who will take care of children, the home, the cleaning, the laundry and the cooking? Can we extend this 'equality' into the home? Obviously not, since the proponents of the Equal Rights Amendment are quick to point out that the Amendment would restrict only governmental action and would not apply to purely private action.

"I am sure my sisters in the Woman's Liberation Movement have reminded you in strong and ominous tones that women represent the majority of voters. True, but there is no more unanimity of opinion among women than among men. Indeed, a woman on welfare in Harlem, a unionized laundry worker in California, an elderly socialite from Philadelphia may be of the same sex and they may be wives and mothers, but they have little in common to cause them to be of one opinion.

"Whatever happens to the structure of opportunity, women are increasingly motivated to work—and they want to work short hours on schedules that meet their needs as wives and mothers. They want fewer hours a week because emancipation, while it has released them for work, has not released them from home and family responsibilities.

"I oppose the Equal Rights Amendment since the equality it may achieve may well be equality of mistreatment."

Judicial Revolution:
The Warren Court

*Although the Warren Court passed into history only six years
ago, upon the retirement of the late Chief Justice in 1969,
scholars have already marked his fifteen-year tenure as one of
the most decisive in the nation's history. The Warren Court's
interpretation of the Bill of Rights and the Fourteenth Amendment, as Harry N. Scheiber remarks in the article reprinted
below, "furthered the establishment of true equality under the
law for persons of all races and in all economic circumstances."
Scheiber, professor of history at the University of California,
San Diego, assesses the broad impact of the Warren Court's
"judicial revolution."*

*Predictably, such far-reaching decisions provoked bitter—but
not unprecedented—controversy. From the Marshall era to the
present, critics of the Supreme Court have repeatedly attacked
its members for "making" social policy under the guise of
"interpreting" the Constitution. Such criticism reached one
crescendo during the 1930s, when the Court struck down numerous state and Federal laws aimed at combating the Great Depression. The Court, detractors claimed, imposed its own subjective estimate of desirable economic policy upon other institutions of government. Many decisions by the Warren Court in
the 1950s and 1960s inspired similar denunciations.*

*Can the Court, in fact, avoid "making" policy when it
decides a particular Constitutional issue? Does not the Court
"make" policy even when it refuses to decide a case, thereby
allowing the decision of another tribunal to stand? Is there a
clear boundary between creative Constitutionalism and judicial
usurpation? Leonard Levy, a Constitutional historian, and
James Kilpatrick, journalist and political commentator, debate
many of these questions with respect to the Warren Court.*

Selection 1   Harry N. Scheiber

Seldom in the history of the United States has the Supreme Court played
so prominent a part in the governance of this nation as it did from 1953 to
1969, when Earl Warren served as Chief Justice. Indeed, the Warren Court's

decisions on vital questions of constitutional law were fully as important a source of national policy as the decisions of either Congress or the Presidents who served during that period. To appraise the Warren Court in historical perspective, one must also recognize the fact that it was in the expansion of individual rights that the Court's record of bold innovation was most controversial and most likely to have enduring consequences for American society. The Warren Court defended the citizen's Bill of Rights freedoms against the power of government, and furthered the establishment of true equality under the law for persons of all races and in all economic circumstances. It also sought to extend guarantees that the agencies and officers of government—in the individual states as well as at the federal level—would be held to high standards of fair procedure. . . .

The first great decision of the Warren Court was *Brown* v. *Board of Education,* decided on May 17, 1954, a day that the Court's critics would call "Black Monday." The *Brown* decision, written by Chief Justice Warren for a unanimous Court, came face to face with the issue of segregation of black people in America. It flatly overruled a doctrine held by the Court since 1896 as the "law of the land" that segregated public facilities were not in violation of the Constitution so long as blacks and whites had access to facilities of equal quality. Warren and the Court upset this "separate but equal" doctrine with a single stroke. The Court ruled that public educational facilities that are segregated are "inherently unequal.". . .

Of the state school segregation laws that had long been in effect in the southern and border states, it may be said that no other feature of American law so blatantly conflicted with the nation's political ideals of human dignity for all. Indeed, even while hesitating to confront the school segregation issue over the years, the Supreme Court had been moving slowly toward a change in doctrine. In 1948 the Court had decided that the state courts could not constitutionally enforce racial covenants (barring blacks from purchase) in real-estate contracts. In other cases, culminating in 1953, the exclusion of blacks from voting in southern states' primary elections had been ruled unconstitutional. In 1950 the Court had struck down the policy of maintaining segregation in public law schools. With those Court decisions, Professor Charles Black has observed, "the clock began to tick on segregation. It struck in the School Segregation Cases," with the 1954 *Brown* decision.

What is perhaps most important of all, however, is the fact that, while the judicial clock was ticking, in the political system at large—that world of political realities in which a Supreme Court must operate—there was widespread lack of interest in desegregation at best, and deep popular hostility at worst. . . . President Harry S. Truman had failed to persuade Congress to enact civil rights laws that would assure blacks of their voting rights and uproot the system of legalized discrimination. Truman's endorsement of civil rights legislation had succeeded, at least, in bringing advocacy of racial equality within the perimeter of "respectable" political ideas. But the volatility of his initiatives was proved when a massive walkout of southern delegates occurred in the 1948 Democratic convention, fracturing the party's historic alliance with pro-segregationist Southerners and providing the occasion for a third-party State Rights presidential campaign. . . .

Therefore, when the Court decreed in the *Brown* decision that segregation was unconstitutional, it was not casting out upon calm political waters. Rather, it was risking its prestige and venturing to correct the most pervasive and deeply rooted social ill in American life. . . . From the perspective of more than twenty years, what is the significance of the school desegregation cases in the history of the Warren Court?

First of all, with *Brown* the Court demonstrated that it would not shrink from playing a bold, activist role in the governance of American life when the basic liberties of the individual were at stake. In that sense, the Court's decision, as Professor Philip Kurland has written, "set the tone for the entire judicial era.". . .

Secondly, there was long-term significance and a portent of future decisions when the Court followed its ringing affirmation of basic principles, in the 1954 decision, with *"Brown II,"* a year later. In *Brown II* the Court refrained from an insistence upon total, immediate school integration. Instead, it left the door open for gradual social and legal adjustment, mandating that schools must be integrated "with all deliberate speed." Many years later, Chief Justice Warren, who by then had retired from the Court, reflected on why his Court had adopted the "all deliberate speed" formula in 1955:

> . . . We realized that under our federal system there were so many blocks preventing an immediate solution of the thing in reality, that the best we could look for would be a progression of action; and to keep it going, in a proper manner, we adopted that phrase, all deliberate speed. . . .
>
> . . . We knew that covering all the school districts in the country, and under different statutes and different organizations of the educational process, it would take a long time to work out.
>
> I remember the first time we discussed how long we thought it would take. I remember one Justice suggested . . . wouldn't it be wonderful if on the centennial of the Fourteenth Amendment, that is, 1968, that it would be a reality all over this country. . . .

Many critics had contended that the Court was kicking over the historic features of American federalism—the division of governmental responsibilities between the states and the Federal government, with school policy traditionally left in the hands of local and state officials. But Warren's version (if accurate) suggests that the Court was extremely sensitive to the imperatives of federalism. While it was setting a new, dramatically different national standard by requiring integration, it was leaving maximum room for individual states and school districts to move by their own routes and at varying rates of implementation toward true integration. . . .

The long-term significance of the school desegregation cases has a third dimension in the dynamics of resistance and reaction that *Brown* set in motion. Probably the key to what followed was in large measure a "vacuum of leadership," resulting in an erosion of the moral authority of the Court's doctrine. President Dwight D. Eisenhower did not make any public appeal for support of the *Brown* decisions. Eisenhower's silence was easily interpreted as disapproval. At best, it raised serious doubts as to whether the Justice Department and the full force of executive authority would supply the federal courts with serious, effective aid in enforcement. Meanwhile pro-segregation Southerners seized the initiative in Congress and in national debate. They raised the banner of states' rights, and hysterical charges of communism were hurled at the Court.

The result of this initial reaction was a pervasive crisis of the rule of law. Many southern state judges and even a few federal district judges in the South openly denounced the *Brown* decision. When the southern state legislatures began to enact laws designed to evade or openly resist school integration, the anti-Warren Court attitude of these judges challenged the "legitimacy" of the *Brown* doctrine. It also lent respectability to racist-motivated resistance. The *Brown* decision itself, however, lent contrasting, authoritative respectability to the NAACP and other organizations that had been pressing for racial integration. In the short run, the dramatic shift in constitutional law triggered an increasingly activist trend on the part of blacks who sought to assert their rights throughout the South. . . . There arose a reaction of heightened fears, racial tension, and determination on the part of many southern whites to hold back the tides of change. . . .

In the long run, the pattern of resistance to the school desegregation rulings was important because it became part of the larger civil rights struggle in America. By standing consistently behind its initial premise of 1954, that the Fourteenth Amendment forbade the states to discriminate against black people, the Court set the stage for further legal challenges to the historic structure of legalized segregation in public facilities of all sorts. The Civil Rights Acts of 1957, 1960, and 1964 finally brought the power of Congress behind this revolution in constitutional principle. These acts vindicated the claim of the Warren Court's admirers that the Supreme Court does have a role to play in serving as the "nation's conscience" and helping to define moral principle. . . .

Legislative Reapportionment

A second great area of American law in which the Warren Court acted to expand individual liberties is that of legislative reapportionment. Here the doctrinal and political background, the degree of unanimity in the Court itself and the variety of judicial activism exercised by the Court were quite different from those in the school desegregation cases. But the pattern of political reaction became closely interlaced with the earlier reaction to *Brown.* The result was to deepen further a crisis of "legitimacy" that had already gathered great momentum when the first reapportionment case, *Baker* v. *Carr,* was decided in 1962. Reapportionment meant the redrawing of the boundaries of legislative districts in order to achieve greater equality of representation. . . .

A system of apportionment which gives some districts with few residents (say, white, suburban, or rural voters) a greater number of representatives in a state legislature than other districts with far larger numbers of residents (say, black, urban, or poor) damages the workings of the ordinary political processes, and subordinates the interests of minorities. That is the situation that prevailed in the United States in 1962. In nearly all states, the legislatures suffered from gross inequalities of representation because of population disparities among districts. Yet the Supreme Court had consistently refrained from exercising its judical power to satisfy the claims of voters who complained of discrimination (inequality under the law, in violation of the Fourteenth Amendment, as was argued) because of malapportionment. The Court's traditional refusal to take jurisdication over such cases was based upon the doctrine of "political questions." This doctrine held that certain issues were by their nature meant to be settled by the states themselves or by the other branches of the Federal Government. They were "non-justiciable," not of a type that lent themselves to the application of consistent judicial standards. . . .

Unlike the *Brown* decision, both the 1962 and subsequent reapportionment cases found the Warren Court divided. The majority took what may be termed an activist-egalitarian position. They asserted the Court's jurisdiction and the propriety of judicial intervention in bold terms, and they rested their decision on the basic notion of equality in the Constitution, under the Fourteenth Amendment. The minority dissenting Justices, Frankfurter and Harlan, regarded the Court's decision as a blow struck at the heart of state rights. They explicitly stated their fears that it would "add a virulent source of friction and tension in federal-state relations to embroil the federal judiciary in them."

In subsequent years, the Court heard numerous cases testing its doctrine of "one man, one vote." The result was that the Court moved ahead on the course it had initially set, broadening the doctrine to cover apportionment in local units of government as well as state legislatures. Even some of the Warren Court's most outspoken defenders in public discussion began to express concern that the Court was moving too fast on too wide a front. Journalist Anthony Lewis, for example, wrote that while Chief Justice Warren read the decision of *Reynolds* v. *Sims* in 1964, "some listeners . . . felt as if they were present at a second American Constitution Convention." If friendly observers welcomed the vigorous, eloquent application of egalitarian ideas, many others wondered aloud whether the Court was the proper vehicle for their application. . . .

There was a striking paradox in the broader public reaction to the reapportionment cases. On the one hand, the attack on the Court failed to arouse much popular concern. . . . On the other hand, behind closed legislative doors an orchestrated and immensely effective "quiet campaign" to call a constitutional convention—the first since 1787—was set in motion under Senator Everett Dirksen's leadership. Although the campaign to overturn the reapportionment and other decisions by this extraordinary device was nearly successful, the general public was largely unaware of the situation. The quiet campaign lost, falling just short of plunging the nation into the most perilous constitutional crisis from the Civil War until then. . . .

Criminal Due Process

By the early 1960's, the Warren Court's activist tendencies had already stirred up troubled political waters. But the Justices continued to meet head-on what they believed was unfinished constitutional business. For nearly half a century the Supreme Court had been reappraising "criminal due process" in the states—that is, the rights and immunities of persons who found themselves in the hands of the police, in state criminal court proceedings, or in prison as the result of criminal convictions in the states. The Court's dilemma turned on the question: To what degree did the Fourteenth Amendment's "due process" clause apply rights enumerated in the first eight amendments to governmental proceedings in the states? As of the mid-1950's, the Court was still committed to the view—essentially a view based on the doctrine of judicial self-restraint—that the states were to be held only to a basic "fairness" test. . . . The balance shifted in favor of the "liberal" bloc when Arthur Goldberg, who had made a brilliant career as a labor union lawyer and as President Kennedy's Secretary of Labor, succeeded the staunch apostle of self-restraint, Felix Frankfurter, in 1962. The new majority greatly broadened the constitutional definition of "due process" guarantees as applied to the states.

The Court abandoned with astonishing speed the vague "fairness" test and applied the first eight Amendments to the states. Gaining some unanimous decisions at first, then increasingly acting with a divided Court, from 1962 to 1968 the Justices transformed the basic ground rules of police and criminal-court procedures in the states. The landmark decision of *Gideon* v. *Wainwright* (1963) jarred observers who believed that the Court should adhere to its own precedents whenever possible. It flatly reversed the holding in a 1942 case, *Betts* v. *Brady,* that "the appointment of counsel is not a fundamental right, essential to a fair trial." In a dramatic extension of its egalitarian principles, the Court in *Gideon* ruled that poor (indigent) defendants must be allowed the same standing and advantages as defendants with the means to hire an attorney. To make "equality before the law" meaningful, the state must provide a lawyer to the poor person standing trial. Then the Court extended new guarantees to the police station as well as the courtroom: the *Escobedo* decision in 1964 and the *Miranda* decision in 1966 gave people in the hands of the police, prior to being brought to trial, new guarantees which Anthony Lewis has observed came as "an earthquake in the world of law enforcement." . . . Further decisions broadened the application of Bill of Rights prohibitions against arbitrary search and seizure of evidence, extended procedural rights to juvenile defendants, and placed limits on government's wire-tapping power.

To many Americans, it appeared that the Warren Court was finally closing the gap between the ideal of equality before the law and the realities of everyday police activity and criminal justice. Such Court supporters contended that these decisions merely gave concrete, specific form to the "basic fairness" requirement that had long been held applicable to the states. But criticism of the Court came from many sources, not least important of whom were police officials and members of Congress who took a "get-tough" stand on law enforcement, accusing the Court of "coddling the criminal." The climax of the resulting debate came in 1968. Presidential candidates Wallace and Nixon, already trading on hostility to the Court sparked by the desegregation and civil rights decisions, opened their big political guns against the Court as an alleged enemy of "law and order" in America. Against this background, Congress enacted the "Omnibus Crime Control and Safe Streets Bill" in 1968. The debate over the crime bill was a response not only to sharply rising crime rates but also to the public mood of alarm and anger over social disorders ranging from the ghetto riots and political assassinations of the 1960's to the widespread demonstrations associated with popular opposition to the Vietnam War. But debate over the crime bill mushroomed into a heated clash over the Court, its specific rulings, its motives, and the proper future role of judicial review in the federal system.

Desegregation, reapportionment, and criminal "due process" exemplify well the "activism" of the Warren Court. But they do not make up the whole range of individual rights and liberties with which the Court concerned itself as it broadened the range of freedoms in American life. Perhaps the boldest demonstration of the activist philosophy was in the birth control case, *Griswold* v. *Connecticut*, in 1965. In an opinion for the majority, Justice Douglas asserted that within marriage people enjoy a "right to privacy" in matters, such as birth control, that might not be directly specified in the Bill of Rights but still come within "penumbras, formed by emanations" from the Constitution's literal guarantees."

This sort of doctrine astonished and alarmed observers who viewed the Court's activism as a growing "intoxication with its own power," as one prominent academic critic said with blunt directness. If *Griswold* represented perhaps an extreme expression of the activist philosophy, there were other areas of the law in which the Court's initiatives served as a lightning rod for conflict and attack. A series of decisions banning religious-type prayers from public school classrooms and limiting the degree of government aid to religious education formed an outstanding example. Other decisions sparked efforts in Congress to curb the Court's jurisdiction and reverse some of its rulings. Among these were a group of decisions that placed strict limits upon government's power to exact loyalty oaths and enforce "security" regulations aimed at persons deemed subversive . . . .

By the late 1960's, then, the cumulative efforts of the Warren Court to maintain a society protective of individual freedom and dignity for unpopular minorities had embroiled the Court in treacherous political difficulties. The whole society was suffering from dangerous tensions. Racial confrontations flared into violence at various times in the 1960's. Rising crime rates frightened many. New militant political tactics by the poor, the disfranchised, and the anti-war dissenters heightened internal divisions. These things made it easy to single out the Supreme Court as an alleged cause of, and ultimately as a scapegoat for, the society's problems.

In 1968, President Johnson, Attorney General Ramsey Clark, and other administration spokesmen sought to defend the Supreme Court. They were soon joined by Chief Justice Warren, who spoke out amidst continuing attacks on the Court by Presidential candidates Nixon and Wallace. "The greatest adhesive power we have," warned the Chief Justice, "is the profound belief of the American people in our constitutional system, the dedication of our public servants to observe its injunctions, and the independence of our judiciary. If one of our three coordinate branches of government is discredited, the entire structure of government is weakened. None of them can strengthen the democratic process by climbing over the weakened body of another."

Legal scholars and others who advocated "judicial self-restraint" could reply that respect for the judiciary depended upon the people's belief that the Supreme Court itself understood and paid some respect to the popular will. But the unspoken premise of Chief Justice Warren's plea was, of course, that some political leaders attacking the Court were not interested in strengthening the democratic process or respect for law. They were interested, instead, in turning the clock back upon the Warren Court's expansion of individual liberties. They sought to do so because they regarded the people who benefited most immediately from that expansion as dangerous—as people whose liberties ought to be curbed in the interest of maintaining social order. . . .

Selection 2   James Jackson Kilpatrick

Perhaps the most famous observation in judicial history, dealing with the Supreme Court's role in shaping our fundamental law, came from John Marshall in *M' Culloch* v. *Maryland*. When it comes to defining the powers of state and federal governments, said the venerable Virginian, "we must never forget that it is a constitution we are expounding."

And perhaps the second most famous observation came almost ninety years later from Charles Evans Hughes in a speech at Elmira, N.Y. "We are under a Constitution," said the famed New Yorker, "but the Constitution is what the judges say it is."

. . . Our Constitution is indeed what the judges say it is. It is more than that, of course, but it is at least that. And during the Warren years—the sixteen years from 1953 to 1969, identified with the Chief Justiceship of Earl Warren—the Constitution was pre-eminently that : An instrument pounded, shaped and refashioned by the hands and minds of the Chief and his activist bloc.

Consider. When the Warren years began, the power of the states to operate racially separate schools, so long as the schools were substantially equal, was "well settled" as a matter of law. The question had been "many times decided," and the decisions had formed a gloss on the Fourteenth Amendment.

It was equally clear that nothing in the Fourteenth Amendment prohibited the states from fixing their own boundaries for legislative districts. Questions of apportionment were not justiciable ; these were political questions beyond the reach of judges.

When the Warren years began, there was little doubt that "obscenity" could be reasonably well-defined, and punished, under both state and federal law. The right of public schools to conduct voluntary religious observances, such as class prayers and baccalaureate sermons, was not challenged. The admissibility of certain evidence in criminal proceedings, even if police had obtained it unlawfully, was widely sanctioned. Evidence obtained through electronic detecting devices also was acceptable, provided the device had not actually penetrated an area protected under the Fourth Amendment. The right to have the assistance of counsel, the right to avoid self-incrimination, and the right to be free from unreasonable searches and seizure were strictly construed. Only a small part of the Bill of Rights had

---

From James Jackson Kilpatrick, "The Warren Legacy: A Very Different Constitution," *National Review*, August 12, 1969, pp. 794–800. Reprinted by permission of *National Review*.

been bodily "incorporated" into the prohibitions imposed upon the states by the Fourteenth.

That was how Earl Warren found the Constitution when he came on the bench. It was a very different Constitution when he left. . . .

. . . The record of the Warren years is a record of judicial activism without parallel in the Court's long history. It is a trail of abuses, usurpations and invasions of power. One pursues the departed Chief along a littered road of fallen landmarks and abandoned precedents. Here every principle of jurisprudence lies discarded. It is as if gypsies had passed through, leaving a bad picnic behind. . . .

The same harsh judgment of the Warren years comes from every corner of the bench and bar; it runs through countless law reviews; it comes most damningly from within the Court itself. To be sure, Warren had his ardent defenders also, and if one is indifferent to the means employed to reach an end, it is possible to admire many of the new landmarks erected . . . .

. . . As a working, practical matter, day in and day out, the Court's unwritten rules of self-restraint provide the only effective rein upon life-tenured judges who hold a virtually final power to say what the Constitution *is*. These rules ought to be rigidly observed. And the first and greatest count in an indictment of the Warren years is that under Warren, the rules were wantonly disdained. . . .

. . . The code of self-restraint holds firmly that in questions of constitutional adjudication, members of the Court must never yield to personal convictions. As Black has said, this is "the essence of judicial duty." It is the one rule that towers above all others . . . .

The charge against Earl Warren is that . . . he presided over a Court in which the subjective views of the judges figured constantly and critically in the disposition of the cases before them. Warren's first landmark opinion, in *Brown* v. *Board of Education*, was a portent of things to come. It was short on law, but long on compassion. His first premise appeared to be that segregation is morally wrong; therefore, he concluded, it must be unconstitutional. Repeatedly in the years that followed *Brown*, the Warren bloc found other wrongs that shocked its conscience and had to be set right; but as Justice Black kept insisting, that which shocks the conscience does not necessarily offend the Constitution.

'Judicial Usurpation'

In one of the last cases to be decided under Warren's regime, the Court, speaking through Justice Douglas, over-turned a garnishment law in Wisconsin as a violation of "fundamental principles of due process." Justice Black filed a stinging dissent. . . .

". . . Made in a Court opinion, holding Wisconsin's law unconstitutional . . . [the statements] amount to what I believe to be a plain, judicial usurpation of state legislative power to decide what the state's laws shall be."

In an addendum, Justice Black renewed his assault upon the whole business of deciding constitutional issues on the basis of a shock-the-conscience test. A judge's concept of "fundamental fairness" has no place in determining the validity of a state law. In its delegation of powers, the

Constitution speaks for itself; the meaning of "due process" must be found within the Constitution, and not, as Justice Frankfurter once suggested in a dreamy moment, in "those canons of decency and fairness which express the notions of justice of English-speaking peoples.". . .

Pole Star

This personal aspect of the code of self-restraint—that judges ought never to confuse their own conscience and the country's Constitution—is paramount. But the code is supplemented by many other traditions of procedure, of comity and of prudence. Together, these form a body of principles for Supreme Court jurisprudence; and these are the principles repeatedly abandoned in the Warren years.

Thus, the Court will not hear cases that are moot. It will not decide issues that have been neither briefed nor argued. It will not take state cases until final judgments have been entered down below. It will not take dummy cases, lacking a genuine adversary interest. It will insist upon strict obedience to its fixed rules of pleading and practice . . . .

Many other self-imposed rules have guided the Court. Out of respect for co-equal branches, the Court will stay clear of political thickets: "Questions of political expedience," said Justice Bradley in the Legal Tender Cases, "belong to the legislative halls, not to the judicial forum." The Court will accord a decent respect to the doctrines of *stare decisis*. . . .*

All these are rules of self-restraint. Their object, in part at least, is to maintain the role of the Court as the most conservative of the three branches. . . .

The Court functions "as the brake on the other men's conduct," Frankfurter once observed. While Congress and the White House are plunging full speed ahead, the Court historically has chugged gently astern.

This tradition, jettisoned so rudely in the Warren years, is echoed in the oldest of all rules of constitutional law. Jefferson described this canon of jurisdiction in 1823: "On every question of construction, carry ourselves back to the time when the Constitution was adopted, recollect the spirit manifested in the debates, and instead of trying what meaning may be squeezed out of the text, or invented against it, conform to the probable one in which it was passed."

To Judge Cooley, most famous of the professors of constitutional law, this rule of strict construction—to go first to the intention of the framers and ratifiers—was the very "pole star" of constitutional adjudication. Such an adherence to fixed meanings does not exclude the proposition that ours is a "living Constitution." Of course the Constitution lives, in the enduring structure of government it created, in the separation of powers, in the spirit of human liberty that gives life to the Bill of Rights. But especially in questions of power, and in the meaning to be attached to particular words and phrases, the intention of the framers is critical. If this is scorned, judges become not interpreters, but amenders.

Ed. Note: The doctrine that principles of law established by judicial decision be accepted as binding in cases similar to those from which such principles were derived.

Landmark Cases

And this, of course; is the grave offense imputed to the Warren Court in its handling of the Constitution: The Court did not interpret; it amended. Not only in the school case, but in many other areas of the law, the Court overturned constructions that in effect had become part of the Constitution itself. . . . In their impatience with Congress, the states and the people, they could not wait upon solutions to public problems through statutory enactment or constitutional amendment. And in their obsession for equality—an absolute equality never intended and impossible of achievement—they often abandoned both common sense and the needs of society as a whole. . . .

*   *   *

. . . In the *Brown* case of 1954 . . . Warren [wrote] "we cannot turn the clock back to 1868 when the Amendment was adopted, or even to 1896 when *Plessy* v. *Ferguson* was written. We must consider public education in the light of its full development and its present place in American life throughout the nation."

The question was asked at the time, but must be asked again and again in different contexts: In the name of the founding fathers, why *not* turn back the clock? In questions of constitutional construction, this is the first duty of appellate judges. The Court in the *Brown* case had no obligation to "consider public education" in the light of its full development or in any other light. It was a compassionate thought on the Chief's part that segregated schools may affect the hearts and minds of children in a way unlikely ever to be undone; but compassion has no place in construing a constitution. As far back as 1795, Justice Paterson stated the rule: "Motives of commiseration, from whatever source they flow, must not mingle in the administration of justice." But under Warren, such motives were mingled time after time.

The race relations cases, born of *Brown*, formed the first of the three great landmarks left by the Warren years. Many of the same criticisms that are made of *Brown* apply with equal force to the second milestone—the reapportionment doctrines laid down in *Baker* v. *Carr*, and the cases that came thereafter. Here, too, as in the case of the South's Negro schools, the facts formed a canvas of palpable wrongs. Tennessee had not permitted a reapportionment of seats for sixty years. Moore County, with a population of 2,300, had two representatives, so did Rutherford, with a population of 25,000. The 34,000 residents of Anderson County had the same representation allocated to the three thousand residents of Houston County. As Justice Clark remarked, it was a "topsy-turvical of gigantic proportions."

Blows for Democracy?

The trial court acknowledged these inequities, and condemned them, but dismissed the complaint: "The remedy in this situation clearly does not lie with the courts." A fragmented majority of the Warren Court, erupting with six opinions in splitting 6-2, tossed precedent aside and reinstated the suit. In a superb dissenting opinion—one of the best he ever wrote—Frankfurter denounced the majority's action as "a massive repudiation of the experience of our whole past." . . . In his view, it simply was not the

294

proper business of the Court to inject itself into the political problems of a state, no matter how malapportioned Tennessee might be.

"There is not under our Constitution a judicial remedy for every political mischief, for every undesirable exercise of legislative power. . . . In this situation, as in others, appeal for relief does not belong here. Appeal must be to an informed, civically militant electorate. In a democratic society like ours, relief must come through an aroused popular conscience that sears the conscience of the people's representatives."

Frankfurter and Harlan could not persuade their activist brothers. With *Baker* v. *Carr*, the Court launched itself upon what Harlan later would describe as a "pervasive overlordship" by the federal judiciary of the apportionment of state legislatures across the land. . . .

The third great landmark of the Warren years arises from a series of interlocking opinions having to do with the criminal law. Every outcry against the Warren Court, and every kind word also, come together in the criminal cases. . . .

By Warren's own evaluation, *Gideon* v. *Wainwright* in March of 1963 ranks with *Brown* and *Baker*. He views them as the most memorable three cases of his term as Chief. Clarence Earl Gideon was a small-time operator who broke into a poolroom with intent to commit a misdemeanor. When he came up for trial, he asked for a lawyer to defend him. Florida's law made no provision for indigent counsel except in capital cases. Gideon undertook to defend himself. He was found guilty and sentenced to five years. What the Sixth Amendment says is that in "all" criminal prosecutions, a right to counsel obtains; and if one accepts the proposition *arguendo*, that a right to counsel is among the "privileges and immunities" incorporated in the Fourteenth Amendment, Florida should have provided Gideon with a lawyer. That is what a unanimous Court held in the *Gideon* case. In terms of equal justice under the law, it was a fine ruling; but it overturned a precedent of 21 years, and it created formidable problems in the courts of fifty states.

Gideon led to *Escobedo* in June of 1964, and this time the Court was not unanimous. It divided 5-4. There was no question that the Chicago police had behaved badly in refusing Danny Escobedo a chance to confer with his lawyer prior to questioning in a murder case. But there was great question in the minds of Harlan, White, Clark and Stewart that the *Gideon* rule should be expanded as widely as the Warren bloc expanded it. The majority held that a criminal prosecution begins whenever a police inquiry focuses upon a particular suspect; the right to counsel thus comes into play; and unless this right is fully respected by police, no statement elicited from the accused may be used at his trial. . . . Two years later, in reversing the rape-kidnapping conviction of Ernesto Miranda in Arizona, Warren himself still further broadened the *Escobedo* rule. In effect, the activist majority prohibited *any* questioning of a suspect unless his right to counsel—and his right to stand silent— are fully explained to him. The four dissenters of *Escobedo* protested anew: "The Court is taking a real risk with society's welfare," Clark objected, but the new rule of *Miranda* came into being.

Three years earlier, Clark had complained of the majority's tendency to make a "fetish of indigency." In *Douglas* v. *California*, the liberal bloc had ruled against a preliminary screening process used by California in its appellate procedures. The system appeared to create one opportunity for the rich, and a lesser one for the poor. But the equal protection clause, said Harlan in dissent, "does not impose on the states an affirmative duty to lift the handicaps flowing from differences in economic circumstances. . . ."

'Hurdles and Barriers'

No field of criminal law saw greater upheaval in the Warren years than the Fourth Amendment law on search and seizures. Precedents that had governed the admissibility of evidence for many years went one by one to the scrap heap. A series of opinions reversed the convictions of criminal defendants whose guilt, as Black objected in one case, was "open and shut."

On the whole . . . the line of Fourth Amendment cases followed a consistent course, by which the majority demanded perfect warrants, pefectly executed, issued on affidavits of overwhelming probable cause.

Well, it may be asked, what is so wrong with that? Is not the citizen's right to privacy a precious right? The answer is simply that the Court's increasingly impossible demands are remote from reality; they require ordinary cops to act as constitutional lawyers. A form of extremism comes into play: The Court would not absolutely prohibit the use of confessions; it would merely make confessions impossible to obtain. The Court would not ban electronic detection devices in theory; it would ban them only in fact. The Court would not object to reasonable searches; but it would find nine of ten searches unreasonable.

During the Warren years, the ends of justice, and the needs of society, thus disappeared into a rarefied gas of vaporized rhetoric. Newly-fabricated rules on self-incrimination, on confessions, on jury trials, on rights to counsel, on post-conviction remedies, suddenly have been imposed on police and prosecutors. In North Carolina, a brute criminal goes free: He had twice raped a girl, shot her and her escort with a rifle, and left them to die; but the rifle, obtained without a proper warrant, was inadmissible. In California, a bank robber gets off; it was unconstitutional for police to obtain a sample of his handwriting. . . . Eddie Harrison, who *three times* confessed to murder, could not be sent to prison; none of the three confessions could pass the purity test.

Scores of such cases run through the records of the Warren years. In the view of experienced police officials, struggling to cope with accelerating rates of crime, there is no question that the decisions, taken as a whole, have seriously hampered law enforcement. The majority's doctrinaire pronouncements have played havoc with long-established principles of federalism. . . .

Warren as Dissenter

It is not only in criminal law, to be sure, that the Warren Court exhibited its contempt for the wisdom of the past. Copyright law, labor law, patent law, antitrust law—all these have witnessed a drastic reshaping. A disgusted Justice Stewart, in one such case, denounced his brothers for "judicial legerdemain." . . .

It would be an error, it seems to me, to read into any account of the Warren years an implication that Warren ranked with John Marshall as a controlling figure on the bench. "There was never a Warren Court in the sense that he dominated it," Professor Alexander Bickel has written. "But there was a Warren Court in the sense that starting, by accident, with his assent, and accelerating, there was clearly a different attitude, a new outlook."

Warren did not always have his way in the great cases of his time. Especially in the early years, when Frankfurter, Whittaker and Clark were still around, the Chief was often on the losing end. Over a span of eight years, between 1955 and 1963, Warren dissented almost 150 times. Between 1957 and 1961, by my count, he stood 48 times with Black, Douglas and Brennan on the bottom side of 5-4 decisions.

Warren v. Burger

Neither should an impression be left that Warren was always, in every case, on the activist side. In the area of obscenity censorship, he stood close by the Harlan conservatives. He frequently cast his vote, as in the Maryland blue law case, on the side of 'states' rights." . . . In the stop-and-frisk case, *Terry* v. *Ohio*, the Chief resisted the howls of his bleedingheart brothers in order to write an opinion of help to police. When it served his purpose, he could defend the Court's rules with steadfast reserve.

Yet the big trends toward activism persisted throughout the Warren years, and the big opinions that were written—*Brown, Baker, Gideon, Escobedo, Miranda*, the New York prayer case, the decisions that liberalized pornography and rewrote the Bill of Rights—will have a lasting impact on the law. The presumption is strong that as suitable cases come along, presenting better facts to work with, a reconstituted court under Burger will clip the wings of some of these spread-eagled doctrines, especially in reapportionment and in some areas of criminal law. But few persons imagine that Burger will seek to overturn the monuments. More likely, the Court of 1969-70 will undertake chiefly to tidy up the grounds. . . .

Selection 3   Leonard Levy

When Earl Warren became Chief Justice of the United States in 1953, American constitutional law, like the nation that it served, stood poised at the brink between two worlds. One, which nothing short of lethal action could move or remove, deserved a speedy, contemptible death; it was the world of racism, political rottenboroughs, McCarthyism, discriminations against the poor, puritanism in sexual matters, denial of the suffrage, and egregious infringements on the rights of the criminally accused. The other was a world struggling to be born, in which injustices would be remedied and the fundamental law of the land would have a liberating and egalitarian impact. The Supreme Court under Warren was a midwife to the newer world. Freedom of expression and association, and, even more importantly, racial justice, criminal justice, and political justice became the Court's preoccupation, its meat and drink. Not since the early nineteenth century when the great John Marshall presided had the Court made American constitutional law so generative, even transforming—indeed there were friends and foes alike who spoke of a judicial "revolution"; and not since Marshall's time had the Court, which periodically suffered withering criticism, been so vilified by its critics nor so rapturously acclaimed by its supporters.

Although the Court operates in the main as a judicial team rather than as individual stars, Warren was the symbol of his Court, literally its head, figuratively its heart. He drew the kudos as well as the aspersions, even the psychotic hatreds epitomized by the scream, "Impeach Earl Warren!" . . . President Dwight Eisenhower, who had appointed him, grew to regret his choice of Warren and is supposed to have said it was the "biggest damn fool mistake I ever made." President Lyndon Johnson handed Warren the accolade as "the greatest Chief Justice of them all." . . . Although Warren was not responsible for the judicial "revolution," he was responsive to it, and in the crucial areas of civil rights and electoral representation he led it. . . .

When Warren retired on June 23,1969, Nixon, . . . offering his grudging respect to the departing Warren, declared that the sixteen years during which he had presided "without doubt, will be described by historians as years of greater change in America than any in our history. . . . Change with continuity," he ventured, "can mean progress," and quite remarkably he added that of the three great branches of the government, none had been more responsible "for that continuity with change than the Supreme Court of the United States." The nation already knew what the President belatedly, if only ceremonially, recognized, that the Constitution had triumphantly survived the change and still stood, despite all vicissitudes— but that it most definitely had not stood still: under Warren it had progressed.

In his extemporaneous response, the Chief Justice stressed the theme of continuity with change. . . . "We, of course, venerate the past, but our focus is on the problems of the day and of the future as we conceive it to be." . . . The Court, Warren concluded, had applied constitutional principles, so broadly stated in the document, in a manner consistent with the public interest and with the future "so far as it can be discerned."

Warren's candid and simple valedictory in effect endorsed the view, stated by both the Court's admirers and critics, that the justices seemed to consider themselves as movers and shakers of the country's destiny rather than as impersonal spokesmen of "the law." . . .

In an article on "The Law and the Future," published in *Fortune* magazine in 1955, two years after his appointment as Chief Justice, Warren was characteristically expansive, warm, and idealistic. This public statement confirmed the tenor of his stewardship. His prime concern for the law, Warren noted, was that it adapt to changing circumstances by keeping its rules in harmony with the enlightened common sense of the nation. That meant to him that the Supreme Court faced "a single continuous problem: how to apply to ever changing conditions the never changing principles of freedom." . . . Significantly he fastened upon "the 462 words of our Bill of Rights" as "the most precious part of our legal heritage," yet he presided over the Court at a time, he said, when the Bill of Rights was under subtle and pervasive attack. Turning to needed reforms of our constitutional system, he noted that the proud inscription above the portals of the Supreme Court Building—"Equal Justice Under Law"—described a goal by no means secured for all citizens. The rights due them, particularly oppressed minorities and the poor, had been infringed, neglected, or unperfected. Our system of criminal justice was "pockmarked with. . . procedural flaws and anachronisms," making for unequal access to justice. . . . The remarks foreshadowed some of the most disputed reforms inaugurated by the Warren Court.

Freedom, like justice, the Chief Justice continued, requires constant vigilance. . . . Warren's statement implicitly recognized that the Supreme Court had a crucial responsibility, one that could not be evaded, to help regenerate and fulfill the noblest aspirations for which the nation stood. In effect he was saying that the law, though remaining constantly rooted in the great ideals of the past, must change in order to realize them. Thus, when posterity receives the Bill of Rights from the present generation, the document will not have the same meaning as it had when we received it from past generations. "We will pass on a better Bill of Rights," he asserted, "or a worse one, tarnished by neglect or burnished by growing use. If these rights are real, they need constant and imaginative applications to new situations." Such "constant and imaginative applications" earned for the Warren Court its reputation for "activism."

The Constitution contains not a word about . . . most of the subjects of great import with which the Court must deal. The framers of the Constitution had a genius for studied imprecision and calculated ambiguity. Their document . . . thereby permitted, even encouraged—in fact necessitated—continuous reinterpretation and adaptation. . . .

"Strict constructionists" to the contrary, the Supreme Court is and must be for all practical purposes a "continuous constitutional convention" adapting the original charter by reinterpretation. One who used that phrase was James Beck, a Solicitor General of the United States and a very conservative one at that. He described the duties of the Court as "political in the highest sense of the word as well as judicial." . . . The reason is simply that the Constitution, as Jefferson said in exasperation, is "merely a thing of wax" which the Court "may twist and shape into any form they please." . . .

Judicial self-restraint and strict constructionism are at best factors that merely temper the inescapable activism needed for decision in constitutional adjudication. . . . Judicial activism, not restraint, has been our experience with the Supreme Court literally from the time of its very first decision.

Activism has certainly characterized the Warren Court, a galloping, hyperthyroid activism. But that occupational disease of the highest judicial process is not at all what distinguished the Warren Court from its predecessors. Activism in the past was associated in the main with the Court's invalidation of federal or state acts and its construction of statutes in a manner that changed their meaning or robbed them of it. . . . Historically the Court sought to redirect the course of public policy into more conservative channels by interposing its highly legislative judgments against those of the popularly elected and politically responsible agencies of government. . . . What made the Warren Court so different is that it sought to *enlarge* the political capacity of the people and to heighten their sense of moral responsibility. . . .

Taken as a group, the cases in which the Warren Court voided acts of Congress are of greater symbolic than practical importance. None of them received much attention from the press or Congress. The cases which evoked great public interest and were most significant involved judicial review of state action, chiefly the racial discrimination and legislative apportionment cases whose transforming effects upon American life are not yet played out. Similarly, the state cases on censorship of obscenity and freedom of the press, on church-state relations and freedom of religion, and on criminal justice loom larger in the public mind and have had a more far-reaching influence than the cases in which the Court invalidated congressional legislation. Under the Warren Court the constitutional law of civil liberties and civil rights enjoyed a golden age in our history. Never before was the Court so bold and vigilant in its defense of constitutional freedoms in so many diverse fields. The various First Amendment liberties, the great procedural rights of the criminally accused, and equal justice under the law for racial minorities, for political lepers, and for the poor have flourished mightily in the pages of the Court's opinions, with considerable fallout in the world beyond.

Often the Court held "the standard aloft" when all other agencies of government, pressed by more expediential or parochial considerations, had lost sight of it. The controversial reforms in state criminal procedure would not have been necessary had local police officials, prosecutors, and courts done their jobs with respect for the Bill of Rights. The reapportionment revolution would not have been imposed by the Supreme Court had state legislatures and state courts discharged their obligations under their own laws and under the equal-protection clause of the Fourteenth Amendment. The Supreme Court would not have had to serve as a sword for the destruction of racial discriminations that had been compelled by law if Congress had passed civil rights acts or if the state legislatures and courts had not sustained local prejudices against constitutional rights. What made the Warren Court so different from its predecessors and vulnerable to criticism was its enthusiastic willingness to play St. George in defense of constitutional rights.

In short, the special character of the Warren Court derived from the fact that it was the first *liberal* activist court in our history. Because it was libertarian and egalitarian in its judicial activism, and because it dared to lead the way, redressing injustices to which state courts, policemen, and politicians both state and national had been stone blind, neglectful, or unable to redress, the Warren Court became the conscience of the country. Its moralistic admonitions and appeals to national ideals, joined to judicial "thou-shalt-nots," provoked feelings of guilt and resentment, even outrage. Even within its own ranks, the Court's departure from its traditional role as a defender of the status quo and its novel assumption of the role of St. George exposed it to scathing criticisms.

The trenchant, intramural discord in the Warren Court was reflected in bruising opinions by dissenting justices. In anguished and angry words they accused the majority, time and again, of making new law, departing from precedent, deciding on the basis of personal predilections, acting as a superlegislature, and disregarding conventional canons of constitutional construction. . . . The public, which has little understanding of and even less patience for constitutional niceties, cares only about the results of cases, and so the Court was accused in irresponsible and misleading terms of having coddled criminals and communists, outlawed God from the public schools, legislated morality and sociology in its desegregation decisions, and intruded into the political thicket of legislative apportionment. Dissenting opinions, sometimes quite openly, fed such charges, but the chief complaint of the dissenters turned on the overbreadth of many of the Court's opinions and the failure of the majority justices to confront complicated constitutional issues with appropriate professional expertise and consistency.

Consistency has rarely been a virtue of the Supreme Court, and under Warren its record in this regard was no worse than in the past. . . . On balance, liberal activism characterized the work of the Court during its sixteen years under Warren; but there were many decisions that libertarians deplored as encroachments on constitutionally protected freedoms.

The Warren Court is associated, for example, with a broad view of First Amendment rights, enabling obscene literature to escape censorship. Yet the Court's leading decision on the subject, in the *Roth* case, sustained the constitutionality of both state and federal obscenity laws; and in several other cases, convictions for violating state laws against obscenity were sustained. . . .

In the *Perez* decision dealing with the right to citizenship, the Court, though it subsequently overruled itself, supported the power of Congress to denationalize native-born citizens who voted in foreign elections. In *Zemel* v. *Rusk* the Court decided that the Secretary of State could ban passports for travel to Cuba, notwithstanding claims, based on due process and the First Amendment, of a right to travel freely. Against a First Amendment challenge based on freedom of expression, the Court in the *O'Brien* case of 1965 sustained a congressional statute making it a felony deliberately to destroy or mutilate a draft card. In four other First Amendment cases, decided in 1961, the Court upheld Sunday closing laws. . . . In the area of criminal justice, despite charges that it was handcuffing the cops, the Court in *Terry* v. *Ohio* sustained a "stop and frisk" law and the conviction obtained under it, although the police officer lacked probable cause to seize, search, and arrest. Reversing the conviction before it in the *Katz* case, the Court nevertheless indicated that evidence secured by electronic bugging, judicially authorized and not involving physical trespass, would not violate the Fourth Amendment.

The Court sustained the government in numerous internal-security cases. . . . Against Fifth Amendment claims that the right against self-incrimination was violated, the Court's *Ullmann* decision sustained the constitutionality of a congressional immunity act forcing witnesses to testify concerning subversive activities; and in three cases the Court upheld the dismissals from public service of persons who refused to answer concerning their communist affiliations. . . .

In these various cases that do not square with the reputation of the Warren Court for unadulterated and consistent support of Bill of Rights claims against the government, the Chief Justice himself sided with the government in the obscenity, stop-and-frisk, Sunday-closing, travel-to-

Cuba, electronic bugging, and immunity cases. In the others he dissented. In the late 1950's the liberal activist group on the Court met frequent defeat, particularly in internal-security cases, because of the defections of Justices Frankfurter and Harlan. When Justice Goldberg succeeded Justice Frankfurter at the beginning of the 1962-1963 term, the balance of power shifted for the remainder of the Chief Justice's incumbency to the liberal activists. In the preceding term, however, Justice Clark's votes insured two victories that will always be identified with the Warren wing. One, *Mapp* v. *Ohio*, overruled a 1948 precedent and extended the Fourth Amendment's guarantee against unreasonable search and seizure to the states, making the fruits of an illegal search as excludable as evidence in a state trial as it would be in a federal one. In the other precedent-shattering case, *Baker* v. *Carr*, the Court sustained the jurisdiction of federal tribunals to require state legislatures to redistrict themselves on an equitable basis. Both cases spawned a progeny of remarkable decisions in the 1960's. By the conclusion of Warren's tenure as Chief Justice the Court had incorporated into the Fourteenth Amendment most of the provisions of the Bill of Rights applicable to accused persons—indeed, all the essential ones except the right against excessive bail. In sum, the Court abolished the double standard that had formerly existed by requiring that state criminal procedures conform to federal ones. In the long line of reapportionment decisions following *Baker* v. *Carr*, the Court ordered an end to the existing malapportionment schemes in federal, state, and local governments that had reached such proportions as to mock the integrity of representative government. When Warren, nearing his retirement, was asked which were the most important decisions of his time, he chose, in rank order, the reapportionment cases, the school desegregation cases, and *Gideon* v. *Wainwright*, the case in which the Court, adding representation by counsel in all felony prosecutions to the list of incorporated rights, required the states to provide counsel to defendants too poor to hire their own.

Warren's choice of the most important decisions of his time was surprising only because he did not rank the school desegregation cases first. These were, after all, the only cases during his sixteen years of which it may be said that had the decisions gone the other way, the United States would have been morally bankrupt and unfit to survive under the pretense that it was a democracy. The nation would have been a far poorer place had the Court ducked the reapportionment issue and had it decided the criminal procedure cases wholly on the side of the government, but on the issue of racial justice, any opinion other than or even narrower than the one handed down by Warren would have been unthinkable, unbearable, unspeakable. . . .

After his retirement, Warren in a public address declared that many people had told him that they opposed discrimination and favored equal treatment under the laws—but "Don't you think that we are moving too fast?" The question, replied Warren, was "an escape from responsibility" and assumed that the Court "had the right to ration freedoms, and that it should go slow enough so as not to offend anyone in doing so. Of course, no such power exists in law or morals. Either all rights of citizenship belong to them or they are entitled to none. . . ." It was Warren's opinion in the 1954 case that sparked the civil rights revolution which led to the series of civil rights acts belatedly passed by Congress.

That opinion also marked the beginning of a profound commitment by the Warren Court to the achievement of racial justice. American constitutional law has always had a central interest to guard. Throughout most of American history that interest had been the rights of property; sometimes it has been the Union, the state police power, the rights of labor, or internal security. During Warren's chief justiceship that central interest was, broadly speaking, the Bill of Rights; more particularly it was racial justice. The unifying theme that runs through a variety of the Court's opinions is that all Americans, including Negroes, are entitled to the same constitutional rights.

The theme of equal rights and racial justice even underscores the Court's various decisions on criminal procedures and reapportionment, because Negroes constitute a disproportionate number of the criminally accused and are increasingly concentrated in metropolitan centers. Racial justice, criminal justice, and political justice were interrelated though different facets of the Warren Court's dedication to passing on to future generations a better Bill of Rights, burnished by growing use and imaginatively applied to new situations.

★ ★ ★

UNIT FOUR
"A MORE PERFECT UNION":
THE
AMERICAN GOVERNMENT

★ ★ ★

Members of House Judiciary Committee during hearing on Articles of Impeachment, July 29, 1974.

"Perhaps a new generation . . . will restore Congress to a vigorous role in an ever-expanding government."—Kurland

"IT'S AWFUL THE WAY THEY'RE TRYING TO INFLUENCE CONGRESS. WHY DON'T THEY SERVE COCKTAILS AND MAKE CAMPAIGN CONTRIBUTIONS LIKE WE DO?"

"It's awful the way they're trying to influence Congress. Why don't they serve cocktails and make campaign contributions like we do?" from *The Herblock Gallery* (Simon & Schuster, 1968)

*"The Presidency had been in crisis before. . . .
It was nonsense to suppose that its fate as an
institution was bound up with the fate of the
particular man who happened to be President at
any given time."*—Schlesinger, Jr.

*"That he was honest,
all admitted. . . . This is a general
characteristic of all new presidents. . . .
He came to Washington determined
to be the Father of his country."*—Adams

FARMER GARFIELD
Cutting a Swath to the White House.

Theodore Roosevelt Addressing a Gathering of the Bull Moose Party, 1912.

"There must be a real choice presented at election time."—Broder

Is Congress Moribund?

Philip B. Kurland

The twentieth century has witnessed a centralization in the powers of government: Within the American federal system, the national government has grown at the expense of state and local governments. And within the national government, Presidential power has increased—usually at the expense of the Congress, particularly in foreign affairs. In the following selection, Philip B. Kurland, professor of law at the University of Chicago, examines the decline of Congressional influence relative to the executive branch in many areas of domestic policy as well.

Revitalizing Congress' role, Kurland argues bluntly, will not be easy because the national legislature "does not have the guts to stand up to its responsibilities. And the American electorate does not have the interest to see that Congress does so."
Despite this pessimism, Kurland also believes that rejuvenation of Congressional authority is indispensable to the continuation of a free and stable American government.

When this country was founded, a written Constitution was drawn in part as an attempt to prevent the concentration of power in a tyrannical executive, from which the colonies had but recently freed themselves. At the same time, the experience under the Confederation had made it clear that a powerless central government would not be conducive to the creation of a nation. American constitutionalism was born with three distinctive features. First the national government was to be tethered in such a way as to assure freedom of the individual. This was to be accomplished by giving the national government only limited powers and then by fencing in those powers with a bill of rights. Second, government power was to be divided between the national and state governments in order to prevent the monopoly of authority that the people feared. Federalism, too, rested on a concept of freedom. Third, within the national government itself, power was to be divided among the three branches in such manner as to prevent the hegemony of any of them. This was to be attained by a separation of the executive, legislative, and judicial powers

From Philip B. Kurland, "The Impotence of Reticence," in *Duke Law Journal*, August, 1968, pp. 619–36. Copyright 1968 *Duke Law Journal*. Reprinted by permission of the copyright holder. Original citation 1968 *Duke Law Journal* 619.

and by affording checks on the powers that each of these branches was to exercise. Separation of powers and checks and balances were also concerned with freedom.

I do not intend . . . to discuss the limitation on governmental authority afforded by the Bill of Rights or the theory of the limited role of government. Of federalism as a viable constitutional principle, I would say only two things. First, that federalism is moribund if it is not dead. Second, that federalism is beginning to be mourned, with all the regrets that mourners usually have about not having treated the deceased better during his lifetime.

. . . A recent report of the Advisory Commission on Intergovernmental Relations came to the shocked conclusion that the great American population centers are threatened by total domination by the national government. In fact, there no longer is any question of the power that the national government has over state and local government. The sole question that remains is when that power will be exercised. And that choice rests in the national capital and nowhere else.

Why did federalism succumb? There were many contributing factors. One was the nationalization of our economic and social life. Another was the abuse of the doctrine by reactionaries who would put it to their own nefarious ends. A third was the pressure by liberals to place power where they thought they could control it. And, not the least important, was the unwillingness of the states and their people to assume the responsibilities that have always been the necessary concomitants of power. Power moved to Washington in part because Washington was prepared to exercise it for the solution of the problems that the American people faced. The states were not.

. . . I would take you with me on a visit to the sickbed of another constitutional concept—the notion of separation of powers. . . . I am not . . . sanguine about the patient's chances, largely because it has lost the will to live. In any event, it is certainly too late to expect that it will be restored to full health.

Responsibility for Foreign Affairs

. . . Let me turn first to the problem of separation of powers in the field of foreign affairs. For here, if anywhere, the power of the executive branch is believed to be justified in constitutional terms. And yet a look at the Constitution hardly affords an answer to the question of where the foreign affairs power is properly to be located. Certainly the Constitution speaks about the Presidential authority to make treaties, but only with the advice and consent of two-thirds of the Senate. The chief executive has the power to appoint ambassadors, other public ministers, and consuls, but only with the consent of the Senate. And he was given the power to receive ambassadors and other public ministers. A general grant of executive power and the power as commander-in-chief were also to be exercised by the President.

On the other hand, it was left to Congress to regulate commerce with foreign nations, to define and punish offenses against the law of nations, to declare war, to raise and support armies, to provide and maintain a navy, to control the purse strings, and "To make all Law which shall be necessary and proper for carrying into execution the foregoing powers, *and all other powers vested by this Constitution in the Government of the United States, or in any Department or Officer thereof.*"

. . . The rationalizations in support of the power of the President to control the conduct of foreign relations—empty rhetoric aside—are two. First, that only the President can speak as the chosen voice of all the American people and it must be the whole American people that speaks when addressing foreign countries. Second, that only the President of the United States has access to all the information necessary to fashion an appropriate foreign policy.

The first rationalization, that the President must be the sole spokesman for all the American people, is difficult to justify. It rests, in part, on the theory that the election or re-election of the American President depends on his announced foreign policy. And yet it is hard to find elections in American history that have turned on such matters. . . . The truth of the matter, of course, is that the United States has no foreign policy or alternative foreign policies that might be offered to the people for them to choose. . . .

Moreover, the rationale that the President is the only proper voice for all the people would justify his power not only in the field of foreign affairs but in all national governmental enterprise. It is the second argument that creates more of a difficulty for Congressional participation in the conduct of foreign affairs—the argument that only the President has access to the necessary data on which to base a judgement. But I submit that this is a statement of fact rather than a reason for action or inaction. If the executive branch alone is privy to the appropriate information, it is largely due to the fact that it is unwilling to share its information with Congress. And, in part, it is due to the fact that Congress is unprepared to set up the machinery necessary to keep itself informed. Both facts are true. Neither is necessary.

The fact of the matter is that Congress has the power to be informed if it would only exercise the authority that it has. So long as it appropriates funds on the say-so of the executive; so long as it remains silent while the executive carries on a war that only Congress is authorized to declare; so long as the executive is permitted to enter into secret agreements with foreign countries, just so long will Congress continue its decline and fall as an essential element in our national government.

Let me make clear that I am not referring to a condition that is peculiar to the present administration. Roosevelt's destroyer deal with Great Britain was recognized as an illegal act of war several years before the Japanese bombed Pearl Harbor. Truman's use of American troops in Korea, ultimately blessed by the United Nations, was a commitment to war without Congressional approval. The martyred President Kennedy almost blew us to bits by sanctioning an invasion of Cuba, only at the last moment withdrawing American air power and thus assuring the failure of the action. Nor should it be forgotten that our military commitments in Viet Nam were initiated by Kennedy under a guise that could hardly fool the Communist world since they make such great use of it themselves, *i.e.,* the guise of "military advisers.". . .

Essentially, our difficulty derives from the fact that we are unconcerned about institutional problems. We are prepared, according to our loyalties, to back a President that we admire and condemn the one that we dislike, when what we should be doing is to recognize the wisdom of the Constitutional provisions that would preclude the unlimited exercise of power that we have witnessed by each of our recent chief executives and the unalloyed cowardice of the Congress in allowing such arrogation of power to the executive branch. . . .

Professor Robert A. Dahl [of Yale University] in his admirable book, *Congress and Foreign Policy,* published in 1950, states the three possibilities for administering our foreign affairs. Only one of them is consistent with our constitutional precepts. And yet, it is that one that seems to have been rejected by the office of the chief executive, even if with the silent advice and consent of the Congress. Dahl put the choices this way:

> The first is a frank dictatorship of the modern type: one based upon mass support and employing every technique of manipulating attitudes and personalities of the mass so as to achieve a society unified around a small range of common purposes, including war. . . .
>
> The second alternative is a "democratic" regime with extensive executive discretion. One thinks here of the Weimar Republic in its final stages. . . . In the United States, this solution would imply the broadest sort of presidential control over foreign policy.
>
> The third alternative is a democratic regime under which executive policy rests upon the confidence of the legislative branch. In the United States this would imply a high degree of collaboration between executive and Congress in the formulation and conduct of foreign policy.
>
> It is the recurrent theme of this book that the second of these alternatives—presidential supremacy—inevitably runs afoul of a number of difficulties that are eliminated or mitigated by executive-Congressional collaboration. And to the extent that the executive is capable of solving its problems without accepting congressional collaboration, it must inescapably become more and more the democratic shadow of that first grim alternative.

The Legislative Function

What is true in the field of foreign relations, which for some at least has special qualities calling for executive power, happens also to be true these days in those other areas in which Congress was charged with responsibility by the Constitution. "All legislative Powers herein granted shall be vested in a Congress of the United States. . . ." So says the Constitution. And it also provided, as I have already stated, that "The Congress shall have Power . . . to make all Laws which shall be necessary and proper for carrying into Execution the foregoing Powers, and all other powers vested by this Constitution in the Government of the United States, or in any Department or Officer thereof." The limitations on this power, insofar as they are explicit, are contained in the grant of a veto authority to the President, . . . in the restraints in the ninth and tenth amendments; and in the implicit, if dubious, power of judicial review vested in the courts of the United States.

. . . I would suggest that the time has long since passed when the government of the United States could be described by the adjective "congressional." At least since 1932, the United States has been a "presidential government." . . . It has been benignly described by Clinton Rossiter* as a "constitutional dictatorship." And this permanent transfer of power has been applauded by Louis Heren (the *Times* of London correspondent who sees himself as a modern Lord Bryce**) in his *The New American Commonwealth,* in these terms:

> If a President cannot take his authority for granted, its bounds have been extended beyond the most improbable dreams of any early monarch. . . . Indeed, the imperative of solving nationwide problems at the national level demands Presidential activism. . . . Only the comparatively sudden emergence of the King-President was a surprise, perhaps because of factors no less real because they are intangible.
> If I have emphasized the recent extensions of Presidential power, it is not to suggest omnipotence. That, to say the least, would be misleading. What I do believe is that congressional government, as it flourished with occasional fluctuation from President Andrew Johnson to President Hoover, has had its day.

Even during the heyday of its powers, the period described by Woodrow Wilson in his first book [*Congressional Government*], there was complaint that Congress limited itself to its legislative function. Thus, Wilson wrote:

> It is not surprising, therefore, that the enacting, revising, tinkering, repealing of laws should engross the attention and engage the entire energy of such a body as Congress. It is, however, easy to see how it might be better employed; or, at least, how it might add others to this overshadowing function, to the infinite advantage of the government. Quite as important as legislation is vigilant oversight of administration; and even more important than legislation is the instruction and guidance in political affairs which the people might receive from a body which kept all national concerns suffused in a broad daylight of discussion. There is no similar legislature in existence which is so shut up to the one business of law-making as is our Congress. . . .

Instead of adding to its powers, however, Congress has forfeited its authority even over the legislative process that was once its primary function. The initiation of legislation has been surrendered by Congress to the executive. In fact, almost all that it retains is a veto power, a power to refuse to enact that which the President demands of it. Thus, the roles assigned by the Constitution with regard to legislation have been essentially reversed.

Let me show by example what I may not have been able to convey by

---

*Ed. note: Late John L. Senior Professor of American Civilization at Cornell University; author of *The American Presidency* (1956).

**Ed. note: James Bryce (1838-1922), British historian and statesman, and analyst of American political life. From 1907 to 1913 he served as British Ambassador to the United States.

simple statement. In the early days of the 90th Congress the country was plagued by what appeared to be an unresolvable transportation strike. There were many who believed that the solution was to be found in legislation. . . . How then did Congress approach the problem? More or less the way Senator Javits—not a member of the President's party it should be noted—approached it, by complaining about the President's failure to submit promised legislation for Congressional action. When Javits spoke on the floor of the Senate he said this:

> It is my considered judgment that the reason why we are where we are—to wit, without any adequate remedy in the law—. . .is that, in the opinion of the Attorney General there is no statute to take care of it. This is attributable to the fact that the President of the United States, notwithstanding that he promised it 2 years ago, has not to this hour submitted legislation which would give permanent protection to the public interest in the event of a work stoppage in a major industry.
>
> . . . We have all found ourselves in a position where we have had to bail out the President from a situation in which we had placed himself, and us, by not recommending definitive legislation.
>
> We are here, now, because the President has failed to act. It is somewhat our fault, to, but I think more of the responsibility is on the President's shoulders; he promised to send us legislation a long time ago, and he has not done so to this very day. . . .
>
> It is uniquely the kind of situation where we are entitled to a recommendation from the executive department.

In one sense, Senator Javits, in shunting his authority over legislation to the President, was properly describing the world in which we live. Laws passed despite the lack of executive sponsorship, or contrary to executive wishes have little chance of being effected. For example, there has been much and bitter dispute about the way the armed forces of the United States should be equipped. In the famous B-70 controversy, Congress sought to command the expenditure of moneys that it appropriated for the construction of these super-planes. The executive successfully argued that such directions from Congress would be a violation of the separation of powers, the invasion of a presidential prerogative under the Constitutiton! . . . It is little wonder that when Admiral Rickover came before the Congress to testify on the question of atomic powered ships, he could ask and answer this question:

> Does Congress any longer have anything to say about how the defense of this country is run? Apparently the Department of Defense is operating on the basis that you have abdicated that responsibility, that it is now rightfully theirs. . . .

Executive Orders and Guidelines

Nor is the executive limited in his legislative powers—nowhere to be found in the Constitution—to the introduction of legislation through Congress. Just as the President can avoid the necessity for Senate approval of treaties by signing documents called executive agreements, so too he may legislate for himself by other devices than Congressional action. Two prime means are the executive order, of ancient lineage, and a more modern device, the promulgation of so-called guidelines.

An examination of the multitude of executive orders will reveal four categories. There are some, essentially those following the original purpose for such orders, that are concerned with internal administration of executive departments. Then there are those that are promulgated pursuant to authorizing legislation. But there are those that purport to be based on legislation that really are not so warranted. And also those that do not have even the pretense of congressional authority. . . . An interesting book remains to be written on this form of presidential legislation. The political scientists and academic lawyers have not been prone to launch an attack on rules that, for the most part, they admire.

The more modern and more interesting forms of executive legislation are the so-called guidelines. Here again there are different kinds. The first is exemplified by the price-wage guidelines of recent memory, based on no congressional warrant whatsoever and, indeed, probably in contradiction of congressional decision to leave prices and wages unregulated. The second type is found in the guidelines promulgated by the Department of Health, Education, and Welfare to effect desegregation in the public shcools. Congress authorized these to be issued, but only if they were approved by the President himself. In fact, the evidence reveals that they have been issued by subordinate action of the very kind that Congress sought to preclude. But the most interesting aspect of guidelines is their means of enforcement. For here, what was once regarded as an essentially legislative power is used: the power of the purse. Thus, steel companies that violated the price guidelines suddenly discovered that their product would not be purchased by their biggest customer, the government of the United States, unless and until they conformed with the executive ukase. Similarly, school systems that fail to toe the HEW guidelines find their federal funds cut off or postponed. The power of the purse here, as elsewhere, is utilized by the executive branch as a means of enforcement of rules that it creates for itself whether with or without congressional sanction.

Congressional Oversight

When we turn from the process of legislation itself to the process of Congressional oversight, we find the same sorry spectacle. The essential argument used for the proposition that Congress must legislate in generalities is that government has become too complex to be governed by rigid legislative rules. A corollary of this proposition is that Congress can oversee the administration of the laws to assure that its policies are, in fact, being executed. Again the theories do not square with the facts. Generally, but not universally, Congressional oversight is more a myth than a reality. The best example of effective Congressional oversight is to be found in the annual reviews of tax legislation and the way that it is being enforced by a joint committee of both Houses. The staff appears to be competent to the job of scrutinizing administrative rulings and judicial decisions to determine whether the tax laws are being effected in accordance with the purposes behind their enactments. . . .

More typical, unfortunately, was the provision in the Taft-Hartley Act for a joint committee to study and investigate labor-management relations. The legislation called for a final report of the committee by January 2, 1949. But, except for the surveillance that the courts impose, since 1949 there has been no realistic legislative review of the administration of this important congressional legislation. Judicial scrutiny and Congressional scrutiny do not amount to the same thing. Indeed, most important congressional legislation, once it receives presidential approval, is likely to fall totally beyond the ken of Congress except in terms of appropriations bills. And that mysterious process is not an effective means of control or, rather, it has not been effectively used as a means of control.

Structural changes for congressional oversight are necessary but not sufficient conditions of improvement. Several proposals are pending in Congress including one that calls for a counsel general's office within Congress effectively to supervise the administrative and judicial constructions given congressional legislation. Judge Henry Friendly has suggested another method:

> . . . Could not Congress be persuaded to amend the Legislative Reorganization Act so that each standing committee would be charged not only with the vague mandate to "exercise continuous watchfulness" but with the obligation to render a comprehensive report every ten or fifteen years on each major piece of legislation subject to its jurisdiction, either with specific proposals for amendment or with a considered statement that none is required? It would be provided or at least understood that any such report would be preceded by a true investigation. . . .

Congressional Investigation

Of the investigative role of the United States Congress, I shall say little. Essentially it has been perverted by one or two Congressional committees in such a way as to bring the entire process under opprobrium. Congress has not created effective means for pursuing its investigative functions. Until it establishes for all its committees that minimal decency that is of the essence of due process of law, Congress will find that even the best of them fails to persuade the public or, indeed, to enlighten the Congress.*

This is the sorry state to which Congress has been reduced. Its legislative power has been all but restricted to a veto function. Its duty of oversight has been mostly ignored. Its obligation to investigate has been destroyed by its own not very amusing spectacles, of which the House Committee on Un-American Activities is the worst example. Congress might well choose to put on the facade of the literally crumbling capitol the words: "The fault, dear Brutus, lies not in the stars, but in ourselves, that we are underlings."[1]

Why has Congress failed? The reasons are too many and too complicated even to catalogue here. Let me suggest a few general observations. First, our legislators are too occupied with unimportant matters to be able to devote their attention fully to important ones. there is the visiting constituent to be seen. There are numerous requests for dispensation of

---

[1]Shakespeare, Julius Caesar, Act I, scene 2, lines 140-41.
*Ed. note: This article was written before the Watergate investigations of the Senate Select Committee and the House Judiciary Committee.

the executive power that Congress has delegated, resulting not only in a loss of time but in the creation of a debt to the particular governmental agency involved. The number of private bills enacted is nothing short of shocking. For many, especially members of the House of Representatives, the job is only a part-time job. Congress is both understaffed and improperly staffed. While the executive has learned the lesson of securing experts to assist it in its job, Congress but rarely calls to its aid such expertise as is available, except perhaps in the dubious role of a witness before a congressional committee. Certainly Congress is badly organized to perform its task. And yet no reorganization bill of substantial merit has the slightest chance of passing both Houses of Congress. The perquisites of office under the existing system are too great to dissolve them in the absence of Herculean efforts that are not forthcoming.

Most important, perhaps, is the fact that Congress never adequately decides what it really wants. And it is going to have to do so if its legislative and oversight functions are to be effective. In terms of the latter, Professor James Q. Wilson [of Harvard] put it this way:

> Both the White House and the Congress seem eager to do something about the bureaucracy problem. All too often, however, the problem is described in terms of "digesting" the "glut" of new federal programs—as if solving administrative difficulties had something in common with treating heartburn. Perhaps those seriously concerned with this issue will put themselves on notice that they ought not to begin with the pain and reach for some administrative bicarbonate of soda; they ought instead to begin with what was swallowed and ask whether an emetic is necessary. *Coping with the bureaucracy problem is inseparable from rethinking the objectives of the programs in question.* . . . Thinking clearly about goals is a tough assignment for a political system that has been held together in great part by compromise, ambiguity, and contradiction. . . .

There are reasons, of course, outside the derelictions of Congress itself. The political cartoons recognize that Congress does not have the stature that its constitutionally defined job demands. In part, this is due to the inadequate use of Madison Avenue techniques that are the everyday life of other branches of government. The Presidential Press Secretary and even departmental press officers are intrinsic parts of these governmental offices. . . . They are not always successful. But it is not for want of effort. Even the Supreme Court has a press relations officer these days. Except for those Senators concerned with establishing themselves as candidates for the Presidency, there is no equivalent effort spent on selling Congress to the people of the United States.

Another reason, especially with regard to the House of Representatives, is that congressmen often run for office as tails to the kite of presidential candidates. And the test for nomination is not so often the special capacities of the individual to do the job as the services that he has rendered and is likely to render to the party organizations.

Ultimately, however, the fault lies with the people: Adlai Stevenson's

314

phrase rings loud and true: the American people get the kind of government they deserve. The essential difficulty is that the people—and each segment of them—tend to be concerned with ends rather than means. . . . It is with pained surprise that a group that so blatantly looked upon the presidency as its knight errant suddenly discovered that the man under the iron mask is not really their kind of man at all. And yet, here he is outfitted with all the weapons and powers that they had entrusted to their own champion.

We are at a time when, for good reasons or bad, the primacy of executive power is being questioned even by those who would when their leader held office, have expanded it beyond its present range. Perhaps it is an appropriate time to consider whether these powers should be entrusted even to the idealized, God-like leader of one's own choice. Perhaps we should be reminded of the words of Mr. Justice Jackson: "With all its defects, delays and inconveniences, men have discovered no technique for long preserving free government except that the Executive be under the law, and that the law be made by parliamentary deliberations."

Perhaps a new generation will find value in the discredited concept of separation of powers and restore Congress to a vigorous role in an ever-expanding government. And perhaps they will people it, both its membership and its staff, with the kind of person that is adequate to so important a trust. As of now, however, Congress does not have the guts to stand up to its responsibilities. And the American electorate does not have the interest to see that Congress does so. The failure of Congress is the failure of democracy. The alternatives are not pleasant to contemplate.

The Presidency and the Founding Fathers

Alexander Hamilton

*American revolutionaries in 1776 directed most of their an-
tagonism against the British sovereign, King George III. Indeed, the Declaration of Independence justified the colonists'
rebellion largely in terms of abuses suffered at his hands:
"He has obstructed the administration of justice. . . . He has
kept among us, in times of peace, standing armies without the
consent of our legislatures. . . . He has excited domestic
insurrections amongst us. . . . A prince whose character is thus
marked by every act which may define a tyrant, is unfit to be
the ruler of a free people."*

*In reality, of course, the Americans rebelled not against an
absolute monarch but against a constitutional monarchy in
which, more often than not, Parliament rather than the king
initiated objectionable policies. But George III became a convenient symbol for colonial frustrations and hatred, and, as a
consequence, there developed in America a profound distrust
of the executive. This attitude also reflected colonial disenchantment with British governors and veneration for their own
provincial legislatures. In 1787 and 1788, at the time of debate
over ratification of the new Constitution, Federalist leaders
such as Alexander Hamilton attempted to quiet these fears
with respect to the Presidency.*

The first thing which strikes our attention is, that the executive authority,
with few exceptions, is to be bested in a single magistrate. This will
scarcely, however, be considered as a point upon which any comparison can
be grounded; for if, in this particular, there be a resemblance to the king
of Great Britain, there is not less a resemblance to the Grand Seignior, to
the khan of Tartary, to the Man of the Seven Mountains, or to the governor of New York.

That magistrate is to be elected for *four* years; and is to be reeligible as
often as the people of the United States shall think him worthy of their
confidence. In these circumstances there is a total dissimilitude between
him and a king of Great Britain, who is an *hereditary* monarch, possessing
the crown as a patrimony descendible to his heirs forever; but there is a
close analogy between *him* and a governor of New York, who is elected for
three years, and is reeligible without limitation or intermission. If we

From *The Federalist No. 69*

consider how much less time would be requisite for establishing a dangerous influence in a single State, than for establishing a like influence throughout the United States, we must conclude that a duration of four years for the Chief Magistrate of the Union is a degree of permanency far less to be dreaded in that office, than a duration of *three* years for a corresponding office in a single State.

The President of the United States would be liable to be impeached, tried, and, upon conviction of treason, bribery, or other high crimes or misdemeanors, removed from office; and would afterwards be liable to prosecution and punishment in the ordinary course of law. The person of the king of Great Britain is sacred and inviolable; there is no constitutional tribunal to which he is amenable; no punishment to which he can be subjected without involving the crisis of a national revolution. . . .

The President of the United States is to have power to return a bill, which shall have passed the two branches of the legislature, for reconsideration; and the bill so returned is to become a law, if, upon that reconsideration, it be approved by two thirds of both houses. The king of Great Britain . . . has an absolute negative upon the acts of the two houses of Parliament. The disuse of that power for a considerable time past does not affect the reality of its existence; and is to be ascribed wholly to the crown's having found the means of substituting influence to authority, or the art of gaining a majority in one or the other of the two houses, to the necessity of exerting a prerogative which could seldom be exerted without hazarding some degree of national agitation. The qualified negative of the President differs widely from this absolute negative of the British sovereign. . . .

The President is to be the "Commander-in-Chief of the army and navy of the United States, and of the militia of the several States, when called into the actual service of the United States. He is to have power to grant reprieves and pardons for offences against the United States, *except in cases of impeachment*; to recommend to the consideration of Congress such measures as he shall judge necessary and expedient; to convene, on extraordinary occasions, both houses of the legislature, or either of them, and, in case of disagreement between them *with respect to the time of adjournment,* to adjourn them to such time as he shall think proper; to take care that the laws be faithfully executed; and to commission all officers of the United States." In most of these particulars, the power of the President will resemble equally that of the king of Great Britain and of the governor of New York. The most material points of difference are . . .

The President is to have power, with the advice and consent of the Senate, to make treaties, provided two thirds of the senators present concur. The king of Great Britain is the sole and absolute representative of the nation in all foreign transactions. He can of his own accord make treaties of peace, commerce, alliance, and of every other description. It has been insinuated that his authority in this respect is not conclusive, and that his conventions with foreign powers are subject to the revision, and stand in need of the ratification, of Parliament. But I believe this doctrine was never heard of until it was broached upon the present occasion. Every jurist of that kingdom and every other man acquainted with its Constitution knows . . . that the prerogative of making treaties exists in the crown in its utmost plentitude; and that the compacts entered into by the royal authority have the most complete legal validity and perfection, independent of any other sanction. The Parliament, it is true, is sometimes seen employing itself in altering the existing laws to conform them to the stipulations in a new treaty; and this may have possibly given birth to the imagination that its cooperation was necessary to the obligatory efficacy of the treaty. But this parliamentary interposition proceeds from a different cause: from the necessity of adjusting a most artificial and intricate system of revenue and commercial laws, to the changes made in them by the operation of the treaty; and of adapting new provisions and precautions to the new state of things, to keep the machine from running into disorder. In this respect, therefore, there is no comparison between the intended power of the President and the actual power of the British sovereign. The one can perform alone what the other can do only with the concurrence of a branch of the legislature. It must be admitted, that, in this instance, the power of the federal Executive would exceed that of any State Executive. But this arises naturally from the sovereign power which relates to treaties. . . .

The President is also to be authorized to receive ambassadors and other public ministers. This, though it has been a rich theme of declamation, is more a matter of dignity than of authority. It is a circumstance which will be without consequence in the administration of the government; and it was far more convenient that it should be arranged in this manner, than that there should be a necessity of convening the legislature or one of its branches upon every arrival of a foreign minister, though it were merely to take the place of a departed predecessor.

The President is to nominate, and, *with the advice and consent of the Senate,* to appoint ambassadors and other public ministers, judges of the Supreme Court, and in general all officers of the United States established by law, and whose appointments are not otherwise provided for by the Constitution. The king of Great Britain is emphatically and truly styled the fountain of honor. He not only appoints to all offices, but can create offices. He can confer titles of nobility at pleasure; and has the disposal of an immense number of church preferments. There is evidently a great inferiority in the power of the President in this particular to that of the British king; nor is it equal to that of the governor of New York if we are to interpret the meaning of the constitution of the State by the practice which has obtained under it. . . .

Hence it appears that, except as to the concurrent authority of the President in the article of treaties, it would be difficult to determine whether that magistrate would in the aggregate possess more or less power than the governor of New York. And it appears yet more unequivocally that there is no pretence for the parallel which has been attempted between him and the king of Great Britain. But to render the contrast in this respect still more striking, it may be of use to throw the principal circumstances of dissimilitude into a closer group.

The President of the United States would be an officer elected by the people for *four* years; the king of Great Britain is a perpetual and *hereditary* prince. The one would be amenable to personal punishment and disgrace; the person of the other is sacred and inviolable. The one would have a *qualified* negative upon the acts of the legislative body; the other has an *absolute* negative. The one would have a right to command the military and naval forces of the nation; the other, in addition to this right, possesses that of *declaring* war and of *raising* and *regulating* fleets and armies by his own authority. The one would have a concurrent power with a branch of the legislature in the formation of treaties; the other is the *sole possessor* of the power of making treaties. The one would have a like concurrent authority in appointing offices; the other is the sole author of all appointments. The one can confer no privileges whatever; the other can make denizens of aliens, noblemen of commoners, can erect corporations with all the rights incident to corporate bodies. The one can prescribe no rules concerning the commerce or currency of the nation; the other is in several respects the arbiter of commerce, and in this capacity can establish markets and fairs, can regulate weights and measures, can lay embargoes for a limited time, can coin money, can authorize or prohibit the circulation of foreign coin. The one has no particle of spiritual jurisdiction; the other is the supreme head and governor of the national church! What answer shall we give to those who would persuade us that things so unlike resemble each other? The same that ought to be given to those who tell us that a government, the whole power of which would be in the hands of the elective and periodical servants of the people, is an aristocracy, a monarchy, and a despotism.

The President
and the People

Frances M. Trollope

European observers of American political life in the nineteenth century, accustomed to the pomp and ceremony surrounding other heads of state, frequently remarked upon the public reception given the republic's chief magistrate, the President, whose power came ultimately from the people themselves. With the election of Andrew Jackson in 1828, this intense identification between the occupant of the office and the "common people" reached a high point. In the following passage, Frances M. Trollope, an Englishwoman, comments upon the familiarity surrounding the new President as he enters and departs Cincinnati on a public steamboat, "the decent dignity of a private conveyance not being deemed necessary for the President of the United States."

And now the time arrived that our domestic circle was again to be broken up. Our eldest son was to be entered at Oxford, and it was necessary that his father should accompany him; and, after considerable indecision, it was at length determined that I and my daughters should remain another year with our second son. It was early in February, and our travellers prepared themselves to encounter some sharp gales upon the mountains, though the great severity of the cold appeared to be past. We got buffalo robes and double shoes prepared for them, and they were on the eve of departure when we heard that General Jackson, the newly-elected President, was expected to arrive immediately at Cincinnati, from his residence in the West, and to proceed by steamboat to Pittsburgh, on his way to Washington. This determined them not to fix the day of their departure till they heard of his arrival, and then, if possible, to start in the same boat with him; the decent dignity of a private conveyance not being deemed necessary for the President of the United States. . . .

We accordingly walked to Cincinnati, and secured a favourable station at the landing-place, both for the purpose of seeing the first magistrate, and of observing his reception by the people. We had waited but a few moments when the heavy panting of the steam-engines and then a discharge of cannon told that we were just in time; another moment

From Frances M. Trollope, *Domestic Manners of the Americans*. (London: Whittaker, Treacher, 1832).

brought his vessel in sight. . . .

The crowd on the shore awaited her arrival in perfect stillness. When she touched the bank the people on board gave a faint huzza, but it was answered by no note of welcome from the land: this cold silence was certainly not produced by any want of friendly feeling towards the new President; during the whole of the canvassing he had been decidedly the popular candidate at Cincinnati, and for months past, we had been accustomed to the cry of "Jackson for ever" from an overwhelming majority; but enthusiasm is not either the virtue or the vice of America.

More than one private carriage was stationed at the water's edge to await the General's orders, but they were dismissed with the information that he would walk to the hotel. Upon receiving this intimation the silent crowd divided itself in a very orderly manner, leaving a space for him to walk through them. He did so, uncovered, though the distance was considerable, and the weather very cold; but he alone (with the exception of a few European gentlemen who were present) was without a hat. He wore his gray hair, carelessly, but not ungracefully arranged, and, spite of his harsh gaunt features, he looked like a gentleman and a soldier. He was in deep mourning, having very recently lost his wife; they were said to have been very happy together, and I was pained by hearing a voice near me exclaim, as he approached the spot where I stood, "There goes Jackson, where is his wife?" Another sharp voice, at a little distance, cried, "Adams for ever!" And these sounds were all I heard to break the silence.

"They manage these matters better" in the East, I have no doubt, but as yet I was still in the West, and still inclined to think, that, however meritorious the American character may be, it is not amiable.

Mr. T. and his sons joined the group of citizens who waited upon him to the hotel, and were presented to the President in form; that is, they shook hands with him. Learning that he intended to remain a few hours there, or more properly, that it would be a few hours before the steam-boat would be ready to proceed, Mr. T. secured berths on board, and returned, to take a hasty dinner with us. At the hour appointed by the captain, Mr. T. and his son accompanied the General on board; and by subsequent letters I learnt that they had conversed a good deal with him, and were pleased by his conversation and manners, but deeply disgusted by the brutal familiarity to which they saw him exposed at every place on their progress at which they stopped; I am tempted to quote one passage, as sufficiently descriptive of the manner, which so painfully grated against their European feelings.

"There was not a hulking boy from a keel-boat who was not introduced to the President, unless, indeed, as was the case with some, they introduced themselves: for instance, I was at his elbow when a greasy fellow accosted him thus: —

" 'General Jackson, I guess?'

"The General bowed assent.

" 'Why they told me you was dead.'

" 'No! Providence has hitherto preserved my life.'

" 'And is your wife alive too?'

"The General, apparently much hurt, signified the contrary, upon which the courtier concluded his harangue by saying, 'Ay, I thought it was the one or t'other of ye.' "

"Servants of the Servants of God"

Henry Adams

Biting satire that lampoons the powerful or merely the pompous has always been an important genre of political expression and protest in American life. Henry Adams, a grandson of two Presidents, who in the late nineteenth century found himself isolated from real power in an era of "robber barons" and mendacious politicians, became a master of this technique in his letters, novels, and famous autobiography. Distrustful of the "common man" and his leaders, Adams frequently despaired over the future of politics in a democracy where, he assumed, the representatives of the people and the parties would seldom rise above the narrow self-interest, vanity, and greed characteristic of the electorate at large. In the following passages from his novel Democracy, *Adams aimed his barbed wit at the process of selecting Presidents, the foibles of the country's imaginary new leader, "Old Granite," and the intrigues of his chief rival, Senator Ratcliffe.*

Such was the situation when on Monday afternoon the President-elect arrived in Washington, and the comedy began. The new President was, almost as much as Abraham Lincoln or Franklin Pierce, an unknown quantity in political mathematics. In the national convention of the party, nine months before, after some dozens of fruitless ballots in which Ratcliffe wanted but three votes of a majority, his opponents had done what he was now doing; they had laid aside their principles and set up for their candidate a plain Indiana farmer, whose political experience was limited to stump-speaking in his native State, and to one term as Governor. They had pitched upon him, not because they thought him competent, but because they hoped by doing so to detach Indiana from Ratcliffe's following, and they were so successful that within fifteen minutes Ratcliffe's friends were routed, and the Presidency had fallen upon this new political Buddha.

He had begun his career as a stone-cutter in a quarry, and was, not unreasonably, proud of the fact. During the campaign this incident had, of course, filled a large space in the public mind, or, more exactly, in the public eye. "The Stone-cutter of the Wabash," he was sometimes called; at others "the Hoosier Quarryman," but his favourite appellation was

Excerpted from Henry Adams, *Democracy, An American Novel.* (New York: H. Holt and Company, 1880) pp. 161–86.

"Old Granite," although this last endearing name, owing to an unfortunate similarity of sound, was seized upon by his opponents, and distorted into "Old Granny." He had been painted on many thousand yards of cotton sheeting, either with a terrific sledge-hammer, smashing the skulls (which figured as paving-stones) of his political opponents, or splitting by gigantic blows a huge rock typical of the opposing party. His opponents in their turn had paraded illuminations representing the Quarryman in the garb of a State's-prison convict breaking the heads of Ratcliffe and other well-known political leaders with a very feeble hammer, or as "Old Granny" in pauper's rags, hopelessly repairing with the same heads the impossible roads which typified the ill-conditioned and miry ways of his party. But these violations of decency and good sense were universally reproved by the virtuous; and it was remarked with satisfaction that the purest and most highly cultivated newspaper editors on his side, without excepting those of Boston itself, agreed with one voice that the Stone-cutter was a noble type of man, perhaps the very noblest that had appeared to adorn this country since the incomparable Washington.

That he was honest, all admitted; that is to say, all who voted for him. This is a general characteristic of all new presidents. He himself took great pride in his home-spun honesty, which is a quality peculiar to nature's noble men. Owing nothing, as he conceived, to politicians, but sympathising through every fibre of his unselfish nature with the impulses and aspirations of the people, he affirmed it to be his first duty to protect the people from those vultures, as he called them, those wolves in sheep's clothing, those harpies, those hyenas, the politicians; epithets which, as generally interpreted, meant Ratcliffe and Ratcliffe's friends. His cardinal principle in politics was hostility to Ratcliffe, yet he was not vindictive. He came to Washington determined to be the Father of his country; to gain a proud immortality—and a re-election.

Upon this gentleman Ratcliffe had let loose all the forms of "pressure" which could be set in motion either in or out of Washington. From the moment when he had left his humble cottage in Southern Indiana, he had been captured by Ratcliffe's friends, and smothered in demonstrations of affection. They had never allowed him to suggest the possibility of ill-feeling. They had assumed as a matter of course that the most cordial attachment existed between him and his party. On his arrival in Washington they systematically cut him off from contact with any influences but their own. This was not a very difficult thing to do, for great as he was, he liked to be told of his greatness, and they made him feel himself a colossus. Even the few personal friends in his company were manipulated with the utmost care, and their weaknesses put to use before they had been in Washington a single day. . . .

Every device known to politicians was now in full play against the Hoosier Quarryman. State delegations with contradictory requests were poured in upon him, among which that of Massachusetts presented as its only prayer the appointment of Mr. Gore to the Spanish mission. Difficulties were invented to embarrass and worry him. False leads were suggested, and false information carefully mingled with true. A wild dance was kept up under his eyes from daylight to midnight, until his brain reeled with the effort to follow it. Means were also found to convert one of his personal, confidential friends, who had come with him from Indiana and who had more brains or less principle than the others; from him every word of the President was brought directly to Ratcliffe's ear.

Early on Friday morning, Mr. Thomas Lord, a rival of the late Samuel Baker, and heir to his triumphs, appeared in Ratcliffe's rooms while the Senator was consuming his lonely egg and chop. Mr. Lord had been chosen to take general charge of the presidential party and to direct all matters connected with Ratcliffe's interests. Some people might consider this the work of a spy; he looked on it as a public duty. He reported that "Old Granny" had at last shown signs of weakness. Late the previous evening when, according to his custom, he was smoking his pipe in company with his kitchen-cabinet of followers, he had again fallen upon the subject of Ratcliffe, and with a volley of oaths had sworn that he would show him his place yet, and that he meant to offer him a seat in the Cabinet that would make him "sicker than a stuck hog." From this remark and some explanatory hints that followed, it seemed that the Quarryman had abandoned his scheme of putting Ratcliffe to immediate political death, and had now undertaken to invite him into a Cabinet which was to be specially constructed to thwart and humiliate him. The President, it appeared, warmly applauded the remark of one counsellor, that Ratcliffe was safer in the Cabinet than in the Senate, and that it would be easy to kick him out when the time came.

Ratcliffe smiled grimly as Mr. Lord, with much clever mimicry, described the President's peculiarities of language and manner, but he said nothing and waited for the event. The same evening came a note from the President's private secretary requesting his attendance, if possible, to-morrow, Saturday morning, at ten o'clock. The note was curt and cool. Ratcliffe merely sent back word that he would come, and felt a little regret that the President should not know enough etiquette to understand that this verbal answer was intended as a hint to improve his manners. He did come accordingly, and found the President looking blacker than before. This time there was no avoiding of tender subjects. The President meant to show Ratcliffe by the decision of his course, that he was master of the situation. He broke at once into the middle of the matter: "I sent for you," said he, "to consult with you about my Cabinet. Here is a list of the gentlemen I intend to invite into it. You will see that I have got you down for the Treasury. Will you look at the list and say what you think of it?"

Ratcliffe took the paper, but laid it at once on the table without looking at it. "I can have no objection," said he, "to any Cabinet you may appoint, provided I am not included in it. My wish is to remain where I am. There I can serve your administration better than in the Cabinet."

"Then you refuse?" growled the President.

"By no means. I only decline to offer any advice or even to hear the names of my proposed colleagues until it is decided that my services are necessary. If they are, I shall accept without caring with whom I serve."

The President glared at him with an uneasy look. What was to be done next? He wanted time to think, but Ratcliffe was there and must be disposed of. He involuntarily became more civil: "Mr. Ratcliffe, your refusal would knock everything on the head. I thought that matter was all fixed. What more can I do?"

But Ratcliffe had no mind to let the President out of his clutches so easily, and a long conversation followed, during which he forced his antagonist into the position of urging him to take the Treasury in order to prevent some undefined but portentous mischief in the Senate. All that could be agreed upon was that Ratcliffe should give a positive answer within two days, and on that agreement he took his leave. . . .

*　　　*　　　*

Of all titles ever assumed by prince or potentate, the proudest is that of the Roman pontiffs: "Servus servorum Dei"—"Servant of the servants of God." In former days it was not admitted that the devil's servants could by right have any share in government. They were to be shut out, punished, exiled, maimed, and burned. The devil has no servants now; only the people have servants. . . .

Whether the new President and his chief rival, Mr. Silas P. Ratcliffe, were or were not servants of the servants of God, is not material here. Servants they were to some one. No doubt many of those who call themselves servants of the people are no better than wolves in sheep's clothing, or asses in lions' skins. One may see scores of them any day in the Capitol when Congress is in session, making noisy demonstrations, or more usefully doing nothing. A wiser generation will employ them in manual labour; as it is, they serve only themselves. But there are two officers, at least, whose service is real—the President and his Secretary of the Treasury. The Hoosier Quarryman had not been a week in Washington before he was heartily home-sick for Indiana. No maid-of-all-work in a cheap boardinghouse was ever more harassed. Everyone conspired against him. His enemies gave him no peace. All Washington was laughing at his blunders, and ribald sheets, published on a Sunday, took delight in printing the new Chief Magistrate's sayings and doings, chronicled with outrageous humour, and placed by malicious hands where the President could not but see them. He was sensitive to ridicule, and it mortified him to the heart to find that remarks and acts, which to him seemed sensible enough, should be capable of such perversion. Then he was overwhelmed with public business. It came upon him in a deluge, and he now, in his despair, no longer tried to control it. He let it pass over him like a wave. His mind was muddled by the innumerable visitors to whom he had to listen. But his greatest anxiety was the Inaugural Address which, distracted as he was, he could not finish, although in another week it must be delivered. He was nervous about his Cabinet; it seemed to him that he could do nothing until he had disposed of Ratcliffe. . . .

He was pacing his room impatiently on Monday morning, an hour before the time fixed for Ratcliffe's visit. His feelings still fluctuated violently, and if he recognized the necessity of using Ratcliffe, he was not the less determined to tie Ratcliffe's hands. He must be made to come into a Cabinet where every other voice would be against him. He must be prevented from having any patronage to dispose of. He must be induced to accept these conditions at the start. How present this to him in such a way as not to repel him at once? All this was needless, if the President had only known it, but he thought himself a profound statesman, and that his hand was guiding the destinies of America to his own re-election. When at length, on the stroke of ten o'clock, Ratcliffe entered the room, the President turned to him with nervous eagerness, and almost before offering his hand, said that he hoped Mr. Ratcliffe had come prepared to begin work at once. The Senator replied that, if such was the President's decided wish, he would offer no further opposition. . . .

The President, more convinced than ever of his own masterly statesmanship, breathed more freely than for a week past. Within ten minutes they were actively at work together, clearing away the mass of accumulated business. The relief of the Quarryman surprised himself. Ratcliffe lifted the weight of affairs from his shoulders with hardly an effort. He knew everybody and everything. He took most of the President's visitors at once into his own hands and dismissed them with great rapidity. He knew what they wanted; he knew what recommendations were strong and what were weak; who was to be treated with deference and who was to be sent away abruptly; where a blunt refusal was safe, and where a pledge was allowable. The President even trusted him with the unfinished manuscript of the Inaugural Address, which Ratcliffe returned to him the next day with such notes and suggestions as left nothing to be done beyond copying them out in a fair hand. . . .

The Imperial Presidency

Arthur M. Schlesinger, Jr.

Although the growth of Presidential power has occasioned alarm among Americans from the days of Washington to Franklin Roosevelt's time, this alarm was normally tempered, as Arthur Schlesinger notes, by an equally strong belief in the necessity of "a strong domestic Presidency to hold the country together." The multiple crises of the 1960s and early 70s, including Vietnam, the Watergate scandals, and Richard Nixon's resignation, shattered this loose consensus and called into question as never before the sources and limitations of Presidential authority.

Arthur Schlesinger, Jr., a former Presidential aide and a Pulitzer Prize-winning historian, discusses the impact of the Nixon years on the office in the final chapter of his recent book, The Imperial Presidency. *Writing after the start of the Watergate investigations but before Nixon's resignation, Schlesinger considers various solutions to "the problem of reining in the runaway President."*

"The tyranny of the legislatures is the most formidable dread at present, and will be for long years," Jefferson wrote Madison six weeks before Washington's first inauguration. "That of the executive will come in its turn, but it will be at a remote period." On the eve of the second centennial of independence Jefferson's prophecy appeared on the verge of fulfillment. The imperial Presidency, created by wars abroad, was making a bold bid for power at home. The belief of the Nixon administration in its own mandate and in its own virtue, compounded by its conviction that the republic was in mortal danger from internal enemies, had produced an unprecedented concentration of power in the White House and an unprecedented attempt to transform the Presidency of the Constitution into a plebiscitary Presidency. If this transformation were carried through, the President, instead of being accountable every day to Congress and public opinion, would be accountable every four years to the electorate. Between elections, the President would be accountable only through impeachment and would govern, as much as he could, by decree. The expansion and abuse of presidential power constituted the underlying issue, the issue that. . . Watergate raised to the surface, dramatized and made politically accessible. Watergate was the by-product of a larger rev-

From Arthur M. Schlesinger, Jr., *The Imperial Presidency.* © 1974 by Arthur Schlesinger, reprinted by permission of the publisher, Houghton Mifflin Company.

olutionary purpose. At the same time, it was the fatal mistake that provoked and legitimized resistance to the revolutionary Presidency.

The Crisis of the Presidency

In giving great power to Presidents, Americans had declared their faith in the winnowing processes of politics. They assumed that these processes, whether operating through the Electoral College or later through the congressional caucus or still later through the party conventions, would eliminate aspirants to the Presidency who rejected the written restraints of the Constitution and the unwritten restraints of the republican ethos.

Through most of American history that assumption had been justified. "Not many Presidents have been brilliant," Bryce* observed in 1921, "some have not risen to the full moral height of the position. But none has been base or unfaithful to his trust, none has tarnished the honour of the nation." Even as Bryce wrote, however, his observation was falling out of date—Warren G. Harding had just been inaugurated—and half a century later his optimism appeared as much the function of luck as of any necessity in the constitutional order. . . .

The Presidency had been in crisis before; but the constitutional offense that led to the impeachment of Andrew Johnson was trivial compared to the charges . . . accumulating around the Nixon administration. . . . What was unique in the history of the Presidency was the long list of potential *criminal* charges against the Nixon administration. Even before the various investigations were concluded, it seemed probable that Nixon's appointees had engaged in a multitude of indictable activities: at the very least, in burglary; in forgery; in illegal wiretapping; in illegal electronic surveillance; in perjury; in subornation of perjury; in obstruction of justice; in destruction of evidence; in tampering with witnesses; in misprision of felony; in bribery (of the Watergate defendants); in acceptance of bribes (from Vesco and the ITT); in conspiracy to involve government agencies (the FBI, the CIA, the Secret Service, the Internal Revenue Service, the Securities and Exchange Commission) in illegal action.

As for the President himself, he consistently denied that he had known either about the warfare of espionage and sabotage waged by his agents against his opponents or about the subsequent cover-up. If Nixon had known about these things, he had himself conspired against the basic processes of democracy. If he really had not known and for nine months had not bothered to find out, he was evidently an irresponsible and incompetent executive. . . .

Nixon's responsibility for the White House ethos went beyond strictly moral considerations. In the First Congress Madison, arguing that the power to remove government officials must belong to the President, had added, "We have in him the security for the good behavior of the officer." This made "the President responsible to the public for the conduct of the person he has nominated and appointed." If the President suffered executive officials to perpetrate crimes or neglected to superintend their conduct so as to check excesses, he himself, Madison said, would be subject to "the decisive engine of impeachment."

---

*Ed. note: James Bryce [Viscount Bryce], 1838-1922. See note, p. 310.

Structural Reform: A Plural Executive

The crisis of the Presidency led some critics to advocate a reconstruction of the institution itself. For a long time people had felt that the job was becoming too much for one man to handle. "Men of ordinary physique and discretion," Woodrow Wilson wrote as long ago as 1908, "cannot be President and live, if the strain be not somehow relieved. We shall be obliged always to be picking our chief magistrate from among wise and prudent athletes,—a small class."

But what had been seen until the late 1950s as too exhausting physically was now seen, after Vietnam and Watergate, as too dizzying psychologically. In 1968 Eugene McCarthy, the first liberal presidential aspirant in the century to run against the Presidency, called for the depersonalization and decentralization of the office. The White House, he thought, should be turned into a museum. Instead of trying to lead the nation, the President should become "a kind of channel" for popular desires and aspirations. Watergate made the point irresistible. "The office has become too complex and its reach too extended," wrote Barbara Tuchman,* "to be trusted to the fallible judgment of any one individual." "A man with poor judgment, an impetuous man, a sick man, a power-mad man," wrote Max Lerner,** "each would be dangerous in the post. Even an able, sensitive man needs stronger safeguards around him than exist today."

The result was a new wave of proposals to transform the Presidency into a collegial institution. Mrs. Tuchman suggested a six-man directorate with a rotating chairman, each member to serve for a year, as in Switzerland. Lerner wanted to give the President a Council of State, a body that he would be bound by law to consult and that, because half its members would be from Congress and some from the opposite party, would presumably give him independent advice. Both proposals had, in fact, been considered and rejected in the Constitutional Convention. That was no argument against considering them again.

Still, the reasons why the Founding Fathers turned them down were worth noting. When James Wilson first moved in the Convention that the executive consist of a single person, there ensued, as Madison put it in his notes, "a considerable pause.". . . Wilson said that a single magistrate would impart "most energy, dispatch and responsibility" to the office. Edmund Randolph of Virginia then strenuously opposed the idea as "the foetus of monarchy," proposing instead a three-man magistracy. Eventually the Convention agreed with Wilson, though not before it gave serious thought to surrounding the President with a Council of State, which might include the Chief Justice, the President of the Senate and the Speaker of the House as well as the heads of the executive departments. . . .

Hamilton and Jefferson disagreed on many things, but they agreed that the Convention had been right in deciding on a one-man Presidency. A plural executive, Hamilton contended, if divided within itself, would lead the country into factionalism and anarchy and, if united, could lead it into tyranny. When power was placed in the hands of a group small enough to admit "of their interests and views being easily combined in a common

---

*Ed. note: Pulitzer Prize-winning historian.
**Ed. note: Newspaper columnist and commentator on American society.

enterprise, by an artful leader," Hamilton thought, "it becomes more liable to abuse, and more dangerous when abused, than if it be lodged in the hands of one man, who, from the very circumstances of his being alone, will be more narrowly watched and more readily suspected. . . ."

Jefferson had favored a plural executive under the Articles of Confederation, and, as an American lately in Paris, watched with sympathy the *Directoire* of the French Revolution. But these experiments left him no doubt that plurality was a mistake. As he later observed, if Washington's cabinet, in which he had served with Hamilton, had been a directorate, "the opposing wills would have balanced each other and produced a state of absolute inaction." But Washington, after listening to both sides, acted on his own, providing the "regulating power which would keep the machine in steady movement.". . .

The question remained whether the world had changed enough in two centuries to make these objections obsolete. There was, of course, the burden-of-the-Presidency argument. But had the presidential burden become so much heavier than ever before? The scope of the national government had expanded beyond imagination, but so too had the facilities for presidential management. . . . The contemporary President was really not all that overworked. . . .

As for the moral and psychological weight of these political problems, this was real enough. All major presidential decisions were taken in conditions of what General Marshall, speaking of battle, used to call "chronic obscurity"—that is, on the basis of incomplete and probably inaccurate intelligence, with no sure knowledge where the enemy was or even where one's own men were. This could be profoundly anguishing for reasonably sensitive Presidents, especially when decisions determined people's livelihoods or ended their lives. It was this, and not the workload, that did in Wilson and the second Roosevelt. But was the sheer moral weight of decision greater today than ever before? Greater for Johnson and Nixon than for Washington and Lincoln or Wilson or FDR? One doubted it very much. . . .

Above all, both the plural executive and the Council of State were open to the objection that most concerned the Founding Fathers—the problem of fixing accountability. In the case of high crimes and misdemeanors, who, to put it bluntly, was to be impeached? . . . The more convincing solution surely lay not in diffusing and blurring responsibility for the actions of the executive but in making that responsibility categorical and in finding ways of holding Presidents to it.

Structural Reform: The Six-Year Term

The other change in the institution of the Presidency under discussion in the early 1970s ran in the opposite direction. The idea of a single six-year presidential term was obviously designed not to reduce but to increase the independence of the Presidency. This idea naturally appealed to the imperial ethos. Lyndon Johnson advocated it; Nixon commended it to his Commission on Federal Election Reform for particular study. What was more puzzling was that it also had the support of two eminent senators, both unsympathetic to the imperial Presidency, Mike Mansfield of

Montana and George Aiken of Vermont—support that gave it a hearing it would not otherwise have had. . . .

This argument had a certain old-fashioned good-government plausibility. How nice it would be if Presidents could be liberated from politics for six years and set free to do only what was best for the country! But the argument assumed that Presidents knew better than anyone else what was best for the country and that the democratic process was an obstacle to wise decisions. It assumed that Presidents were generally right and the people so generally wrong that the President had to be protected against political pressures. It was, in short, a profoundly anti-democratic position. . . . "A President immunized from political considerations," Clark Clifford* told the Senate Judiciary Committee, "is a President who need not listen to the people, respond to majority sentiment, or pay attention to views that may be diverse, intense and perhaps at variance with his own.". . .

. . . Six years in the second half of the twentieth century were equivalent in terms of change to a generation in the first half of the nineteenth century; and, given the onward rush of contemporary life, the nation could hardly afford to place in power for so long a time an administration that might lack the capacity of the will to meet fresh problems with fresh solutions. A four-year term gave both the President and the voters a fair test. If they approved his general course, they could then re-elect him for four years more. . . .

Structural Reform: A Parliamentary System

Oddly the crisis of the imperial Presidency did not elicit much support for what at other times had been a favored theory of constitutional reform: movement in the direction of the British parliamentary system. This was particularly odd because, whatever the general balance of advantage between the parliamentary and presidential modes, the parliamentary system had one feature the presidential system badly needed in the 1970s—the requirement that the head of government be compelled at regular intervals to explain and defend his policies in face-to-face sessions with the political opposition. Few devices, it would seem, would be better calculated both to break down the real isolation of the latter-day Presidency and to dispel the spurious reverence that had come to envelope the office.

In a diminished version, applying only to members of the cabinet, the idea was nearly as old as the republic itself. The proposal that cabinet members should go on to the floor of Congress to answer questions and take part in debate, "far from raising any constitutional difficulties," as E.S. Corwin** once observed, "has the countenance of early practice under the Constitution.". . .

But in the 1970s there appeared little interest in reforms that squinted at parliamentarianism. This may have been in part because the parliamentary regimes best known in America—the British and French—had themselves moved in the direction of prime-ministerial or presidential govern-

---

*Ed. note: Secretary of Defense under President Johnson.
**Ed. note: Edward S. Corwin, political scientist, author of *The President: Office and Powers* (1940).

ment and offered few guarantees against the Vietnam-Watergate effect. . . .

Legislative Restraints: On Executive Privilege

The problem of reining in the runaway Presidency, as it was conceived in the 1970s, centered a good deal more on substantive than on structural solutions. Congress, in other words, decided it could best restrain the Presidency by enacting specific legislation in the conspicuous fields of presidential abuse. The main author of this comprehensive congressional attack on presidential supremacy was, well before Watergate, Senator Sam Ervin of North Carolina. . . .

A leading item on Ervin's domestic agenda was executive privilege. This question . . . had been historically one of conflicting and unresolved constitutional claims. In the nineteenth century, while insisting on a general congressional right to executive information, Congress had acknowledged a right, or at least a power, of presidential denial in specific areas. It acquiesced in these reservations because they seemed reasonable and because responsible opinion outside Congress saw them as reasonable. But what Congress had seen as an expression of comity the Presidency in the later twentieth century came to see as its inherent and unreviewable right. Still both Congress and the Presidency had taken care to avoid a constitutional showdown.

The Nixon administration, with its extravagant theory of an absolute privilege covering everything, whether related or not to the performance of official duties, made a showdown almost inevitable. . . . Nixon himself said in early 1973 that, if the Senate wanted a court test, "we would welcome it. Perhaps this is the time to have the highest court of the land make a definitive decision with regard to the matter." But the judiciary had traditionally steered clear of this question. "The federal courts," as Justice Douglas said in another connection in 1972, "do not sit as an *ombudsman*, refereeing the disputes between the other two branches."*

But could not courts handle the denial of executive information to Congress as they were coming to handle denial of such information to the courts themselves—that is, by judicial inspection of the documents *in camera* to determine whether the executive had a case for withholding them? . . . The trend of lower court decisions in the early 1970s was plainly to favor judicial examination of documents, even those allegedly concerned with national security, in order to decide whether or not they were admissible as evidence. "No executive official or agency," the Court of Appeals for the District of Columbia said in 1971, "can be given absolute authority to determine what documents in his possession may be considered by the court. . . . Otherwise the head of any executive department would have the power on his own say so to cover up all evidence of fraud and corruption when a federal court or grand jury was investigating malfeasance in office, and this is not the law." The courts made similar rulings in the case of the Nixon tapes. . . .

Ed. note: The Supreme Court subsequently did rule, 8-0, that Nixon could not legally withhold Watergate tapes under a claim of executive privilege. The Court rejected Nixon's contention that the President alone should determine when to invoke executive privilege. (*Nixon* v. *United States*, July 24, 1974).

Appropriations provided one handle on the problem of executive privilege. Another, and the one favored by Sam Ervin, was to meet the problem head-on. The Ervin bill, based on an earlier bill introduced by Senator Fulbright, required members of the executive branch summoned by a committee of Congress to appear in person, even if they were intending to claim executive privilege. Only a personal letter from the President could warrant the claim; and the Fulbright-Ervin bill gave the committee the power to decide whether the presidential plea was justified. As Fulbright said, it placed "the final responsibility for judging the validity of a claim of executive privilege in the Congress, where it belongs."

A presidential thesis in violation of the traditional comity between the two branches thus produced a congressional answer that would itself do away with what had been not only an historic but an healthy ambiguity. For 180 years the arbiter in this question had been neither Congress nor the President nor the courts but the political context and process, with responsible opinion considering each case more or less on merit and turning against whichever side appeared to be overreaching itself. The system was not tidy, but it encouraged a measure of restraint on both sides and avoided the constitutional showdown. Now absolute presidential claims provoked an absolute congressional response. Would this really be an improvement? Would Fulbright and Ervin themselves twenty years earlier have wanted to give Joe McCarthy and his committee "the final responsibility" to judge whether executive testimony could be properly withheld? In the area of executive privilege as well as of executive agreements, Nixon's revolutionary conception of the Presidency finally forced Congress into sweeping and dramatic proposals of self-defense.

Legislative Restraints: On Impoundment

Next in the Ervin agenda to the achievement of congressional control over executive information stood the restoration of congressional control over something Congress thought peculiarly its own—the power of the purse. This meant a solution of the problem of presidential impoundment. Impoundment had existed before Nixon, but no previous President had used it to overturn statutes and abolish programs against congressional will. For Nixon impoundment had become a means of taking from Congress the determination of national priorities.

The courts were by no means so diffident about impoundment as they had initially been about executive privilege. In decision after decision in 1973, judges declared one aspect after another of the impoundment policy illegal. No judge accepted Nixon's claim that he had a "constitutional right" not to spend money voted by Congress. . . . The decisions were, however, as they should have been, constructions of specific statutes and stopped short of proposing a general solution to the impoundment controversy. . . .

It was a political fact, however, fully recognized by Ervin, that anti-impoundment legislation would have to be accompanied by evidences of congressional self-control in spending. He was personally a budget-balancer anyway. So his impoundment bill included a spending ceiling. The bill, as passed by the Senate in 1973, also had certain eccentricities for a constitutional fundamentalist. After a clear statement in Section 1 that impoundment was unconstitutional, subsequent sections said that nevertheless the President was authorized to commit this unconstitutional act for periods up to seventy days. Thereafter impoundments not covered by the anti-deficiency laws must cease unless Congress specifically approved them by concurrent resolution. . . .

A strong argument could be made for conceding Presidents leeway in the spending and transfer of appropriated funds, so long as they were not thwarting the intent of Congress when it made the appropriations. But this assumed Presidents whom Congress could trust; it assumed, in short, comity. Here as elsewhere presidential abuse produced extreme counterclaims of congressional authority. The revolutionary Presidency had tried to abolish the congressional power of the purse and make spending a matter of executive decree. The congressional reaction was to stop the President by measures that introduced rigidity into a political process which had always prospered by flexibility.

Cutting the Presidency Down to Size

. . . In one area after another, with the concealed passion and will of a deceptively relaxed personality, Ervin moved to restore the balance of the Constitution by cutting the Presidency down to constitutional size. . . .

The Ervin scheme,* in short, was a scheme of presidential subordination. Where presidential abuse of particular powers had harmed the country, those powers were now to be vested in Congress. The authority and discretion of the Presidency were to be held to their constitutional minimum. All this was entirely understandable as a response to the Nixon scheme of presidential supremacy. It had great value both in checking a deluded President and in raising the consciousness of Congress and the people on constitutional issues. But, pursued to the end, it could produce a national polity which, if it had many more roots in the Constitution than the Nixon scheme, would be almost as overbalanced in the direction of congressional supremacy as the Nixon scheme was in the direction of presidential supremacy.

The Ervin counterattack envisaged a general limitation of the Presidency with all functions reconsidered and all powers diminished. It saw presidential power as unitary and indivisible, and therefore to be reduced across the board. Yet the dilemma of the Presidency was surely that presidential power was not unitary. It could well be argued that while the Presidency had come to have too much discretion in foreign affairs, where error was sometimes irreversible, it had too little in domestic affairs, where error could usually be corrected. As President Kennedy used to say, "Domestic policy can only defeat us; foreign policy can kill us." The revolt against the Presidency had begun in reaction against extravagant assertions of unilateral presidential power to go to war. It would be ironic if it were to end in more binding restraints on the Presidency as an instrument of the general welfare at home. . . .

---

*Ed. note: When Ervin retired from the Senate at the end of 1974, most of the work of his Subcommittee on the Separation of Powers was assumed by the Government Operations Committee. In the aftermath of Nixon's resignation, some bills were allowed to lapse. But two important acts curbing the President were passed in 1974. The War Powers Resolution required that the President must terminate the use of American troops in any military engagement within 60 days unless Congress declares war or specifically approves the action. The Impoundment Control Act of 1974, as described above, was also passed.

It was hard to know how literally to take the Ervin scheme. If it sounded at times like an effort to replace presidential government by congressional government, it must be remembered that the proposals were provoked by an unprecedented attempt to alter the political order. Ervin and his colleagues were fighting not to frustrate the leadership of a President who recognized his accountability to Congress and the Constitution but to protect Congress and the Constitution from the revolutionary Presidency. Yet, if taken literally, the Ervin scheme ran the risk of creating a generation of weak Presidents in an age when the turbulence of race, poverty, inflation, crime and urban decay was straining the delicate bonds of national cohesion and demanding, quite as much as in the 1930s, a strong domestic Presidency to hold the country together. . . .

. . . Said Wilson in 1912, . . . "The individual is caught in a great confused nexus of complicated circumstances, and . . . without the watchful interference, the resolute interference, of the government there can be no fair play." And, for the first Roosevelt and for Wilson, as for their joint heir, the second Roosevelt, national authority was embodied in the Presidency.

This had not been a bad thing for the republic. It was presidential leadership, after all, that brought the country into the twentieth century, that civilized American industry, secured the rights of labor organization, defended the livelihood of the farmer. It was presidential leadership that protected the Bill of Rights against local vigilantism and national resources against local bigotry. Congress would have done few of these things on its own; local government even fewer. It would be a mistake to cripple the Presidency at home because of presidential excesses abroad. History had shown the Presidency to be the most effective instrumentality of government for justice and progress. Even Calvin Coolidge, hardly one of the more assertive of Presidents, said, "It is because in their hours of timidity the Congress becomes subservient to the importunities of organized minorities that the President comes more and more to stand as the champion of the rights of the whole country."

The scheme of presidential subordination could easily be pressed to the point of national folly. But it was important to contend, not for a strong Presidency in general, but for a strong Presidency within the Constitution. The Presidency deserved to be defended on serious and not on stupid points. In 1973 Watergate produced flurries of near hysteria about the life expectancy of the institution. Thus Charles L. Black, Jr., Luce Professor of Jurisprudence at the Yale Law School, argued that, if Nixon turned over his White House tapes to Congress or the courts, it would mean the "danger of degrading or even destroying the Presidency" and constitute a betrayal of his "successors for all time to come." The republic, Professor Black said, could not even risk diluting the "symbolism" of the office lest that disturb "in the most dangerous way the balance of the best government yet devised on earth": and it almost seemed that he would rather suppress the truth than jeopardize the symbolism.

Executive privilege was not the issue. . . . Nor, in the longer run, did either Ervin's hope of presidential subordination or Black's fantasy of presidential collapse have real substance. For the Presidency, though its wings could be clipped for a time, was an exceedingly tough institution. Its primacy was founded in the necessities of the American political order. It had endured many challenges and survived many vicissitudes. It was nonsense to suppose that its fate as an institution was bound up with the fate of the particular man who happened to be President at any given time. In the end power in the American order was bound to flow back to the Presidency.

Congress had a marvelous, if generally unfulfilled, capacity for oversight, for advice, for constraint, for chastening the Presidency and informing the people. When it really wanted to say No to a President, it had ample means of doing so; and in due course the President would have no choice but to acquiesce. But its purpose was, as Wilson said, "watchful criticism, talk that should bring to light the whole intention of the government and apprise those who conducted it of the real feeling and desire of the nation . . . in order that nothing which contravened the common understanding should be let pass without comment or stricture, in order that measures should be insisted on which the nation needed, and measures resisted which the nation did not need or might take harm from." It was inherently incapable of conducting government and providing national leadership. Its fragmentation, its chronic fear of responsibility, its habitual dependence on the executive for ideas, information and favors—this was life insurance for the Presidency. . . .

Holding a President to strict accountability required, first of all, a new attitude on the part of the American people toward their Presidents, or rather a return to the more skeptical attitude of earlier times: it required, specifically, a decline in reverence. An insistent theme in Nixon's public discourse was the necessity of maintaining due respect for the Presidency. The possibility that such respect might be achieved simply by being a good President evidently did not reassure him. He was preoccupied with 'respect for the office' as an entity in itself. Can one imagine Washington or Lincoln or the Roosevelts or Truman or Kennedy going on in public, as Nixon repeatedly did, about how important it was to do this or that in order to maintain 'respect for the office'? But the age of the imperial Presidency had in time produced the idea that run-of-the-mill politicians, brought by fortuity to the White House, must be treated thereafter as if they had become superior and perhaps godlike beings.

The Nixon theoreticians even tried to transform reverence into an ideology, propagating the doctrine, rather novel in the United States, that institutions of authority were entitled to respect per se, whether or not they had done anything to earn respect. . . . But should institutions expect obedience they do not, on their record of performance, deserve? To this question the Nixon ideologues apparently answered yes. An older American tradition would say no, incredulous that anyone would see this as a question. In that spirit I would argue that what the country needs today is a little serious disrespect for the office of the Presidency; a refusal to give any more weight to a President's words than the intelligence of the utterance, if spoken by anyone else, would command; an understanding of the point made so aptly by Montaigne: "Sit he on never so high a throne, a man still sits on his own bottom."

And what if men not open and modest, even at the start, but from the start ambitious of power and contemptuous of law reached the place once occupied by Washington and Lincoln? What if neither personal character, nor the play of politics, nor the Constitution itself availed to hold a President to strict accountability? In the end, the way to control the Presidency might have to be not in many little ways but in one large way. In the end, there remained, as Madison said, the decisive engine of impeachment.

The Crucible
Of Leadership

James MacGregor Burns

It is difficult to estimate the long-term impact of the Watergate scandals and the resignation of Richard M. Nixon on public confidence in the Presidency. Will the events of the past few years be looked upon primarily as individual moral disasters or as institutional failures rooted in the structure of the executive branch itself? Even those who are critical of the growth of Presidential influence and who now demand curtailment of executive power in the aftermath of Watergate are forced to concede that the office has been the principal national source of important social and economic reforms in the past half-century. Can America in the last quarter of the twentieth century afford not to have a "strong" Presidency?

In the following selection, James MacGregor Burns, professor of political science at Williams College and a biographer of Presidents Roosevelt and Kennedy, argues the case for presidential government: "a bulwark of individual liberty, an agency of popular representation, and a magnet for political talent and leadership." Although Burns wrote in 1966, long before Watergate and the Nixon resignation, his analysis remains a powerful defense of the modern Presidency. For his post-Watergate views, see the selection following this one.

"I am the President of the United States, the only President you will have, God willing, until January of next year," Lyndon Johnson said a few months after his election, before a group of newspaper editors assembled in the flower garden. "One of the hardest tasks that a President faces is to keep the time scale of his decisions always in mind and to try to be the President of all the people. He is not simply responsible to an immediate electorate, either. He knows over the long stretch of time how great can be the repercussions of all that he does or that he fails to do, and over that span of time the President always has to think of America as a continuing community."

He has to try to peer into the future, and he has to prepare for that future.

From James MacGregor Burns, *Presidential Government: The Crucible of Leadership.* © 1966 by James MacGregor Burns, reprinted by permission of the publisher, Houghton Mifflin Company.

". . . Irresistible forces of change have been unleashed by modern science and technology, and the very facts dissolve and regroup as we look into them. To make no predictions is to be sure to be wrong. . . .

"The President of this country, more than any other single man in the world, must grapple with the course of events and the directions of history. . . . Somehow we must ignite a fire in the breast of this land, a flaming spirit of adventure that soars beyond the ordinary and the contented, and really demands greatness from our society, and demands achievement in our Government. . . ."

No presidential speech could have caught more aptly the paradox of the modern Presidency. To serve the needs of the present and the future, to satisfy current electorates and future ones, to conceive of America as a present community and a continuing one, to anticipate the future by preparing for it now, . . . to foster greatness in the midst of so much that is mediocre and complacent—all these alternatives pose dilemmas for the President who aspires to his own greatness in history but must work in a tangle of day-to-day problems.

The crowning paradox is an old one for the American President—the need to be both the "President of all the people" and yet to respond to the interests and expectations of the majority that elected him. Since the beginning the President has had to serve both as the ceremonial and symbolic head of the whole nation and also as the head politician. He has had to be Chief of State at the same time that he has served as legislative and party chief. He has had to combine roles that are neatly divided in parliamentary countries between a king and a prime minister, or between a largely ceremonial president and a *premier*. He has had to be both a unifier and a divider of the people. . . .

The increasing dominance of the Presidency over the rest of the government, its embodiment of the national purpose, its symbolic expression of the nation's glory and solidarity, its tremendous impact on Americans during their most formative years—what does all this imply for the future of the nation and of the Presidency?

The Presidency and Civil Rights

The old and accepted fears of presidential power. . . do not seem justified on the basis of actual experience. Increased authority and scope have not made the Presidency a tyrannical institution; on the contrary, the office has become the main governmental bastion for the protection of individual liberty and the expansion of civil rights. The office "represents" the electorate at least as effectively and democratically as does Congress, though in a different way. The office has attracted neither power-mad politicians nor bland incompetents but the ablest political leaders in the land, and these leaders in turn have brought the highest talent to the White House. We must, under modern conditions, reassess the old idea that the *main* governmental protection of civil liberty, social and economic rights, and due process of law lies in the legislature or the courts or state and local government. The main protection lies today in the national executive branch. As a general proposition the Presidency has become the chief protector of our procedural and substantive liberties; as a general proposition, the stronger we make the Presidency, the more we strengthen democratic procedures and can hope to realize modern liberal democratic goals.

The danger of presidential dominance lies in a different and more subtle tendency. It lies not in presidential failure but in presidential success. It lies not in the failure to achieve our essential contemporary goals of freedom and equality but in their substantial realization and in the incapacity of presidential government to turn to new human purposes.

The prospects seem good that presidential government will continue to help broaden equality of opportunity at the same time that it protects our basic freedoms. . . . We can expect that the contest between the presidential parties on domestic issues will turn mainly on the incumbent Administration's successes and failures in combating poverty, expanding opportunity, and enlarging civil rights, especially for Negroes. In foreign policy the election tests will be the efficient management of crisis plus the long-run effectiveness of military and economic programs abroad designed to strengthen the foundations of freedom and equality in other nations. Given the harmony between ends and means—between the ends of freedom and equality and the means of presidential government—we can expect that well before the end of this century, and perhaps much sooner, we will have achieved substantial equality of opportunity in this nation. . . .

One might speculate, though, that many of the most crucial domestic problems might revolve around certain old but still compelling value-questions. Given the trends in the nation that one could predict with the greatest certainty—huge population increases in the urban and suburban areas, accelerated social mobility, a constantly enlarging and increasingly homogenized middle-class population, a decline in ethnic solidarity and variety—one might guess that once the old problems of equality and freedom had been subdued, sharper questions might emerge over the possibilities of individuality and privacy in a mass culture. . . . If in past years we have been concerned with mainly quantitative problems—the amount of goods and services produced and how they were distributed—we might be more occupied in the future with the quality of American life in a great, affluent, complacent, and perhaps mediocre society. . . .

The Shift from Quantitative to Qualitative Goals

The crux of the problem is whether a system of presidential government so perfectly adapted to, and so largely facilitative of, quantitative liberalism—that is, of the augmentation and fairer distribution of goods—can redefine its purpose and shift its strategy in order to embrace new values with their implications for changes in means and instrumental goals. Such a shift calls for much more than making the White House into a showplace of the arts, or awarding medals to heroes of culture, or bestowing presidential recognition on private cultural enterprises. . . . It means diverting the kind of resources into cultural, recreational, and educational activities that we have in the past poured into economic recovery, or even into national defense. And such an effort might be controversial and even unpopular. . . .

Above all, the shift from the pursuit of quantitative to qualitative goals would call for comprehensive, sustained, and broadly unified policies—in short, for planning. Effective planning is impossible except in the context of at least a rough ordering of values, instrumental goals, and means. It will be as important to have clearly thought out, long-range priorities in this respect as it would be in planning increased productivity. . . .

Presidential government is a superb planning institution. The President has the attention of the country, the administrative tools, the command of information, and the fiscal resources that are necessary for intelligent planning, and he is gaining the institutional power that will make such planning operational. Better than any other human instrumentality he can order the relations of his ends and means, alter existing institutions and procedures or create new ones, calculate the consequences of different policies, experiment with various methods, control the timing of action, anticipate the reactions of affected interests, and conciliate them or at least mediate among them. If as Hubert Humphrey has said, we need not a planned society but a continuously planning society, the Presidency provides strong and versatile tools for that purpose.

The Need for New Goals

. . . The question is whether presidential government can detach itself enough from set ideas and existing institutions and old ways in order to embrace new goals. . . .

To define new goals, to fashion new institutions to realize those goals, to avoid both utopianism and opportunism, to build popular support without improper manipulation, to allow for flexibility of means and redefinition of ends, and always to elevate purpose over technique—all this is the test of creative leadership. It will be the test of presidential government in the years ahead. To define leadership in this way is to see the importance of a number of proposals that have been made to strengthen the Presidency and hence to enable the President to reshape institutions and processes: four-year terms for Representatives (to bring presidential and congressional constituencies into closer correspondence); the granting of full power to the President to control executive department organization; finding means of attracting the highest talent to the executive department, especially to its major staff positions; efforts to bring into the policy-making process intellectuals with creative and innovative gifts; providing the President with greater discretionary power over fiscal policy, including the item veto and the granting of authority to change tax rates within certain limits; and above all, the further strengthening of the elected leadership of Congress so that it can act more quickly and comprehensively in harmony with the President. But the greatest need of presidential government does not lie in this kind of reform. We can expect many of these changes to take place in any event as the Presidency becomes increasingly institutionalized. Indeed, some are already taking place, in substance if not in form. Some of them at best will simply speed up transitions that already are under way—for example, greater presidential control of fiscal policy.

The Need for a Strong Opposition

The greatest need of the Presidency in the years ahead will not lie in internal changes, important though these are, or even in its relations with

Congress. The greatest need will be an opposition that challenges presidential values, presidential methods, presidential institutions, that is eager to take power and to present its own definition of the national purpose.

Of all the vital elements of American democratic government the national opposition is the most disorganized, fragmented, and ineffective. As a responsible opposition to the President, Congress is an almost total failure. Hostile Senators and Representatives bombard the White House from all directions. Typically they fail to advance alternative proposals and hence they do not provide the voters with an idea as to how the opposition would govern if it got the chance. The congressmen usually prefer to play the game of bargain and even various forms of genteel blackmail with the President rather than to criticize forthrightly and dramatically. No wonder that Presidents in recent years have been far more sensitive to criticism in the press than on Capitol Hill. . . .

The impotence of the opposition becomes more serious as presidential government becomes more powerful. No matter how benign a government may be, it will be tempted to manipulate public opinion, to try to dominate the flow of opinion, to cover up mistakes, and to cast doubt on the patriotism or at least the honesty of outside critics. The more that government represents a consensus, or claims to, the more tempted it may be to succumb to some of these tendencies. Above all a consensus government may become flabby and complacent and lose the cutting edge of energy, initiative, and innovation. The very tendencies toward excessive concern with technique that we noted above can cause a government to lose direction and momentum unless the opposition holds it to its promises and threatens to oust it from power. . . .

The Need for Presidential Government: A Summary

The Hamiltonian President—the resourceful, heroic, opportunistic leader—was from the outset an alternative to the weak Madisonian executive and to the Jeffersonian model of the party chief who both acted for, and was constrained by, the popular majority that he led. The Hamiltonian President aroused ambivalent attitudes among Americans—including many intellectuals—who wanted strong leadership and honored it in past Presidents but who feared that a current or future strong man in the White House might threaten American democracy. The expansion of the President's political, military, diplomatic, and economic power, combined with the huge enlargement of the executive department, posed the threat that an independent leader, manipulating various constituencies, freely wielding his broad executive and emergency authority, and drawing party, Cabinet, Congress, and even the courts into his political orbit, would start the nation on the road to tyranny. But this threat never materialized. On the contrary, the executive and political institutionalization of the Presidency generated internal checks and balances and stable bases of support in the presidential parties in such a way as to channel and stabilize presidential power. And the convergence of the long ambivalent American ideology in the modern doctrines of freedom and equality has both empowered the President to act for quantitative liberalism and set broad limits for his actions.

Hence presidential government, far from being a threat to American democracy, has become the major single institution sustaining it—a bulwark of individual liberty, an agency of popular representation, and a magnet for political talent and leadership. But the situation has its drawbacks and dangers. Presidential government has become such a fitting means of realizing agreed-on ends of freedom and equality that it runs the risk of losing sight of its purpose in its preoccupation with technique and of becoming irrelevant to new ends. As the President comes increasingly to speak for the whole nation in his political and policy and planning role, just as he has always done in his ceremonial role; as he comes to act for the people in general rather than for his party or for Congress or for some particular constituency; as he cultivates a consensus that may become flabby and complacent—presidential government may lose its potency for anticipating new problems and realizing new values. The politics of adjustment and adaptation threatens to take the place of a politics of principle and passion. . . . The future of presidential government turns less on constitutional and other reforms, useful though these would be, than on the access of intellectuals and innovators to the White House and on the creation of a vigorous, coherent, creative opposition. . . .

Tendencies toward executive government can be found in other nations. . . . Whether the executive impetus in the great nations in time will produce systems of executive government—of executive leaders taking their mandates directly from the people, dominating party and parliament, manipulating constituencies and pressure groups, directing huge public agencies and holding at least a veto power over big private bureaucracies—cannot yet be discerned. But to the extent that nations deliberately adopt systems of executive government the American experience may be instructive.

For in presidential government Americans have established one of the most powerful political institutions in the free world. They have fashioned, sometimes unwittingly, a weapon that has served them well in the long struggle for freedom and equality at home and in the search for stable and democratic politics abroad. They have grasped the uses of this power, and as Harold Laski said, great power makes great leadership possible. Yet power alone is inadequate. It must be linked with purpose. Ultimately it must embody a Jeffersonian thrust toward the most elevated goals of man; it must express the single central vision of the hedgehog. But purpose in turn is steeled not amid agreement, adjustment, conformity, but in crisis and conflict; it was out of crisis and conflict that Roosevelt, Nehru, Lenin, Churchill, and the other great leaders of this century emerged.

A great society needs not consensus but creative leadership and creative opposition—hence it needs the sting of challenge in a society rich in diversity and in a politics rich with dissent.

The Presidency After Watergate

As the following selections indicate, the Watergate scandals and Richard Nixon's resignation provoked a great deal of discussion about the future of the American Presidency. What are the lessons that have been learned? What modifications in the institution can be anticipated as a result? James MacGregor Burns, author of Presidential Government, excerpts of which appear as the preceding selection, responded to these and other questions about the post-Watergate Presidency in The Center Magazine, September-October, 1974. Harper's Magazine also asked distinguished journalists and political commentators, including Arthur M. Schlesinger, Jr., to answer similar questions in its issue of October, 1974.

Selection 1   James MacGregor Burns

There are certain things we should not do. We should not abstract the Presidency from history, from politics, and from ideology. All of us, to a lesser or greater degree, are overreacting to the experience of the last three Presidencies.

We should learn from those Presidencies. I have. I thought certain defenses would operate in our system, but they didn't. On the other hand, I don't know how one can deal with a Richard Nixon. If you have a Nixon-and-company onslaught against our government, I don't know if there is any system that ever would protect us. If we could devise one, it would be so elaborate it might fall of its own weight, since it would have been designed to cope with a particular President in a particular historical period.

The Johnson and Nixon Administrations are not representative of the American Presidency. Both were a response to political disarray in this country, which had its roots immediately in Vietnam and, more fundamentally, in such long-term developments as the demoralization of our party system. We could improvise some brilliant responses to the failures of these last two Presidencies, but find ourselves, ten or twenty years from now, looking at the ruins of our Presidential system because things had gone into an even more unhappy state of affairs.

We must ask ourselves whether we are going through a very restricted and unique period in American history. I contend that, of all our institu-

"Don't Go Too Far" by James MacGregor Burns. Reprinted from the September/October, 1974, issue of The Center Magazine, a publication of the Center for the Study of Democratic Institutions, Santa Barbara, California.

tions, the Presidency has represented, on the whole, the most egalitarian and libertarian thrust in this country. We ought to be very careful about threatening this institution, not because we have had egalitarian and libertarian Presidents, but because the very structure of the Presidency, with its electoral, institutional, and behavioral aspects, has made it the kind of institution it is.

We must also ask ourselves to what extent the failures of the last few years have been political rather than Presidential or institutional failures. The impact of Vietnam is still incalculable in so many aspects of American life, but particularly in the Presidency. We must hope that, if only as a result of Vietnam, we will not undergo future Vietnams. Certainly we must provide against excessive Presidential intervention in the making of foreign policy. But on the domestic side we must put reform proposals in historical context.

We must also put them in an institutional context. Of all the quixotic proposals, the most quixotic are those calling for fundamental congressional reform. I argued in a book back in 1949 that Congress cannot reform itself. Congress, despite all the stress and pressure in recent years, has not reformed itself. We are always hearing about the end of the filibuster, for example, and yet the filibuster continues to be very much with us, as do many other congressional "institutions."

In contrast, the Presidency is an infinitely adaptable institution, partly because it is so personalized. Perhaps it is overly personalized. But I would expect that at the least, in 1976, we will have Presidential candidates advocating an open Presidency. And we will see a far more open Presidency, with a leader who will be extremely sensitive to the kinds of searching questions that have been raised in recent years. But I do not think we will see this in the case of Congress. There will be reformers in Congress, but I think its institutional drag is so profound, so insidious, so intensive and unremitting that it is not a good institution on which to place our hopes for the future.

We should maintain the strength of the Executive, perhaps even augment it in domestic matters, not simply so that it can respond to crisis more quickly, but to anticipate and plan against crisis, which is one of the great potential strengths of the Executive.

We should also strengthen the negative power of Congress. We already do this in certain fields. For example, we give Congress an explicit negative power over the President's reorganizing of the executive branch.

Through the years, we have reversed the old relation between Congress and the President. The Presidency has become the great affirmative branch, in both the best and the worst sense of that term. Perhaps we should be more honest about this and frankly acknowledge that in this century the legislature is essentially a checking, vetoing, investigating, and inspecting institution, and that in very few countries has it been an effective source of governmental power.

We must be honest with ourselves and ask whether, in effect, we want to repudiate the main lesson of this century about how our political institutions work. We must not overreact to what I feel—and hope—is a unique period in American history these last five or ten years.

Selection 2 "Rulers v. Reality"

Among the many causes of Richard Nixon's troubles, surely one was that he let himself be isolated in the splendor of the White House. In that Oval Office no voices were heard save those of sycophants, reflecting back his own mood and thoughts—or what the courtiers took them to be. Much could have been avoided if he had heard a few saying this should not be done, that is in error, but all such advice came to him filtered through a glass, darkly. Such isolation feeds upon itself until in time all perception becomes distorted. Whatever else those famed tapes show, they show a man shut off from the world.

In the extreme, this can be fatal. It was thus that Charles I and Louis XVI lost their heads. It was thus that Richard Nixon was brought to the edge of impeachment.

Mr. Nixon was not the first of our Presidents to be so afflicted. It has been a growing problem of the twentieth-century Presidency since the Roosevelt era, when we first began to view the President not merely as first citizen but as the omnipotent leader responsible for all our blessings—or ills. With power come the trappings of power, and with those trappings the inevitable isolation. Lyndon Johnson, once one of the most sensitive of politicians, surely would not have followed his Vietnam policy to disaster had he not been so isolated from the moods, thoughts, and feelings of the people.

How are we to avoid leaders cut off from the led? Inevitably there have been gropings for some new law, some new form of institutionalized arrangement to protect that man in the White House from misperceiving reality, misjudging his options, and so perhaps someday being misled to a fatal misjudgment.

I doubt this can be done by new laws, by new institutional arrangements. The trouble now is too many laws giving the President too much power, too much institutionalizing of the Presidency. The solution, if indeed there is one, is to diminish our expectations of the office and so diminish its powers and its panoply. At the very least, we should cease paying for those multiplying courtiers, that White House staff, those men beholden only to the President. All public servants should be answerable to the public, for so long as we have courtiers so long will we have a court around the President.

But the best hope is that the debacle that has come to Richard Nixon will teach his successors. Let's hope it will remind them of the age-old problem of all leaders, that calamity awaits him who lets his perception of reality be distorted by isolation, however splendid.

—*Vermont Royster, contributing editor of* The Wall Street Journal.

*   *   *

How to make sure that Presidents do not cut their ties to the reality principle? I doubt whether legislative or constitutional solutions to this problem are necessary, or possible. The first answer is surely to elect Presidents who, like most Presidents in our history, have an inner commitment to accountability and understand that their success depends on their capacity to elicit and mobilize informed consent. In the future voters will have to pay more attention than they have in the recent past to personal evidences of this inner commitment: temperamental openness and accessibility; a relish for face-to-face consultation, discussion, and debate; a readiness to meet the press and to level with the people; a belief in reason and persuasion; a dislike of furtiveness and secrecy; and those old-fashioned virtues of integrity and character.

Obviously even rather open Presidents have been corrupted in time by the pleasures and perquisites of the Presidency. The antidote is to reject the latter-day myth of the President as a man above the people, a myth bulwarked by the ghastly contention of the new conservatives that institutions of authority must command respect, whether or not they have done anything to earn it. Nothing is more mischievous than the singular idea of recent years that the President has a sacred right to be protected from secular exposure and confrontation. An American President, let us never forget, is simply a politician luckier than the others—one who has made it to the top of the greasy pole. Shinnying up the pole does not, however, transform a politician into a quasi-deity or carry him out of our sight and jurisdiction; and he can expect to stay on top only so long as he remembers and respects the disciplines of consent. The transubstantiation of the Presidency has gone far enough. It is a recent development; it is not inherent in the process. If the electorate will get the Presidency back into proportion and restore the historic system of accountability, future Presidents will be quite as much tethered to the reality principle as the great Presidents of the past have been.

> —*Arthur M. Schlesinger, Jr., author of* The Imperial Presidency
> (*Houghton Mifflin*).

*   *   *

When I worked with Barry Goldwater, he was accused of simplistic thinking when he said that (1) the American Presidency has become an elected monarchy, (2) secrecy in government is anathema to freedom, (3) secret diplomacy is an affront to democracy, and (4) federal welfare programs do not end poverty, they simply enroll selected dependent populations into new political constituencies.

Now he defends the most absolute privilege of the President, seeks to jail those who penetrate government secrecy, absolutely supports the most secret diplomacy imaginable, and sits in virtual silence while the great corporations become recipients of massive federal welfare. His former detractors, meantime, now echo many of his former supposedly extremist positions.

What has changed? Well, Goldwater is in, and his former detractors are out. So what else is new?

I derive from such experiences the following notion: what is crucially involved in the misperceptions of great leaders is not the isolation of power but the possession of power. Great leaders behave in bad ways not because of some imperfection in the system or even because of imperfections in the souls of the leaders. The system (here or in the U.S.S.R.) is fundamentally hierarchical and representative. It demands that a few rule. Here they are said to rule because they represent "the people." In the Soviet Union they are said to represent a progressive state and a force of history. But what they do is rule. The same thing applies in a commercial empire. The boss may be said to represent the stockholders. What he does is rule the employees.

Everywhere this system works perfectly.

A few *do* rule. They rule because they want to rule. It is their character to do it, not a failure of their character.

Would-be leaders who do not have power are renowned throughout history for their stirring calls for freedom. Leaders who do have power are known for their stern insistence on order, obedience, loyalty, progress, duty (to the institution that *they* represent or embody), and sacrifice (of everyone who isn't doing anything more important).

Dreamy liberal theorists still tell us that baked into some pie in some sky there is a prize way of doing things in which great leaders would not be isolated, would heed wisdom and rule in elegant style. If the Joint Chiefs just read the right journals, they seem to say, they would have showered Cambodia with rose petals. But the Joint Chiefs are hired to kill the enemies chosen by *their* boss, the Commander-in-Chief. And that's exactly what they do—not in contravention of the system, but in exact keeping with it. This seemed clear enough to some of our leading political theorists when the people being killed were John Kennedy's enemies. They supported his war as hotly as they opposed Johnson's.

Rather than moaning about how we are going to get along with great leaders, it seems to me that a millennium or so of experience might urge us to ask how, instead, we can get along *without* great leaders. The anti-Federalists in America had some notions along those lines and it might befit our upcoming Bicentennial to give them some second thoughts. The town meeting and local sovereignty once put these ideas into a real social form. Participatory rather than representative democracy sort of sums up the alternatives. Such ideas, it seems to me, are more realistic than various schemes of how best to speak wisdom to power.

When will we learn? Power is deaf. Not isolated. Stone cold deaf.

—Karl Hess, Barry Goldwater's chief speechwriter during the 1964 Presidential campaign. He is now a commercial welder and community organizer in Washington D.C.

*   *   *

In legend, a young king disguises himself as a beggar and mingles anonymously among his subjects, thus to discover how things in his realm truly are. In the United States today the ruler's problem is quadruply difficult.

First, there is the difference in vantage point: rulers see from the macropicture, but citizens live in the microworld of their own families, neighborhoods, occupations. Technology increases the distance between vantage points.

Second, the United States is not a homogenous country with a single moral culture. What some groups believe to be moral (abortion, gambling, the death penalty), others hold to be immoral. It is difficult for a single personifier of the whole people—a President—to comprehend, let alone to represent accurately, all the diverse groups of this tumultuous yet peaceful land. Which "realities" weigh heaviest in his recognition?

Third, the national press systematically distorts reality. Out of touch with heterogeneous realities, it presents a homogeneous image of the nation. The vast numbers of evangelical, fundamentalist citizens, for example, are treated with condescension. An anti-Catholic bias has been

348

built into the language; although they number one-quarter of the population, Catholics can scarcely feel that one-quarter of the nation's symbols, biases, and preoccupations reflect their own symbols, biases, and preoccupations.

The upshot is that many Americans feel excluded from public presentations of "reality." They feel excluded, not only by the White House, but by the media and other institutions.Indeed, many social institutions—the schools, the universities, the media—seem intent upon *mis*informing us about the variety.

Thus, even if a President wants an accurate view of the United States, he can turn to very few institutional supports.

Fourth, in the Presidency as organized by the Founding Fathers, two quite separate roles are conflated: that of personifying the people, the kingly role; and that of executing the government's business, the executive role. For our own protection, we need to devise a way of separating these roles.

We do need someone to personify the people, to be the mythic link in the nation's narrative history, from Washington through Jefferson and Jackson and Lincoln and Wilson to the present. Our Presidents loom larger than any other figures in the national imagination.

We also need an executive officer who can be held accountable for policies that affect the many diverse publics of the land.

For six years Richard Nixon used the former role as a "cover" for certain activities in the second role. These other activities of his were designed to rearrange the power base of American politics. These activities are in one sense quite traditional for some Americans, as dramatized in Melville's *Confidence Man,* in *The Sting*, and in the history of the building of many great family fortunes; but they are justly feared and disdained in Presidents.

In an odd way, Nixon was more in touch with the messy, multiple realities of American life than his enemies. Yet he committed certain symbolic violations; he violated the nation's kingly ideals. But he still was king.

To impeach a king is more awe-inspiring than to impeach a mere manager. The king can identify as brazenly as he dares with one part of the population, over and against another part. He can use the nation against itself.

Those who hate Nixon don't anymore. Ironically, it was his paranoia regarding his enemies that led him to hand his enemies the dagger of his own undoing. Reinhold Niebuhr used to speak of the one iron rule of human life: each of us is in the end done in by what we take to be our strength. (Neibuhr himself succumbed to this law.)

So it was also with Kennedy and his love for images of the new, the quick, the daring, the aggressive; so it was also with Johnson's unrestrained energy, on which he so prided himself.

There is only one sound political advice: lean, as Aristotle put it, against the wind of your own strength. A pitifully weak instrument against the ironies of history; and yet even attempts to improve upon it are subject to its bite.

The strength of our Presidents is their kingly, symbolic role. The strength of our activists is their moral passion. The strength of our conservatives is their economic power and Protestant symbolism.

No one group perceives realistically the complicated social texture of the entire country. The road to realistic perception is to acquire the perceptions held by our profoundest enemies—and to find ways to negotiate between their perceptions and our own. Respect for diversity is the highest form of politics. When politics declines, moralism rises: enemies are no longer partners in negotiation but objects of retribution. When the effort to respect diversity is more habitual to many in America, it will be easier for our Presidents to manifest it, too. We cannot ask Presidents to do what we do not do ourselves.

Michael Novak, associate director for humanities at the Rockefeller Foundation. His latest book is Choosing Our King (*Macmillan*).

*　　*　　*

Short of a radical change in the form of our government, such as an elected triumvirate to serve as our Executive branch, which might provide better insurance against the possibility of some Hitler-like madman coming to power, I fail to see how to avoid the ills you outline. . . .

However, as I see it, we shall emerge from the morass in which we, as a people, allowed ourselves to be bogged down. The checks and balances written into our Constitution, the moral courage of leaders in our Congress and throughout our nation, and the final arbiter, the common sense of the American people, will suffice to tear apart the veil of self-deluding grandeur of any American chief executive, or other key governmental official, restoring him to a balanced perception of reality and his very small place in the scheme of things. There are signs that the decent-thinking majority of our citizens has been shocked to the point where the downward trend has been halted. This vast majority is determined to start us on the upward path again.

What an opportunity we have in this upcoming Bicentennial era to exemplify again those high principles with which our Founders once ignited a flame that spread throughout the world.

—Matthew B. Ridgway was supreme commander of the Allied Powers in Europe and Army Chief of Staff.

The Fate
of Party Politics

David S. Broder

*A weak party system, non-ideological and decentralized, has fre-
quently been regarded as one of the major virtues of the American
political system because it encourages compromise, pluralism, and
diversity. Except for periods of extreme national emergency, such
as the Great Depression or World War II, party unity on the parliamentary model has been rare in America. As the nation
approaches its Bicentennial, however, it is well to ask, as the
political columnist David Broder does in the following selection,
whether America can solve her pressing national problems without
a stronger party system.*

*Without disputing the values of compromise and pluralism,
Broder emphasizes that many of our social ills demand national
treatment that only national parties with national programs can
begin to implement. "The weakness of our party system," he
suggests, "has made it very difficult to build and maintain
support for the long-term enterprises we need to pursue at home
and abroad."*

Many of the problems confronting America today, many of the shortcom-
ings in the political system . . . were foreseen by a group of scholars twenty
years ago. In its 1950 report, "Toward a More Responsible Two-Party
System," the committee on political parties of the American Political
Science Association said there were four dangers to our democracy which
"warrant special emphasis," dangers which they prophesied would become
more acute unless the forces weakening our party system were combated.

"The first danger," the report said, "is that the inadequacy of the party
system in sustaining well-considered programs and providing broad public
support for them may lead to grave consequences in an explosive era."

The weakness of our party system has made it very difficult to build and
maintain support for the long-term enterprises we need to pursue at home
and abroad. The task of supporting international economic development,
of constructing a stable world peace, of building a strong domestic
economy and equitably distributing its products and wealth, of reforming

From pp. 244–57 in *The Party's Over: The Failure of Politics in America* by David S. Broder.
Copyright © 1971, 1972 by David S. Broder. Reprinted by permission of Harper & Row,
Publishers.

our governmental structures and finding adequate resources for our urgent national needs cannot be accomplished by a single Congress or a single President. We have paid a high price for the instability and weakness of our governing coalitions. Ambitious programs have been launched, but funds to finance them withheld. Commitments made by a President have been undercut by Congress. Funds voted by Congress have been vetoed or impounded by a President. No party has been able to move ahead on its own agenda for very long, and the result has been sixteen years of government by fits and starts, with a mounting backlog of unkept promises and unmet needs.

"The second danger," the APSA committee said, "is that the American people may go too far for the safety of constitutional government in compensating for this inadequacy by shifting excessive responsibility to the President."

We have seen that happen, too. The weakness and frustration of responsible party government at the state and local levels—which is, if anything, even more serious than at the national level—has sent most of our major issues to Washington for resolution. And in Washington power has increasingly been stripped from Congress and the departments and been centralized in the White House. Bereft of the sustained support a responsible party system could provide for passage and implementation of a long-term program, each of the last four Presidents has been forced to improvise his governmental policies and tactics on a day-to-day basis, hoping some temporary alliance would permit him to overcome the inherent immobility of the vast governmental system. As the APSA committee predicted, this situation has produced the type of "President who exploits skillfully the arts of demagoguery, who uses the whole country as his political backyard, and who does not mind turning into the embodiment of personal government." But even the highly personalized presidency of our era has not managed to cope successfully with the problems challenging America.

"The third danger," the APSA committee said in 1950, "is that with growing public cynicism and continuing proof of the ineffectiveness of the party system, the nation may eventually witness the disintegration of the two major parties." That has not yet happened, but we are appreciably closer to that danger than we were twenty years ago. Popular dissatisfaction with the two-party system is manifested in many ways: by the decline in voting; by the rise in the number of voters who refuse to identify themselves with either party; by the increase in ticket splitting, a device for denying either party responsibility for government; and by the increased use of third parties or ad hoc political coalitions to pressure for change.

"The fourth danger," the APSA committee said, "is that the incapacity of the two parties for consistent action based on meaningful programs may rally support for extremist parties, poles apart, each fanatically bent on imposing on the country its particular panacea."

Regrettably, we have seen altogether too much of this kind of political polarization in the past twenty years. This has been an era of confrontation politics: whites vs. blacks; hard hats vs. students; demonstrators vs. police. The extremist parties are yet small, but the extremist movements are growing, and as our domestic political process becomes increasingly polarized, polemicized and violent, there is real danger the end result may be a totalitarian party of the left or right.

What must concern us is the rising level of public frustration with government-and-politics-as-usual. It is not just a few radical students who say and believe the political system is not working; millions of ordinary, hard-working Americans recognize that government is not dealing with the problems that are uppermost in their lives: crime and drugs and war and inflation and unfair tax loads and fear of unemployment and family budgets that do not stretch to meet the housing and education and medical and recreational needs of their families.

The ways in which this frustration is expressed are as various as the men and women who share it, but they were all summed up for me in the words of a retired furniture maker I met while polling in Nashville, Tennessee, in the fall of 1970. He was weeding his garden as we talked, and at the end of the conversation, he straightened up to say goodbye. "I'll tell you this," he said, "I'm glad I'm getting too old to live, because what's going to happen when this bubble bursts? The kettle is starting to boil, brother, and she ain't even heated up good yet."

For most of the last sixteen years, American liberals, of whom I am, I suppose, one, have been most concerned about the outsiders in our society—the black, the brown, the poor, the uneducated, the young—who are the all-but-inevitable losers in the influence game we have substituted for responsible party government. But some of these groups have learned to beat the odds by ignoring the rules. If the "big boys" and the "special interests" control city hall, or the legislature or the capitol, the "outsiders" have learned to control the streets. They have "voted with their feet," as the saying goes, and with their throats, and with their threats. And sometimes the government has responded, as it should have responded to the justice of their cause, if not to the threat of disruption that accompanied it.

But today it is not just these minority-group "outsiders" who are frustrated by the inequities of our society and the laggard performance of our political-governmental system. Millions of middle-aged, middle-class white working Americans are coming to understand that they have been victimized by the irresponsible politics of the recent era. No one asked them if they wanted their sons sent to fight in Vietnam; no one asked them if they wanted to gamble their family security on their ability to keep one step ahead of inflation; no one asked them if they wanted to swap token cuts in their income taxes for walloping hikes in the property taxes on their homes. Yet all these things have been done to them, by their government, and they are not going to take it lying down. Failing any means of registering their views through the political system, they will follow the blacks and the students and the other minority groups into the streets. And confrontation politics—with its constant threat of violence and repression—will increase.

Vietnam and the Political Parties

Is there not a better way to resolve our differences, to move ahead on our common problems? I believe there is. I have argued. . . that the instrument that is available to us—little used in the last sixteen years, at least—is the instrument of responsible party government. The alternative to making policy in the streets is to make it in the voting booth.

But, if that is to be more than a cliche answer, there must be real choices presented at election time—choices involving more than a selection between two sincere-sounding, photogenic graduates of some campaign consultant's academy of political and dramatic arts. . . .

The instrument, the only instrument I know of, that can nominate such candidates, commit them to a program and give them the leverage and alliances in government that can enable them to keep their promises, is the political party.

But, even as I say that, I recognize that the notion will be greeted with enormous skepticism. The parties, it will be said, have been around for years; if they are the answer, then why do we have the problems we have now? My reply, of course, is that we have not seen responsible party government in this country—in Washington or in most states and cities—in the sixteen years I have been covering national politics. Instead, we have had fractured, irresponsible, nonparty government, and we have paid a fearful price for it.

I have dwelled . . . on the domestic consequences of our long period of governmental stalemate: the unmet needs of our major public services, the deteriorated condition of our governmental machinery. . . . But I do not want to leave the impression that the most serious or costly consequences of the breakdown of responsible party government are in the domestic field. Still less do I want to leave unchallenged the argument, so often made, that politics should stop at the water's edge. For it is my firm conviction that if one wants to sum up in one word what can happen in the absence of responsible party government, that word is Vietnam.

For twenty-five years, respectable opinion in this country has held that the great questions of foreign policy should be kept sacred and inviolate, far removed from the sordid considerations of partisan advantage. The notion had a specific historic justification. In 1946, when Democrat Harry Truman was President, the Republicans captured Congress in an election that represented a strong public reaction against the wartime controls associated with the Democratic Administration.

The Republican congressional victory made responsible party government impossible. Faced with the necessity of securing support from a Republican Congress for major postwar international policies—including the Marshall Plan—Truman entrusted his foreign policy to a group of successful lawyers and businessmen, many of them liberal Republicans from the New York Establishment. The prominence given such men as Robert Lovett, Paul Hoffman, John McCloy, Allen and John Foster Dulles facilitated the course of bipartisanship that was necessary under the historical circumstances.

Unfortunately, the notion became permanently enshrined that such nonpolitical men had a natural right to manage the nation's foreign policy. . . . Elections are held and party control of the presidency shifts, but the technicians and "experts"—the Walt Rostows and Henry Kissingers—never seem to lose their grip on the foreign policy machinery.

When protest over foreign policy arises from the ranks of the President's party, as it did from some Democratic senators in the Lyndon Johnson years and from some Republican legislators since Richard Nixon has been in office, it is the nonpolitical "experts" in the key foreign policy jobs who always rush forward to defend existing policies. It is these men, with their marvelous self-confidence and their well-developed contempt for politicians and public opinion, who wrote the clever scenarios and the cynical memoranda that comprise the history of Vietnam policy under three administrations contained in the Pentagon Papers. It is they who stand ready to advise a President how he can dupe the Congress and the public and maneuver the nation into war without disclosing his intentions.

How have they been able to maintain their control over foreign policy? Because the political parties, at critical junctures, have failed to meet their responsibilities. In none of the national elections during the whole course of the escalation and de-escalation in Vietnam were the American people given a choice of defined, coherent policies toward the struggle in Indochina. . . . For six long years—between 1964 and 1970—the leadership of both parties in Congress failed to try to bring to a vote a policy declaration on Vietnam. Vietnam is a classic instance of the costliness of isolating a basic foreign policy question from examination in partisan, political debate. It is a terrible measure of the failure of responsible party government in our time.

Letting the Parties Go

I am not optimistic about the prospects of reviving responsible party government in the near future. The momentum of current trends, the drift of the public mood seem to me to point in the opposite direction: toward the further fracturing of the already enfeebled party structure in this decade. The survey that Haynes Johnson and I did at the time of the 1970 election convinced us that "not only are voters splitting their tickets and moving back and forth from election to election, but their perception of party differences is growing visibly weaker." That habit of partisanship, once lost, may be very difficult to regain.

If that proves to be the case, and if the young people entering the electorate remain as independent of the party system as they now appear to be, the major parties may no longer enjoy a monopoly on high office. Three or four or half-a-dozen serious presidential candidates may run each election year, posing a constitutional crisis whether we are operating under the existing electoral college system or a plan for direct election of the President. More minor party or independent candidates may find their way into Congress, weakening the existing party structure there.

If the distrust of politicians and parties continues to grow, it may be reflected in the deliberate crippling of responsible leadership, by dividing the branches of government between the parties and by turning office-holders out as soon as they show signs of amassing any significant power. While the masses of alienated voters use these tactics to cripple government, the activists for one cause or another may continue to press their demands through confrontation tactics—lawsuits, demonstrations, strikes, boycotts and the other weapons in their arsenal. The result would be an increase of domestic turbulence and violence.

I do not think it is inevitable that we go down this road, but I am afraid that there is as yet no widespread understanding that this is what we face unless we make a deliberate effort to reinvigorate our political party system. There is as yet no broad appreciation of the fact that the aggravations and frustrations each of us feels is part of a single crisis—the malfunctioning of our governmental-political system. We still delude ourselves by thinking we can treat the symptoms and ignore the cause. . . .

. . . Unless our basic population patterns are reversed, most of us will find ourselves living in a compact mass of humanity in one of the concentrated metropolitan clusters, where we will have only the choice of trying to solve our problems on a community basis or attempting to survive by the law of the jungle. When the time comes—and it is not that far off—when most Americans live constantly with the threat of breakdowns that have plagued New York City residents in recent years, when teachers and policemen and sanitation workers and subway and bus and taxi operators strike, when taxes rise while municipal services deteriorate, and filth piles up in the streets, when jobs become more scarce and inaccessible and welfare rolls soar, while schools turn out more addicts than graduates, when personal security is no greater than one's own strength or weapons provide, then we may recognize that we face a genuine crisis of government.

If we are very fortunate at that moment, we may find leadership in one party or the other capable of mobilizing the nation through democratic means to confront what will by then be an almost overwhelming challenge. In our desperation, we may by our ballots give that party a mandate for governing commensurate to its task, and we may even be fortunate enough to find its leaders responsible and responsive in office. . . .

But there is a darker possibility we cannot overlook. When frustration reaches the breaking point, . . . a different sort of man with a different solution may present himself. A plausible demagogue may appear and say, "Give me power and I will make things work again. I will restore order to your lives. I will see that there is discipline again. I will make the streets safe and I will remove those who are disturbing our peace of mind. It may not be pleasant, but I promise you it will be effective. . . . Congress will pass the necessary laws, because its members will understand it will not be wise for them to go home unless they act. And the press will cooperate with us, and stop its carping and sniping, if it understands what is good for it. And we will save our country"—but, of course, destroy freedom and democracy in the process.

That possibility sounds like scare talk. Some will dismiss it as apocalyptic nonsense. But things have been happening in this country that I would not have believed when I came to Washington sixteen years and four Presidents ago. I have seen a President and his brother, a presidential candidate, murdered by assassins. I have seen the Capitol of the United States blasted by explosives, on one occasion, and ringed by arson fires on another. I have circled our national monuments in an airplane carrying the Vice President of the United States and watched the tears in his eyes as he saw the magnificent capital city set to the torch by its black residents, venting their rage and frustration at the murder of Martin Luther King, Jr.

I have seen speakers shouted down and heckled into silence by student mobs at our oldest university, and I have seen police in a dozen cities use their clubs with savage delight on the heads and arms and backs of peaceful demonstrators.

356

Above all, I have heard the conversations of hundreds of average Americans, who see their world, their plans, their hopes crumbling, and do not know where to turn. . . . I remember all too well the young husband in New Rochelle, New York, with his arm around his wife's shoulders, who told a visitor of the fears for the future that have caused them to delay starting a family. "We've even thought seriously of moving to some other country," he said, "but we don't know where to go."

Taking the Political Option

Where do we turn? To ourselves. Obviously, that must be the answer. There is no solution for America except what we Americans devise. I believe that we have the instrument at hand, in the party system, that can break the long and costly impasse in our government. But it is up to us to decide whether to use it.

What would it entail on our part if we determined to attempt responsible party government? First, it would mean giving strong public support to those reform efforts which in the recent past have been carried on entirely by a small group of concerned political insiders, aimed at strengthening the machinery of political parties and government. *

We should seek to strengthen the liaison between the presidency and Congress, on a mutual basis, and between the presidency and the heads of state and local government. We should elect the President in the same way we elect all other officials, by direct vote of his constituents, with high man winning.

We should expand the role and responsibilities of the party caucuses and the party leaders in Congress. The caucus should choose the floor leaders and policy committee members, the legislative committee chairmen and committee members, not on the basis of seniority but on the basis of ability and commitment to the party program. That leadership ought to be held accountable for bringing legislation to which the party is committed to a floor vote in orderly and timely fashion, with adequate opportunity for debate and particularly for consideration of opposition party alternatives. . . .

In state government, we need to reduce the number of elected officials, to provide governors with adequate tenure and staff to meet their responsibilities, and particularly to strengthen the legislatures, by limiting their size and by improving their pay, their facilities and their staffing, and to recognize they have a full-time job to do each year.

In local government, too, we need to reduce drastically the number of elected officials and make sure the jurisdictions they serve are large enough to provide a base for two-party competition and to bring resources together

---

*Ed. Note: Several major reforms have been effected since Mr. Broder's book was written. These include provisions for a Democratic national "miniconvention" to be held midway between Presidential election years, and for representation of women and minorities among delegates "as indicated by their presence in the Democratic electorate." Reform proposals in the Republican party would require that the Republican national chairman approve campaign expenditures of more than one thousand dollars and that the states report to the National Committee on efforts to open the Party to women and minorities.

The Federal Elections Campaign Act of 1974 set an absolute ceiling on individual campaign contributions and on campaign spending for a Presidential candidate ($20,000,000). It also provided for optional public financing of Presidential campaigns and established a Federal Elections Commission to enforce the law.

with problems along a broad enough front to give some hope of effective action.

We need to take every possible measure to strengthen the presidential nominating convention as the key device for making the parties responsible. The current effort to open the Democratic delegate-selection process to wider public participation is a promising start, and its emphasis on the congressional-district nominating convention offers corollary benefits for integrating congressional and presidential constituencies. Both parties should experiment with devices for putting heavier emphasis on the platform-writing phase of the convention's work, including the possibility of a separate convention, following the nomination, where the party's officeholders and candidates debate the program on which they pledge themselves to run and to act if elected.

Most important of all the structural reforms, we need to follow through the effort to discipline the use of money in politics, not only by setting realistic limits on campaign spending and by publicizing individual and organizational gifts, but also by channeling much more of the money (including, in my view, all general election spending) through the respective party committees, rather than through individual candidates' treasuries.

We need to strengthen the party organizations and their staffs, and recapture for them the campaign management functions that have been parceled out to independent firms which tend to operate with a fine disdain for the role of party and policy in government. We need to devise ways to make television—the prime medium of political communication—somewhat more sensitive to the claims of the parties to be a regular part of the political dialogue, and to protect the vital institution of the nominating convention from being distorted by the demands of the television cameras.

All these reforms would help, I believe, but they would not accomplish the invigoration of responsible party government unless they were accompanied by a genuine increase in the participation by the public in party affairs. The cure for the ills of democracy truly is more democracy; our parties are weak principally because we do not use them. To be strong and responsible, our parties must be representative; and they can be no more representative than our participation allows. Millions more of us need to get into partisan political activity.

We need also to become somewhat more reflective about what we do with our votes. We need to ask ourselves what it is that we want government to accomplish, and which candidate, which party comes closest to espousing that set of goals. . . .

Finally, we need to examine some of our habits. It seems to me we should ask, before splitting a ticket, what it is we hope to accomplish by dividing between the parties the responsibility for government of our country, our state or our community. Do we think there is no difference between the parties? Do we distrust them both so thoroughly that we wish to set them against each other? Do we think one man so superior in virtue and wisdom that he must be put in office, no matter who accompanies him there? Why are we splitting our tickets? My guess is that, if we asked those questions, we would more often be inclined to give a temporary grant of power to one party at a time, rather than dividing responsibility so skillfully between the parties that neither can govern. If we were willing to risk this strategy, knowing that we would be able to throw the rascals out if they failed, we might even discover to our amazement that they are not always rascals.

Diagnosing
The Body Politic

During the past decade, a striking convergence of opinion has taken place among both conservatives and liberals who analyze the present condition and future prospects of government in American society. Liberals, who since the emergence of the welfare state in the 1930s have generally supported the expansion of centralized governmental control over the economy, have become somewhat less sanguine about this process. If the institutions of laissez-faire capitalism could be callous and insensitive toward the individual, so, too, it seems are the regulatory agencies of the welfare state, in which the instruments of domination have become more pervasive.

Conservatives, long critical of the welfare state, have enjoyed greater influence than ever before by concentrating their attack upon the excesses of bureaucratic government. Peter F. Drucker, professor of management at the Claremont Graduate School in California, provides a scathing indictment of many liberal assumptions about "big government" in the following selection. He urges a deliberate strategy of "reprivatization" to restore vitality to the system.

Richard N. Goodwin, former speech writer and special assistant to Presidents Kennedy and Johnson, echoes many of Drucker's concerns. He, too, deplores the centralization of authority which, since the Great Depression, has expanded official governmental power in Washington at the expense of private, voluntary groups and local political institutions. Goodwin calls for a program of decentralization to "enlarge the sense and reality of individual relevance and participation" in the decision-making process. "Both burden and enterprise," he concludes, "must be shifted into units of action small enough to allow for more intimate personal contact and numerous enough to widen the outlets for direct participation and control."

Selection 1. Peter F. Drucker

Government surely has never been more prominent than today. The most despotic government of 1900 would not have dared probe into the pri-

From Peter F. Drucker, "The Sickness of Government," *The Public Interest* (Winter, 1969) pp. 3–23. Reprinted by permission of the author.

vate affairs of its citizens as income tax collectors now do routinely in the freest society. Even the tsar's secret police did not go in for the security investigations we now take for granted. Nor could any bureaucrat of 1900 have imagined the questionnaires that governments now expect businesses, universities, or citizens to fill out in ever-mounting number and ever-increasing detail. At the same time, government has everywhere become the largest employer in the society.

Government is certainly all-pervasive. But is it truly strong? Or is it only big?

There is mounting evidence that government is big rather than strong; that it is fat and flabby rather than powerful; that it costs a great deal but does not achieve much. There is mounting evidence also that the citizen less and less believes in government and is increasingly disenchanted with it. Indeed, government is sick—and just at the time when we need a strong, healthy, and vigorous government. . . .

The disenchantment with government cuts across national boundaries and ideological lines. It is as prevalent in Communist as in democratic societies, as common in white as in nonwhite countries. This disenchantment may well be the most profound discontinuity in the world around us. It marks a sharp change in mood and attitude between this generation and its predecessors. For seventy years or so—from the 1890s to the 1960s—mankind, especially in the developed countries, was hypnotized by government. We were in love with it and saw no limits to its abilities, or to its good intentions. . . . Anything that anyone felt needed doing during this period was to be turned over to government—and this, everyone seemed to believe, made sure that the job was already done. . . .

Disenchantment

But now our attitudes are in transition. We are rapidly moving to doubt and distrust of government and, in the case of the young, even to rebellion against it. We still, if only out of habit, turn social tasks over to government. We still revise unsuccessful programs over and over again, and assert that nothing is wrong with them that a change in procedures or a "competent administrator" will not cure. But we no longer really believe these promises when we reform a bungled program for the third time. Who, for instance, any longer believes that administrative changes in the foreign aid program of the United States (or of the United Nations) will really produce rapid world-wide development? Who really believes that the War on Poverty will vanquish poverty in the cities? Who in France believes that one more commission on administrative reform will really change the system? Or who, in Russia, really believes that a new program of incentives will make the collective farm productive? . . .

We expected miracles—and that always produces disillusionment. Government, it was widely believed (though only subconsciously) would produce a great many things for nothing. Cost was thought to be a function of who did something rather than of what was being attempted. There is little doubt, for instance, that the British, in adopting the "free health service," believed that medical care would cost nothing. . . . At the least, everyone expected that under a "free" health service the taxes of the rich would pay for the health care of the poor. But there never are enough rich people around to carry the burden of any general service. . . .

Abolishing "Vested Interests"

This belief has been, in effect, only one facet of a much more general illusion from which the educated and the intellectuals in particular have suffered: that by turning tasks over to government, conflict and decision would be made to go away. Once the "wicked private interests" had been eliminated, a decision as to the right course of action would be rational and automatic. There would be neither selfishness nor political passion. Belief in government was thus largely a romantic escape from politics and from responsibility . . . .

There is still a good deal of resistance to the responsibility of politics, and resentment of the burden of political desicion. Indeed, the young today want to "drop out" altogether—in a frightening revival of the hostility to responsibility that made an earlier young generation, forty years ago, so receptive to totalitarian promises and slogans. But no one, least of all the young, believes any longer that the conflicts, the decisions, the problems would be eliminated by turning things over to government. Government, on the contrary, has itself become one of the wicked "vested interests" for the young.

A Case of Nonperformance

The greatest factor in the disenchantment with government is that government has not performed. The record over these last thirty or forty years has been dismal. Government has proven itself capable of doing only two things with great effectiveness. It can wage war. And it can inflate the currency. Other things it can promise, but only rarely accomplish. Its record as an industrial manager, in the satellite countries of Eastern Europe as well as in the nationalized industries of Great Britian, has been unimpressive. . . .

The best we get from government in the welfare state is competent mediocrity. More often we do not even get that; we get incompetence such as we would not tolerate in an insurance company. . . . It is true in education. It is true in transportation. And the more we expand the welfare state, the less capable even of routine mediocrity does it seem to become. . . .

. . .During the past three decades, federal payments to the big cities have increased almost a hundred-fold for all kinds of programs, whereas results from this incredible dollar-flood are singularly unimpressive. What *is* impressive is the administrative incompetence. We now have ten times as many government agencies concerned with city problems as we had in 1939. We have increased by a factor of thousand or so the number of reports and papers that have to be filled out before anything can be done in the city. . . . As James Reston reported in *The New York Times* (November 23, 1966), there were then 170 different federal aid programs on the books, financed by over 400 separate appropriations and administered by 21 federal departments and agencies aided by 150 Washington bureaus and over 400 regional offices. . . .

362

Power Without Policy

Modern government has become ungovernable. There is no government today that can still claim control of its bureaucracy and of its various agencies. Government agencies are all becoming autonomous, ends in themselves, and directed by their own desire for power, their own narrow vision rather than by national policy.

This is a threat to the basic capacity of government to give direction and leadership. Increasingly, policy is fragmented, and execution is governed by the inertia of the large bureaucratic empires, rather than by policy. . . . As a result the Welfare State cannot set priorities. It cannot concentrate its tremendous resources—and therefore does not get anything done. . . .

Not so long ago, policy control by the policital organs of government could be taken for granted. Of course . . . a Franklin Roosevelt or a Winston Churchill could get things done that weaker men could not have accomplished. But this was, people generally believed, because they had the courage of strong convictions, the willingness to lay down bold and effective policies, the ability to mobilize public vision. Today, a ''strong'' president or a ''strong'' prime minister is not a man of strong policies; he is the man who knows how to make the lions of the bureaucracy do his bidding. . . .

This growing disparity between apparent power and actual lack of control is perhaps the greatest crisis of government. We are very good at creating administrative agencies. But no sooner are they called into being than they become ends in themselves, acquire their own constituency as well as a ''vested right'' to grants from the treasury, continuing support by the taxpayer, and immunity to political direction. No sooner, in other words, are they born than they defy public will and public policy. . . .

What Government Cannot Do

Yet never before has strong, effective, truly performing government been needed more than it is in this dangerous world of ours. Never before has it been needed more than in our pluralist society. Never before has it been needed more than in the present-day world economy.

We need government as the central institution that expresses the common will and the common vision, and enables each organization to make its own best contribution to society and citizen while expressing common beliefs and common values. We need strong, effective governments in the international sphere so that we can make the sacrifices of sovereignty needed to give us working supranational institutions for world society and world economy. We cannot wait until we have new political theory or until we fully understand this pluralist society of ours. . . .

Certain things are inherently difficult for government. Being by design a protective institution, it is not good at innovation. It cannot really abandon anything. The moment government undertakes anything, it becomes entrenched and permanent. Better administration will not alter this. Its inability to innovate is grounded in government's legitimate and necessary function as society's protective and conserving organ.

A government activity, a government installation, and government employment become immediately built into the political process itself. This holds true whether we talk of a declining industry—such as the nationalized British coal mines or the government-owned railroads of Europe and Japan. It holds equally true of Communist countries. . . .

The inability of government to abandon anything is not limited to the economic sphere. . . . The same inability to abandon applies to research projects supported by government. It holds true as soon as government supports the arts. Every beneficiary of a government program immediately becomes a "constituent." He immediately organizes himself for effective political action and for pressure on the decision-maker. . . .

Welfare, Farms, and Depressed Areas

Nothing in history, for instance, can compare in futility with those prize activities of the American government, its welfare policies and its farm policies. Both policies are largely responsible for the disease they are supposed to cure. We have known this for quite some time—in the case of the farm program since before World War II, in the case of the welfare program certainly since 1950.

The problem of the urban poor is undoubtedly vast. No city in history has ever been able to absorb an influx of such magnitude as the American cities have had to absorb since the end of World War II. Wherever it happened in the past, there was the same collapse of family, community, and local government. . . . The influx of almost 2 million rural Negroes and Puerto Ricans into New York City alone, in less than a fifteen-year period, . . . is unprecedented in the history of cities.

But we certainly could not have done worse if we had done nothing at all. In fact, the nineteenth-century cities that did nothing, did better.

And so, these last twenty years, has São Paulo in Brazil, which, inundated by similar floods of rural, illiterate Negroes, fresh from serfdom, did nothing—and is in better shape than New York City.

Our welfare policies were not designed to meet this problem. They were perfectly rational—and quite effective—as measures for the temporary relief of competent people who were unemployed only because of the catastrophe of the Great Depression. Enacted in the mid-1930s, the relief policies had essentially finished their job by 1940. But being government programs, they could not be abandoned. Far too massive a bureaucracy had been built. The emotional investment in these programs and in their slogan had become far too great. They had become "symbols" of the "New Deal."

Small wonder, then, that we reached for them when the entirely different problems of the 1950s arose, that is, when the rural Negro moved into the core city in large numbers. And small wonder that these programs did not work, that instead they aggravated the problem and increased the helplessness, the dependence, the despair of the Negro masses. But all we could do when relief failed to relieve was to double the budget and to double the number of people engaged in filling out forms.

The farm program tells the same story. It was designed—also in the 1930s—to save the family farmer and to restore his economic and social health. Instead it has subsidized his replacement by large, heavily capitalized and highly productive "industrial farms." This may well be a more desirable result than the one the farm program was meant—and is still meant—to produce. But it was abysmal failure in terms of the program's announced objectives. Yet the program goes on, with an increased budget, and increasingly perverse consequences. . . .

Government and Mismanagement

Government is a poor manager. It is, of necessity, concerned with procedure, just as it is also, of necessity, large and cumbersome. Government is properly conscious that it administers public funds and must account for every penny. It has no choice but to be "bureaucratic"—in the common usage of the term. Every government is, by definition, a "government of paper forms." This means inevitably high cost. . . . And the reason is not just "bureaucracy" and red tape; it is a much sounder one. A "little dishonesty" in government is a corrosive disease. . . . To fear corruption in government is not irrational. This means, however, that government "bureaucracy"—and its consequent high costs—cannot be eliminated. Any government that is not a "government of paper forms" degenerates rapidly into a mutual looting society. . . .

We have built elaborate safeguards to protect the administrative structure within government against the political process. This is the purpose of every civil service. But although this protects the going machinery from the distortions and pressures of politics, it also protects the incumbents in the agencies from the demands of performance. . . .

We can—and must—greatly improve the efficiency of government. There is little reason these days to insist on "100 per cent audit," for instance. Modern sampling methods based on probability mathematics actually give us better control by inspecting a small percentage of the events. But we need something much more urgently: the clear definition of the results a policy is expected to produce, and the ruthless examination of results against these expectations. This, in turn, demands that we spell out in considerable detail what results are expected rather than content ourselves with promises and manifestos. . . .

We may even go further—though only a gross optimist would expect this today. We may build into government an automatic abandonment process. Instead of starting with the assumption that any program, any agency, and any activity is likely to be eternal, we might start out with the opposite assumption: that each is short-lived and temporary. . . . We may, let us hope, eventually build into government the capacity to appraise results and systematically to abandon yesterday's tasks.

Yet such measures will still not convert government into a "doer." They will not alter the main lesson of the last fifty years: *government is not a "doer."*

What Government Can Be

The purpose of government is to make fundamental decisions, and to make them effectively. The purpose of government is to focus the political energies of society. It is to dramatize issues. It is to present fundamental choices. The purpose of government, in other words, is to govern. This, as we have learned in other institutions, is incompatible with "doing." Any attempt to combine government with "doing" on a large scale paralyzes the decision-making capacity.

There is reason today why soldiers, civil servants, and hospital administrators look to business management for concepts, principles, and practices. For business, during the last thirty years, has had to face, on a much smaller scale, the problem that government now faces: the incompatibility between "governing" and "doing." Business management learned that the two have to be separated, and that the top organ, the decision-maker, has to be detached from "doing." Otherwise he does not make decisions, and the "doing" does not get done either.

In business this goes by the name of "decentralization." The term is misleading. It implies a weakening of the central organ, the top management of a business. The true purpose of decentralization, however, is to make the center, the top management of business, strong and capable of performing the central, the top-management task. The purpose is to make it possible for top management to concentrate on decision-making and direction, to slough off the "doing" to operating managements, each with its own mission and goals, and with its own sphere of action and autonomy.

If this lesson were applied to government, the other institutions of society would then rightly become the "doers." "Decentralization" applied to government would not be just another form of "federalism" in which local rather than central government discharges the "doing" tasks. It would rather be a systematic policy of using the other, *the nongovernmental* institutions of the society—the hospital as well as the university, business as well as labor unions—for the actual "doing," i.e., for performance, operations, execution.

Such a policy might more properly be called "reprivatization." The tasks that flowed to government in the last century, because the family could not discharge them, would be turned over to the new, nongovernmental institutions that have sprung up and grown these last sixty to seventy years.

Reprivatization

Reprivatization would give us a different society from any our *social* theories now assume. In these theories, government does not exist. It is outside of society. Under reprivatization, government would become the central social institution. Political theory and social theory, for the last two hundred and fifty years, have been separate. If we applied to government and to society what we have learned about organization these last fifty years, the two would again come together. The nongovernmental institutions—university, business, and hospital, for instance—would be seen as organs for the accomplishment for results. Government would be seen as society's resource for the determination of major objectives, and as the "conductor" of social diversity....

Reprivatization, therefore, may create social structures that are strikingly similar, though the laws in respect to ownership differ greatly from one country to another and from one institution to another. *What they would have in common is a principle of performance rather than a principle of authority.* In all of them the autonomous institution created for the performance of a major social task would be the " doer." Government would become increasingly the decision-maker, the vision-maker. It would try to figure out how to structure a given political objective so as to make it attractive to one of the autonomous institutions. It would, in other words, be the "conductor" that tries to think through what each instrument is best designed to do. . . .

Toward a New Politics

We do not face a "withering away of the state." On the contrary, we need a vigorous, a strong, and a very active government. But we do face a choice between big but impotent government and a government that is strong because it confines itself to decision and direction and leaves the "doing" to others. We do not face a "return of laissez-faire" in which the economy is left alone. The economic sphere cannot and will not be considered to lie outside the public domain. But the choices of economy—as well as for all other sectors—are no longer *either* complete governmental indifference or complete governmental control. In all major areas, we have a new choice: an organic diversity in which institutions are used to do what they are best equipped to do. In this society all sectors are "affected with the public interest," whereas in each sector a specific institution, under its own management and dedicated to its own job, emerges as the organ of action and performance. . . .

Reprivatization will not weaken government. Indeed, its main purpose is to restore strength to sick government. We cannot go much further along the road on which government has been traveling these last fifty years. All we can get this way is more bureaucracy but not more performance. We can impose higher taxes, but we cannot get dedication, support, and faith on the part of the public. Government can gain greater girth and more weight, but it cannot gain strength or intelligence. All that can happen, if we keep on going the way we have been going, is a worsening sickness of government and growing disenchantment with it. And this is the prescription for tyranny, that is , for a government organized against its own society. . . .

Selection 2 Richard N. Goodwin

Centralization of Power

Over the past several decades much of the world has been experiencing the growing power and dominion of centralized national leadership. The word "nation" itself, having once described a loosely governed confederation of territories or people, now increasingly refers to a fixed geographical area where a central authority assumes mounting responsibility for a range of social and economic activities formerly left to localities, tribal groups, or individuals. . . .

This process of centralization has not been confined by ideology. It has occurred under democracy and dictatorship; it has been guided by capitalism and socialism, Communism and Fascism. For it is imposed by the

From Richard N. Goodwin, "The Shape of American Politics." Copyright © 1967 by Richard N. Goodwin. Reprinted by permission of the Sterling Lord Agency, Inc. This article first appeared in *Commentary*, June, 1967.

fusion of technology with the psychology of power. In making the concentration of power possible and expanding its uses, technology helps to liberate more forceful and sweeping impulses in those individuals who seek authority.

The process is global and differently shaped by the innumerable varieties of culture and circumstance. My discussion, however, will be restricted to the United States. It is what I know, and it best illuminates the most troubling political fact of our age: that the growth in central power has been accompanied by a swift and continual diminution in the significance of the individual citizen, transforming him from a wielder into an object of authority. . . .

The growth of central, or federal, power in America during the past few decades has been phenomenal. Only thirty-five years ago, Mencken could write: "The rewards of the Presidency are mostly trashy. . . ." He describes a typical Presidential day: "All day long the right hon. lord of us all sits listening to bores and quacks. Anon a Secretary rushes in with the news that some eminent movie actor . . . has died, and the President must seize a pen and write a telegram of condolence to the widow. Once a year he is repaid by receiving a telegram on his birthday from King George. . . . It takes four days hard work to concoct a speech without a sensible word in it. . . . Four Senators get drunk and try to neck a lady politician. . . . The Presidential automobile runs over a dog. It rains."

We still mock our Presidents, sometimes brutally, but not because they are futile, comic, or unimportant. The springs of today's satire are fear and rage rather than condescension. For the target is immense.

The federal govenment spends about one-seventh of our national wealth and creates more of it. Between 1950 and 1960, nine out of ten new jobs were created by the public and the private not-for-profit sectors, and only one out of ten by private enterprise. Today, one-third of the entire labor force works for someone other than a profit-making institution. The towering apparatus of scientific and technological research which is remaking our society, and causing apprehension in Europe, is increasingly fueled by federal funds. It is the government, not private business, that is held responsible for the condition of the economy: credited with prosperity; blamed for recession and inflation; expected simultaneously to make the country prosper, end unemployment, and keep prices down. . . .

But today's government is not only expected to maintain prosperity; it is also expected to ensure justice. . . . Social ills, from benighted cities to polluted air, are regarded as the charge of government; and Washington is also expected to lead the way out of the automobile-choked tunnels in which we are incarcerating ourselves.

Augmenting the swelling domestic authority of government, there is the conduct of foreign policy, which gives to a few men, often acting in partial secrecy, the power to commit our country to action in all parts of the world, send hundreds of thousands to fight in distant lands, and entangle the resources and honor of the nation in adventures, promises, programs, and acts in every continent. This control culminates in the numbly familiar power to decree our destruction—a power less real because it is beyond the grasp of consciousness, but present and infusing all the other acts of government with majesty and terror.

We usually associate all this centralization with the Presidency, both because the power of that office has increased disproportionately and because the President is most visible to our expectations and our rage: we find a personal target more congenial than an institutional one. Most of our discontents are therefore directed at an individual's defects of character, temperament, or intelligence, rather than at the structure which permits such qualities to rule or, at least, leaves a great deal of our welfare in the hands of chance. The more that power is concentrated, the greater the stakes on the always obscure gamble of selection.

Yet the Presidency is not the only part of our government whose power has grown. The Supreme Court helped lead the social revolution of the Negro: an astounding role for an institution whose previous incursions into the political process had nearly always been to check the affirmative action of government. . . . Sharing in the general euphoria of power, the nine justices of the Supreme Court make major political decisions, unresponsive to the democratic process, in secret meetings on Friday afternoons. Both the number and the scope of such decisions steadily mount. Liberal critics have generally approved this development because they approve the content of the decisions, while the fundamental reshaping of an important institution seems not to trouble them. But it is a transformation which almost certainly will come back to plague us as judicial personnel and social attitudes change, and as an institution which has become more and more political develops an even greater sensitivity to transitory shifts in the political temper.

Congress, too, shares in the mounting power of the federal government, exercising its authority to frustrate the will of the President, or to collaborate with him in denying redress. Congressional action is often spoken of as negative power, a sort of reverse veto. But that is because we are trapped in the liberal rhetoric which defines positive action as increased spending, greater regulation, or new programs. . . .

Causes: Historical and Psychological

The reality of increased federal power is undeniable. The events and circumstances which have created it are more tangled and ambiguous. Most obvious is the necessity for federal leadership in the conduct of foreign affairs, accepted by even the most conservative. Thus, as America became a global power with swiftly spreading burdens and ambitions, government waxed. Our relations with other countries, deeply and even mortally consequential in themselves, inevitably seep into a hundred areas of national life, shaping the structure of our industrial system, setting priorities for education and scholarship, pushing us toward technology and away from other pursuits. . . .

In some measure the increase in central power is atributable to the converging flow of historical and psychological factors. The New Deal, out of necessity, created large new authority for government. More importantly, it led citizens to expect a great deal more than they previously had from Washington. Once this process had begun, it could not easily be arrested. . . . As demands increased, the central government was compelled to seek fresh authority. Those who chose conservative principle over political response met the fate of Taft and Goldwater.

Strengthening this domestic "revolution of rising expectations" is the natural tendency of political leaders to add to their power, to relish the "anguish" of decision, and to resent any effort to oppose their will. . . . Our system is deliberately and instinctively designed to restrain this ominous psychological inclination. The great number of institutional "checks and balances" are combined with less formal limitations grounded in national traditions and values, political realities, popular sentiment, and the power of the press to criticize and expose. These are often the most potent restraints, not only limiting what a leader can do, but what he would think of doing. They are accepted and even cherished by men whose indoctrination in the American system is stronger than inner drives to power. . . .

The price of this system is often inaction, or very slow progress. For radical and swift changes require great and concentrated authority, which, in turn, is extraordinarily dangerous in the wrong hands. We can see today how the concentration of power over foreign affairs in a single man—long a goal of that liberal thought which was contemptuous of congressional conservatism—has dissolved the normal checks of our institutional structure. And these restraints have been neutralized precisely in the area where political checks—public opinion and the press—are weakest, poorly informed, most prone to emotional reaction (especially since personal economic interests are rarely affected in any obvious way), and most willing, in resigned bafflement at complexities, to accept Presidential direction on faith. . . .

This interlocking psychological and historical process has been given a greater momentum by our increasing ability to shape events from the center. Economics and, to a far lesser extent, other social sciences have enabled us to achieve an improved mastery over the operations of society. We now try to control economic conditions in every section of the country, using newly refined tools of fiscal and monetary policy. . . . Mass communications and swift transportation have enabled government to bring its authority and assistance to bear in a detailed and specific manner, allowing it to construct the rapidly responsive bureaucracy hitherto thought impossible in a nation of continental dimensions, and encouraging the natural tendency of local officials to turn to the federal government. . . . Computerization of government, the next stage, will increase the possibilities of central control and influence and, unless we make some fairly radical structural changes, will in fact bring about such an increase. . . .

Access and communication, however, also work in reverse, occasionally yielding a political influence to disadvantaged groups greater than their economic and social power. . . . For example, the civil-rights movement owes much of its impact to the television cameras which displayed the cruelties of Bull Connor and the violence of Selma to an audience for whom racial injustice in the South had seemed as remote as apartheid in South Africa. . . .

The Dissolution of Alternatives

These varied forces contributing to central power have a unifying theme: The mutually reinforcing concurrence of national demand and expectation with the assertion of power and the capacity to exercise it. There is, however, a more subtle, pervasive, and probably more significant factor. It is the gradual dissolution of alternative outlets for grievances, demands, ambitions, and inner needs. It is as if many small magnets and a single large one were scattered on a floor. If the smaller magnets steadily lost their force, particles would break away and take their place in the stronger field of force. Something like that has happened to American political life.

There are, after all, many ways for a man to change the conditions of his life or modify his environment. He can act through local government, social institutions, and private organizations. Or he can gain access to opportunities which do not rest on official action—by, for example, "going West" to an unsettled frontier.

All these possibilities have been dissolving. Large-scale opportunity outside settled institutions began to disappear when the West was closed. After that, migrants and minorities sought a path into society through unskilled labor. Its virtual elimination in modern times may prove as momentous an event as the end of the frontier. . . . Today it is no longer possible to avoid conflict with society while gathering strength to force an entrance. The confrontation must be direct and immediate. . . .

More important to the growth of central power than the destruction of frontiers is the dwindling influence of local government and private associations. This erosion has been produced by two major social changes. The first, and most obvious, is the enormous resistance and complexity of many modern problems, requiring an antagonist of great force and resources. The second is a loss of connection: the fraying of human, ethnic, and territorial bonds between the individual and the disembodied structures which surround him. In consequence, the individual loses confidence in the capacity of local structures to modify the political conditions of existence, a self-fulfilling distrust which accelerates the weakening process. Diminishing faith turns people, not away from authority, but toward a more powerful center. This is certainly one of the reasons that totalitarianism finds its moment of opportunity at times of relative chaos.

Added to the many social and psychological conditions which have assaulted these historic structures are the growth in population (diluting participation in local government) and our fantastic mobility (making it hard to retain local allegiances). Therefore, individuals again turn toward the central government where, it seems, grievances and hopes can be effectively aired, and to which citizens in all parts of the country, even the rootless and displaced, feel some connection.

These weakened structures confront a social order whose growing rigidity closes off many traditional non-governmental outlets for change and for those personal ambitions which depend on social justice. The power of large corporations, the sanctity of the search for profits, the desirability of swift economic growth (we measure our success by our Gross National Product), and the exaltation of technology, are all virtually beyond serious challenge. . . . Since so much of our system is fixed, it is necessary to turn to the one authority still capable of channeling our institutions, through coercion or guidance, toward desired change: the central government. . . .

Significance of the Individual

Central power is not in itself contemptible or hazardous, but must be judged by the extent to which it enlarges or constricts the possiblities of individual existence. Difficult as it is to untangle relationships and sources, we can be certain that rising central power has been accompanied by the diminishing significance of political man. In part this human lessening flows from the increase in central power itself; in part from the changes contributing to that increase; and, in incalculable part, from the general nature of the modern world.

The individual's confidence in his own significance rests on the share of mastery he possesses over his life and environment. . . . As political affairs become more centralized and as personal, group, and local responsibilities are absorbed, this vital sense of mastery is eroded. For, in fact, the individual's ability to control circumstances is diminished.

This is not simply a political phenomenon. It saturates our philosophical, technological, and social environment; and even as politics, it cannot be discussed apart from the commanding values of the time. These values differ radically from those which in one form or another have been dominant since the Renaissance—a historical moment, Michelet explained, that was characterized by "man's discovering of the world and of man." . . . There was an effort to comprehend the essence of man, along with a search for a fresh synthesis of the new "spiritual individual" with the world around him. There was a growing faith that incomplete human understanding resulted from an imperfect knowledge we could labor to complete.

One of the last glories of the Renaissance, and one of its destroyers, Albert Einstein, when faced with theories that assumed the essential role of chance in describing the existence of basic units of the material world, asked: "Do you really believe God resorts to dice playing?" He spoke in the tradition which encouraged the conviction that the free play of the inquiring mind would lead to a complete and harmonious account of reality. . . . Now the belief in the possibility of such unity and wholeness is fading. We live, instead, at a time of fragmentation and dissection, in search of the components of our sensible world. The concept of God as a source of moral authority dissolves into mystical generalizations or disappears. Efforts at systematic philosophy are scorned, ignored, or become the province of esoteric technicians. Saint Augustine and Spinoza become Norman O. Brown and Marshal McLuhan. . . .

Frustration and Alienation

Whether or not the foregoing description has psychological and philosophical validity, it provides an analytic lens through which we can view our political and social institutions. More conservative than science or thought, they still reflect—as already suggested in the above account of the forces behind rising central power—the more profound contemporary currents of fragmentation and dissolution. Family ties stretch and break as the gap between the experience of the generations widens, and as more spacious possibilities of geographical and occupational mobility remove the pressure to reconcile natural hostilities and make it easier to indulge them. The community disappears, as the comprehensible unit of living blends

372

into the huge, accidental monstrosities our cities have become. Science describes our world in terms beyond all but the most specialized understanding, dissolving control in mystery. . . . Cities and technology, production and population, grow and change, powered by forces which seem beyond the control, and even the desire, of the individual person. A handful of men in remote capitals hold our existence hostage to their wisdom or impulse or sanity. The small groups where we could once achieve a sense of belonging and of being needed, because we could encompass them with our knowledge and presence, are disappearing, while the activities they once guided—the life of a town and of its citizens—now seem hopelessly beyond their competence.

As these myriad enemies assault the private stronghold of influence and importance, alienation, rage, desperation, and a growing sense of futility increasingly scar our political life. Two principal forms of reaction emerge. Violent protests and extreme convictions reflect the frustration of many at their inability to assert their significance and to share in the enterprise of society. . . . The history of the civil-rights movement reveals how helplessness can drive the pursuit of unexceptionable goals toward violent rhetoric. "Black power" is more a cry of despair and a plea for attention than a signal for battle. Among larger numbers, less endowed with vitality and conviction, there is a rising determination to protect and conserve. They seek security for their present position in the face of receding confidence in their own ability to shape the future.

We see these basic impulses in manifold, sometimes terrifying, forms: more reasonably in the New Right and the New Left, irrationally violent among Minutemen and John Birchers, Black Muslims and Southern Secessionists. They are reflected in the compulsive search for a hero or an enemy, and in a deepening disgust with political life itself. . . . All these conflicting movements help serve the single purpose of giving the individuals who belong to them the inner sense of significance that comes from being a part of some larger purpose. They reveal how a feeling of impotence is charged with danger, polarizing groups and individuals and creating a nation of strangers, until even those with whom we sympathize glare at us across an impassable barrier of hostility. . . . The result is not merely extremism, but resignation and lassitude embodied in an unwillingness to face problems, make personal commitments, or to act until difficulties have all but overwhelmed us.

Thus, whatever our particular political positions, the one overriding goal of political life must be to help restore and strengthen that faith of the individual in himself which is the source of national direction and generosity of deed.

This may be an illusory goal. Perhaps the machine is already out of control, hurling us toward a future where we will all blend into some grotesque organism, our sensations absorbed by discordant sound and flashing light—where life itself is an endless "trip." Yet no one who pursues the profession of politics can permit himself to regard the goal as illusory, any more than a novelist can permit himself to believe that the form in which he works is obsolete. Politics alone cannot remedy a condition whose causes are so manifold. But it is a least partly a political task. . . .

Decentralization

As important as the content and direction of public policies are the methods and structures used to carry them out. Initially, the elaborate structure of American federalism mirrored the judgment that a great deal should be left to local authority. For decades we have been moving in the other direction. Not only is this a dangerous and, as I believe, a mistaken course, but it is becoming clearer that certain substantive objectives utterly depend upon fashioning fresh techniques. Modern poverty, for example, cannot be abolished by friendly edicts from remote officials, and even if it could, the result would be sterile, vacuous, and purely material.

The blended goal of structure and policy alike must be to meet specific ills through methods which can in themselves enlarge the sense and reality of individual relevance and participation. The way to accomplish this, at least on the political front, is through decentralization—by assisting and compelling states, communities, and private groups to assume a greater share of responsibility for collective action. In other words, both burden and enterprise must be shifted into units of action small enough to allow for more intimate personal contact ·and numerous enough to widen the outlets for direct participation and control. . . .

Although decentralization is designed to help combat the social and spiritual ills of fragmentation, it also responds to the fact that centralized bureaucracies tend to become increasingly ineffective and coercive in direct proportion to the scope and intricacy of the problem they are established to solve. . . . Now . . . we must apply complete technical and planning skills to wide-ranging difficulties. One need only look at the fantastic labyrinth of welfare programs, the monstrous incapacities of the Department of Health, Education and Welfare—operated by one of the best teams of executives in government—as well as the foreseeable futilities of the new Departments of Housing and Urban Development and Transportation, to realize that something is wrong with the old approach. . . .

Decentralization is not abdication. It is possible . . . to set standards for local action and by enforcing these standards to raise the level of performance. Different problems will call for different structures, requiring a great deal of political creativity and experiment. But there are common obstacles and methods of approach. . . . We are already doing this, to some extent, in programs ranging from the war against poverty to the construction of waste treatment plants on our rivers. (Standards, incidentally, can be educational rather than coercive. Often local groups are unaware of the dimensions of a problem, nor can they command the technical and intellectual resources necessary to devise solutions. . . .)

Another prospect for decentralization, and one closer to home, is the American city. We know that the problem of the cities is enormously complex. It is not one problem but a hundred: urban renewal and rehabilitation of rundown structures, new financing techniques and private development corporations, control of land speculation and new suburban slums, breaking up ghettos and giving people a place to play in, efficient transportation and mastery of the automobile. We may need to rebuild entire central cities or construct huge new satellite metropolises. The condition and future prospect of our cities are the greatest single threat to the quality of American life. Many who live in major urban areas are already the victims of conditions which confine, stifle, and degrade their daily existence to an extent unthinkable half a century ago. Nor is this a problem for the poor alone. They are the chief victims, but all must breathe the air, fight the traffic, do without nature, and worry about violence.

Instead of a scattered attack on particular problems, we must begin by asking what kind of city we want to live in, and what kind of city we want for our children. As we approach the problem on this spacious scale, we see immediately that uncontrolled growth and change must be replaced by long-range planning which encompasses the entire urban area across municipal and state lines. And we see, too, that the cities do not have the money to meet their problems.

I believe we should adopt a Marshall Plan approach to the problems of the American city. Resources on a large scale would be made available to those urban areas which prepared a comprehensive program for future development, embracing urban policies as diverse as land use, housing codes, tax structures, and water systems. The federal government could give technical assistance in planning, set certain standards, and ensure that the program was being carried forward. But the basic responsibility for decision and action would rest with the city and its people. This would not only help meet the more general imperatives of decentralization, but would provide a powerful incentive for the cooperation across historic political jurisdictions which is the condition of effective action.

There are many other areas in which decentralization is possible. Anti-poverty and job-retraining programs should be increasingly handed over to community groups instead of being drawn, as they now are, closer to the federal government. Aid to education might well be administered to a far larger degree by local boards, subject only to the most general standards. Instead of threatening to draft all young Americans for public service, we could encourage and finance a host of varied volunteer groups to perform public services at the state and community level in order to provide an outlet for those many citizens still anxious to find an answer to the question, "What can you do for your country?" Many federal installations and services could well be subject to greater local supervision. For example, we might establish local boards of directors for post offices, permitting the community to decide, within the limits of available resources, the kind of postal service they require, even hire and fire postmasters and, at least, to air their complaints.

Much of this will appear sloppy and chaotic. Some of it will certainly be confused. It is always easier to yearn for the illusory neatness of central direction and control, under the assumption that it is more effective. That assumption has often proved wrong in the past, and it must now be questioned across the board of federal activity. Even if we do add to confusion, that is a small price to pay for the benefits of decentralization. Confusion may even turn out to be creative. In fact, I cannot remember a single unconfused government organization that ever produced an important new idea.

I do not assume that proposals such as these will cure what Norman Mailer calls "the plague" of modern life or halt the flow toward fragmentation and futility. Politics is only part of the story. The values, ideas, and instincts of our modern condition may be too relentless to yield, even slightly, to leadership and political invention. Perhaps the changes required are far more convulsive and profound than most of us can formulate. As a practicing politician, I can only hope for and speak of those things which seem to reach toward the limits of foreseeable possibility.

THE AUTHORS

HENRY J. ABRAHAM (1921–   ), who was a member of the faculty of the University of Pennsylvania from 1949 to 1971, is currently Doherty Professor of Government and Foreign Affairs at the University of Virginia. A native of Germany, he has been a visiting professor at several universities in Europe as well as in America. His particular concern with the judicial process is reflected in his many books on this subject, including *The Judicial Process, Freedom and the Court, The Judiciary,* and, most recently, *Justices and Presidents.*

HENRY BROOKS ADAMS (1838–1918), the grandson of President John Quincy Adams and son of Charles Francis Adams, the diplomat, was an historian and philosopher. In *The Education of Henry Adams,* which won a Pulitzer Prize in 1919, he developed his theory that human institutions, like the human body, are subject to aging and decay. Among his other books were a nine-volume *History of the United States* and *Mont Saint Michel and Chartres,* a study of medieval life and art.

MARY ANTIN (1881–1949) was born in Polotzk, Russia, and emigrated to the United States in 1894. Her books, including *From Polotzk to Boston* (written in Yiddish), *The Promised Land,* and *They Who Knock at Our Gates,* dealt with the immigrant experience. She campaigned actively against proposals in Congress to pass restrictive immigration legisltaion.

DANIEL J. BOORSTIN (1914–   ) is director of the National Museum of History and Technology of the Smithsonian Institution in Washington, D.C. He has practiced law in addition to teaching history at Harvard, Swarthmore, and the University of Chicago, where he taught from 1944 until 1969. His many books include *The Lost World of Thomas Jefferson, The Genius of American Politics,* and the multi-volume study of *The Americans,* which won the Bancroft and the Francis Parkman Prizes.

WILLIAM BRADFORD (1590–1657) was governor of the Plymouth Colony for thirty of the first thirty-five years of its existence. Born in England, he migrated with the Puritans to Holland in 1609 and then sailed to America on the *Mayflower* in 1620. His *History of Plymouth Plantation, 1620–1647* contains the best account of the early days of the settlement; it was not published in full until 200 years after his death.

DAVID S. BRODER (1929–   ) is a syndicated columnist and a reporter for the *Washington Post.* He was previously with the *Congressional Quarterly,* the *Washington Star,* and the Washington bureau of *The New York Times.* In 1973 he received the Pulitzer Prize for journalism. He is the author of *Republican Establishment* and *The Party's Over.*

JAMES MacGREGOR BURNS (1918–   ) has been a member of the political science faculty at Williams College since 1941. He has also been active in politics, serving as a Massachusetts delegate to the Democratic national conventions from 1952 to 1964. He is the author of two major biographies of F.D.R., *Roosevelt: The Lion and the Fox,* which treats the New Deal period, and *Roosevelt: The Soldier of Freedom,* a study of the war years, which won the Pulitzer Prize and the National Book Award. Among his many other books are *Government by the People, Presidential Government: The Crucible of Leadership,* and *Uncommon Sense.*

WITTER BYNNER (1881–1968), a poet, lived in New York and Santa Fe, New Mexico, and several of his poems are about the Indians of the Southwest. He was elected Chancellor of the American Academy of Poetry, and in 1954 he received the Gold Medal of the Poetry Society of America. His writing spanned a period of more than fifty years and included *The Beloved Stranger, A Book of Plays, Indian Earth, Take Away the Darkness,* and *New Poems.*

EVE CARY is currently a staff attorney at the New York Civil Liberties Union, for which she has handled several women's-rights law suits. A graduate of the New York University Law School, she is a former editor of *Civil Liberties in New York* and of several handbooks for the American Civil Liberties Union, including *The Rights of Prisoners, The Rights of Poor People,* and *The Rights of Students.*

WILLA S. CATHER (1873–1947), a novelist, was born in Virginia and moved to frontier Nebraska when she was nine. From 1906 to 1912 she was managing editor of *McClure's Magazine*. Much of her best work, including *O Pioneers!* (1913), *My Antonia* (1918), and the Pulitzer Prize-winning *One of Ours* (1922), dealt with pioneer themes. Her later novels—*Death Comes to the Archbishop* (1927) and *Shadows on the Rock* (1931)—reflected her disillusionment with the modern world.

C. C. COFFIN was a correspondent for *Harper's New Monthly Magazine* in the late nineteenth century.

PADRAIC COLUM (1881–1972) was a poet, playwright, and popular author of young people's books. Born in Ireland, he was an original member of the group of Irish writers that brought fame to Dublin's Abbey Theatre. In 1914 he emigrated to the United States. His verse includes *Wild Earth* (1907) and *Collected Poems* (1953).

JAMES FENIMORE COOPER (1789–1851) grew up in Cooperstown, New York, a frontier village founded by his father. He began his literary career in 1820, and his novels soon made him the preeminent American literary figure of his day. Having trained as a seaman himself, he invented a new type of adventure story, the sea romance. Cooper wrote fifty books, but he is best known for his *Leatherstocking Tales* (*The Pioneers*, 1823; *The Last of the Mohicans*, 1826; *The Prairie*, 1827; *The Pathfinder*, 1840; and *The Deerslayer*, 1841), which trace the archetypal frontiersman from his youth through his prime, as he retreats from civilization, and finally into old age, as a trapper among the Great Plains Indians.

RAYMOND F. DASMANN (1919–   ) has been senior ecologist of the International Union for the Conservation of Nature in Morges, Switzerland, since 1970. He was previously a member of the Humboldt State College faculty for many years and an ecologist with the Conservation Foundation in Washington. Among his books are *Environmental Conservation, Destruction of California, A Different Kind of Country, Planet in Peril,* and *Ecological Principles for Economic Development.*

PETER F. DRUCKER (1909–   ) was born in Vienna, Austria, and came to the United States in 1937. He taught at Bennington College and was a professor of management at New York University for more than twenty years before assuming his current position as Clarke Professor of Social Sciences at the Claremont (California) Graduate School. He is the author of many books on management, economics, and the future, including *America's Next Twenty Years; Technology, Management and Society; Men, Ideas and Politics; The Age of Discontinuity;* and *Management.*

SAMUEL JAMES ERVIN, JR. (1896–   ) retired in 1974 after twenty years as U.S. Senator from North Carolina. He was a member of the Senate Armed Services Committee and the Judiciary Committee, and chairman of the Separation of Powers Subcommittee of the Government Operations Committee. He became a familiar national figure as chairman of the Senate Select Committee on Presidential Campaign Activities (the Watergate Committee). Prior to becoming a Senator, Ervin was a Congressman and a judge of the North Carolina Superior and Supreme Courts.

ALEXANDER FORBES (19th century) was an Englishman of a prominent family who spent approximately thirty years in Spanish America. Prior to 1825 he was engaged in the mercantile business in Buenos Aires. He then established the house of Barron, Forbes & Company, which became the largest mercantile concern on the Pacific Coast of Mexico. In addition to trade, the company engaged in the manufacture of cotton fabrics. He also operated the New Almaden quicksilver mine in Santa Clara County (California), from which he reaped huge profits. His history of California is one of the most detailed descriptions available of the period of the 1830s. Forbes retired to England in 1856.

BARRY M. GOLDWATER, JR. (1938–   ) has represented the 27th District of Southern California in the U.S. Congress since 1969. He is a member of the House Committee on Science and Astronautics and the Committee on Interstate and Foreign Commerce.

RICHARD N. GOODWIN (1931–   ), who received his law degree from Harvard, served as law clerk to Supreme Court Justice Frankfurter from 1958 to 1959. He was an assistant to John F. Kennedy when he was a U.S. Senator, and when Kennedy became President, Goodwin served as special counsel to the President, deputy assistant secretary of state for inter-American affairs, and special assistant to the President. He subsequently was a fellow at the Center for Advanced Studies at

Wesleyan University and a visiting professor at MIT. His books include *The Sower's Seed* and *Triumph of Tragedy: Reflections on Vietnam*.

JEAN GOTTMANN (1915–   ) was born in Russia and educated in Paris. A geographer, he was a member of the Institute for Advanced Study at Princeton and of the faculty at Johns Hopkins University. He became professor of geography at Oxford University in England in 1968 after teaching for many years at the University of Paris and École des Hautes Études in Paris. His findings as research director for the Twentieth Century Fund's study of megalopolis were published in 1961. He also authored *A Geography of Europe* and *The Significance of Territory*.

ALEXANDER HAMILTON (1755–1804), the first U.S. Secretary of the Treasury, was a leading supporter of a strong national government. With James Madison and John Jay, he authored *The Federalist Papers*, a series of eighty-five essays published in New York newspapers between 1787 and 1788. Appearing under the signature *Publius*, they supported the new Constitution then before the states for ratification.

BRET HARTE (1836–1902) was born in Albany, New York, and moved to California as a young man. He became the first editor of the *Overland Monthly*, for which he wrote several short stories about life in the mining camps, including "The Luck of Roaring Camp" and "The Outcasts of Poker Flat." His humorous poem, "Plain Language from Truthful James," commonly known as "The Heathen Chinee," appeared in 1870. Harte served briefly as a consul in Germany and Scotland, and he lived in London from 1885 until his death in 1902.

KARL HESS (1923–   ) has been, at various times, a journalist, politician, businessman, and welder. He served as press editor of *Newsweek* from 1950 to 1955, and he was one of the founders of the conservative *National Review*. He drafted the platform for the Republican National Convention of 1960, served as director of special projects at the American Enterprise Institute for Public Policy Research in Washington, and was chief speech writer for Senator Barry Goldwater in his 1964 Presidential campaign. Partly as a result of U.S. actions in Vietnam, he became disillusioned with politics and advocated resistance to the draft and to paying taxes. A leading spokesman now for the "New Right," or Libertarians, he is the author of *The Death of Politics* and co-author of *The End of the Draft*.

JOHN HIGHAM (1920–   ) is the John Martin Vincent Professor of History at Johns Hopkins University. He previously taught at UCLA, Rutgers, and the University of Michigan, where he was Moses Coit Tyler University Professor and Chairman of the Program in American Culture. His *Strangers in the Land: Patterns of American Nativism, 1860–1925*, won the Dunning Prize of the American Historical Association; his new book on immigrants, *Send These to Me: Jews and Other Immigrants in Urban America*, is scheduled for publication in 1975. His other books include *The Reconstruction of American History*, *History*, and *Writing American History: Essays on Modern Scholarship*. He recently served as President of the Organization of American Historians.

NATHAN HUGGINS (1927–   ) became professor of history at Columbia University in 1970, after previously teaching at California State College, Long Beach, Lake Forest College, and the University of Massachusetts, Boston. He also served as president of the Museum of Afro-American History in Boston. He is the author of *Protestants Against Poverty* and *Harlem Renaissance*, and co-editor of *Key Issues of the Afro-American Experience*.

JOHN B. JACKSON (1909–   ) holds a joint appointment from the University of California, Berkeley, where he is adjunct professor in the College of Environmental Design, and from Harvard University, where he is lecturer in the Visual and Environmental Studies Department. From 1952 to 1968 he was editor and publisher of *Landscape Magazine*. He is the author of *Landscapes* and *American Space*.

EDWARD JOHNSON (1598–1672) was a prominent figure in the Massachusetts Bay Colony. Born in England, he came to America in 1630, traded briefly with the Indians, and returned to England in 1631. However, in 1636 he returned with his family to Massachusetts, where he was one of the founders of the new town of Woburn. He remained a leader of Woburn, sometimes representing the town in the General Court, until his death in 1672. His *Wonder-working Providence of Sion's Savior in New England*, published in 1653, was an attempt to demonstrate God's approval of the Massachusetts settlements; it is the oldest published history of the early years of the colony.

ALVIN M. JOSEPHY, JR. (1915–   ) has had a varied career as a screen writer, radio-station news director, and editor. After serving as editor of *Time* magazine from 1951 to 1960, he became vice president and senior editor of American Heritage Publishing Company. He has been active in many organizations concerned with the American Indians, and served as a commissioner of the Indian Arts and Crafts Board, a consultant to the National Congress of American Indians, and as member of the Council of Indian Affairs. A prolific writer, he is the author of *Uncommon Valor, The Patriot Chiefs, The Nez Perce Indians and the Opening of the Northwest, The Indian Heritage of America,* and *Red Power,* among others.

HORACE M. KALLEN (1882–1974) was a philosopher and a leader in the adult education movement in America. Born in Germany, he came to the United States as a small chld. In 1917 he helped found the New School of Social Research in New York City, where he taught philosophy for many years. In addition to several influential essays on immigration, Americanization, and democracy, Kallen authored many books, including *The Structure of Lasting Peace; Education, the Machine and the Worker; Individualism; A Free Society;* and *Americanism and Its Makers.*

JAMES J. KILPATRICK, JR. (1920–   ) was a newspaperman with the Richmond, Virginia, *News-Leader* from 1941 until 1967, serving as reporter, chief editorial writer, and editor. He received the Sigma Delta Chi award for editorial writing in 1954. For the last ten years he has been associated with *The National Review,* and he is a frequent television commentator. He is author of *The Sovereign States, The Smut Peddlers,* and *The Southern Case for School Segregation.*

PHILIP B. KURLAND (1921–   ) is both a practicing lawyer and the William R. Kenan Professor at the University of Chicago Law School. Since 1967 he has been chief consultant for the subcommittee on separation of powers for the U.S. Senate Judiciary Committee. He has argued and briefed many cases for the Supreme Court, and in 1960 founded *The Supreme Court Review,* which he edits. He has authored more than 100 articles in law reviews and other journals, as well as several books, including *Frankfurter: Of Law and Life; The Supreme Court and the Constitution; Politics, The Constitution and the Warren Court;* and *Mr. Justice Frankfurter and the Constitution.* He was a contributor to the first Course by Newspaper.

LEONARD LEVY (1923–   ), who was born in Canada, is currently William W. Clary Professor of History and chairman of the graduate faculty in history at the Claremont (California) Graduate School. From 1951 until 1970 he taught at Brandeis University, where he was first incumbent of the Earl Warren chair in constitutional history. In 1969 he won the Pulitzer Prize for his *Origins of the Fifth Amendment.* His many other books include *Legacy of Suppression: Freedom of Speech and Press in Early American History; Jefferson and Civil Liberties; Judgements: Essays on American Constitutional History;* and *Against the Law: The Nixon Court and Criminal Justice.*

DAVID E. LILIENTHAL (1899–   ) is a lawyer and public administrator. He was appointed to the three-member board of the Tennessee Valley Authority when it was created in 1933, and served until 1946—after 1941 as chairman. His account of the project, *TVA: Democracy on the March,* was published in 1944. Lilienthal was also the first chairman of the Atomic Energy Commission, serving from 1946 until 1950. In addition to five volumes of his *Journals,* his works include *Big Business in a New Era* and *Change, Hope and the Bomb.*

JERRE MANGIONE (1909–   ) has been a member of the faculty at the University of Pennsylvania since 1961. His account of the Federal Writers' Project, *The Dream and the Deal,* grew out of his experience as national coordinating editor of the Project from 1937 to 1939. He also served as special assistant to the U.S. Commissioner of Immigration and Naturalization from 1942 to 1948. The son of Sicilian immigrants, he has frequently written about this national group. His books include *Mount Allegro, Reunion in Sicily, Life Sentences for Everybody, A Passion for Sicilians,* and *America is Also Italian.*

GEORGE PERKINS MARSH (1801–1882) was a diplomat, linguist, and conservationist. Born in Vermont, his varied career also included teaching and law. He served in the House of Representatives and as U.S. Minister to Turkey and to Italy. His books include *The Goths in New England, The Origin and History of the English Language,* and *Man and Nature: Or Physical Geography as Modified by Human Action.*

D'ARCY McNICKLE is professor of anthropology at the University of Saskatchewan, the Regina campus. A member of the Confederated Salish and Kootenai Tribes of Montana, he formerly served as a staff member of the Bureau of Indian Affairs and was director of American Indian Development, a program in community development. His books include *They Came Here First; The Indian Tribes of the United States, Ethnic and Cultural Survival;* and *Indian Man: A Life of Oliver LaFarge.*

BARBARA MIKULSKI (1936–   ) has been City Councilwoman in Baltimore since 1972, and in January 1973, she became chairperson of the Democratic Party's Commission on Delegate Selection. Her grandparents immigrated from Poland at the turn of the century, and she grew up in a mixed Irish-Polish-Greek area of Baltimore. She had an early career as a social worker, became involved in the civil rights movement of the sixties, and turned to community organization and politics following the assassinations of Martin Luther King, Jr., and Robert Kennedy in 1968.

GOTTLIEB MITTELBERGER, a native of Württemberg, Germany, came to Philadelphia in 1750. After working for four years as an organist and schoolmaster, he returned to Germany, where he lived in obscurity. His *Journey to Pennsylvania,* published in 1756, was an attempt to portray accurately conditions in America.

LEWIS MUMFORD (1895–   ) is generally considered the leading American critic of twentieth-century architecture. His books range from art and architecture to literature, history, and the impact of technology on human life. Among the most influential have been *The Story of Utopias, Technics and Civilization, The Culture of Cities, The City in History, The Highway and the City,* and *The Myth of the Machine.*

THOMAS NAIRNE (late 17th to early 18th century) was a Swiss who wrote a promotional tract, *A Letter from South Carolina,* advertising the advantages of the colony.

GARY B. NASH (1933–   ) was an assistant professor of history at Princeton University from 1964 to 1966 before joining the faculty of the University of California at Los Angeles, where he is now a professor of history. He is the author of *Quakers and Politics, The Great Fear: Race in the Mind of America, Class and Society in Early America,* and *Red, White, and Black.*

MICHAEL NOVAK (1933–   ) has had a varied career as writer, lecturer, professor, and an editor of *Christianity and Crisis* and *Christian Century.* He is currently associate director for humanities at the Rockefeller Foundation. In addition to two works of fiction, he has authored many books on philosophy, religion, and politics, among them *The Open Church, Belief and Unbelief, The Experience of Nothingness, The Rise of the Unmeltable Ethnics,* and, most recently, *Choosing Our King,* about the Presidential election process.

LEO PFEFFER (1910–   ) came to the United States from Hungary in 1912. He has practiced and taught law in New York City, and served as a lecturer at the New School for Social Research and at Mt. Holyoke College. Since 1964 he has been chairman of the Political Science Department at Long Island University, and his work on behalf of religious freedom has earned for him several civil liberties awards. Among his books are *Church, State and Freedom; The Liberties of an American; Church and State in the United States;* and *This Honorable Court.*

THOMAS PHILLIPS (late 17th century) was a ship's captain in the service of the Royal African Company of England. He was engaged in the trade of ivory, gold, and slaves.

MATTHEW B. RIDGWAY (1895–   ) entered the Army upon graduation from West Point in 1917, and advanced through the ranks to general in 1951. He served as United Nations commander in Korea, Supreme Commander in Europe, and from 1953 to 1955 as Army Chief of Staff. He published his memoirs, *Soldier,* in 1956.

JACOB RIIS (1849–1914) was a journalist and social reformer. Born in Denmark, he came to the United States in 1870. As a police reporter for the *New York Evening Sun,* he became familiar with the horrors of slum life. *How the Other Half Lives,* published in 1890, was largely responsible for stimulating the first reform movement to improve conditions in the tenements. His later books included *The Children of the Poor, Children of the Tenements,* and an autobiography, *The Making of an American.*

VERMONT C. ROYSTER (1914–   ) has been associated with the *Wall Street Journal* since 1936, serving as Washington correspondent, editorial writer, and editor. He is currently contributing editor and columnist, and a professor of journalism and public affairs at the University of North Carolina. A commentator for CBS radio and TV, he has won several awards for his journalism, including the 1953 Pulitzer Prize for editorial writing and the Sigma Delta Chi Award. He is the author of *Main Street and Beyond, Journey Through the Soviet Union,* and *A Pride of Prejudices.*

RUBEN SALAZAR (1928–1970) was born in Juarez, Mexico. He joined the Los Angeles *Times* as a reporter in 1959. He was a correspondent for the *Times* in the Dominican Republic and Vietnam, and served as bureau chief in Mexico City. In 1968 he returned to Los Angeles and specialized in coverage of the Mexican-American community. At the time of his death during a demonstration in Los Angeles, he was news diretor of KMEX, a Spanish-language television station in Los Angeles, and he was contributing a weekly column to the *Times.*

CARL O. SAUER (1889–   ) was professor of geography at the University of California, Berkeley, from 1923 until his retirement in 1957. In addition to dozens of articles on humans and their environment, some of which were collected into a volume titled *Land and Life,* Sauer has written *The Spanish Main* and *Sixteenth-Century North America.*

HARRY N. SCHEIBER (1935–   ) is professor of history at the University of California, San Diego. A specialist in American legal-constitutional history and economic history, he served on the Dartmouth College faculty for eleven years. Among his published works are *The Wilson Administration and Civil Liberties, The Condition of American Federalism, Ohio Canal Era: A Case Study of Government and the Economy,* and *Law in American History,* to which he was a contributing author.

ARTHUR M. SCHLESINGER, JR. (1917–   ) is currently Schweitzer Professor of Humanities at the City University of New York, having taught history at Harvard University from 1946 to 1961. From 1961 to 1964, he served as special assistant to Presidents Kennedy and Johnson. He won the Pulitzer Prize in history for *The Age of Jackson* (1945); his *A Thousand Days: John F. Kennedy in the White House* (1965) won both the Pulitzer Prize in biography and the National Book Award. His other books include a multi-volume history of the *Age of Roosevelt; The Crisis of Confidence: Ideas, Power, and Violence in America;* and *The Imperial Presidency.*

JOHN STEINBECK (1902–1968) was born in California, which is the setting for many of his novels. *Grapes of Wrath,* his novel about the "Okies" during the Depression, won the Pulitzer Prize in 1940. Other books, most of which deal with the poor and down-trodden, include *Of Mice and Men, Cannery Row,* and *The Winter of Our Discontent,* which earned for him the 1962 Nobel Prize for literature.

MARY HELENA STEPHENSON emigrated with her family from Sweden to the United States in the 1860s. She settled on a farm in Mt. Pleasant, Iowa, an area that attracted many other Scandinavian immigrants.

FRANCES M. TROLLOPE (1780–1863) was an English novelist and the author of several travel books. *Domestic Manners of the Americans,* which she published in 1832 after a trip to Cincinnati, Ohio, aroused considerable resentment in the United States. Her many novels include *The Vicar of Wrexhill, The Widow Barnaby,* and *The Widow Married.* Her son, Anthony, was also a famous novelist.

MARK TWAIN (1835–1910) was the pen name for Samuel Clemens. Born in Missouri, he grew up along the Mississippi River, which was the setting for many of his later writings. In 1861, Twain headed west to the Nevada Territory. His unsuccessful attempts at prospecting and mining left him without finances but provided the experience that formed the basis for *Roughing It.* He traveled widely, and his travel report, *Innocents Abroad,* was a great success. In 1870 he settled in Connecticut to begin a highly productive period, which saw the publication of the *The Gilded Age, Tom Sawyer, Huckleberry Finn,* and *A Connecticut Yankee in King Arthur's Court.*

THOMAS JEFFERSON WERTENBAKER (1879–1966) taught history at Princeton University from 1910 until his retirement in 1947. A specialist in American colonial history, he lectured at universities around the world. He authored hundreds of articles and more than a dozen books, including *The Shaping of Colonial Virginia, The First Americans, The Golden Age of Colonial Culture,* and *Give Me Liberty: The Struggle for Self-Government in Virginia.*

MYRA K. WOLFGANG is Vice President of the Hotel and Restaurant Employees and Bartenders International Union, AFL-CIO. She also is a member of the Michigan State Minimum Wage Board and the Michigan Women's Commission.

C. VANN WOODWARD (1908–   ) has been Sterling Professor of History at Yale University since 1961, having previously taught for many years at The Johns Hopkins University. In 1968–69 he served as president of both the American Historical Association and the Organization of American Historians. His writings on the South and on blacks have been particularly influential. They include *Tom Watson: Agrarian Rebel, Origins of the New South, Reunion and Reaction, The Strange Career of Jim Crow, The Burden of Southern History,* and *American Counterpoint: Slavery and Race in the North-South Dialogue.*

ISRAEL ZANGWILL (1864–1926) was a British author and leader in the Zionist movement. His novels portrayed Jewish life in a sympathetic light. He also wrote light comedies and social plays, including *The Melting Pot* and *The War God.*

A special STUDY GUIDE has been designed to accompany this Course by Newspaper, "American Issues Forum I: American Society in the Making." If you are taking this course for college credit, you will find the STUDY GUIDE an indispensable companion to the material covered in this course. Prepared by academic experts, the STUDY GUIDE contains brief summaries of key concepts; commentaries relating the newspaper articles and articles in the READER; review questions; and bibliographies to guide the interested reader to additional materials. The STUDY GUIDE will enable you to gain the maximum benefit from the course materials and will make your study of these materials both more efficient and rewarding.

To order the STUDY GUIDE for AMERICAN ISSUES FORUM I: AMERICAN SOCIETY IN THE MAKING, use the coupon printed below. Include the list price, $2.95. Please send *check* or *money order*—no currency or C.O.D.'s. Additional copies of AMERICAN ISSUES FORUM I may also be ordered at $4.95.

PUBLISHER'S INC.
243 12th Street
Del Mar CA, 92014

Please send me ____copy/copies of AMERICAN ISSUES FORUM I *STUDY GUIDE*($2.95). I am enclosing a total of ____ (Calif. Residents add 6% Sales Tax).

Name _____

Address _____

City _____ State _____ Zip _____
